DOVES OF WAR

DOVES OF WAR

Four Women of Spain

PAUL PRESTON

NORTHEASTERN UNIVERSITY PRESS

Boston

First published in 2002 in England
by HarperCollins*Publishers*.
Published in 2003 in the United States of America
by Northeastern University Press by arrangement
with HarperCollins*Publishers*.

LIBRARY OF CONGRESS
CATALOGING-IN-PUBLICATION DATA

Preston, Paul, 1946–
Doves of war: four women of Spain/Paul Preston.
p. cm.   Includes index.
ISBN 1–55553–560–7 (cloth : alk. paper)
1. Spain—History—Civil War,
1936–1939—Women. 2. Scott-Ellis,
Priscilla, 1916-1983. 3. Green, Nan.
4. Sanz Bachiller, Mercedes.
5. Nelken, Margarita, 1896–1968.
6. Women—Spain—Biography. I. Title.
DP269.8.W7P74 2003
946.081′082—DC21 2003001047

Printed and bound by
The Maple Press in York, Pennsylvania.
The paper is Sebago Antique, an acid-free sheet.

MANUFACTURED IN THE UNITED STATES OF AMERICA

07 06 05 04 03   5 4 3 2 1

CONTENTS

ACKNOWLEDGEMENTS

One of the more agreeable duties involved in producing a book is paying tribute to the friends and colleagues who have helped the author in one way or another. As always, without their help in terms of suggestions, documents, and critical readings of the text, this book would have been much the poorer. I would like to thank several people for their readiness to share with me their memories of the principal protagonists of the book: the late Bill Alexander, Noreen Branson, Santiago Carrillo, the late Len Crome, the late Irene Falcón, Milt Felsen, Dr Donald Grant, Avis Hutt, Lou Kenton, Rafa Kenton, Francis K. S. Khoo, Hans Landauer, Gerarda de Orléans-Borbón, Tatiana Orloff-Davidoff, Enrique de Rivas Ibáñez, Rosaleen Ross, Charmian Alaric Russell, Sam Lessor, the late Fred Thomas and Sadie Thomas.

I would also like to acknowledge my good fortune in having friends and colleagues who discussed aspects of the book with me, helped me find material and, in some cases, read sections of the text. Their advice and readiness to discuss the problems of researching the lives of these four women were invaluable and I would therefore like to recognise my debts to: Alicia Alted, Trinidad Barbero, Nicolás Belmonte, Victor Berch, Rafael Borràs Betriu, Anny Brooksbank Jones, Michael Burke, Peter Carroll, Julián Casanova, Norman Cooper, Giuliana Di Febo, Sheelagh Ellwood, Ana Ena Bordonada, Jerónimo Gonzalo, Lord Nicholas Gordon Lennox, Gina Hermann, James Hopkins, Gerald Howson, Amparo Hurtado, Emilio Majuelo, Shirley Mangini, Marisa Maldonado Blanco, Aurelio Martín Naquera, Enrique Moradiellos, Mario Ojeda, Kathleen Richmond, Susana Tabera and Pablo Villalaín García.

A number of friends provided invaluable help by seeking out extremely recondite documentation – Richard Baxell in Moscú,

Iván Pliego in México, Michael O'Shaughnessy in New Zealand and Jim Carmody in London. In this respect, my greatest debt is to Mariano Sanz, a peerless research assistant, an excellent historian and an even better detective, tirelessly travelling around Spain in search of lost documents. In England, three friends provided priceless assistance. Helen Graham, Angela Jackson and Lala Isla read various drafts of each chapter and their commentaries were always as astute as they were generous. Jonathan Gathorne-Hardy read the entire book and his comments on style were, as always, an education in themselves. At HarperCollins, I have been extremely fortunate to have as my editor and friend Philip Gwyn Jones who has always been unstinting in his support. I would also like to thank Georgina Laycock for her sensitive work on the book.

Finally, it is obvious that in the case of a book like this, the author's reliance on the relatives of the protagonists for access to diaries, letters, notes, unpublished memoirs and other documents has been considerable and that, without their help, the research would simply not have been possible. Accordingly, I would like to express my warmest thanks to the following persons: for the chapter on Mercedes Sanz-Bachiller, Mercedes Sanz-Bachiller herself and her daughter Mercedes Redondo Sanz-Bachiller; for the chapter on Margarita Nelken, her granddaughter Margarita Salas de Paúl and to her great granddaughter Ana de Rivas Salas; for the chapter on Nan Green, her son Martin Green and her daughter Frances Brouard; for the chapter on Priscilla Scott-Ellis, her sister Gaenor Heathcoat-Amory, her son Juan Alfonso de Vilallonga and her daughter Carmen Foster de Vilallonga. They were all prodigal in their help, providing documents and photographs as well as putting up with interminable, and often indiscreet, questions from me. To some extent, the book is theirs and I hope that they will not be disappointed by it.

As a man trying to write about what it was like to be a woman in the Spanish Civil War, I owe most to my wife Gabrielle, whose sharp comments and suggestions, as well as her constant moral support, helped more than I can say. The book is thus dedicated to her.

ILLUSTRATIONS

Actresses knitting and crocheting for the militia
Anti-fascist guerillas
Priscilla Scott-Ellis (Pip) in Argentina
Pip in Scotland in her uniform as honorary colonel of the Polish
    Army
Pip with Prince Ataúlfo at the Feria de Sevilla
Pip with the nurses of the Hadfield-Spears Mobile Hospital Unit in
    France
Pip and José Luis de Vilallonga
Pip's wedding in Sanlúcar de Barameda
Pip in her cabin en route to Buenos Aires
Combatants on the Republican side
Pip with her son John and her daughter Carmen
Pip in 1951
Nan Green in 1925
Nan and George Green in the Peak District
Nan, Frances and Martin, Grandpa Green, and a friend
Nan, Frances and Martin on the steps of their house
Nan and visiting Labour M.P., Leah Manning
Nan on board the *Normandie*
George's improvised band at the International Brigades Hospital at
    Huete
Nan in China in 1954 with Ted Brake
Nan joins in with a Chinese band
Militia men and women standing on a home-made tank

Women enthusiastically salute Franco's troops as they enter
    Barcelona
Mercedes Sanz-Bachiller and Franco's wife, Carmen Polo
Mercedes uncomfortable with the fascist trappings given to her
    welfare organisation

Mercedes Sanz-Bachiller and Pilar Primo de Rivera
Mercedes surrounded by children being cared for by Auxilio Social
Mercedes Sanz-Bachiller in Hamburg
Mercedes visits Fascist Italy
Carmen Polo, Mercedes Sanz-Bachiller and Evita Duarte de Perón
Franco receives Mercedes at a late 1960s audience
Margarita Nelken in 1923
A rare 'glamour' shot of Margarita Nelken from 1926
Margarita with Magda and Santiago
Margarita with Santiago in Madrid
Margarita in exile in Russia in 1935
Margarita in August 1938 at the Ebro front
Margarita's husband Martín de Paúl with her daughter Magda
Margarita with the officers of the Margarita Nelken battalion of the
    Republican Army
Margarita with her granddaughter Cuqui
Margarita pictured in her study in Mexico City in 1941
The recently engaged Magda, six months before her death
Margarita, aged seventy-four, and seriously ill. She died in Mexico
    City on 9 March 1968

PROLOGUE

Fears and Fantasies

IN LATE SEPTEMBER 1937, two English women arrived in Paris. One, a penniless housewife and Communist Party militant from London, had travelled on the crowded boat train from Calais. Despite being exhausted after her trip, she left her luggage at the station and got a bus straight to the recently inaugurated Great Exhibition. The other, the daughter of one of the richest aristocrats in England, accompanied by a princess, the granddaughter of Queen Victoria, arrived in a gleaming limousine. After checking in at their luxurious hotel in the Rue de la Paix, she dined out. The next day, after a little shopping, she too visited the exhibition. So great was the bewildering cornucopia spilling out of the two hundred and forty pavilions jostling along the banks of the Seine that only a small part of their wonders could be seen in a few hours. The two women had to make choices. What they decided revealed much about where they had come from and about where they were going.

The Communist made a beeline for the pavilion of the Spanish Republican Government and 'stood spellbound at Picasso's *Guernica*'. She was repelled by 'the competitive vulgarity' of the German and Soviet pavilions which glared aggressively at each other at the end of the Pont d'Iéna on the Rive Droite of the Seine. In contrast, the society girl was captivated by the great German cubic construction, designed by Albert Speer, over which flew a huge eagle bearing a swastika in its claws. Although, like her poorer compatriot, she was en route to the Civil War raging to the south, she did not bother to visit the pavilion of the Spanish Republic. They did both share utter contempt for the British display. The Communist 'snorted in disdain at the British contribution – mostly tweeds, pipes, walking sticks and sports gear'. The aristocrat considered the British pavilion's displays of golf balls, marmalade and bowler hats to be 'very bad'.

The two English women never knew that they had coincided at the Paris exhibition any more than that their paths had crossed before. Three and a half months earlier, the aristocrat had emerged from a cinema in Leicester Square and watched a Communist demonstration protesting about the German navy's artillery bombardment of Almería in South Eastern Spain. Amongst those chanting 'Stop Hitler's War on Children!' was the left-wing housewife. For both women, Paris was just one stop on a longer journey to Spain. Their preparations in August 1937 could hardly have been more different. The Communist had thought long and hard about leaving England and her son and daughter to volunteer for the Spanish Republic. With trepidation, she sold what she could of her books and household chattels and deposited the rest in a theatrical skip. At Liverpool Street Station in London, she bade a painful farewell to her two children and then put them on a train to a boarding school paid for by a wealthy Party comrade. A month before her thirty-third birthday, the petite brunette leftist had little by way of possessions. She had hardly any packing to do for herself, just a few clothes – her two battered suitcases were crammed with medical supplies for the Spanish Republican hospital unit that she hoped to join. Clutching her burdens, she took a bus to Waterloo Station to catch the train to Dover.

Her counterpart's preparations were altogether more elaborate. For more than six months, she had dreamed of nothing else. She was in love and hoped that by going to Spain she would win the attention of her beloved, a Spanish prince serving with the German Condor Legion. During the summer of 1937, in the intervals between riding, playing tennis and learning golf, she took Spanish lessons with a private tutor. In London's West End, her punishing schedule of shopping was interspersed with inoculations, and visits to persons likely to be useful for her time in Spain. These included one of the four men with principal responsibility for British policy on Spanish affairs at the Foreign Office and the ex-Queen Victoria Eugenia of Spain. Not yet twenty-one, the blonde socialite, rather gawky and deeply self-conscious about her weight, desperately haunted the beauty salons in preparation for her Spanish adventure. She left England in the chauffeur-driven limousine belonging to Victoria Eugenia's cousin, Princess Beatrice of Saxe-Coburg. The car was overloaded with trunks and hatboxes containing the trophies of the previous four weeks' shopping safaris. After being ushered by the station master at Dover into a private compartment on the boat train, they crossed the channel then motored on to Paris – to their hotel, more shopping and the visit to the Great Exhibition. On the following morning, she set off on the remainder of her journey south to the Spanish border, enjoying an extremely pleasant tour through the peaceful French countryside.

After seeing the Picasso, her left-wing compatriot hastened to collect her heavy cases and catch the night train to Spain. Crushed into a third-class carriage, she was able to reflect on the horrors that awaited her on the other side of the Pyrenees. She was an avid reader of the left-wing press and had received painfully eloquent letters from her husband. He was already in Spain, serving as an ambulance driver with the International Brigades. By contrast, the young occupant of the limousine bowling along the long, straight, tree-lined French roads was blithely insouciant. Her knowledge of the Spanish Civil War was based on her reading of a couple of right-wing accounts which portrayed the conflict in terms of 'Red atrocities' and the knightly exploits of Franco's officers. She sped towards Biarritz like a tourist, in a spirit of anticipation of wonders and curiosities to come. Her mind was on the object of her romantic aspirations, and she was thinking hardly at all of the terrors that might lie before her.

Both women were sustained by their fantasy of what their participation in the Spanish war might mean. For the aristocrat, it was about love and a chivalric notion of helping to crush the dragon of Communism. The Communist's hopes were more prosaic. She wanted to help the Spanish people stop the rise of fascism and, deep down, vaguely hoped that doing so might be the first step to world revolution. Neither the aristocrat setting out to join the forces of General Franco nor the Communist could have anticipated the suffering that awaited them. Even the gruesome picture of the bloodshed at the front provided by the graphic letters from her husband had not fully prepared the left-winger en route to serve the Spanish Republic for the reality of war. By that late summer of 1937, however, the women of Spain had already been coming to terms with the horrors of war for over a year. For most of them, there had been no question of volunteering to serve. They had little choice – the war enveloped them and their families in a bloody struggle for survival. For two Spanish mothers, in particular, the war would have the most wildly unexpected consequences in terms of both their personal lives and the way in which they were dragged into the public sphere. Both were of widely differing social origins and political inclinations and had different hopes for what victory for their side might mean for them and their families. Their lives – and their fantasies – would be irrevocably changed by the war.

In the first days of the military uprising of 18 July 1936, one, a young mother of three, who had just turned twenty-five, had every reason to expect dramatic disruption in her life as a consequence of the war. She lived in Valladolid in Old Castile, at the heart of the insurgent Nationalist zone, and her husband was a prominent leader of the ultra-rightist Falange. Already, as a result of his political beliefs, she had experienced exile and political persecution. She knew what it was like to be on the run and to keep a family with a husband in jail. Because of his political activities, she had endured one childbirth completely alone and, in exile, had undergone a forceps delivery without anaesthetic. Nevertheless, she had stifled whatever resentment she might have felt as a result of her husband's political adventures and supported him unreservedly. Now four months pregnant, the outbreak of war brought all kinds of possibilities and dangers. She rejoiced at his release from prison as a result of the military uprising and shared his conviction that everything for which they had both made so many sacrifices might come to fruition within a matter of weeks, if not days. Not without anxiety about the final outcome, she could now hope that her husband's days as a political outlaw were over, that they could build a home together and that they and their children would be able to live in the kind of Nationalist Spain to which he had devoted his political career.

Within less than a week of their passionate reunion, both her husband and her unborn child would be dead. The reality of the war had smashed its way into her world and shattered her every hope and expectation. In an atmosphere charged with hatred, calls for revenge for her husband's death intensified the savage repression being carried out in Valladolid. Confined to bed, she found little consolation in the bloodthirsty assurances of his comrades. She faced a bleak future as a widow with three children. Her own parents were long since dead and the best that her in-laws could suggest was that she earn a comfortable living by getting a licence to run an outlet for the state tobacco monopoly (*un estanco*). To their astonishment, after a relatively short period of mourning, she renounced both thoughts of vengeance and of a quiet life in widow's weeds. She dug deep into her remarkable reserves of energy and embarked on a massive task of relief work among the many children and women whose lives had been shattered by the loss of fathers and husbands through death at the front, political execution or imprisonment. By the time that the two English women were packing their cases for Spain, she had fifty thousand women at her orders and was being feted in Nazi Germany by, among others, Hermann Göring and Dr Robert Ley, the head of the German Workers' Front. By the end of the war, she would be – albeit briefly – one of the most powerful women in Franco's Spain. Such triumphs, at best poor consolation for her personal losses, would see her embroiled in an unwanted rivalry with the leader of the Francoist women's organisation, Pilar Primo de Rivera, and in the ruthless power struggles that bedevilled both sides in the Civil War.

In Republican Madrid, another mother, a distinguished Jewish writer and art critic, and a Socialist member of parliament for a southern agrarian province, was beset by a tumultuous kaleidoscope of feelings as a result of the outbreak of war. On the one hand, she hoped that the military uprising would be defeated and that a revolution would alleviate the crippling poverty of the rural labourers that she represented. On the other, she felt both pride and paralysing anxiety as a result of the wartime activities of her children. As soon as the military rebellion had been launched, militiamen had raced to the sierras to the North of Madrid to repel the insurgent forces of General Mola. Among them was the woman's fifteen-year-old son. Despite her desperate pleas, he lied about his age and enlisted in the Republican Army. After three months training, he received a commission as the Republic's youngest lieutenant. She tried to use her influence to keep him out of danger, but he successfully insisted on a posting in the firing line and took part in the most ferocious battles of the war. Her twenty-two-year-old daughter was a nurse at the front. Conquering her worries, their mother threw herself into war work, collecting clothes and food for the front, giving morale-raising speeches, organising the evacuation of children, and welfare work behind the lines. Like her Nationalist counterpart, she too would travel to raise support for her side in the war. And she too would find herself in an inadvertent rivalry – in her case, with the most charismatic woman of the Republican zone, Dolores Ibárruri – Pasionaria. Unlike the mother from Valladolid, for her there would be no victory, even a tainted one. The defeat of the Republic meant, for her, as for the many thousands who trudged across the Pyrenees into exile, incalculable personal loss and the crushing of the hopes which had underpinned her political labours. With the end of the war, her troubles were just beginning.

These four women, despite their different nationalities, social origins and ideologies, had much in common. They were brave, determined, intelligent, independent and compassionate. To differing degrees, all were damaged by the Spanish Civil War and its immediate and long-term consequences. As a direct result of the war, two would be widowed, two would lose children. Two would be deeply traumatised by their experiences in the front line. The shadow of the Spanish Civil War would hang over the rest of all their lives.

This book has no theoretical pretensions. Its objective is quite simple – to tell the unknown stories of four remarkable women whose lives were starkly altered by their experiences in the Spanish Civil War. All of them are relatively unknown. Neither of the two English women who served in the medical services of each zone had any political prominence at all. The two Spanish women who did have a notable public presence, the one in the Republican zone, the other in Nationalist Spain, were involved in tasks at some remove from the decision-making of the great war leaders of the two sides in conflict. Moreover, both at the time and subsequently, they functioned in the shadow of more famous rivals. None the less, for the purposes of this book, that is an advantage. Political detail takes a back seat, or is at least considered in the context of other personal relationships – with lovers, husbands and children. In that sense, this is a work of emotional history. It follows them from birth to death, in an attempt to show how, as women, wives and mothers, they were affected by the political struggles of the 1930s, how their lives were altered for ever by the political conflicts of the 1930s, by the Spanish Civil War and by its consequences. It is hoped thereby to cast light into some unfamiliar corners of the conflict.

Writing the book has been a singularly emotional experience as well as a major effort of detective work. It is not the first time that I have written biography but my previous efforts have focused on more politically important figures. National prominence provided a chronological framework lacking from the material left behind by the four women whose lives are reconstructed here. The diaries and letters written by women tend to be much more intimate than those left by men. Accordingly, in the lives of all four of the women portrayed in this book, the personal has considerable priority over the public. Deeply aware of the problems of being a man writing about women, in the course of writing them, I asked many friends to read drafts of the different chapters. One of these readers is well-versed in both feminist and postmodernist theory. I was much heartened when she remarked encouragingly about one of my chapters that 'even the theoretically illiterate can occasionally arrive at important insights by the use of anti-quated empirical methods'. The implication is that it could all have been worked out by theory without all the messy biographical details. Even had I known how to do so, I fear that I would have thereby missed out on a moving experience and the reader would have missed the opportunity to know about four remarkable lives.

PRISCILLA
SCOTT-ELLIS

PRISCILLA SCOTT-ELLIS

All for Love

T HE SPANISH CIVIL WAR has given rise to a gigantic
bibliography running into more than fifteen thousand
books. In 1995, a remarkably original addition to the literary
legacy of the conflict passed almost unnoticed. Its importance
was obscured by the fact that it appeared on the list of a small
English publishing house in Norfolk. *The Chances of Death*
consisted of an edited selection from a voluminous diary written between the autumn of 1937 and the end of the war by
Priscilla Scott-Ellis.[1] The author, who had died twelve years
earlier, was one of only two British women volunteers who
served with Franco's Nationalist forces during the war. Her
vibrantly written and transparently honest account of her
experiences is a mine of original insights into life behind the
lines of the Francoist zone. Gut-wrenching descriptions of the
front-line medical services alternate with accounts of the lux-
ury still enjoyed in the rearguard by the Spanish aristocracy.
Although highly readable, and deserving of a wider audience,
there was every chance that this remarkable book would be
a reference only for scholars.

However, an appreciative article published in the Madrid
daily *El País* by the British historian Hugh Thomas provoked
an astonishing polemic which in turn guaranteed that the book
would be translated and published in Spain. Once at the centre
of the ensuing scandal, the book, taken up by one of the

country's most prestigious publishers, achieved considerable popular success. Hugh Thomas's glowing review, entitled 'Sangre y agallas' (blood and guts), gave an entirely accurate picture of the book's merits. He praised its vivid portrayal of life in an emergency medical unit and its equally fascinating account of high society behind the lines. He also commented rightly that the diary presented an image of a brave, self-sacrificing but fun-loving girl, tirelessly driven by curiosity and enthusiasm.[2] Nine days later, a disputatious reply was published in the pages of *El País*'s Barcelona rival, *La Vanguardia*. Entitled 'Un enigma', its author was José Luis de Vilallonga y Cabeza de Vaca, the Marqués de Castellvell, a playboy and journalist, known for his appearance in several Spanish and French films, for several successful novels published in France and for a semi-official biography of the King of Spain, Juan Carlos, with whom he claimed friendship.[3]

Vilallonga attacked the editor of Priscilla Scott-Ellis's diary, Raymond Carr, claiming that it was a forgery 'written by God knows who and with what sinister intentions'. Accordingly, he dismissed Hugh Thomas's remarks as the fruit of ignorance. Vilallonga justified these assertions by the fact that he had been married to Priscilla Scott-Ellis for seventeen years, from 1945 to 1961. He found it incredible that she had never mentioned such a diary to him. He now demanded to know the identities of 'the real author of this diary' and of the beneficiary of the book's profits. Along the way, he presented a cruelly dismissive account of Priscilla Scott-Ellis and her family. He asserted that the author was incapable of writing a diary, claiming that her prose was 'infantile'. He described her father, the Lord Howard de Walden, as a whisky-sodden alcoholic. He alleged that Priscilla Scott-Ellis was in fact illegitimate and really the fruit of an adulterous affair between her mother and Prince Alfonso de Orléans Borbón, a cousin of Alfonso XIII and a close friend of her parents. He further insinuated that the great love of her life, Ataúlfo de Orléans Borbón, who was in some ways inadvertently responsible for her decision to go to Spain, was a homosexual. His own marriage to her was thus presented as a way out of an embarrassing situation for Prince Alfonso. He stated that his own parents never approved of the marriage 'to a foreigner through whose veins there coursed Jewish blood'.

Some weeks later, Vilallonga's diatribe brought forth a dignified reply from Sir Raymond Carr.[4] He pointed out that Vilallonga's questions about the authorship and the royalties constituted an accusation that, for money, he had knowingly undertaken to prepare an edition of a forgery. Carr gave an account of the genesis of the diary and an explanation of the circumstances whereby it had lain unpublished for half a century. In fact, it had been on the point of publication in the autumn of 1939 but the project was aborted because of the outbreak of the Second World War. Carr also published in facsimile a section of the diary. He then went on to underline some of the inaccuracies of Vilallonga's account of Priscilla Scott-Ellis's experiences during the Spanish Civil War. Finally, in a spirit more of sadness than of anger, he expressed his surprise that 'a Spanish gentleman should assert in a newspaper that his wife, deceased and unable to defend herself, was a bastard and her father a drunk'. He found it tragic that Vilallonga's article should thus 'defame the memory of a valiant and indomitable woman'.

Who then was this remarkable woman? Esyllt Priscilla Scott-Ellis – known as 'Pip' – was the daughter of two remarkably creative and eccentric parents, Margherita (Margot) van Raalte and Thomas Evelyn Scott-Ellis, the eighth Lord Howard de Walden and fourth Lord Seaford. Margot was born in 1890, the daughter of an extremely wealthy banker of Dutch origins, Charles van Raalte, and Florence Clow, an English women with some talent as an amateur painter. Florence van Raalte was such a snob that she was known in the family as Mrs van Royalty. From her parents, Margot had inherited money and both musical and artistic talent. She was a good painter and an accomplished musician. Her singing voice was good enough for her to be trained for the opera with Olga Lynn and she often gave concerts, even being conducted – in Debussy's *La Demoiselle Élue* – by Sir Thomas Beecham. These interests would provide a formative influence in Pip's childhood. Margot's family lived at Aldenham Abbey near Watford in Hertfordshire, where they were often joined by members of the Spanish royal family. The Infanta Eulalia, Alfonso XIII's aunt and a woman of scandalous reputation, was a friend of Margot's parents. Princess Eulalia's two sons, Prince Alfonso and Prince Luis de Orléans Borbón, were being educated at English boarding schools and often spent summer holidays with the family. In the late 1890s, the Van Raalte family bought the paradisical Brownsea Island in Poole harbour. With its medieval castle, two fresh-water lakes and dykes and streams, it was a wonderful place for children. Margot spent many idyllic summers there with other children including Prince Ali and Prince Luis. It was on Brownsea Island that Lieutenant-General Baden-Powell, a friend of Margot's father, launched his Boy Scout Movement in 1907.[5]

Tommy Scott-Ellis was born in 1880. A soldier and a great sportsman, he was educated at Eton and Sandhurst. He was commissioned into the 10th Hussars in 1899 and fought in the Boer War. The man presented by Vilallonga as a helpless sot was actually a good cricketer and boxer and was the English amateur fencing champion. In 1901, he became an immensely rich man at the age of twenty-one when he inherited his father's title and the fortune of his grandmother, Lady Lucy Cavendish-Bentinck. He then bought a racing motorboat and competed in highly perilous cross-Channel races. He also bought a yacht and was a member of the British Olympic Team in 1906. He then acquired racing stables. In his childhood, he too had spent happy summers at Brownsea Island which was then owned by the Cavendish-Bentinck family. Having had a bitterly miserable time at various boarding schools, Brownsea became a haven for him. He now tried unsuccessfully to buy it. Deeply disappointed, he was consoled when the new owners, Charles and Florence van Raalte, turned out to be friends of his mother, Blanche. He was thus invited to Brownsea to sail in summer and to shoot in winter.[6]

Shortly after marrying Margot van Raalte, Tommy, anxious to keep a link with the Army, joined the Westminster Dragoons. Their first children, twin sister and brother, Bronwen and John Osmael, were born on 27 November 1912. When the First World War broke out, Tommy left for Egypt as second-in-command of his regiment. At the time Margot was pregnant with their third child, Elizabeth, who was born on 5 December 1914. At the first opportunity, however, she arranged to join Tommy in Egypt. As was commonplace among the upper classes at the time, Margot thought it normal to leave her three children with a nurse. At Chirk Castle, the family's country seat near Llangollen in North Wales, they were neglected to the extent of contracting rickets.[7] At first Margot was rather bored in Egypt but after Tommy volunteered to go with the British invasion forces to Gallipoli, and casualties began to arrive from Turkey, she joined a friend, Mary Herbert, the wife of Aubrey Herbert, a contemporary of Tommy's at Eton, in setting up a hospital. One of the Herberts' daughters, Gabriel, was also to work with Franco's medical services during the Spanish Civil War; the other, Laura, was to be the second wife of the novelist Evelyn Waugh. At the end of 1915, Tommy was posted back to Egypt and Margot was able to live with him there until in May 1916, they returned to England. She was by then pregnant once more. In November 1916, Tommy got himself transferred to the Royal Welsh Fusiliers in order to serve in France. Two days after he left, Priscilla was born in London on 15 November 1916. The real sequence of events undermines Vilallonga's accusation that her father was Prince Alfonso de Orleáns Borbón.[8] Margot and Tommy would have two further daughters,

Gaenor, born on 2 June 1919 and Rosemary on 28 October 1922.

In later life, when she had become addicted to drama and excitement, Pip would attribute her taste for adventure to having been born during an air raid; more likely it was inherited from her parents. According to her brother, when she was a toddler, the family called her 'Chatterbox'. Ensconced in her high chair, she would chunter away irrespective of anyone listening or understanding. As a child, she used her Welsh name of Esyllt (the equivalent of Iseult or Isolde). However, she quickly became irritated when people twisted this to Ethel, so she switched to Priscilla, which in turn became reduced to Pip. Her mother remembered how useful she always made herself with her younger sisters: Rosemary was a rascal, 'Pip alone could manage her with loving ease.' Pip was an affectionate child, always desperate to please and to be liked – and thus hurt by the coldness of her parents. Gaenor recalled that Pip was 'a very pretty girl with golden curls and blue eyes, and bitterly resented the disappearance of the curls and her entry into the comparative drabness of schoolroom life'. She was brought up in the splendour of Seaford House in Belgrave Square until she was nine, attending a London day school – Queen's College in Harley Street. While still a child in London, she suffered a distressing riding accident in Rotten Row in Hyde Park. She was thrown from her horse and when her foot was caught in a stirrup she was dragged some distance. She was nervous about riding for a while but, according to her sister, 'she grew up to become an extremely brave horse-woman, and to show courage in all sorts of difficult and dangerous situations'.[9]

Withal, it was a privileged existence. Margot was concerned that her children be independent and resourceful which was difficult given the legions of servants whose job it was to make life easy for the family. With a great imaginative leap, considering her own station in life, Margot supposed that 'some, if not all, of the girls might have to cope and "manage" in later life'. To create a contrast with the world of housemaids who cleared up books and toys and grooms who saddled and rubbed down horses and ponies, a little house was built at Chirk called the Lake Hut. There, the girls made do on their own, cooking, washing–up, and looking after themselves. Pip took to this very well. When their parents took the children on trips on their sixty-foot motor launch, *Etheldreda*, Pip and Gaenor would do the cooking. In her mother's recollection, 'when it was rough it was Pip who managed to produce food for us all. She was gallant and highly efficient at ten and twelve years old.' Holidays at Brownsea were enlivened by days camping at nearby Furzy Island. Indeed, Chirk, Brownsea and Furzy provided the basis of blissful fun for the children. They had considerable independence to wander the fields, the woods and streams. When they were required for meals, if Margot was present, she would unleash the power of her soprano in Brünnhilde's call from *Die Walküre* and they would come scampering home.[10]

All in all, there were idyllic elements but there remains a question mark about the impact on the children of the lengthy separations from both Margot and Tommy. The Scott-Ellis girls saw relatively little of their parents, particularly of their father. When they did, emotional warmth was in short supply. Tommy and Margot were, according to their son, incapable of showing emotion. They both seemed totally remote, capable of impersonal kindness but not of understanding. Pip's cousin Charmian van Raalte, who was brought up with the Scott-Ellis girls, having been abandoned by her own mother, recalled that 'neither Tommy nor Margot ever showed a grain of affection to any of the children'. Indeed, when Thomas Howard de Walden returned from France, where he had fought in the mass slaughter of Passchendaele, he was dourly taciturn, in shock from the shelling and the butchery. In his own description, part of him had died in the war and the part

that survived was 'no more than a husk, living out a life
that he finds infinitely wearisome'.[11] However, on the rare
occasions when their parents did acknowledge the existence
of the children, they seemed, fleetingly, to have fun together.
Lord Howard de Walden had a burning interest in the theatre
as well as being a musician of some talent. At Chirk, he would
often delight guests with his playing in the music room. He
wrote the libretto for three operas by Joseph Holbrooke. He
ran the Haymarket Theatre for several years. He often organised theatrical events involving his children and their friends,
writing six plays for them. With professionally produced costumes and scenery, these were exciting enterprises. In one, a
part was taken by Brian Johnston, later famous as a broadcaster.
Moreover, baskets of costumes from old productions at the
Haymarket, with armour and helmets, ended up in the family
home, swelled the dressing-up basket and transformed many
childhood games.

Although he seemed always to have more of a bond with
Pip, Tommy did not, in general, have much time for girls.
He once wrote of his granddaughters: 'The girls are alright
but they are girls and there is no more to be said about that.'
He rarely spoke to his daughters and Pip was the only one
not to regard him as a complete stranger. His conversation
was too erudite and dismissive, his interests too varied. When
in England, Tommy and Margot had an astonishing array of
friends and acquaintances that included G. K. Chesterton,
Hilaire Belloc, George Bernard Shaw, Diaghilev, Augustus
John, Jacob Epstein, Thomas Beecham, Rudyard Kipling, Cole
Porter, Ivor Novello, Alicia Markova, Arturo Toscanini,
Richard Tauber, James Barrie, P. G. Wodehouse, Arthur
Rubinstein and Somerset Maugham. He was President of the
London Symphony Orchestra. In Wales, he was an especially
generous patron of the arts and was made a Bard at the
Eisteddfod. With his wife, he shared a passion for opera and
they had their own box at Covent Garden.[12]

Tommy was a major expert in medieval weaponry and heraldry about which he wrote a number of important reference works. He even had his own suit of armour made in order to assess the difficulty of swordplay. On one occasion, the painter Augustus John, while staying at Chirk Castle, was quite taken aback to find his host reading *The Times*, dressed in a suit of armour. The reason for this eccentricity was that Lord Howard de Walden wished to ascertain how easily an armour-clad man could get up from a prostrate position. To avoid spending hours helplessly trapped on the floor, he was awaiting a companion before beginning the experiment. Tommy was deeply interested in falconry and regularly went hawking. He had farming interests in East Africa including a coffee farm in Kenya and he was often away for long periods on safari. In 1926, however, he took Pip with him for several months. Her bravery during brushes with wild animals in Kenya reinforced his pride in her. She would later describe to Gaenor her terror on the walk in the dark to the outside lavatory. On another occasion, he took her on a lengthy sailing trip to the north of Scotland. In contrast, Margot got on less well with Pip because, as her sister recalled, they were so alike in their energy, practicality and impetuousness that they irritated each other.[13]

While Margot and Tommy enjoyed the London season or were travelling abroad, Pip, Bronwen, Elizabeth and Gaenor spent much of their childhood in the grandeur of Chirk Castle. Chirk had been an old border castle on Offa's Dyke. There, they were educated by a series of governesses, usually two at a time. The life in the castle fed Pip's taste for adventure. An ancient castle full of armour and swords and shields inspired games of make-believe involving knights and dragons, fairies and damsels in distress. The fact of having ponies and vast tracts of Welsh hillside on which to roam also encouraged her imagination. The governesses were easily typecast as ogres and giants. These different women each had to stand in for the girls' frequently absent mother whose social commitments were extraordinarily time-consuming. Moreover, their regular replacement added an element of insecurity into Pip's early life. At least she had avoided the worst childhood wounds of the repeated separations of boarding school. Only in early 1932 when she was fifteen, and Gaenor twelve, was Pip – to her delight – sent away to Benenden.[14] Pip was a sensitive girl and the consequence of this upbringing was that, for all the protection provided by money and class, not to mention her indisputable bravery, she was always rather insecure and eager to please. She could be easily humiliated by the verbal cruelty, or simple thoughtlessness, of others. Nevertheless, as her voluminous diaries show, she was an indefatigable optimist. Her brother remembered her as always 'of a cheerful and jolly disposition'.[15]

The patrician atmosphere in which Pip was brought up was characterised by a degree of paternalism towards the less privileged. Both Tommy and Margot were active patrons of hospitals. Tommy, however, was, outside the arts, a considerable snob. He once reprimanded Margot after a visit by the Prime Minister, the Conservative Stanley Baldwin, and his wife. Tommy commented to Margot: 'You really should not ask those sort of people.' That was an indication of his snobbery rather than of his political orientation which was inevitably very right-wing. In early May 1926, during the nine days of the General Strike, the ballroom of Seaford House was home to about two hundred undergraduates from Oxford and Cambridge who had volunteered to join a special police force. Effectively, they were engaged in strikebreaking. From 4 to 12 May, for twenty-four hours every day, they were on call. Telephoned news of a demonstration or clashes with pickets would see lorry engines roar to life. The enthusiastic scions of middle-class families, armed with truncheons and well fed by Margot's caterers, would set off for some sport.[16] Similar attitudes underlay Pip's later involvement in the Spanish Civil War.

In 1932, during holidays from Benenden, Pip had learned to fly in a Gypsy Moth bought by her mother. Nervous because Pip was already showing signs of the wanderlust that would characterise her later life, Margot prevented her taking her pilot's certificate.[17] She remained at Benenden for a year and two terms before going on to a finishing school in Paris in the autumn of 1933. When Pip left Paris in early 1934, her already good French was much improved. After skiing at Mürren in Switzerland, she spent time with an Austrian aristocratic – and anti-Nazi – family, the Harrachs, in Munich. In 1931, before going up to Oxford, John had gone to Munich to learn German. On his first day, driving his car, he ran over a man who turned out to be Adolf Hitler. The future Führer was, unfortunately, unhurt. Shortly afterwards John met, and fell in love with Irene 'Nucci' Harrach and in 1934, they were married. Elizabeth, Pip, Gaenor and Rosemary were all bridesmaids at the wedding.[18] Pip's first interest in boys was focused on a handsome young flyer called William Rhodes Moorhouse. They went out together a few times but her adolescent crush on him was not reciprocated. In any case, Pip was about to become involved in a relationship with the Orléans Borbón family that would erase thoughts of William and dramatically affect the remainder of her life.

Alfonso de Orléans, who had established a friendship with Margot van Raalte during the summers that they spent at Brownsea, was married to a beautiful German princess, Beatrice Saxe-Coburg-Gotha, a granddaughter of Queen Victoria. Prince Ali, as he was known in the family, was an intrepid aviator and also a cousin of the King of Spain, Alfonso XIII. His wife was a cousin of Alfonso XIII's consort, Queen Victoria Eugenia. Prince Ali was a fitness fanatic and an enthusiastic military man who was determined to prove that being of royal blood imposed an iron duty to be useful to his country.[19] From 1909 until 1914, and then again from 1917, he and Princess Bea – as the family knew her – spent their summers at

Brownsea Island with the Van Raalte family. After Margot married Tommy Scott-Ellis, the children of the Orléans and the Scott-Ellis families spent summers together at Brownsea.[20] Prince Ali and Princess Bea had three sons, Álvaro (b. Coburg, 1910), Alfonso (b. Madrid, 28 May 1912) – known always as Alonso to distinguish him from the several other Alfonsos in the Royal Family, and Ataúlfo (b. Madrid, 1913). When in Spain in 1924, they lived in their palace at Sanlúcar de Barrameda, in the province of Cádiz. The Palacio de Montpensier consisted of three different buildings combined in the mid-nineteenth century into a pseudo-Moorish palace. About half a mile away, the family also had a huge English garden called 'El Botánico' within which there were two houses.[21] Alfredo Kindelán, the head of the Spanish air force and a close friend of Alfonso de Orléans, was a frequent visitor.

After the flight of Alfonso XIII on 14 April 1931, Alfonso de Orléans Borbón regarded it as his duty to resign his commission and accompany the King on his painful journey from Madrid, via Cartagena, into exile in France.[22] Prince Ali's properties having been confiscated by the Republican Government, his family settled in Switzerland. He reconciled himself to living on his wits – and his not inconsiderable talents as an aeronautical engineer and a linguist (he spoke fluent English, French, German and Italian as well as Spanish). For Alfonso de Orléans, it was always a matter of principle to demonstrate that royal personages were not all effete and useless. Energetic and resourceful, remembering that he had once met Henry Ford, he wrote and asked him for a job. While awaiting a reply, he worked sweeping up in bars. The American magnate replied quickly and instructed him to report for work at the Ford factory at Asnière, outside Paris. He did so first as a cleaner, then as a salesman. Then he was soon transferred to the Ford headquarters at Dagenham in England where he worked variously, under the pseudonym Mr Dorleans, in stock control, accountancy and public relations. Within four years, his dynamism and initiative saw him made director of the company's European operations. Princess Bea had moved from Zurich to London and kept in close touch with the Howard de Walden family. During this time, the Howard de Waldens commissioned Augustus John – who had set himself up as a kind of artist-in-residence at Chirk – to paint a portrait of Princess Bea.[23]

Pip had inherited from her mother a passion for the opera although her own violin studies had not borne great fruit. Wherever she went, she was always accompanied by a gramophone and a box of records. That Pip was a cultured and witty girl is amply illustrated by her diary. The extant part dates back to August 1934. She describes a stay in Salzburg with her mother and her sisters Gaenor and Elizabeth who, at the time, was being wooed by the great cellist Grigor Piatigorski. There Pip revelled in a performance of *Don Giovanni* conducted by Bruno Walter in which the Don was sung in Italian by Ezio Pinza. She was also entranced by the playing of Piatigorski when he serenaded Elizabeth. The family was en route to Munich for the wedding of Pip's brother John to Nucci Harrach.[24] In 1934, Princess Bea and her son Prince Ataúlfo stayed at Seaford House when they came over for the marriage of the Duke of Kent to Princess Marina. Pip also made her début in 1934. It was probably at this time that she began to notice Ataúlfo – or Touffles as he was known in the family, seeing him not as the child with whom she had played at Brownsea but as a charming young man. Both Gaenor and Pip's cousin Charmian van Raalte recalled Ataúlfo as 'definitely not good-looking'. He had a round and podgy face but women liked him for his gentle manner and his amusing conversation. He played the piano and danced with extraordinary delicacy. If to some this denoted effeminacy, Pip did not notice.[25] At this time, Pip was gawky and unattractive. She was worried about her weight – nearing thirteen stones (83 kilos). A photograph of her at a ball in May 1935 shows her looking frumpy, nervous and ill-at-ease.

When the military rebellion of 18 July 1936 precipitated the Spanish Civil War, Prince Alfonso de Orléans Borbón was in Bucharest on Ford business. He hastened to Burgos where he arrived on 2 August 1936. He offered his own and his sons' services as pilots and was bitterly disappointed to be told that General Mola wished to avoid the uprising having a monarchist character. He was ordered to leave Spain. He then wrote to his friend, General Alfredo Kindelán, who had been named head of the rebel air force, and to Franco himself, pointing out that his two elder sons, Álvaro and Alfonso Orléans y Coburgo, had earned pilots' licences in England in the Officers' Training Corps. In consequence, at the beginning of November, they were able to join the Nationalist forces. However, Franco considered that Prince Ali himself was more useful to his cause in London. There he was able to facilitate the delivery of Ford trucks to the Nationalists. Moreover, Princess Bea was carrying on effective propaganda on behalf of Franco in establishment circles in Britain. She was also raising significant sums of money for food and hospital supplies for the Nationalist cause. Alfonso Orléans y Coburgo was killed on 18 November 1936. Flying as observer, his Italian Romeo Ro37bis biplane crashed while flying from Seville to Talavera de la Reina. The aircraft flew into a mountain at Ventas de Culebrín near Monesterio in the south of the province of Badajoz. In consequence, his younger brother Ataúlfo immediately volunteered.[26] Pip was devastated when, at a dance in New York in January 1937, she had been told of Alonso's death.[27]

In November 1936, Pip had sailed with her father for New York to stay with friends, a Mrs Wagner and her daughter Peggy. The trip would expand her horizons considerably. 'I wonder what this year will bring me. I have a feeling lots. I hope so. I do wish Touffles would write.'[28] He was constantly on her mind. 'Last night', she wrote on 3 January 1937, 'I dreamed Touffles was terribly ill and all tied up in bandages and as white as a sheet. Oh dear oh dear. I wish he was not out in Spain in the war. God how foul wars are. Every time I think of Alonso it makes me feel sick and think of the cruel futility of it all. What a mess human nature is.' The 'divine' Tyrone Power in a movie reminded her of Touffles. 'I don't suppose even if Touffles gets back from Spain alright he would ever want to marry an unattractive fool like me so I might as well stop wishing.' Letters from him merely left her miserable and worried.[29] She wrote on 22 January, 'I have put my new photo of Touffles up on my bed table and simply adore it. I am silly to let myself go on pretending he might love me one day because I know he won't but I can't stop myself being nuts over him so I might as well enjoy it as much as I can.' New York was a regular round of cinema, theatre and nightclubs, punctuated by having her fortune told at the Gypsy Tearooms. As always, she maintained her interest in music, attending a concert by the violinist Josef Szigeti. Among several historic performances at the New York Metropolitan, she attended *Rigoletto* with Lawrence Tibbett in the title role, *Die Walküre* with Kirsten Flagstad and Lauritz Melchior, and Saint-Saëns' *Samson et Dalila* with Gertrud Wettergren, as well as a *Cavalleria Rusticana* and *Le Coq d'Or*.[30] Nevertheless, she was restless. 'Life here is so idle and pointless that I am pining to have some work or something to occupy me. We just do nothing.' She managed to persuade the Wagners that she had to leave in case Touffles returned from Spain.[31] While waiting for her passage home, she worried about her weight, and danced and flirted with an eligible young Cuban called Alvaro García.

Her passion for Touffles was boosted by the flirtation with García whom she had met at the Wagners' home in New York. On 26 January 1937, the twenty-year-old Pip wrote in her diary:

I am so shocked at myself by my behaviour tonight and so bewildered by it all that I don't even know if

I enjoyed it. I went out with Alvaro to a Cuban place where we danced mambas (*sic*) until 4 o'clock in the morning. He dances divinely and it was grand fun. He made violent love to me the whole time and kissed me and I kissed him in the taxi home. But then he saw me up to the apartment and made such passionate love to me I was scared stiff. He even pulled down my dress and kissed my bosom which horrified me but I could not stop him. He did everything under the sun and I let him. I am certainly gaining experience but I don't know if I like it.

By the next day, reflecting on the incident, she wrote: 'The trouble with my flirtation is that all it has done is to wake me up and make me want Touffles to make love to me even more than I did before. Oh hell and damnation.'[32] 'Make love', of course, meant rather less then, as this passage illustrates, than it does now.

Day after day, she wrote of missing Touffles. On 2 February, she wrote perceptively: 'I think the trouble with all of us is our age and suppressed sex. I would like to have a hectic affair with someone but of course never will.' The next night, however, she came very near. After a cocktail party and dancing into the early hours, 'Alvaro took me home and came into the apartment where he made love to me on the sofa too divinely for words. It was heaven and again I behaved outrageously and let him do even worse things than before.' She refused to have sex with him and was amused by the fact that he clearly believed her to be much more experienced than was actually the case.[33]

On her return passage on the SS *Paris*, she wrote: 'I hate to be all alone, I feel scared and depressed.' Her essential insecurity was revealed in other diary entries. 'Everyone on board is sweet to me and they all seem to like me so much. It is so lovely to know people like you. If only I have changed enough to make Touffles like me too.' The round of cocktail parties and dancing terminated on the last night on board in a dramatic encounter with a French diplomat. 'God knows why but this evening I went off the rails and was mildly raped. I can't think why I let Mr Brugere do such a thing, I must have been crazy.' Having been assaulted by the man on deck, she later went to his cabin, 'so now I don't know whether I am still a virgin or not. I think not. It was heavenly but frightening.' She left his cabin 'feeling very ashamed and yet all excited and happy in a way'. The event seemed to unleash a hitherto repressed passion. After a 'hot' encounter in a taxi with a film director 'Frenche' whom she met on the ship from New York, she wrote: 'I seem to have become so damn oversexed that I just can't stop myself. I don't know whether it is suppressed sex bursting forth or my thyroid pills or what, but the effect is incredible for the erstwhile priggish me.' On returning to Chirk, she took up riding with a vengeance. She started to dream about Touffles again. Life in London was an endless kaleidoscopic social round in which she occasionally bumped into 'that filthy fucking Frenche'. She took singing and piano lessons, fenced most days, regularly went to the theatre and the cinema, often visited the hairdresser and fashion shows and consulted more fortune-tellers. Despite her sexual progress, she was still young enough to sit with friends and be scared by talk of ghosts.[34]

In early March, Prince Ali appeared in London. Revealingly, Pip refused his dinner invitation to spend time with her father. 'Papa and I get on so well. We talk for hours every evening. He knows so much about every subject. I wish I had his brains.' When she did go to see Princess Bea, she found her heartbroken by the death of her son Alonso. Pip got news of her beloved Touffles who, as befitted the son of a German princess, had joined Hitler's Condor Legion and was now flying as an observer in German bombers. As always, being reminded of Touffles provoked her into a flirtation. At a society hostess's dance, she 'spent most of the evening dancing with crazy Francis Cochrane to whom I got engaged just for fun. He is great fun and dances quite well. So now I have a fiancé for a change. I shall break it off again soon.' Nothing more was heard of him thereafter. Her social life was more of a whirlwind than a roundabout. When she was not in the country, at the races or at Brooklands, she took every advantage of what London had to offer. A typical day would see her rise late, and after breakfast, practise fencing or do some work in relation to the small stud farm at Chirk. She would then lunch at the Ritz or the Savoy with friends. Lunch would be followed by shopping, a dress fitting, the hairdresser and then tea with some family friend. In the evening, she would attend one or more cocktail parties, a dance in the home of some society hostess or the theatre, the ballet or the opera, then dinner, perhaps at Quaglino's or the Savoy Grill, then on to the Café de Paris or a nightclub. She attended a number of legendary operatic occasions, including Eva Turner and Giovanni Martinelli singing Puccini's *Turandot* at Covent Garden. Dancing until the early hours of most mornings, she met lots of attractive men but nothing came of her flirtations with them.[35] When, on 24 March, she finally got a letter from Touffles requesting her photograph, she pranced down the passage 'singing at the top of my voice'. Already thinking of going to Spain, she started Spanish lessons.[36]

The ceaseless round of fun was beginning to pall when her life was changed by a chance conversation with her mother – 'so nice the way she leaves me to myself, no advice, no orders, just perfectly sweet'. On Easter Sunday, 28 March 1937, she wrote: 'This evening after dinner we began to talk about Spain and Mama suddenly said that Gabriel Herbert was out there doing nursing and smuggling medicines etc. I said, "God I wish I was" so Moke (Monica FitzClarence, a friend of Margot's) said "Why don't you?" I explained I would have long ago if I had thought for a moment Mama would let me.'

To her astonishment, her mother said that she would give Pip permission if she produced proper plans mapped out and aimed to do important work out there – 'but I must find out and arrange it myself and she can't help me. So now I must see Mrs Herbert and Princess Bea and see what I can do to help. My chance at last I hope!' Margot had not expected such a burst of focused energy and was horrified. She regarded Pip as 'both frivolous and pretty. She loved hairdressers, young men and cream buns. She would go to several cinemas in one afternoon and I deplored that she would not face up to anything serious.' The Spanish Civil War was rather too serious even for Margot. Pip herself was enthused by the idea of going to Spain and determined to overcome all obstacles. She was desperate to be of some use. 'It is a bore to look so young and silly, it will be very difficult to make anyone think I really mean it and am capable of doing it.' She now asked her mother to let her take first-aid classes as well as Spanish lessons. She also spoke to Mrs Herbert and her daughter Laura, who was soon to be married to Evelyn Waugh. Presumably on the basis of communication with her sister, Gabriel, Laura told Pip that 'it was awfully difficult to get in now'.[37]

Perhaps she was inspired by her mother's earlier example running a hospital in Egypt. It is an extraordinary coincidence that the mother of the only other British woman to volunteer to work for Franco, Gabriel Herbert, had also worked in that Egyptian hospital. Gabriel Herbert herself was a competent and energetic young woman. In September 1936, she had gone to Burgos and returned to London with a list of medical supplies requested by the Junta. She then returned to Spain with an ambulance. With a second vehicle sent in November, it became the Equipo Anglo-Español Móvil de Servicio al Frente. Gabriel Herbert herself acted as an intermediary between the medical team in Spain and the London committee of the Catholic Bishops' Fund for the Relief of Spanish Distress. Pip's reference to her 'nursing and smuggling medicines' was a misunderstanding of Gabriel's activities in taking supplies into Spain.[38]

Pip's Spanish progressed quickly. Nevertheless, while she tried, in a desultory fashion, to find out more about going to Spain, she began to see a lot of 'the most gorgeous tall hero called John Geddes', a fashionable young man–about–town. They danced together, got drunk together and talked about their respective broken hearts, she about Touffles and he about a girl named Ann Hamilton Grace who had ditched him. They walked their dogs and within a couple of weeks of knowing him, she could write: 'I dote on him and hope I will see him again soon.'[39] By 13 April, they were lovers. She found the experience physically painful 'but it was fun'. 'I still don't feel even a twinge of conscience or remorse. And oddly I don't like him any more or less.' After sleeping with him a second time, she wrote: 'He is an absolute darling although definitely rather a cad.' She was taken entirely by surprise, at the end of April, when he asked her to marry him. She was emboldened to refuse after being told by her cousin, Charmian van Raalte, that she had had a letter from Touffles 'who is livid because I have not written for ages'.[40] She was also distracted by Gaenor's coming-out dance at Seaford House which was to be attended by 650 people including the Duke and Duchess of Kent. At dinner beforehand, she was delegated to look after the then seventeen-year-old King Faroukh of Egypt whom she thought 'a dear and we got on like billyoh'. Rather alone in London, he was taken by Pip to Regent's Park Zoo, the Tower of London, St Paul's Cathedral and several theatres.[41]

The big event was the coronation of George VI on 12 May. Pip was as bedazzled by its magnificent pageantry as the rest of the world. She attended the first court ball of the new reign which she found 'heaven'. On returning home 'I put on Mama's tiara and earrings and looked too regal for words. How I wish I had one.'[42] She had started writing to Touffles again and, on the strength of hearing that he might come to

London on leave, had begun to diet. Her diary at this time began to have increasing references to her hating 'that filthy smelly town London' and even 'I hate social life.'[43] Frantically hopeful of seeing Touffles, Pip was further reminded of the ongoing Civil War on 1 June. Two days before, the German navy had mounted a large-scale artillery bombardment of the Mediterranean city of Almería in southeastern Spain. Coming out of a newsreel with some friends, Pip ran into a Communist demonstration chanting 'Stop Hitler's War on Children!' Nan Green was among the demonstrators. However, she was discouraged when, accompanying her mother to lunch at the Herberts', she met Gabriel who 'was very interesting but convinced me more that there is no point in my going out there as a nurse or anything else. Damn it.'[44]

Just when she was on the verge of abandoning thoughts of Spain, Touffles turned up unexpectedly in London. On Wednesday 23 June, she wrote: 'He rang me up this morning and we lunched out together at San Marco and spent the afternoon buying records and talking. He is exactly the same as he always was and I like him as much as I always did.' The next day he broke a date to take her to an air show. She now admitted to herself what had been obvious for some time. 'I can't pretend to myself any longer. I know I am just as much in love with him as I always have been for the last three years. Oh God what hell it is, all so pointless, just lack of control.' On 29 June, he flew back to Spain from Croydon. After seeing him off, Pip was desperately miserable.[45]

However, for all her distress at seeing him go back to the war, his visit had reawakened her interest in Spain. Her notions of what was going on there derived almost entirely from Princess Bea 'who really knows what she is talking about. I simply adore her and admire her enormously for her courage about everything.' Her new-found determination to go to Spain roused her from her misery. Her hopes were raised on 6 July when she heard that she had passed her first aid and nursing exams with high grades. Nevertheless, bored with her social life in London and still unsure how to get to Spain, she fell into a limbo. 'I am in a very odd sort of numb way. I don't mind much what I do or where I go as long as it is more or less peaceful.' She was concentrating on her Spanish lessons with some dedication. On 22 July, without much expectation of a helpful reply, she wrote a long letter to Touffles asking him how to go about getting a posting in Spain.[46] Her interest in Spain was further fired by a book by an aviation journalist, Nigel Tangye, *Red, White and Spain*. Tangye had got into Nationalist Spain on the basis of letters attesting to his pro-Nazi sympathies. His entirely pro-Nationalist account probably confirmed for her things that she had already been told by Princess Bea. After lurid tales of Red atrocities, it related that, if the 'Reds' won, there would be a 'Communist State, complete suppression of the Church, mass-murder of land-owners and employers, officers and priests, and abolition of all freedom'. Tangye asserted that 'The Government, or Red, forces are entirely controlled and supplied by Russia.' Coincidentally, Tangye travelled for part of his time in Spain with a cavalry officer, the Barón de Segur, whose son was that same José Luis de Vilallonga who would later denigrate Pip's diaries.[47]

Things began to move a little faster when Prince Ali returned briefly to London. At dinner, Pip told Princess Bea of her firm intention to go to Spain and asked for her help. Pip's new-found determination and recently acquired nursing qualifications impressed the Infanta that she was serious. Accordingly, she concluded that Pip could be useful and undertook to find out where she should go as well as getting someone with whom to practise her Spanish. Pip was so heartened that she determined once more to 'get thin and fit and learn more Spanish'. She went up to Chirk in her Super Swallow Jaguar. She found her mother was making plans for her twenty-first birthday party on 16 November. Accordingly,

Pip reminded her of her Spanish project and Margot van Raalte was far less insouciant than she had been three months earlier. Now, she was concerned about her daughter's safety in the midst of so many men and decided to write to Princess Bea. Pip, confident that she could bring her mother around, had begun to read another blood-curdling account of Nationalist heroism, Major McNeill-Moss's *The Epic of the Alcazar*, which she found 'very interesting and exciting'. McNeill-Moss's book consisted of a romantically heroic account of the Republican siege of the Nationalist garrison in the Alcázar of Toledo from July to September and a notoriously mendacious white-wash of the Nationalist massacre of the civilian defenders of the town of Badajoz on 14 August 1936.[48]

The big leap forward in Pip's plans came when Princess Bea replied to Margot Howard de Walden's letter. Her enquiries had revealed that the level of confusion in Nationalist Spain was such that nothing for Pip could be organised from London. However, a change in her own circumstances opened the way for Pip. Prince Ali had been bombarding Franco with pleas for an active role in the fighting. Through the intercession of General Kindelán, the head of the Nationalist air force and the most prominent monarchist among the Nationalist generals, his wish had finally been granted. Accordingly, Princess Bea was going to return to Spain in the autumn to be near her husband's air base in the south. To Pip's intense delight, the Infanta proposed that she accompany her, assuring Margot that she would look after Pip 'as if she were her own daughter'. Under these circumstances, her parents did not object. Half a century later, her brother was still perplexed by their lack of anxiety.[49]

Pip's girlish joy was all too understandable since she was not only going to Spain but proximity to Touffles was virtually guaranteed. 'Princess B really is a saint,' she wrote on 8 August. 'It will be so nice to go with her.' She had little notion of the horrors that she would encounter. On 26 August, she wrote:

'What an adventure though a gruesome one.' With her Spanish future apparently resolved, she devoted much of the summer at Chirk to riding, playing tennis and learning golf. Princess Bea arranged a Spanish teacher, named Evelina Calvert, and Pip set herself a tough schedule in preparation for the journey. She was ecstatic when she learned that Princess Bea planned to take her to Sanlúcar by car on 22 September, via Paris, San Sebastián, Salamanca and Seville.[50]

Her preparations became frantic – increased efforts to improve her Spanish and some half-hearted dieting which got her weight down to 12 stone 3 pounds. A daily round of shopping, visits to the hairdresser (on one occasion to have her eyelashes dyed), inoculations, arrangements for her passport and visa for Spain. This included a visit to the Foreign Office where she was interviewed by William H. Montagu-Pollock, one of the four men with principal responsibility for British policy on Spanish affairs. That she was received by a functionary of such eminence was an indication of her social, if not her political, importance. On 18 September, she went with Princess Bea to Portsmouth to meet ex-Queen Victoria Eugenia of Spain. As the day for her departure drew near, she began to worry – 'I am almost frightened of going to Spain now' (19th); 'Somehow now the great moment has come, I feel almost scared and rather depressed' (20th); 'I wish I knew exactly what I was going to and where . . . I still can't really believe that this time next week I shall be in the middle of war. A strange and exciting life.'[51] What a contrast with Nan Green who knew rather more, from her husband's letters, about the hell into which she was going.

Pip's reasons for going to Spain had little to do with the real issues being fought out there. She lacked the ideological conviction of either Nan Green or even Gabriel Herbert who was a devout Catholic and believed that Franco's war effort was a crusade to save Christian civilisation. According to her sister Gaenor, Pip's views were 'a simple expression of support for her friends, and therefore pro-monarchy and anti-Communist'. In the case of one friend, Ataúlfo de Orléans Borbón (Touffles), much more than friendship was at stake. There can be no doubting that Pip went to war for love. It helped that her parents had been much taken by Prince Ali's repetition of the canard that the military had rebelled in July 1936 because a Communist takeover in Spain had been imminent. However, her plans would probably have come to nothing if her adored Princess Bea had not taken a hand. Pip's eventual placement as a nurse would owe much to the Infanta's prominent position in the Nationalist organisation known as La Delegación Nacional de Asistencia a Frentes y Hospitales, a patrician welfare operation headed by the Carlist María Rosa Urraca Pastor and largely run by monarchists.[52]

Complete with trunks and hatboxes containing the accumulated fruits of her last months' shopping trips, Pip left England in some style in Princess Bea's chauffeur-driven limousine on 21 September 1937. At Dover, they were met by the station master in his top hat and were swept into a private compartment on the boat train.[53] Then it was on to Paris for some more shopping and a visit to the World's Fair. This was the great exhibition for which Picasso's *Guernica* was commissioned by the Spanish Republican Government.[54] Interestingly, for someone just off to the Spanish Civil War, Pip did not see it, instead spending her time at the German and English pavilions. On one side of the Pont d'Iéna on the Rive Droite of the Seine, the German pavilion, designed by Albert Speer, glaring at its equally pugnacious Soviet rival, was an architectural representation of Nazi aggression. Huge, thirty-three-feet-high statues of muscle-bound Soviet heroes strode triumphantly forward, their way apparently blocked by the naked Teutonic heroes guarding the German design, a huge cubic mass, erected on stout pillars, and crowned by a gigantic eagle with the swastika in its claws. For Pip, this was 'the best'. The British pavilion symbolised the tired gentility of

appeasement. The British displays were of golf balls, pipes,
fishing rods, equestrian equipment and tennis rackets while
the German and the Italian were of military might. Pip thought
the British pavilion 'very bad'.[55] She and Princess Bea were
then driven on 23 September to Biarritz where Pip was
delighted to discover that she could understand most of the
Spanish that she began to hear. They were received by Sir
Henry Chilton, the British Ambassador to Republican Spain.
The pro-Nationalist Chilton had been on holiday in San Sebastián when the Civil War broke out and had refused to return
to Madrid. With the aid of the French Ambassador to Spain,
they managed to get across the frontier to San Sebastián on
the following day. With the beautiful resort bathed in sunshine,
it was like being on holiday.

The unwarlike nature of the trip continued when she and
Princess Bea were joined for dinner by one of General Alfredo
Kindelán's sons, Ultano. Pip went to the cinema with him,
then for a long walk and a mild flirtation – 'If it had not been
for the fact that he has known Ataúlfo and Alvaro all his life
and would certainly have told them I would have had a spot
of fun but I would have been ragged for the rest of my life
so I refrained and bade him a polite goodbye at the hotel.'
Pip saw her first sign of the war when they drove to Santander
along the route that the Nationalists had taken on their campaign in the north earlier in 1937. They met Touffles, 'much
thinner and very sunburnt . . . Madly attractive.' He went out
of his way to talk to her and she admitted that 'alas I still like
him more than I want to'. He told her about the capture of
Santander and took her to the German airbase from which he
flew as a navigator. 'They fly huge Junkers. His is a beauty
with two engines and a retractable undercarriage.' This means
that he must have been flying in the experimental Junkers Ju
86D-1. It was a curious time for Pip, a mixture of tourism
and initiation into the war. They visited the beautiful medieval
village of Santillana del Mar and La Magdalena, the great

English-style royal country residence on a hill overlooking the bay of Santander. 'It had been ruined inside by the Reds and is still being cleaned up by Red prisoners who are camped in the park. They all looked well and happy.'[56]

Sad to leave Touffles, she continued her journey on 28 September, moving on to Burgos where she toured the great cathedral, then onto Valladolid and to Salamanca. Pip was entranced by Spain, the only drawback being the fleas awaiting her in every hotel bedroom. She and Princess Bea stayed with General Kindelán. Kindelán was a man of great rectitude and austerity. Nevertheless, to Pip's young eyes, oblivious to his moral and political merits, he was just 'rather fat and sloppy'. At the Grand Hotel in Salamanca, she caught a glimpse of the 'stunning looking' Peter Kemp, whom she knew vaguely from London. In a Carlist regiment, he was one of the very few English volunteers on the Nationalist side. On 1 October, the first anniversary of Franco's elevation to the headship of state saw a major display of pageantry. Pip was elated by being able to witness history being made – 'a parade of soldiers led by the Moors in their wonderful coloured cloaks on Arab horses with golden trappings. The leaders rode white Arabs with silver hooves and gold-embroidered medieval trappings which looked beautiful with the men's white and orange cloaks, behind them were men in green cloaks on black horses got up the same but with golden hooves.' Her concern that the Nationalist forces might be antiquated was redressed when Álvaro, Princess Bea's eldest son, took her to inspect the Italian Savoia Marchetti tri-motored bombers at his air base. This was the Base Aéreo de Matacán, built in October–November 1936. Afterwards Álvaro took her to see the fierce fighting bulls at the estate of Antonio Pérez Tabernero, a bull-breeder friend of the Kindelán family.[57]

On 2 October, she was thrilled when Touffles unexpectedly showed up in Salamanca although her delight was tempered when he spent their brief time together teasing her about her figure. She also wrote to her father and asked him to buy her a Ford 10 and have it sent to Gibraltar. 'I hope you do as I must have a car if I am here alone.' On 4 October, they left Salamanca and, after a spectacular journey south through the harsh and arid hills of Extremadura, they reached Sanlúcar de Barrameda – the family's Palacio de Montpensier having been returned to Prince Alfonso by Franco. Pip found its crazy mixture of styles hideously ugly but fascinating. Prince Ali, now a lieutenant colonel in the Nationalist airforce, was stationed at Seville and so was often able to visit his home. Inevitably, she imbibed the family's views on the Reds.[58]

By mid-October, everything had been arranged for her to go and stay with the Duquesa de Montemar in Jérez while attending a nursing course at a hospital there. Lord Howard de Walden cabled that her car would be sent to Gibraltar in a few days. When it arrived at the end of the month, she thought it 'heaven. Black with green leather inside and a dream of beauty.' At first she found the hospital 'splendid fun' and 'not in the least disgusting'. The bulk of the patients were Moorish mercenaries whom she found 'perfectly sweet but like a lot of children and rather dirty'. When her course proper began, she was shocked by the appalling wounds that had to be treated. 'I did not feel sick at all but afterwards when I left the hospital I kept seeing the wounds all day and hearing the screams of agony.' She was fully aware that she would see far worse sights at the front. 'I understand now why nurses are so often hard and inhuman.' While in Jérez, she got gathered up in the local social whirl. She was mortified when it was suggested to her by her hostess, the Duquesa, among others, that it was obvious that she was in love with Ataúlfo and ought to marry him. This was not because the idea displeased her. Quite the contrary, but she was embarrassed that her infatuation should be so obvious. Despite her emotional preoccupations, she made good progress with her nursing skills. She loved the work and was beginning to be able to witness without distress the most hair-raising wounds being treated.[59]

There were now two parallel strands in her life. One was training to be a nurse at the front and the other was her deepening passion for Touffles. When he returned to Sanlúcar and telephoned to invite her over, she skipped her classes to go and see him, 'hopping with life and merriment'. When she got back to the Orléans household, her happiness knew no bounds. The life of the well-to-do in the Nationalist zone had no equivalent in the Republican ranks. Touffles arrived with nine Luftwaffe pilots for a bout of entertainment and relaxation that included swimming, a flamenco fiesta at one of the Jérez bodegas and a visit to a stud farm for Arab steeds. There was then a trip to Gibraltar to collect Pip's car and to do shopping, during which she bought a white kimono embroidered with golden dragons. She spent a lot of time with Touffles drinking and dancing. After one late night, she wrote: 'I adore Touffles more every day and only wish I could just stay with him for ever.' He bought her a radio in anticipation of her imminent twenty-first birthday. It was to accompany her throughout the Spanish Civil War. Loaded with shopping, including 3,000 cigarettes, she drove her new car back into Spain. Her social position ensured that she had no difficulty getting through the border control. 'They had been warned to expect us and refused to let us declare anything. So we just sailed through with no trouble at all. It was very nice of them to be so kind as it saved a packet of trouble as my car has no triptyque [a document permitting the transit of a car from one country to another] or insurance, and I have no licence.'

Ecstatically happy to be spending time with Touffles, she had no desire to return to the hospital at Jérez. However, her views were somewhat altered when she came face to face with the arrogantly sexist mentality of the Andalusian aristocratic *señorito*. Pip and the family went to Seville to stay at the Hotel Cristina, which was 'crammed full of Germans on leave'. Touffles met up with his Luftwaffe comrades and announced that they were off to a brothel. 'Of course it is damn stupid of me to mind as it won't be the first or last time he sleeps with a tart but if he liked me the weeniest bit the way I want him to, he could not have told me he was going to without a qualm. However, who cares. I'm damned if I'm going to. I knew he was not in the least in love with me before so it does not make any difference. Oh hell and damn.' When he and his German cronies did the same on the following night, she decided that she would rather be at the front nursing. She did not know, of course, whether he did anything more than play the piano and dance.[60]

Feeling rejected by Ataúlfo, she began to get involved in her hospital work. On 10 November, she attended her first operations which she found enthralling. Touffles went back to his unit on the next day, leaving her 'with that grim feeling of emptiness and the awful wartime pessimism of wondering at the back of my mind whether I will ever see him again'. One and all continued to enquire as to when she would marry him. She wrote in her diary: 'But why bother, at this very moment he is almost certainly tootling around Seville with a tart but why should I care. Of course I do but it is very stupid.' She was finding some consolation in nursing. She loved the work although 'I am beginning to loathe the Moors. They are so tiresome always quarrelling and yelling at one. It makes me mad to have a lot of filthy smelly Moors ordering me about.' On the eve of her twenty-first birthday, she wrote: 'I feel awfully small and young tonight. In a new country talking a strange language and only understanding half of what is said to me, doing a new kind of work amongst new people and about to prance off on my own to the middle of the war. Sometimes I feel an awful long way from home but who cares. It is the first adventure I have ever undertaken and so far I love it.' When Princess Bea returned to England on 20 November, Pip went back to Jérez where she waited anxiously for her nursing examination. She was keen to get to the front –

'I am tired of waiting around doing nothing much. I want action.' Every day, her diary recorded her anxiety to be off to war. However, this required the permission of Mercedes Milá, the head of the Nationalist nursing services. The ordeal of the examination on 1 December passed off less traumatically than she had feared. In fact, she was amazed by how much she was left to do in the hospital without supervision.[61]

Her social life was hectic; late nights consisting of cinema, dinner, protracted dancing and drinking. On 6 and 7 December, she was given a tour around the German battleship *Deutschland* which she thought 'a lovely boat'. On 20 December, Touffles and one of his German friends took her for a spin in a Junkers 52 bomber. Despite the distractions, she was becoming deeply impatient with Mercedes Milá's failure to respond to her request to go to the front. She was all the more unsettled because of rumours about major action on the Aragón front – an echo of the Republican offensive against Teruel. As her Spanish improved and she got to know more people, her social life was coming to resemble her life in London albeit on a narrower scale. She had a couple of superficial flirtations, her blonde hair and blue eyes – and probably her plumpness too – making her very attractive to Spanish men. Finally, knowing that Princess Bea was in Burgos, she decided to leave the hospital at Jérez and make the hazardous eleven-hour 1000-kilometre car journey to join her for Christmas. It was a courageous – or irresponsible – initiative since attractive young women travelling alone in Spain were usually at risk from sexually frustrated soldiers. With typical self-reliance, she coped with running out of petrol on remote roads and the car's sump springing a leak.[62]

When, after driving for two days, she finally arrived at Burgos on 23 December, she could not find Princess Bea and was desperate to have come so far only to be all alone. Princess Bea had moved on to the Palacio de Ventosilla at Aranda de Duero where her family would be staying. This was because the front-line units of the Nationalist air force were being regrouped as the Primera Brigada Aérea Hispana at Aranda, alongside the Italian Aviazione Legionaria in Zaragoza and the German Condor Legion in Almazán, the walled medieval town due south of Soria. General Alfredo Kindelán, with overall command over all three forces, had established his headquarters at Burgos. It was Pip's good fortune to get a room in the hotel where General Kindelán's family were staying. They told her that Mercedes Milá planned to send her to a front-line hospital. There was a terrible scare when word was brought to the hotel that Álvaro de Orléans had crashed. His Italian wife Carla Parodi-Delfino was hysterical and Pip had to calm her down. She then went on to the Palacio de Ventosilla. To the relief of Álvaro's escape, there was added the dual pleasure of resolving her future as a nurse at the front and of seeing Ataúlfo. Touffles told her that she was much thinner and very beautiful. However, that delight was dampened by Princess Bea, who knew that Pip was in love with him. The Infanta told her the first of a series of slightly conflicting stories by way of breaking to her gently that Ataúlfo would never marry her. She said, rather implausibly, that he would never recover from having his heart broken by the daughter of Alfonso XIII, Beatriz. The romantic in Pip was both intrigued and devastated to be told by Princess Bea that Touffles was so affected by this that she was 'afraid he will never fall in love or get married and will just get more and more the young man about town and have mistresses'.[63]

Meanwhile, the men of the family were flying bombing missions against the Republican forces that were closing in on Teruel. The proximity to the war was beginning to affect Pip. 'It really is an awful life when you know your friends are risking their lives every single day and every time you say goodbye or just goodnight you think you may never see them again.' Her diaries reflected her links with senior officers of the Nationalist air force. She felt an ever closer identification

with the cause: 'Today [28 December] we lost one machine
and shot down seven reds.' Today [30 December] they brought
down eight Reds, four Curtis, two Martin bombers and two
others and we did not lose one. Good work!' 'We shot down
eleven Reds today [4 January 1938].' 'We shot down eight
Reds today. The right spirit. [5 January 1938].' The strain of
seeing Touffles only fleetingly as he often popped in between
flights was trying her nerves and increased her determination
to get to the front line. Her wish was granted, in mid-January,
by a telegram instructing her to go to the hospital at Alhama
de Aragón, southwest of Zaragoza on the road to Guadalajara.
She was reluctant to leave the Orléans family but a move
was inevitable because of a reorganisation of the Nationalist
air force. Prince Ali's air force unit (escuadra) of Savoia-
Marcchetti 79s was moving to Castejón while Ataúlfo's Condor Legion bomber unit was moving to Corella. Both Castejón
and Corella were between Alfaro and Tudela in Navarre and
Princess Bea was going to Castejón in order to set up a house
for her husband and son.[64]

In fact, when the orders came, the entire household was
plunged into various forms of colds and influenza. The worst
hit was Ataúlfo and Pip decided to stay on and nurse him.
However, proximity to her loved one did not bring happiness.

> I am in the depths of depression and so nervous that
> I don't know what to do with myself. I can't sleep
> and have not done so for three nights which is not
> surprising when I have to spend my whole day keeping
> a firm grip on myself not to appear to be in love
> with Ataúlfo. I don't know whether I am getting less
> controlled, more frustrated or more alone but it is
> pure hell whatever it is and leaves me in a state of being
> unable to sleep, unable to eat and feeling miserable.

The imminent upheaval meant that Pip would have to leave
anyway. The malicious gossip about her relationship with him

made it impossible for her to stay and nurse Ataúlfo without Princess Bea in the house as chaperone. Pip's misery was dissipated by a meeting with Bella Kindelán, the general's daughter, who was a nurse at Alhama. When Bella told her that it would be possible to go from Alhama with a mobile unit right up to the front, she cast off her melancholia and threw herself into nursing.[65]

By 24 January 1938, Pip's prolonged Christmas holidays were over and she was ensconced along with the other nurses in the grim hotel in Alhama de Aragón which partly served as the local hospital. It was bitterly cold and depressing. The winter of 1937–8 was one of the cruellest Spain had ever suffered, the bitter cold at its worst in the barren and rocky terrain of Aragón with temperatures as low as −20° centigrade. Pip was missing Ataúlfo and there was nothing for her to do. She had been joined by Consuelo Osorio de Moscoso, the daughter of the Duqesa de Montemar. Alarmed at the prospect of spending time in their tiny unheated room, they impetuously decided to take matters into their own hands and go to Sigüenza where Consuelo knew some doctors. They hoped thereby to get to the front. However, when they reached the emergency hospital there, they were told that the front-line mobile units were fully staffed and had very few wounded. On their return to Aragón, they fell into an even worse gloom. 'There is nothing to do anywhere. The war seems to have paused and no one wants nurses.'[66] This was far from true. The battle for Teruel was still raging. Within ten days of the city falling into the hands of the Republic, the advancing Nationalist forces became the besiegers. The scale of the fighting can be deduced from Franco's remark on 29 January to the Italian Ambassador that he was delighted because the Republic was destroying its reserves by throwing them into 'the witches' cauldron of Teruel'.[67] Astonishingly, this was not reflected in the traffic through the hospital at Alhama where Pip was now assigned to a ward.

Much of her work was routine and unpleasant. One of her patients had a spinal injury – 'as he has lost all sense of feeling, he pees in his bed and we have to change the sheets which is both difficult and messy as he can't move at all, also he has no pyjamas and boils all over his bottom which is most unappetising. As for the other part of him, it is definitely an unpleasing spectacle which somehow always manages to be just where I want to take hold of a sheet.' However, the routine was short-lived. On 28 January, Mercedes Milá arrived to assign nurses to other hospitals. Consuelo and Pip pestered her to be sent to the front. At first, their pleas fell on deaf ears and the head of the Nationalist nursing services said that Pip was too young to be given responsibility in a dangerous position. However, with more senior nurses reluctant to go to the front, they were picked with three others to go to Cella, eight kilometres from Teruel, the nearest hospital to the front. Pip was excited and immediately thought of Ataúlfo, 'I shall see them all going over to bomb everyday perhaps. I can't wait to go, my spirit of adventure is aroused.' Although she was aware the hospital might be shelled and bombarded, her principal concern was whether her nursing skills would be adequate when the lives of the seriously wounded were at stake.[68]

After a perilous journey on mountain roads, Pip and Consuelo reached the bombed-out village of Cella. Their welcome was muted since there was neither food nor accommodation to spare. The officers refused to believe them when they said they would willingly sleep on the bare floor. They were eventually put in a room with three others, without proper bedding or window panes and only the most minimal sanitation. Pip's spirit of adventure and her country background helped her make light of the situation: 'The town itself is crammed with soldiers and mules, and ambulances come and go in a continuous stream. I am so enchanted with the place that I long to stay but we are terribly afraid that they will send us back when the others come as they have precedence over us. It is a shame as they will hate the discomfort and dirt and all and we don't mind it.' Indeed, she was anxious to join a mobile unit leaving for a position at Villaquemada, even nearer to the front line. Just when Pip thought that she would have to go back to Alhama, a need arose for two nurses so she and Consuelo were able to stay. They also found accommodation in a peasant farmhouse. Possessing a car made a colossal difference, since she could drive to nearby towns to shop for household necessities to make their room more comfortable and also for food. In the operating theatre itself, Pip was shocked by the doctor's ignorance of basic procedures of hygiene, 'His ideas of antisepsia were very shaky and it gave me the creeps to see the casual way they picked up sterilised compresses with their fingers.' She was equally alarmed to see their peasant hostess dipping into their food fingers 'black with years of grime'.[69]

The Nationalists were mounting a major attack on Republican lines at Teruel and Pip's medical unit was moved nearer the front. On 5 February, she was in attendance for 'one elbow shrapnel wound, three amputations, two arms and one leg, two stomach wounds, one head and one man who had shrapnel wounds in both legs, groin, stomach, arm and head. They were vile operations. The stomach ones were foul. One had to be cut right down the middle and his stomach came out like a balloon and most of his intestines; the other had a perforated intestine so had all his guts out, looking revolting.' Things were made more difficult by the fact that the doctor for whom she worked was both incompetent and perpetually irritable. 'It is perfectly grim having to work as operation sister to a man one does not trust, who is brutal and shouts at one all the time. It is nerve-wracking and leaves me all of a flop.' Pip discovered that she had type O blood and therefore could give blood for transfusions. At massive cost to both sides, the battle swayed back and forth until finally, on 7 February 1938, the Nationalists broke through and the Republic lost a huge swathe of territory and several thousand prisoners as well as tons of valuable equipment. Pip was delighted: 'The news of the war last night was stupendous. We have advanced to Alfambra, twenty kilometres in two days, taking fifteen villages, 2,5000 prisoners and 3,000 dead, not to mention lots of war material.' It was the beginning of an inexorable advance which in two weeks would lead to the recapture of Teruel on 22 February, the capture of nearly fifteen thousand prisoners and the loss of more equipment.[70]

The appalling conditions in the operating theatre could be mitigated by the trips in the car. Only with considerable resourcefulness had she kept it on the road, changing wheels, repairing punctures and getting it started in sub-zero temperatures. She drove to Alhama to collect her belongings which had been sent there from Aranda. Having a gramophone and lots of new records sent out by her family made life all the more tolerable. She also was able to see some beautiful countryside. Buying presents for the family with which she was billeted, she was surprised at their reaction – 'Unlike English poor class they were so proud they would hardly accept them.' The gruesome sights that she was seeing each day in the operating theatre were so distressing that she needed every possible distraction. Her diary faithfully recorded the details of horrendous surgical interventions often carried out without anaesthetic. After an operation on a young boy wounded in the stomach only three days after being conscripted, she broke down and cried. 'He was so white and pathetic with an expression of such pain and sorrow and he never made a sound.' The accumulated horrors were beginning to get to her and she began to question the wisdom of coming to Spain. However, by the following day she had recovered her usual good spirits. A lunch which would have been the envy of the entire Republican zone helped. It consisted of 'poached eggs, tinned salmon with mayonnaise, albóndigas (meatballs in rich gravy) and fried potatoes, cheese and chocolate pudding, not to mention foie gras and oporto as an aperitif and coffee and coñac to finish with'. Even better was an unexpected – and poignantly short – visit from Touffles. Despite the cold, in a room with no panes in the windows, having to sleep fully dressed in tweeds, she sewed and ironed and maintained her essential cheerfulness. Inevitably she faced many of the same problems as Nan Green and the front-line nurses on the Republican side. 'The thought of a hot bath, a comfortable bed, a good meal that we did not have to cook ourselves or watch cooking and a w.c. instead of a pot seemed distinctly pleasant.'[71]

On 17 February, there was a big Nationalist push and Pip went to watch the battle from a German anti-aircraft battery. 'The noise was incredible, a continual roar like thunder with intermittent different-toned bands. The sky was full of aeroplanes shooting up and down the Red trenches and the whole landscape all around was covered with pillars of smoke.' 'At about 11.30 the bombers began to arrive and came in a continual stream for hour after hour till the Red lines were black with the smoke of the bombs.' Pip thought it was 'the most thrilling thing I have ever seen'. The counterpart to the exhilarating sights was an increase in traffic in the operating theatre. Her compassion for the wounded and dying was unrelated to any analysis of the reasons for the war. Indeed, by 20 February, she was exhilarated by the possibility of going to see Nationalist troops entering Teruel. Although not allowed to enter the city, she and her fellow nurses found a vantage point from which, 'to our great joy', they watched Nationalist aircraft bombing the Republicans retreating towards Valencia.

Yet on the next day, after ten hours' non-stop effort in the operating theatre, she could write that 'it is demoralising to live in an eternal whorl of blood, pain and death'. Reflecting on the daily deaths of casualties in the operating room, she wrote: 'I don't know how there is anyone left.' There was still house-to-house fighting in Teruel. On 22 February, awakened by bells ringing for the Nationalist capture of the city, she walked through the battered remains of the city. 'I didn't see a single whole house, they are all covered in bullet holes and shot to bits by cannons with great gaping holes from air bombardments.' In the midst of the rubble, she found an undamaged grand piano in a bar and played tunes while the soldiers stopped looting in order to dance. She rejoiced at the Nationalist advance that was chasing the retreating Republicans to the south. Three thousand prisoners were taken and two thousand dead according to the official radio. The next day, back in the hospital, she was covered in blood from the operations and, on the day after that, back in Teruel. She was flushed with excitement by a Republican artillery bombardment – 'I admit I was terrified myself but I like being frightened.' Her emotional highs and lows were intense.[72]

Unsurprisingly given the daily horrors that she was facing, Pip was outraged to learn from her cousin Charmian that her brother John disapproved of her being in Spain and was determined to get her back home. 'Bloody interfering nonsense. I should like to see him try anyhow.'[73] In mid-February, John did come to Spain in search of Pip. Since she was on duty in the midst of the Battle of Teruel, he did not get to see her. He was rather shocked by this since, as he recalled later, 'I don't think that my parents had visualised anything more than her being in some base camp, helping a bit with bandages.' John Scott-Ellis did meet Peter Kemp who gave him news of Pip. He also met Ataúlfo and struck up a friendship with the German pilots of his unit. Shortly afterwards he continued his journey on to Munich. When John spoke to his wife's family there, they categorically refused to believe that he had met German pilots in Spain because, after all, Hitler had declared that there were none.[74]

Pip's diary is remarkable for the wealth of detail with which she described her days. It is therefore all the more puzzling that her future husband, José Luis de Vilallonga, claimed to have bumped into her in Teruel, some hours after the recapture of the town by the Francoist forces. No such incident is mentioned by Pip in her diary, in which there are no gaps during this period. Nevertheless, the 'meeting' is described with a wealth of salacious detail in his memoirs. Entertainingly written, like all his work, this account is full of the most unlikely particulars. After one of the bloodiest battles of the Civil War, fought in sub-zero temperatures, the Republicans had to give up their costly defence of the provincial capital captured on 8 January. They retreated on 21 February 1938, when Teruel was on the point of being encircled. According to Vilallonga, at the time, just eighteen,[75] he was wandering around the recently captured city in search of his father, the Barón de Segur, a staff officer with the great cavalryman General José Monasterio Ituarte. 'And suddenly, as I turned a corner, I saw her. It was like an advertisement torn from *Harper's Bazaar*. A tall, blonde woman, in an immaculate white nurse's uniform with a great blue cape that reached down to her feet. Around her neck, curled with studied negligence, she wore a Hermés *foulard* that brought out the clear blue of her eyes.' José Luis recalled being entranced by this vision of loveliness. Allegedly, she was smoking while leaning nonchalantly on the bonnet of a new ambulance with a London number plate. All around, the aftermath of the battle in the streets could be seen. A woman knelt next to the still-warm corpse of a man whose throat had been cut by one of the Moorish mercenaries. While excited Moors were looting houses, carrying out the most bizarre objects from mattresses to bidets, Pip is described as simulating total indifference to what was going on around her, an oasis – or perhaps a mirage – of calm in the midst of chaotic slaughter and mayhem.[76]

The Pip of this account has nothing of the girlish spontaneity and good-hearted sincerity that speaks out from every page of her diary. When José Luis de Vilallonga walked up and began to speak to her, in English he later claimed, she offered him a cigarette then slid a silver hip flask from under her cape and invited him to take a swig of Beefeater gin. She then said peremptorily, 'Have lunch with me' and introduced herself. 'I'm Priscilla Scott-Ellis, but all my friends call me Pip. I'm half-Welsh, half-Scottish, but of course I was born in London.' After a short pause, she announced, 'My mother is Jewish.' It is highly questionable that she would say any such thing but José Luis, who seems to be transferring many of his attitudes onto her, repeatedly makes reference in his works to her Jewish blood. She then opened the chest on the side of the ambulance, rummaged around in a pile of packages and emerged clutching a tin of foie gras and a bottle of excellent claret. For pudding, she managed to come up with a packet of Fortnum and Mason chocolate liqueurs. She explained how she came to be involved in the Spanish Civil War, commenting: 'Most of my friends and some of my relatives have joined the Republicans and the Communists.' Just as she was assuring him that the British Government would never help the Republic on the grounds that the British always support the forces of order, they heard the sound of shots from behind a nearby church. 'They're shooting people. That means that the Falangists have arrived. They are always the ones who come to shoot the reds left alive in the cities occupied by the Army.' 'The forces of order,' commented Vilallonga sarcastically. 'No,' she replied with devastating insight, 'just people who like killing. They're just loud-mouthed rich kids who say they are fighting for the workers but, as soon as they find one alive, they put him up against a wall and shoot him.'

By this time, a bottle of Johnny Walker had both appeared and as quickly half-disappeared. Apparently, this sumptuous lunch had been taken over the bonnet of the ambulance despite the presence all around of starving desperados. According to Vilallonga, whose memoirs are replete with assertions of his sexual magnetism, his new acquaintance informed him that there were bunks inside the ambulance. On repairing within, he discovered couchettes of roughly the size of a first-class cabin on a transatlantic liner. This facilitated an afternoon of ecstatic lovemaking. On dressing, he asked her, 'Do you do this kind of thing often?' With an uncharacteristically dismissive tone, the Pip of this account replied, 'Only when I feel I need it and not always for pleasure. But it's good for my physical and mental health.' That was the last time that he saw her until the end of the Second World War. He often thought of her. With his wonderfully snobbish and sexist hauteur, he wrote: 'I kept the memory of someone out of the ordinary who had provoked my curiosity. She was a long way from being beautiful, but she had the unmistakable style of certain women, especially in England, who immediately attract the attention of those of us who are great enthusiasts for horses, creatures that, along with the bull, I regard as being among the most splendid products of nature. I have never made a mistake whenever I have judged a woman by comparing her with a pure blood mare.'[77]

The account is certainly untrue. Vilallonga claims that Pip was driving an ambulance sent out by her father and describes it as having been specially constructed by Daimler to the most luxurious standards. Elsewhere, he describes the ambulance as a Bentley. On other occasions, José Luis de Vilallonga claimed that his first meeting with Pip took place during the battle of the Ebro in the summer and autumn of 1938.[78] It is possible that the entire story is a fictional amalgamation of the experiences of both Pip and Gabriel Herbert. Pip's only vehicle in Spain up to this time was her by-now battered Ford. There is no record of Pip ever owning or driving an ambulance in Spain.

Her hesitant sexual behaviour at the time had nothing in common with the cold-hearted and voracious siren depicted in his account. It is a regular lament in her diary that she was rarely able to wash, invariably slept in her crumpled clothes and that her nurse's uniforms were spattered with blood and mud. It is therefore not plausible that she could have been seen in the streets of Teruel looking like a model from the pages of a fashion magazine. Moreover, at this time, the conditions in which she lived and worked had left her with a chronic throat infection which left her completely run down. In any case, her otherwise copiously detailed diary makes no mention of the incident. Her days were usually occupied fully either in the operating theatre, in her billet or else travelling in her car. Such an erotic encounter might have been expected to be mentioned. She describes in full her constant efforts to fend off the frequent approaches of amorous, or more aggressively predatory, soldiers in the streets and once, by drunken intruders into the room she shared with Consuelo. For this reason, she had been given by Álvaro de Orléans a pistol with which to defend her virtue.[79]

After Teruel, Pip's unit was ordered to move on to Cariñena. After the recapture of the city, Franco lost little time in seizing advantage of the massive superiority in men, aircraft, artillery and equipment that the Nationalists now enjoyed over the depleted Republicans. He assembled an army of two hundred thousand men for an offensive across a 260-kilometre-wide front through Aragón following the eastwards direction of the Ebro valley. Loading up the car with her gramophone, records and radio, Pip set off in a convoy after the rapidly advancing Nationalist troops. Thereafter, they were sent northwards to Belchite which had been recaptured by the Nationalists on 10 March. The town was virtually destroyed. There, she and Consuelo cleared rubble and scrubbed floors to make one of the less damaged buildings usable for the unit. Queuing for water at a fountain, she was told that there were eighty-five prisoners of the International Brigades nearby, mostly Americans but also some English. 'They will all be shot as foreigners always are.' It is an indication of her identification with the Francoist cause, the brutalising effects of the war and, perhaps, her basic class prejudices, that she could seem so unaffected by the atrocity about to be committed. At the end of the day, she merely commented, 'I have never enjoyed a day more but I have never been dirtier.' Her good spirits were shattered on the following day. While she was working in the operating theatre, looting soldiers stole a case of records, 1000 cigarettes, her pistol and, the worst blow of all, the radio that Ataúlfo had given her in Gibraltar for her twenty-first birthday. She then had to spend a day kneeling at the riverside scrubbing bloodstained operation sheets in the icy water. Her distress was compounded by news of the German advance into Austria. It provoked agonies about her understandable identification with the Nationalist cause, which was, at the time, also the cause of the Axis. 'Oh God, I hope there won't be another war. What can I do if there is, as all my sympathies will be against England. What hell life is.'[80]

The speed of the Nationalist advance required them to move on to Escatrón, forty kilometres further east, in a bend in the River Ebro. This involved a journey over stony roads through scenes of desolation littered with corpses, dead horses, barbed wire and abandoned trenches. It was rendered somewhat more tolerable for Pip by the recovery of her radio and the news that Ataúlfo was not far away. She was thrilled when he visited despite it being so long since she had been able to have a bath: 'my uniform was black, and my hands too, as well as swollen and rough, my face dusty and unpainted and my hair all dirty and tangled'. Unlike the dirty soldiers by whom she was normally surrounded, Ataúlfo 'was looking very clean and smart' and Pip thought him 'devastatingly attractive and goodlooking despite the fact that he is really quite ugly'. Escatrón was near enough to the front to be within artillery range. Pip found the bombardments enthralling. 'I was scared pink, but of course did not say so.' She was about to experience several days' carnage that would see her remarkable powers of endurance pushed to the limit. Badly wounded casualties began to pour in. Illuminated by oil lamps, she and her unit worked incessantly throughout the daily bombardments. Since most of her fellow nurses were terrified and took shelter, she stayed up entire nights at a time to be with the patients, sleeping in her uniform in the ward. There was little food for either the staff or the wounded. 'It is awful being here bombarded all day in a ward of wounded begging to be moved, and so petrified that they pretty well die of fright.' Her indefatigability was remarkable: 'Well, everything stops sooner or later one way or another, though I hope this won't stop by us all being killed, which is quite probable if they go on bombarding every day.'[81]

Despite the appalling existence in a virtual hecatomb, Pip was alarmed by suggestions that her unit should be withdrawn further away from the front. She was delighted to have to advance, in the middle of the night, to Caspe which had been captured by the Nationalists on 16 March. Driving in pitch darkness over boulder-strewn tracks, her car hit a huge rock and was badly damaged. On the verge of nervous as well as physical exhaustion, at Caspe they had to create a new hospital. As more casualties flooded in, she learnt that her car (which she called Fiona) had been stolen. She had hardly slept for a week: 'I finally got to bed semi-conscious at about eleven after more casualties had arrived. If life goes on like this much longer we will all die. It is more than any one can stand.' Yet, after a night's sleep, she was back in the fray. Ataúlfo appeared with biscuits, chocolate, shortbread and wine and a message from Princess Bea that it was time for Pip to stop risking her life. Yet, far from taking the opportunity to leave, she was determined to stay at the front.

The strain remained intense. Just when she thought that she could go to bed, a large number of wounded were brought in. 'The floor was covered in stretchers, blood everywhere, everyone shouting, the poor patients moaning and screaming, and so instead of going to bed it started all over again.' The experience was, not surprisingly, changing Pip. She wrote on 21 March: 'Six months today since I left home and it seems like six years! Home seems so far away, and such a completely different world that I cannot imagine ever going back.' Two days later, she wrote: 'How any nurse can look at a man, let alone touch him, I don't know after all the unattractive things one has to do with them.' As she became more skilled as a nurse, she got more exasperated with the village girls who came in to help. In the light of the tribulations that she had undergone, she was mortified when, on an unannounced inspection, Mercedes Milá raged that the hospital was untidy and the nurses were wearing make-up. 'After all the weeks of filth we have been through, the very first time we have time to make ourselves respectable she has to come and tell us we are too painted.' Milá's reprimand was outrageously unfair. The endless stream of casualties meant that the nurses were going for days on end without sleep. Pip described herself as looking 'like a dead cat'. On some nights, she could find no time to write up her diary.[82]

The attrition took its toll. Already shocked and still reeling from the shelling at Escatrón, in the last six days of March, Pip got to bed twice, for six hours on each occasion. She was working shifts of forty-two hours with six-hour breaks that were often interrupted by the unexpected arrival of horrendous casualties. In the midst of this, she was invited to dine with some of Consuelo's friends on the staff of General José Monasterio Ituarte. Monasterio was the head of the Nationalist cavalry. At the battle of Teruel, he had led the last major cavalry charge in Western Europe. During the current Aragón offensive, his mounted brigades, supported by the Condor Legion, were running ahead of the main advance. Pip found him charming, 'although very quiet and serious'. She was particularly delighted when he announced that her car had been found abandoned by a roadside. The occasion recharged her batteries for the unit's next move behind the rapidly advancing Nationalists. They were sent on to Gandesa to the southeast, in the province of Lérida in Catalonia.[83]

Yet again miracles of improvisation were required to pack up the entire unit, including making arrangements for the twenty-seven seriously wounded men who had to be left behind. In Gandesa, Pip's group had to share an abandoned school building with an Italian unit. It was a startling change of personnel and of scenery, as spring took over from the ferocious winter conditions in which she had worked. She found the Catalans in Gandesa irritating and, along with virtually everyone in the unit, was frustrated by an inability to understand the Catalan language. The Italians in the other part of the hospital seemed to confirm everything that is said about their presence in Spain – 'very amiable and fearfully smart, but over-amorous'. A lull in the endless arrival of casualties allowed her to come to terms with the attrition of the previous month. 'I was in the depths of despair, sick of life and all I am doing, and wondering what has happened at home. I decided I was either going to go crazy or get tight.' She opted for the latter and drank herself sick on sherry and brandy. When she came to, she wrote: 'What I am turning into I don't like to think, getting so tight that I am sick at 6 o'clock in the evening. I went through half an hour of pure hell, being sick at intervals, with the world spinning round me.' That episode had to be put immediately behind her. A massive influx of casualties saw her drawing on astonishing resources of stamina and competence.[84]

Finally, she got a weekend's leave. Princess Bea had moved into a requisitioned palace at Épila, thirty kilometres to the southwest of Zaragoza, in order to be near the men in her family who were posted nearby. Ataúlfo was now a pilot. Pip arrived at Zaragoza too late to travel on to Épila, so she stayed at the Grand Hotel. She lamented: 'I was very ashamed of turning up to dinner at the Grand Hotel in my filthy uniform, with burst shoes and torn stockings, my face unpainted and my hair on end.' Nonetheless, to get away from the front in such circumstances was something rarely vouchsafed to her counterparts in the Republican nursing services. Pip had dinner with the prominent British Conservative, Arnold Lunn, a Catholic and an old Harrovian, who was in Spain writing articles about 'Red horrors'. Lunn was one of the English pro-Nationalist propagandists who had been involved in supporting the cover-up of the bombing of Guernica. For Pip, the main thing about being with him was to be able to eat 'good food with the right amount of knives and forks'. When Pip got to Épila, she luxuriated in her 'first bath for more than two months' and in the opportunity to relax in comfort with her friends. Ataúlfo took her to recover her car, which she found minus windows, number plates, tools, papers and her passport. General Kindelán's driver fixed her car. Of course, what she valued most about this period was to be clean, warm and well fed. She was able to go to the hairdresser and also went shopping with Últano Kindelán. A greater change from the horrors of her unit could hardly be imagined. The combination of uninterrupted nights and cleanliness made for 'a short piece of heaven'. In the Grand Hotel in Zaragoza, she met two aristocratic acquaintances, Alfonso Domecq and Kiki Mora 'who were both tight as usual and had just bought a large white rabbit and a white duck'. After chasing the two animals around the hall, Últano caught the duck and tied string around its neck and wings so that he could take it for walks. The sense of wild release after the tribulations of the front left Pip disorientated – 'I have never hated anything more in my life than the idea of going back to the *equipo*. I don't want ever to see a hospital again in my life.'[85]

Nevertheless, she did return to her unit, which had now moved south to Morella in the harsh and arid hills of the Maestrazgo between Aragón and Castellón. The return was a rude shock: 'How I hated the jerk back to this life, stretchers being carried in dripping blood all over the front doorstep, the smell of anaesthetic, the moans and shouts. I have gone all squeamish in my few days away.' Her depression was perhaps linked with the fact that she was laid low by an illness which saw her confined to bed with a raging fever. She was finally diagnosed with the beginnings of paratyphoid – a fever resembling typhoid but caused by different bacteria.[86] In consequence, she was allowed a few days' convalescence in Épila. She drove there in her car and it was severely damaged along the way by unmade roads. Princess Bea was back from the recently captured Lérida. As part of her work with Frentes y Hospitales, the relief organisation which provided welfare for the old, women and children, she would enter occupied areas with the Nationalist forces.[87] Still very weak, Pip was able to stay because her car was not ready for the return journey. She managed some relaxation, gossiping with Princess Bea, playing cards and ping pong with visiting German and Italian aviators. She even had an evening out in Zaragoza with Ataúlfo. They went to a sleazy cabaret in 'an old theatre with semi-naked women who came out on stage and who could neither dance nor sing. A fair smattering of peroxided tarts and swarms of dirty, tight and noisy soldiers all singing and shouting lewd remarks at everyone.'[88]

During her stay at Épila, Pip met Juan Antonio Ansaldo, one of Spain's most famous aviators. Ansaldo was a monarchist air ace and playboy who had once organised Falangist terror squads. He had piloted the small De Havilland Puss Moth in which General Sanjurjo had perished on 20 July 1936 when leaving Portugal to take charge of the military uprising.[89] Ansaldo now commanded one of the two Savoia Marchetti 79 squadrons of the First Brigade of the Nationalist Air Force (Primera Brigada Aérea Hispana) while Prince Alí commanded the other. Ansaldo's wife Pilarón was both a flyer and a nurse who had just been asked to work in the Ciudad Universitaria on the outskirts of Madrid. On the very edge of the besieged capital, it was the most dangerous area and women were not usually allowed to work there. Pip hoped to find out how to volunteer to go too.[90]

Inevitably, after the pleasures of Épila – ping pong, music, decent food, whisky and even a flight in a Luftwaffe aircraft – the return to hospital duty was depressing: 'Morella is the lousiest, most boring place in the world, and not a thing to do all day.' She felt low because she was still suffering from paratyphoid. She was pleased, however, by the possibility that she and Consuelo, for their gallantry under fire, would both be proposed for the Cruz del Mérito Militar con Distintivo Rojo, the highest award for bravery that could be awarded to a woman. It was eventually awarded in May 1939.[91] She was also cheered by a letter on 5 May from her mother who was delighted by some articles about Pip in the British press. Margot promised her a new car and a full bank account when she returned home and announced an imminent visit to Spain. In fact, Pip, always her best when the going was most difficult, perked up when the hospital got busy again about a week later. A stream of wounded saw her attend fourteen operations in thirteen hours. She was irritated by the petty jealousies among the nurses and felt put upon by the hostility of Captain Ramón Roldán, the hospital chief surgeon. As a Falangist, he deeply resented the aristocratic origins and monarchist connections of both Pip and Consuelo. Just as she got the news that her mother was arriving on 19 May, the entire hospital had to move with the advancing Nationalist forces nearer to the province of Castellón, to the village of La Iglesuela del Cid. When her martyred car got there, she and Consuelo were billeted by Roldán in the most dingy dungeon just off the operating theatre. However, on the following day, 23 May, she was able to go on leave to see her mother who had arrived with her brother John at Princess Bea's home in Épila.[92]

Margot was obliged to wait until Pip was 'disinfected and de-loused' before she could see her. When she remonstrated with Princess Bea about the horrors being experienced by Pip, the Infanta replied, 'I promised you, dear Margot, that I would look after her as my own daughter; and if I had a daughter

she would surely be at the front.'[93] Pip spent ten days with
her mother in Zaragoza with daily visits to Épila. One evening,
she met Peter Kemp, the Englishman who had volunteered
for Franco and was now a lieutenant in the Spanish Foreign
Legion. He told her a gruesome tale about the sadism of
his colonel. An Englishman had crossed the lines claiming
plausibly to be a sailor who had ended up at the front after
getting drunk in Valencia. When Peter Kemp requested permission to set him free, the colonel ordered him to shoot the
sailor. When Kemp stared unbelievingly, the colonel shrieked,
'What is more, shoot him yourself or I will have you shot.'
He duly took the man into the countryside, they shook hands
and he was shot. Pip commented, 'A nasty thing to have to
do.' Her account implies that Kemp shot the man himself.[94]
There was a standing order from Franco that all captured
foreigners be shot. This was rescinded on 1 April 1938 when
he needed prisoners to exchange for the 497 Italians captured
at Guadalajara.

On her return to her unit, still weak from the paratyphoid,
Pip was driven by the constant humiliations to which Captain
Roldán subjected her and Consuelo to contemplate leaving.
Once more, her mind was taken off the problem by her work.
She took part in an operation on a twelve-year-old girl who
had been playing with a hand grenade that had exploded –

> I think I minded seeing her being treated and operated
> on more than anything else I have seen so far. I can't
> bear to see children hurt. She was blood from head to
> toe, her whole body one mass of burns and superficial
> wounds, both her knees had to be operated, one arm
> amputated above the wrist as her hand had been blown
> clean off, the thumb of the other hand (or what was
> left of it) amputated and two holes in her forehead
> and all one side of her face sewn up. Apart from which
> she is temporarily blind in one eye and permanently

in the other. She is getting on quite well now but moans and shouts all day as she is in awful pain. I had a terrible quarrel with Roldán yesterday evening to get him to allow her aunt to stay with her all night.

To Pip's horror, Roldán planned to leave Consuelo behind when the unit made its next move. However, Pip was prostrated with a fierce attack of the paratyphoid that had afflicted her for the previous two months. Left behind, she and Consuelo found refuge in another hospital and volunteered to work at an emergency clearing station right at the front. However, Pip's delight at this opportunity was short-lived. With her temperature at 39.8°, she was sent to rest at Épila. She stayed there for a month and then, on 7 July, she returned to England for five weeks of convalescence. Exhaustion, the trauma of her front-line experiences and serious illness had at last brought her down.[95]

Pip reached England completely drained. She spent six weeks recuperating mainly at Chirk and more briefly in London. In the capital, she attended the lavish society wedding of her sister Gaenor and Richard Heathcoat-Amory on 18 July. She was the first of eight bridesmaids attired in 'picture dresses of white chiffon, the bodices made with heart-shaped necklines and short, puffed sleeves, with narrow waist-belts of silver ribbon and headdresses of stephanotis with bows of blue ribbon'.[96] With her health restored, Pip set off back for Spain on 19 August 1938, accompanied by Consuelo, who had joined her in London. They travelled by sea with sixteen pieces of luggage 'including two packing cases'. Pip was heartened to have been told by a fortune-teller that, within six weeks, she would be engaged to be married. 'I hope she is right because that is exactly what I intend.' It was a slow and boring trip to Gibraltar where she was cheered by the prospect of seeing Princess Bea and even more delighted to collect a new car, 'very large and impressive, black with pale brown leather inside and all its gadgets attached'. Her old car, already without wheels, had met an untimely end in Épila when the garage roof had collapsed on it. Spending time with Princess Bea and anticipating seeing Ataúlfo, her spirits soared. En route to Épila, they stayed at the ancient Roman town of Mérida in Badajoz. It was crammed with aviators who had been moved down because of the minor Republican counteroffensive in Extremadura. 'I do love being back here. I adore seeing everyone in uniform and a vague atmosphere of war.' In her absence, Prince Ali had been promoted to full colonel and was now in charge of the newly created Segunda Brigada Aérea Hispana, which was about to go into action on the Ebro front.[97]

Once at Épila, Pip was overjoyed to discover that Ataúlfo had fourteen days' leave which he planned to spend driving around southern Spain with one of his German fellow aviators, named Koch. She and Consuelo were invited to accompany them. Pip wrote in her diary: 'I really must marry that man but my luck does not seem quite to run to that as yet, but as I have waited four years now I suppose I can wait longer.' She had a wonderful time on the trip, driving over dusty roads through villages of white houses shimmering in the blazing sun passing donkeys laden with panniers overflowing with grapes. 'I am so pleased with life that I don't know what to do with myself. It is fun to feel like this. It must be years since I last felt such an untroubled confidence in Life. I love every moment of it.' The idyll was nearly interrupted when Koch was summoned to Zaragoza because of the simmering Munich crisis. It seemed that Ataúlfo would have to drive him there. However, a return to Épila would mean that Pip and Consuelo would need to seek a new medical unit and return to front-line duty. The danger was averted when Koch flew back to Zaragoza and Pip was able to go on falling deeper in love with Ataúlfo. Unfortunately, when driving from Seville to Malaga, things came to a head. He told her that her mother had tried to get him to marry her sister Elisabeth and called him a pansy when he demurred. He then said, 'After Alonso died, I promised Mama that I would only marry a Princess.' She was devastated – 'Such a simple sentence and it just sent all my hopes and the foundations of my life crashing. I had not realised until he said that, just how much I had been building on the chance of my marrying him one day.' Ataúlfo's was a noticeably different version of the story about the Infanta Beatriz told to Pip by Princess Bea and was probably an equally feeble subterfuge to avoid telling her that he just had no inclination to marriage.[98]

Pip went through agonies trying to pluck up the courage to ask Ataúlfo if he would have married her if he had not made the vow. If he said 'yes', then she would try to get Princess Bea to release him from the promise and, if 'no', then try to get on with the rest of her life. They had moved on to Torremolinos, then a tiny and beautiful fishing village. On the following day, driving to Malaga to go shopping, she asked the fateful question and he replied in the negative. Deeply embarrassed, he told her that he was not in love with her. She answered, 'I knew that. I just wanted to know exactly how things stood. Please forget I ever asked you.' Then their aristocratic training came to the rescue and they reverted to amiable small talk. 'And thus ended all my hopes and longings and ambitions.' On their return to the hotel in Torremolinos, she broke down and cried 'with a feeling as if there was no world left'. Pip then spent the day with their friends putting on a brave face. She determined to use every resource of self-control to hide her despair and avoid jeopardising her friendship with Ataúlfo. By the end of the day, she wrote: 'Today has been the longest and most miserable day I have ever spent. Never again in my life am I going to give life such another chance of kicking me.' Nevertheless, by the following day, her irrepressible optimism had reasserted itself and she was determined to keep on hoping as long as Ataúlfo remained single. 'I won't be depressed or take life seriously and tragically,' she wrote. 'Life can kick me all it likes but I shall go on laughing and pretending whatever happens.'[99] In fact, this was bravado. She showed no sign of being able to relinquish the agonising bliss of her unrequited love.

In September 1938, the Munich crisis gave rise to talk of a European war. British reinforcements were arriving at Gibraltar, down the coast, and Ataúlfo's German comrades were being recalled to Germany. In such company, Pip's inclination was to blame Britain. Together with her emotional setback, the ambiguity of her political position left her feeling confused and miserable. The holiday in Torremolinos over, she and Consuelo returned to Zaragoza and Épila in an eventful journey accompanied by two flatulent priests. Continued news of Hitler's determination to take the Sudetenland did nothing to cheer up the company. Pip's particular unhappiness was not helped when she was bluntly urged by Juan Antonio Ansaldo to marry Ataúlfo as soon as possible. Despite her efforts to remain stoical, she was deeply miserable. Perhaps in an effort to justify telling Pip that he did not love her, Ataúlfo was giving vent to his viperous tongue. His thoughtless mocking shrivelled her and brought out all her insecurity. 'God how I hate Ataúlfo sometimes. Why in heaven's name did I have to fall in love with a louse like him. Now I want to get married and I can't because I just could not marry anyone else. I want to have lots of children and I can't. I can't even have an affair to relieve my feelings.' The situation became so intolerable for her that she was desperate to get back to the front despite what she took to be hints from Princess Bea that she actually favoured her marrying Ataúlfo.[100]

A return to the front was rendered more difficult by a requirement for certificates of qualifications and proof of previous service. Nevertheless, she and Consuelo went on to Castellón which was near the Valencia front. There they made contact with Roldán and got certificates of their service in his unit. They then found an opening at a hospital at Calaceite

on the Ebro front. They returned to Épila where they partici-
pated in a big party given by Princess Bea for the German
aviators. Pip got pleasantly drunk but then was made to feel
bad by vain flirting with Ataúlfo. On the following day, 26
September, they listened to a speech by Hitler giving the
Czechs until 1 October to capitulate. It lasted two hours and
Pip found it 'good and moderately disturbing'. Again, her
situation made her miserable. She was in the company of
Francoists who were fighting alongside German and Italian
units. 'If there is a big war I am completely sunk. I can't
stay here and I won't fight with France against Germany.'
Contemplating the possibility of war, she wrote: 'God only
knows what I shall do if there is a war. I suppose I shall have
to go home but what hell it will be to have to be on the
wrong side and with no news of Ataúlfo and the rest of the
people out here.'

Starting to work at Calaceite on 29 September did little to
animate her. There was little activity in the hospital and, at
first, she did not like the other nurses, 'a pretty gloomy lot'.
The 'wounded' seemed to be suffering mainly from stubbed
toes and scratched fingers. Pip was desperate to prove herself
and to be useful. In fact, despite her self-deprecating remarks,
describing herself at one point as feeling 'like a lunatic worm',
reading between the lines of her diary makes it clear that she
was extremely competent and hard-working. She rather liked
the director of the unit, a lieutenant Magallón, but basically
she moped for Ataúlfo. Gradually, she bucked up as the hospital got busier. Twenty-nine-hour stints were not unusual. As
before, some of what she had to cope with was deeply distressing – most horrifically, a four-year-old boy who had been
playing with a hand grenade that exploded in his face. She
and the diminutive Magallón were often thrown together on
night duty. 'I would rather listen to the radio with one man
than gossip with eleven women.' She liked him because he
gave her interesting work and explained things in a way that

improved her nursing skills. He began to groom her as his theatre assistant. She also began to get along with the nurses with whom there were some riotous meals. In reaction to the horrors of the operating table, they drank, sang and danced noisily. One moonlit night, after a hard day, she set up her gramophone and danced the rumba alone on the veranda while open-mouthed patients and colleagues gawked from the windows. Pip was regularly teased about her weight. 'I am the size of a house now and can hardly do up my uniform.' 'I am as fat as six pigs.' She was working on trying to forget Ataúlfo without great success. She attended a number of bull-fights in Zaragoza which she did not much enjoy. She was also distressed to discover that some of her patients who had wounds in the hand were suspected of shooting themselves to get away from the front and would thus be executed.[102]

At one point, Pip accompanied Dr Magallón on his rounds in the village. Walking around the cobbled streets of Calaceite, she was fascinated by her introduction to village life about which she wrote amusingly. Their patients ranged from an 'adorable baby' to a grandmother in bed in the midst of piles of stored fruit – 'one of those tough, bald, scraggy old hags of about a hundred'. At one house, 'I could not make out if the patient was male or female as it had a large, black moustache.' The patient was, in fact, a woman. The interlude was brief. Pip now picked up a liver infection and was soon extremely ill. Just as she was recovering, after passing ten wretched days, she discovered that another nurse, Maruja, was spreading gossip about her relationship with Magallón in order to promote the career of her own beloved, a Dr Torrijos. On Pip's side, the relationship was entirely innocent but she was aware that Magallón was deeply smitten by her. During her illness, he took personal charge of her care and would sit by her bedside stroking her face and hair. Then the front moved. Franco passed through Calaceite to direct the decisive Nationalist counteroffensive at the Battle of the Ebro which was

launched on 30 October 1938. Within twenty-four hours, Pip
was installed in a new hospital. She was thrilled when, while
out with Magallón and another nurse looking for a place on the
river bank for the hospital linen to be washed, the Caudillo's
cavalcade roared by and Franco himself saluted them.[103] On
other days, Magallón led fishing expeditions using hand gren-
ades to stun the fish. Her health continued to give cause for
concern. In addition to liver problems and dysentery, she had
a persistent cough that led Magallón to believe she might be
tubercular. She also had abscesses on her legs and bottom.
Consuelo was threatening to write to Margot to come and
collect her daughter.[104]

The continuing relationship between Maruja and Torrijos
led to Pip writing cattily in her diary: 'Romance in a hospital
between a jellified skeleton and a prize sow'. She continued
to flirt mildly with Magallón. 'Magallón seems to spend his
life tickling me which I admit he does well and with a uniform
and starched apron he can't go too far if he wants to, which
he does.' That was as far as it went at first, but the gossips in the
hospital enjoyed making up more scurrilous stories. Maruja, in
particular, was determined to get both Pip and Consuelo out
of the hospital and to cause trouble for Magallón. Maruja had
reported Consuelo as a drunkard and drug addict. This led to
Mercedes Milá visiting the hospital and threatening to throw
them both out. Eventually, after considerable humiliation, they
managed to persuade her of the truth. To be assailed by such
nonsense when all she wanted to do was nurse was deeply
frustrating for Pip. 'Why, oh why did I ever come here? Won't
life ever be fun again, however hard one tries to enjoy it. God
I hate wars and all they entail.' As she reflected on the gratuitous malice of Maruja, she was briefly gladdened by a letter
from Ataúlfo asking her to come to Épila. However, as she
contemplated how pointless it was to go and see him,
depression descended again. She had a fight with the deeply
jealous Magallón and wrote bitterly of Ataúlfo: 'Why did I ever

have to fall in love with a red nosed, begoggled, mother-ridden poop?' Feeling frustrated, and suffering even more from boils and abscesses, she wrote with characteristic self-deprecation: 'I expect I will soon have to flirt with Magallón. It would be so enjoyable to have a spot of mild sex once more only I am not so sure it would stay mild for long. Only no one can come to much harm with the knowledge that they have their bottom covered with growths!'[105]

At last, the guerrilla war with Maruja was ended by the arrival of a new head nurse named Isabel. A close friend of Consuelo's mother, she turned out to be very experienced but puritanically strict. Pip gave in to her frustration and she spent the afternoon of 14 November, her last day of being twenty-one, 'having an enjoyable spot of slap and tickle with Magallón, mostly tickle but a nice bit of slap too. His technique is hot even though he is teeny, and one must admit doctors know their way about.' Her twenty-second birthday was miserable since there was no post other than a telegram from her mother. Her life was rendered more gloomy by a reprimand from Isabel who ordered her not to smoke, drink, swear, sing or fraternise with the doctors. 'I might just as well be a nun, and it is not my form. I can't help having been brought up to a lot of liberty and it drives me mad to be spied on and followed about and treated like either a child or a bloody tart who must be reformed. I am quite willing to behave like a nun in the hospital from eight in the morning till nine at night, but at least I might have some enjoyment afterwards.' In despair at the pettiness around her, she was invigorated by a visit from Ataúlfo and Princess Bea who came loaded with ham, cheese, chocolates, vermouth, brandy, magazines and some correspondence. Ataúlfo was sufficiently nice to her to start her longing for him again. That, plus news from home that her sister Gaenor was pregnant made her sorry for herself. 'Why oh why can't the goop realise he is as much in love with me as he is ever likely to be with anybody. My younger sister is married and having a baby, why in hell can't I do the same. But I can't and that is that and I shall just have to put up with it.'[106]

By the third week of November, the Nationalists had pushed the Republicans out of the territory captured in July. The Republicans retreated back across the Ebro into Catalonia. Pip's hospital was to be moved again. As she thought about leaving the hospital, a drunken Legionario told her that he regarded her as his mother. The Pip who was always eager to please was moved to reflect on the consolations of her work.

> It really is awfully nice to be able to do things for people and them be grateful even if I do have to lose my temper with them often. I like being relied on for everything. Whatever bothers them, they ask me. Sometimes it is to do with their wound or illness, sometimes clothes, sometimes a quarrel which I automatically have to decide for them, sometimes I am a go-between to get them leave to visit relations or friends. I pretty nearly am their mother, though God forbid I ever have forty-seven children.

These satisfactions were little enough consolation for the petty jealousies that surrounded her. 'Everyone thinks I am so calm and unemotional; that I don't mind all the rows and muddles there are but it is driving me potty. Only seeing everyone else in such a state makes me pretend to be even calmer than I would normally appear.'

By the end of November, she was in a country house called Monte Julia in the deserted hills near Tremp in the north of Lérida. She threw herself into converting it into a hospital, rounding up charladies in nearby villages and requisitioning furniture from deserted houses. Her ownership of a car put her right at the heart of the operation. 'I am going to buy myself a chauffeur's uniform and give up being a nurse. All I seem to do is drive my car.' She was also, as a result of her various ailments, getting a lot thinner. Moreover, shrugging off the injunctions of the head nurse, Isabel, she was now flirting very heavily with Magallón who claimed to be in love with her. Although Isabel rightly suspected the relationship, she said nothing to Pip who regarded her as 'that damn, filthy-minded, frustrated, cackling old hen'. 'It makes me livid because I know that even if I had sat all night on duty in complete silence knitting the matter would be exactly the same. And what right has she to think the worst of me?'[107]

Pip was disgusted by the strange combination of spiteful gossip and reformatory school atmosphere at the hospital. She found it difficult to relate the petty jealousy behind the denunciations to

> the pretty illusions of heroism and justice with which
> I came to this filthy country. Everyday I think more
> of giving up the whole thing and going home. Why
> should I go on helping such a set of swine at the cost
> of feeling continually ill and tired and being covered
> in boils and lice. And yet I know that if I go home
> and have no worries, I shall worry so much about
> Ataúlfo that it will be worse, and I am too much in
> all this war to be able to walk out and leave it flat for
> good.

Pip continued to get thin since everything she ate nauseated her. Much as she delighted in weight-loss, she was concerned by the fact that she got palpitations just from walking up stairs. She infinitely regretted her flirtation with Magallón and tried to break it off gently. Even though his wife came to join him, he continued to importune Pip.

Driving to Prince Ali's base at Fraga, twenty-five kilometres to the south east of Lérida, she saw convoys of lorries. Franco was preparing the final offensive of the war, against Barcelona, which suggested that the hospital would be moved again.[108] On 22 December, she drove to Épila and immediately began to feel better. She went to a hairdresser in Zaragoza, lounged around with Ataúlfo and briefly put the horrors of the hospital behind her. Christmas Day was organised on totally English lines, complete with turkey and plum pudding and a tree with lights. However, it did not feel like Christmas – partly because, despite the Orléanses' hospitality, she was depressed to be an outsider at another family's festivities. 'The only thing that makes me realise it really is Christmas Day is that I have eaten too much and feel sick.' In fact, she was also downcast by a letter from her mother. Recounting a conversation that she had had with the Infanta in London, Margherita van Raalte relayed yet another version of the Orléans family explanation for Ataúlfo's disinclination to marry Pip: 'she says that Princess Bea is terribly fond of me but Prince Ali is set on royalty and that Ataúlfo is not in love with me as he knows me too well, but is fonder of me than anyone else.' Despite again being told that it was futile to hope, her interminable optimism came to the fore again. 'I can't help my feelings and unless something unexpected happens I shall just go on waiting until the day he marries someone else. I have bloody little hope but still a lot of patience and no other desire in life to fix myself to.' At least she had the brief consolation that, at midnight on 31 December 1938, Ataúlfo kissed her for the first time in all the years that she had known him. They danced until dawn on New Year's Day.[109]

By 2 January 1939, Pip and Consuelo were back at Monte Julia where there were no wounded since the Nationalist advance had moved on so rapidly towards Barcelona. The food was almost as poisonous as the atmosphere among staff with little else to do but gossip. The love-sick Magallón had boasted to his wife Mercedes that he had slept with Pip. Mercedes, in turn, had discovered from Consuelo that this was untrue. Consuelo wanted Pip to confront him but she could not see the point of having a row. She wrote phlegmatically in her diary:

I would get him slung out willingly if it was not that I am fond of his wife and don't see why I should hurt her for pride's sake. God, what filthy swine men are. The trouble is the lousy brute is quite capable of getting angry and going to other people with the story. I would like to reassure his wife that I think him an ugly, slimy, oversexed little pimp so she need have no fear. I would also like to tell him just what I think of him and that one more word out of him and I will go straight to the Teniente Coronel.

She decided to sleep on it. In fact, she did nothing. In any case, she was too occupied with the altogether more exciting news that Princess Bea and Prince Ali were moving to Monzón, forty-eight kilometres to the northwest of Lérida, and barely half an hour's drive away. Princess Bea asked her to help with the move and also to accompany her on an inspection of the front.[110]

Pip was even more delighted with the war news – 'our advance is simply shooting along to Tarragona; each day is better than the other'. By the time that she set out with Princess Bea, the Nationalists had already captured Tarragona and Reus. Writing at Mora del Ebro of her satisfaction at the speed of the advance on Catalonia, she noted: 'The amount of prisoners taken daily is colossal and there is hardly any fighting and very few wounded especially down here.' They drove to Reus along tranquil lanes through ochre hills dotted with blossoming olive and almond trees. Their idyllic journey belied the fact that they were only a couple of days behind Franco's forces. As they caught up with the troops marching on Barcelona, Pip began to record fascinating details. At a factory, the returning owner was greeted with pleasure – real or feigned? – by 'all his workmen and servants'. Outside one of the factory sheds lay the corpses of six Republican soldiers: 'They were killed yesterday evening so are quite harmless as they don't smell or anything.' The roads were packed with troops 'in groups of about fifty, each with its flag, hundreds and hundreds, dirty, unshaven, carrying guns with their pack and blankets tied round them, all terribly tired, as they had averaged thirty kilometres per day for three days'. Through Pip's innocently enthusiastic eyes a unique picture emerges.

> It is fun to see newly taken big towns. Auxilio Social distributing bread from lorries, men sticking up anti-Red and up-with-Franco posters everywhere, people clearing up debris in the streets, putting down telephone wires, looking for houses for hospitals and offices, and dozens of simple sightseers. Unluckily the fun of a frantically pleased population waving flags and making whoopee was missing as all the Catalans are red so don't look on us very much as heroic liberators.[111]

Despite the comfort of travelling as Princess Bea's companion, Pip made the courageous decision to join a unit of Franco's Moroccan Army Corps. It meant risking the Infanta's displeasure and giving up the possibility of frequent meetings with Ataúlfo, but 'after all, I came here to work'. To her chagrin, Mercedes Milá would not permit her friend Consuelo to join the same unit. 'God knows that I don't want to go all alone to a new *equipo* miles from Princess Bea and her family where I know no one and there is no one who can speak a word of English or has anything even distantly to do with my previous life.' Her decision was all the more plucky given her own war-weariness.

> This time last year I was in Ventosilla wildly excited that at last I was off to the front. How much one year can wear out one's enthusiasm and vitality. It seems at least five years since I left Ventosilla and God how sick I have got of the war in that time . . . if I have to spend another wartime Christmas here I shall die

of depression and worries and illnesses . . . If only the
war could be over so that I could stop worrying about
Ataúlfo and go away somewhere and never move,
speak or think for a month. I am tired out both morally
and physically.

Her new unit was in the agreeable surroundings of the
elegant resort of Sitges to the south of the Catalan capital.
Billeted in a fashionable hotel, the sun and the beach cheered
her as did the news that Barcelona had fallen on 26 January
1939. The prospect of being among the first to enter the city
excited her and her morale was further bolstered by the fact
that she was the most competent of the nurses in her new
unit and was given plenty of responsibility. On 27 January she
visited Barcelona with the rest of her unit.

It is a lovely big spacious town and quite unharmed
though very dirty. We drove madly all round it. The
port is a shambles due to the hard work of aviation.
The streets were crowded with people showing considerable enthusiasm. Everyone shouting and cheering
and all the girls parading up the streets with flags.
The troops marching through were surrounded by
cheering crowds and everyone was in splendid form.
And yet as soon as one was out of the main streets,
where all the fun was going on, the people looked
surly.

To her disappointment, her unit was ordered to stay in Sitges
as the Moroccan Army Corps was not participating in the rest
of the advance. There, with astonishing energy, she single-
handedly created a functioning hospital out of the chaos of
broken beds, tangled bed linen and boxes of utensils dumped
by a convoy of lorries. There being little military activity she
was able to drive to the Orléans house in Monzón and to
marvel at Ataúlfo's brand-new grey Condor Legion uniform.

In Barcelona, she was regaled with horror stories of the Communist '*checas*', the dungeons in which political prisoners
were tortured and interrogated. Her hospital was moved to
a lunatic asylum at San Baudillo de Llobregat and Pip was
delighted to be in sole charge. In fact, the war was virtually
over in Catalonia and there was talk of her unit being sent to
Extremadura.[112]

While awaiting orders, she spent her time ferrying the
officers and nurses of her unit to and from Barcelona. Her
description of a journey with one of the chaplains is worth
repeating.

> Matute is a dreadful bore and can't see a car without
> getting into it. He always wants to go somewhere.
> We stopped in Vilanova i la Geltrú for petrol and my
> car was immediately surrounded by children as always.
> To my surprise, the priest, who had alighted leaps
> forward and starts to deal blows all around with his
> rolled-up newspaper. The little crowd dispersed in a
> moment. I was furious, as I thought it very unnecessary
> as they were doing no harm.

When the priest launched himself at the children a second
time, Pip remonstrated with him. He skulked off while she
entertained the children with a concert on her car radio. 'They
were sweet, all peering in through the windows and hushing
each other and dancing and pretending to play the violin.' On
his return, he reaffirmed the marriage of Church and Francoist
State by obliging the dumbfounded children to sing the Falangist hymn, 'Cara al sol' (face to the sun) and delivering a
sermon on the meaning of its words.[113]

The extent to which Pip had changed was illustrated on
one of her frequent journeys. She had always been intrepid
and was not fazed by hair-raising trips alone across mountain
tracks in thick fog or through floods. The war had hardened
her. On 16 February, she had an accident. Driving into Bar-

celona, intent on manoeuvring her car through convoys of lorries on narrow roads, she did not notice an old lady wandering into her path and could not brake in time. The woman was scared and bruised but otherwise unharmed. At one level, Pip was horrified but quickly recovered, commenting later, 'I have gained an instantaneous cold-bloodedness in this war from having to show no feelings in my work when my insides are writhing. And ever since I was shelled at Escatrón I have a complete cold control over myself which is very useful.'[114]

Pip got her mother to send out 500 bedcovers, lots of white material, cloaks, boots together with some peach brandy and 10,000 cigarettes. She drove for twenty hours to Sanlúcar to spend her leave with Ataúlfo. She finally began to recover from the ravages of the war.

> I live in a sort of peaceful haze of pleasure. The continual trouble of having to watch my step with Ataúlfo so as never to appear more than good friends when I really long to be close to him, to touch him and so on is amusing despite its unpleasantness and frustration. It is like a continual game. I let myself go as close to flirting as I dare but without ever going a step too far, not even by so much as a look. I don't know how long I shall have the self-control and placidity to be able to go on like this but for the moment it hardly disturbs my happiness at all, rather adds a flavour to it if anything. Neither the past nor the future exist and I live gloriously in the present here with Ataúlfo.

They spent idyllic hours gardening in El Botánico. The only cloud on the horizon was the amount that she was drinking – 'a disgrace. I even take brandy to finish off my breakfast.' It was an indication of the toll taken on her by the war. On Saturday, 25 February, she spent the night in Seville and got riotously drunk and danced with Ataúlfo in a nightclub until dawn. 'It was a heavenly evening, nobody existed in the world as far as we were concerned.' They paid the price the following morning when they set out for the long drive to Épila with the corresponding hangovers. They arrived just as the radio was announcing that Britain and France had recognised Franco. The end of the war was imminent. This elated her immensely but the shadow of a general war soon dampened spirits. It was a reflection of the Germanophile and anti-Semitic ambience of Prince Ali's household that she could write in her diary: 'The news from England tonight was once more all about war preparations in view of the imminent crisis. There is no crisis but as the Jews have sworn to have a European war this spring come what may, I suppose there soon will be.'[115]

With the war effectively over, there was little for Pip to do. Inevitably, away from the chaos of the front, her mind focused on Ataúlfo and she saw him frequently. Her pleasure in this was negated by signs that Princess Bea was starting to worry about their relationship. 'Somehow a strange feeling seems to have crept into the atmosphere. It is impossible to explain and may be all my imagination but there have been so many tiny probings and pointed remarks and meaning looks.'[116] There are various reasons why this might have been the case. If Ataúlfo was getting attached to her, that would challenge Prince Ali's hopes for his son to marry a royal. It is more likely that Princess Bea knew instinctively that her son had no real interest in women, would never marry and perhaps wanted to avoid Pip being hurt. All this was going on while the Republican zone was disintegrating into a mini civil war between the Government and the anti-Communist forces of Colonel Casado. Her unit had been sent to Don Benito in the province of Badajoz – at the best of times, a drab town. Now, pockmarked by shells and bombs, it was without any charm. To make matters worse, she was worried that she would miss the triumphal Nationalist entry into Madrid. In the event, her time there was made pleasant by sunbathing and horse riding. It was also just about near enough for visits to the Orléanses who were now in Talavera de la Reina. Her peace of mind was briefly disturbed by news of the Germans marching into Slovakia in mid-March.[117]

On 22 March 1939, her unit moved to Pueblonuevo in Córdoba – 'a filthy little dump'. She was depressed. 'God I wish this war would stop. I am fed up to the back teeth and will go raving mad soon.' The Nationalists were preparing for the final march on Madrid. Conditions in Pip's new hospital were primitive. 'It is hell having to start this war again when we all thought it was over and finished. I am sick of it and never want to work again in my life. My worst worry is my terror of there being a European war although things are temporarily quieting down.' Pip dreaded moving from one bleak village to another although in fact the end was nigh. She was released from her unit and, after a difficult search through the frozen sierras near Ávila, she managed to rejoin Princess Bea. The Infanta was about to enter Madrid with Frentes y Hospitales and Pip became one of her staff preparing food and blankets to take into the starving city that had been besieged for two and a half years.[118]

On 26 March, a gigantic advance was virtually unopposed across a wide front. Franco's forces entered an eerily silent Madrid on 27 March. When Pip heard the news, she was exultant: 'A day no Spaniard will ever forget nor I either. It has been so unbelievable that I don't know how to begin to describe it. At last, at last I am in Madrid, and I doubt if any other English person has entered it for the first time in their lives under similar conditions.' On 28 March, the Infanta, with Pip and a convoy of lorries containing supplies, were into Madrid before the main Nationalist forces. They drove through the lunar landscape of the Ciudad Universitaria, the front line marked by huge fortifications and smashed buildings. As they drove slowly into the centre, starving children jumped for joy as they handed out chocolate. There were emotional scenes as right-wingers who had been in hiding since the beginning of the war staggered out into the light from the embassies and legations where they had been buried alive. Pip was distressed by the damage to the magnificent Orléans Palacio in Madrid. Much of the façade had been damaged by shell-fire. A *tabor* (battalion) of Moorish mercenaries had been billeted there and filled the patio with sheep, goats and bullocks. However, the upstairs apartments and most of the furniture was intact.[119]

On the following day, they drove northeast out of Madrid past Guadalajara to inspect Princess Bea's estate at Castillejo. In the course of a drive of one hundred kilometres between Guadalajara and Tarancón, they saw no Nationalist troops yet passed without incident through 40,000 demoralised Republicans. 'All along the road, some going one way, some the other, in groups of twos and threes, or tens and twelves. They all looked dead tired, pale and exhausted, but quite cheerful. Lots were limping and hardly able to walk. All carrying their rugs and packages on their backs, but no arms at all.' The estate at Riba de Saelices which Bea had not seen since the family's departure from Spain in April 1931 was a ruin, its miles of woodland cut down, the house turned into a stable. On her return to Madrid, Pip accompanied the Infanta on an endless round of visits to hospitals, emergency stations and canteens. The weather was cold and wet and in the aftermath of the war, most people seemed to be suffering from colds or flu. Boredom briefly set in and, like others, Pip began to 'think of the filthy war which we loathed as "the good old days"'. Ataúlfo was similarly affected and was surly and bad-tempered with both Pip and his mother. The entire air force was depressed by the death, in an exhibition flight, of Joaquín García Morato, the Nationalists' great air ace.

Pip was at least cheered by moving into the new quarters of the Orléans family, a magnificent house that had been the Turkish Legation. She was busy establishing the canteen at the air base of Barajas, on the Guadalajara road out of Madrid.

She wrote of her relief work with Frentes y Hospitales: 'Always the same rows and bothers. Oh my kingdom never to see a hungry person or a tin of milk or Bovril again.' She was suffering the common letdown of the soldier's return to a squalid normality in a war-ravaged country. The end of hostilities meant no longer living on adrenaline. For Ataúlfo and Prince Ali and others, it meant the space to think about dead comrades. The atmosphere was not helped by the fact that there was little food. Pip was still losing weight but, unusually, not pleased by the fact. The relief work was certainly tedious – 'I am so sick of all this fussing and bothering and wearing uniform and never doing anything amusing.' The emergency stations provided horrendous sights and smells. Yet there was nothing to stop Pip returning to London to the glittering social life she had left behind eighteen months earlier. 'I can't bear the thought of leaving this, because after all I not only could but should go home, but it will be so hard to have to start life again.' She meant 'life far from Ataúlfo'. On the dark afternoon of Easter Saturday, he played the piano to her and the thought of eventually being separated from him left her tearful.[120]

Despite a telegram from her mother ordering her to return home, Pip lingered on doing ever-more relief work. Prince Ali was involved in organising various triumphal parades of the Condor Legion and the Italian Regia Aeronautica. On 20 April, Pedro Chicote, owner of Madrid's most fashionable bar, gave a cocktail party for Frentes y Hospitales. The hostess was Pilar Franco Bahamonde, the Caudillo's sister. Pip met her daughter, Pilar Jaraiz-Franco, who had spent much of the war in Republican prisons. She thought that 'she looks the silliest, most uninteresting girl, who has never done anything but amuse herself'. Pip could hardly have been more mistaken. Pilar Jaraiz would later become a Socialist and write a cuttingly acute critique of the Franco family and regime. Other days involved visits to hospitals and desperate efforts to get supplies for them. Pip found a cancer hospital 'too dreadful for words. All dying and pale green and half-mad.' Tuberculosis was rife in Madrid. With 70,000 cases, the hospitals could not cope. Despite serious risk of infection, Pip was occupied making regular house calls to the seriously ill, distributing food and dressing ulcers and sores. In the working-class quarter of Vallecas, she came across scenes from a medieval plague.

> We found a married couple of fifty-six and sixty years old in bed, black with dirt and just like skeletons. Their hands and legs were covered with ulcers and blisters, pouring blood, pus and water, tied in dirty rags. For two months they have lived on orange peel and a few onions they found fermenting in a manure heap. A woman of forty-eight looking about seventy, a skeleton with scabs all over her hands and face and the pus running into her eyes so that she could not open them.

Starving consumptives and people deranged by hiding for years became common sights for her. After hours of visits, she would work long into the evening typing reports for the hospitals.[121]

Princess Bea wrote to Margot Howard de Walden of her admiration for

> Pip's character and work . . . Here now in Madrid we found the population in a deplorable condition, sights like in an Indian famine. We had to visit separately as there was so much work. Pip nursed these people and gave them injections and took food to them. In the evenings she typed reports for the Hospitals all on her own and in perfect Spanish . . . Where there was no doctor to hand, she did the diagnosis . . . got the cancer patients into the Cancer Hospital, the tuberculosis patients into the Sanatorium . . . She never made a mistake . . . Her intelligence and patience have been

astounding. All this without an audience, or a single
day off for fun. She is known from one end of Spain
to the other ... never flurried or impatient. I want
you to know all this as in tidy England you may never
have seen her tackle a burden of work single-handed
like she has in Madrid.[122]

Occasional visits from Ataúlfo merely left Pip – and indeed
his mother – feeling tense. Not being involved in their frenetic
relief work, he moped around the house and picked quarrels
with Princess Bea who would take out on Pip her consequent
distress. Pip wrote in her diary: 'Life is so hopeless anyhow.
I almost wish Ataúlfo had not come at all. I am just about at
the last gasp as it is. I don't want to see Ataúlfo. I want to be
left in peace with no more work and no more emotions.' In
early May, Pip was awarded her military cross for her bravery
at Escatrón. She also served drinks at the Barajas aerodrome
when Franco came to preside at a fly-past of the Nationalist
air force, including Germans and Italians. She was not
impressed by the Caudillo: 'Franco is a weeny little man, the
size and shape of a tennis ball and looked too funny beside
huge stooping lanky old Kindelán and even taller, lankier
Queipo de Llano.' In fact, the round of victory parades and
march-pasts, of celebratory dinners and cocktail parties,
heralded the inexorable approach of Pip's return home.
At a dinner at the Ritz, she sat disconsolately watching others
dance, longing for Ataúlfo and reflecting 'it is going to be one
hell of an effort to get used to enjoying dancing with anyone
else again'. After a visit to Philip II's palace at the Escorial on
Sunday 14 May, she wrote: 'Everyday I love Spain more and
hate more having to leave it. I will visit it again but it will
never be my country like now.' On the following day, she
was even more down. Ataúlfo was going to Germany with
the Condor Legion. She was anything but resigned as she
wrote:

I can't bear the thought that this is all over. I can never be of the family here again. I will stay with them and them with us but it won't ever be the same. God knows how, when and where Ataúlfo and I will meet again once I leave Spain. And I must go. How I hate life for doing this to me. I want to be married and have lots of children and lots of fun. And I can't do it and can't even be happy.[123]

On 17 May, Pip was exhilarated when Prince Ali took her flying in a Savoia Marchetti 79 bomber and let her take over the controls for ten minutes. On the same day she had dinner with Peter Kemp, who introduced her to Major Hugh Pollard. Pollard was a retired army officer, secret-service agent and sexual adventurer. He had helped make the arrangements for the Dragon Rapide that flew from Croydon on 11 July 1936 to collect Franco in the Canary Islands and take him to Morocco to join the military uprising.[124] He lived up to his image by making indecent advances to Pip. Kemp was rather more romantic and declared his love for her. This provided her with an opportunity to make Ataúlfo jealous although it backfired, souring things between them. Her last days in Madrid were beginning to resemble her life in London before she came to Spain – a wild round of cocktail parties, dinners and her ongoing flirtation with Peter Kemp. That ended when she was outraged by his persistent attempts to prise bits of military information out of her friends in order to pass it on to the British military attaché. When she said farewell to Ataúlfo on the eve of his departure for Germany, they spoke of their next meeting. Pip said that it would be in the air in the next war and he replied that he would shoot her down. 'And so endeth both the happiest, unhappiest and most eventful chapter in my life up to date.'[125]

Frentes y Hospitales was dissolved in late May and there was nothing left for Pip to do. On Monday 5 June, she took

ship for England and was back in Seaford House four days
later on Friday. One of her first tasks was to report on the
situation in Spain to the exiled Queen Victoria Eugenia, Princess Bea's cousin. Reflecting the patrician prejudices of the
Orléanses, she told her 'how Red the Falange is and that
Serrano Suñer is ambitious, self-seeking and not to be trusted'.
She busied herself but felt desperately lonely. She wrote of
the contrast between her armies of friends and the fact that
'inside of me there is nothing more than just a lonely emptiness'. It was all to do with Ataúlfo and now there was no war
or relief work to distract her. 'I wish to God I could get him
out of my head for five minutes of the day. If I buy clothes
it is because he might see them, if I hear jazz I want to be
dancing with him; if I hear a joke I want to tell it him; if I
see something nice I wish he was there to see it too.'[126]

Certainly, after her experiences both in the war and in the
Orléans household, life in London would never be the same
again. There could be no going back. Pip felt completely lost.
Gaenor, her sister, compared it to those who returned from
France after the First World War. Many years later, Pip's son
concluded from conversations with her that she had been
burned out. It was certainly not uncommon for those who
had been in Spain to find their contemporaries incapable of
understanding what had happened there during the Civil War.
Even her sister, with whom she had been very close, now
seemed a stranger, having grown up and married. After the
rigours of Spain, Pip busied herself with the usual distractions
– the races, cocktail parties, dances, and pampered herself with
visits to hairdressers, dressmakers and shopping. For all that it
was infinitely more pleasant than life in a front-line hospital,
she found it meaningless. On 19 June, she met the great theatrical stars, Flora Robson and John Gielgud. She acquired a new
car but her thoughts were really set on a possible visit from
Ataúlfo.

She worked on censoring her diary for publication. Pip was

persuaded that it was publishable and she set about editing it. Her blue pencil seemed to have had two principal concerns. She was anxious to ensure that nothing said about Prince Ali, Princess Bea or the rest of the Orléans-Borbón family could embarrass them. On the eve of war, she also eliminated references to the Luftwaffe pilots she had known through Ataúlfo and to her distress at the prospect of going to war against people she considered to be her friends. The outbreak of the Second World War led to the prospective publishers pulling back. Thereafter, she said that she could not bear to look at the diary. It was her edited text that was published in 1995.[127]

Ataúlfo arrived in London at the beginning of July, 'looking very handsome and sunburned and healthy'. However, since his German comrades had been asking him why he had not married Pip, he had become careful not to spend too much time with her lest 'people should start talking here too'. Pip realised once more that he had no intention of marrying her: 'Firstly, he is not in love with me, secondly he has no money so can't marry anyone, thirdly he has promised P. Bea only to marry a Princess.' With the brilliant sophistry of the self-deceiver, she consoled herself that 'if he was sure he really did not want to, he would not have to make his mind up about it so often'. In fact, they had such a good time together that she was emboldened to raise the subject of their future. She was devastated again when he told her what she already knew – that he didn't love her and would not marry her. She thought of travelling to get him out of her mind. Bizarrely, on 19 July, she drove to Sanlúcar with Consuelo.[128]

In fact, the warmth of her friendship with Ataúlfo was undiminished. They were together in Sanlúcar when the Danzig crisis broke. She mistakenly believed that the Nazi-Soviet pact made war less likely. Things went well enough until Ataúlfo had to leave for Yugoslavia on 30 August. On the following day, Germany declared war on Poland. Taking her cue from Prince Ali, Pip was inclined to blame Poland for the entire crisis. When war was declared on Germany, she felt she had to return to Britain. She was distraught at the prospect of another war. 'I am sick to death of hospitals, of uniforms, of corpses, of everything to do with it. I loathe it all.' She bravely set off to drive across Spain and a now belligerent France, reaching London on 9 September. The family home at Seaford House had become the Red Cross headquarters.[129]

Pip took the war badly. It definitively separated her from Ataúlfo and she felt suicidal – 'I'd die tomorrow with pleasure if I had not been brought up to think it cowardly to commit suicide. I never thought I should really want to. But what on earth is there worth living for? I have lost the one person I love and always will love. I may get used to the hurt but I will never forget or lose it.'[130] She rejected out of hand any possibility that Ataúlfo's behaviour might have been occasioned by homosexuality. She was still fuming because, four years earlier, Moke FitzClarence had put round a story that Ataúlfo was 'a pansy' because he had not taken the opportunity to kiss her in a taxi.[131] To break out of her black mood, Pip threw herself into socialising and drank too much. At one point, she met a man called Christopher Hobhouse who asked her to consider working for British Intelligence in Spain, a suggestion she rejected indignantly as snooping on her friends. She had a perpetual hangover, alcohol being increasingly her response to the emptiness of life after Spain. She wrote: 'I wish I could stop myself bounding into these fits of hectic gaiety when I am sick of life.' Her gloom was intensified by news that a decline in the family fortunes might mean the loss of Seaford House and maybe also Chirk Castle.[132]

Pip found the phoney war unbearable. Ataúlfo remained foremost in her thoughts. She was obliged to attend lectures about the war and longed to interrupt and tell the ignorant lecturers about the real effects of being shelled. A visit from her ex-lover John Geddes did nothing for her and she found herself becoming hard and bitter. 'I can't stick this continual ache much longer. I can't eat, I can't sleep, food just makes me feel sick and every time I shut my eyes I think I see Ataúlfo.' Brief telegrams and letters from him did reach her but merely set her off weeping and aching when she considered that it might be years before they could meet again. She continued to drink far too much – whisky and brandy by night alternating with Bromo-Seltzer by day. The men that she met just bored her.[133]

At the beginning of November, she started to train formally as a nurse at St Thomas's Hospital. After her experience in Spain, she was mortified to be treated as a total novice. She wrote on 8 November, 'no one can stand getting up at 7.30, spending the day in a hospital, dancing till 6 in the morning, sleeping one hour, eating one meal only and drinking too much, for long. I shall have to sober up or I will crack up. I already look like the wrath of God.' After virtually running a hospital at the front, to be prevented from doing anything more complex than making beds severely dented her morale: 'I have lost everything in the world I wanted since then [the last time that she had seen Ataúlfo], most depressing of all, my optimism. A year ago today, Consuelo and I were running single-handed a hospital of eighty-two beds and we had thirty-six new patients. This year I went to St Thomas's Hospital and made two beds in an empty ward and was taught a few things I have already done hundreds of times.' The next day was her twenty-third birthday, enlivened by telegrams from Princess Bea, Prince Ali and Ataúlfo. Suggestions that she return to Sanlúcar cheered her up as did a stint on the men's surgical ward at the hospital. 'There is something very funny about scrubbing the bottom of a London policeman.'

Her dejection finally began to dissolve after an invitation by a social acquaintance, Maureen Schreiber, to join a field hospital leaving for France in January 1940. Presented to the French by Lord and Lady Hadfield and organised by Mary, the wife of Brigadier-General Spears, it was large and well-equipped, with thirteen doctors, x-ray facilities, one hundred beds, trucks and tents. Pip agreed – with no illusions. There was no excitement, just a sense of duty and a desperate need for something to distract her from the endless longing for Ataúlfo. 'I must do something and that will be about the best. I would far rather go to Spain and ignore the whole thing for evermore, but I can't do that so I had better work . . . Am I going to spend all my life drifting about in wars from one hospital to another with no aim and no ambition . . . I am tired out from war already and I *know* what it is going to be like so it is no adventure any longer.' She really wanted to go to Sanlúcar but dared not, knowing she could spend only a finite period there and that the pain of separation would be ever more unbearable. It was thus with dread in her heart that she accepted the invitation to join the Hadfield-Spears ambulance unit.[134] Burnt-out by her front-line experience, she wrote: 'I suppose I ought to be glad to have had six months rest since I left Madrid, but it has not been a very happy one and soon I must go back to the sickening smell and sound of it again.'[135]

To say that she had left her heart in Spain was an understatement. In mid-December, she received a visit from Últano Kindelán and his English wife Doreen. Most of her diary entries recount a lively social life that left her deeply miserable and a sense of alienation. Now 'a breath of my beloved Spain' filled her with joy. 'The realisation that Spain is not all a dream, that they all exist and want me back and that one day I can go. It was wonderful and I felt alive and interested in life again for a moment.' She wished she could accept their invitation to go back to Spain with them. As it was, she had to meet her colleagues from the medical unit: 'hard-faced wispy old hags except one pop-eyed nit-wit'. She was gratified by a telegram on 16 December from Ataúlfo: 'Thanks letters. Can't see why you shouldn't come here for next five years.'

On the following day, it was backed up by another from Consuelo which read: 'For the Lord's sake do what Ataúlfo says in his telegram. You will regret it all your life if you don't come.' Her reaction – that, despite her longing, to go without a prospect of fulfilment would just be to condemn herself to unhappiness – was both courageous and momentous. 'For five years I have chased after Ataúlfo like a fool. Now if he wants to, he can come and fetch me but if he does not want me I won't go back.' She began sporadically to get angry with Ataúlfo by way of reconciling herself to what was likely to be a final break. Her wretchedness was not diminished by the packing-up of Seaford House in advance of it being abandoned by the family for good.[136]

Nineteen-forty started with more telegrams from Ataúlfo, more heartache for Pip and relief that she would soon be off to France. The telegrams provoked tears and intense hurt by forcing her to contemplate her impossible situation. As departure for France beckoned, she began to regret rejecting the invitations to Sanlúcar. In bitterly freezing weather, she left London on 29 January 1940. She spent a pleasant fortnight in Paris, shopping and taking advantage of well-stocked and cheap restaurants. With the war seemingly a long way off, she bought clothes, gramophone records and 'material for curtains etc for my future rooms'. On 12 February, the unit moved to northeast France, setting up a hospital between Nancy and Sarrebourg in the Moselle. Although the hospital was near the front, there was virtually no military action and the work was inconsequential and tedious. It was enlivened by one daring visit to the Maginot line to peer at the Germans and by occasional concert parties.[137] Her hopes were raised by a possibility that Ataúlfo would come to London as adjutant to Juan Antonio Ansaldo who had been named Spanish Air Attaché.[138] She was pleased too when her experience and her good French and English saw her given considerable responsibility. As the work increased, she was moved to write: 'I am gradually get-

ting happier here and more or less contented. All bothers of
life are so far away from one here that one can't worry so
very much.' She forged a friendship with another English
woman in the unit, Dorothy 'Dodo' Annesley, and even had
a mild flirtation with an American officer called Etienne
Gilon.[139]

However, Pip's version of the phoney war was coming to
an end. On 22 April, the hospital was shelled, which stirred
unpleasant memories of her ordeal at Escatrón. Her combat
experience in Spain singled her out in the unit and gave her
a maturity not shared by her older companions. On the other
hand, she never entirely escaped from her time and class,
writing after one day in the operating theatre, 'We had two
buck niggers today. I hate niggers.' Rumours of Mussolini
joining the war at Hitler's side led to speculation that Franco
would not be far behind. The idea caused her deep disquiet.
'I can't imagine anything very much more hellish than fighting
against Spain. It was bad enough worrying about Ataúlfo when
I was on the same side, but it will be far worse when we are
on opposite sides with no news.' The German assault on the
Low Countries provoked an ambiguous reaction – 'Altogether
the Germans have been very spirited. They have bombed
masses of French towns last night . . . Winston Churchill is
now Prime Minister of England instead of Chamberlain. I
think he is dreadful but perhaps he will do something for a
change because so far the Germans seem to be having everything all their own way.' She was quite blasé about the advancing Wehrmacht. 'Evidently the Germans have dropped some
men in parachutes near here and they have not been caught. So
we are all to expect to be murdered in our beds or something.'

The surrender of the Dutch on 15 May did not affect her
good humour. A newly arrived and pompous new nurse, a
friend of Lady Hadfield, seemed to Pip to be 'an awe-inspiring
old hag if I ever saw one'. As the Germans reached Amiens
and Arras, the stream of casualties increased somewhat. When

they took Abbéville and were closing in on Boulogne, she began to get concerned for the British Expeditionary Force – 'Hopeless pansy performance we are putting up.' She bitterly regretted not being nearer the front line and felt that her unit, being 'smart', would never be put in serious danger. When wounded German prisoners came in, Pip was appalled by the hostility that they provoked. 'We are nurses. And to a nurse, there is no such thing as nationality. One patient is the same as another whether black or white, a Frenchman or a German.' The fall of Belgium at the end of May left her worried about the BEF being cut off and massacred. Orders came on 30 May for the unit to be evacuated but nothing happened for a week. With the patients packed off, the nurses spent the time drinking, partying, picnicking, fishing and squabbling, with Pip distributing succour to those who had lost fiancés. With no newspapers and only sporadic news on the radio, it was an idyllic interlude – 'I have not been so happy since goodness knows when.'[140]

The unit left Alsace for the south on 7 June. Pip found it all a great adventure until Mussolini's entry into the war on 10 June once again provoked her worries that Franco would not be far behind. The unit was to set up as a *poste d'embarquement*, with two hundred beds in a tent at a railway station near Rosnay. However, the speed of the German advance saw them swept up in the flood of refugees heading south. The German occupation of Paris forced the abandonment of plans to set up a new hospital to back up a French defensive stand. The group moved on, staying in requisitioned chateaux. By 16 June, they were near Vichy. News of Pétain's request for an armistice left Pip weeping with 'the sudden feeling of the bottom dropping out of one's world'. As they neared Bordeaux, there was deep anxiety that their convoy would run out of petrol or be cut off by the vertiginous German advance. In either case, Pip was determined to start walking along with other refugees and head for Spain. Depressed and frightened by the prospect of being captured and sent to a German concentration camp, they pressed on, without food, towards Bordeaux.

On 22 June, with wounded British soldiers and a motley group of refugees, they were taken out to sea. There they were picked up by the British light cruiser, HMS *Galatea*, which took them to St Jean de Luz to pick up the British Ambassador. By 24 June, the unit was on board a troop carrier, the SS *Ettrick*, en route to England. Among those on board were a group of Polish troops. Pip was instantly entranced – 'wonderful tall, dark, strong-looking people'. She nursed the wounded soldiers on board and, since her friend Dorothy was ill, Pip also looked after her. Despite her lack of sleep and the cramped conditions, her irrepressible optimism reasserted itself – 'the Polish troops on board are heaven and have wonderful singing orgies on deck every evening'. The ship reached Plymouth on 26 June. She reached Chirk only to discover, to her horror, that her mother was in Liverpool on the point of leaving for Canada with her four granddaughters.[141]

Chirk and London were equally depressing. On arrival in the capital, she was told that a young man, James Cassell, who had written to her in France and proposed to her, had committed suicide, leaving a note which read simply 'Goodbye, Pip.' When she made enquiries about the Orléans family, she was devastated to be told that they were so pro-German that the British Royal family was livid with them and that Ataúlfo had not been allowed into the country as assistant air attaché to Juan Antonio Ansaldo. Such gossip was wildly exaggerated but it was true that the Civil War had left enormous admiration for the Third Reich on the Spanish Right. The men of the Orleans family had flown with German and Italian aviators throughout the war. Although upset by these rumours, Pip's reaction was not without shrewdness.

> Why do I have to go on being nuts about a man who has always behaved like a prize shit to me and is now violently pro-German. I ought to be furious but it is

exactly what I expected of him, the great spineless sod. He is led by his parents wherever they fancy. And to think that we have all been brought up together for two generations and that they are monarchists and Catholics and yet pro-German. They deserve all they would get if the Nazi regime spreads to Spain.[142]

The mental turmoil occasioned by the Catholic royalist Orléanses' pro-German stance helped Pip to see Ataúlfo in a slightly harsher light – 'I still like him better than anyone else in the world which is probably why I mind so terribly his upholding the other side. I hope I never have to see him again, the filthy bastard.'[143] Her mind was taken off Ataúlfo by an encounter with 'Dodo' Annesley and Marjorie Fielden who had been with her in the nursing unit in France. Dodo intended to organise a hospital for the Poles in Scotland and wanted Pip to take charge of the nursing staff. In fact, she had to do everything – find suitable premises, raise the necessary funds, purchase surgical equipment. Having committed herself to Dodo, she was then offered a job in Spain by a man called Hugh Smyth. He told her, implausibly, that it would be with the British diplomatic corps. Other evidence suggests that this was a tentative approach by the intelligence services. She felt relieved that the Polish undertaking saved her from making a fool of herself with Ataúlfo. By 3 August, she was on her way to Glasgow where it was arranged that there would be a mobile field hospital, half surgical and general medical complete with operating theatre, laundry and fumigating plant. It was eventually to accompany the Polish units into battle in Italy but by then Pip would have moved on. The entire enterprise was going to be extraordinarily expensive and the initial costs were readily met by Margot Howard de Walden. Pip looked for locations, continued further fund-raising and started learning Polish.[144]

It was sufficiently hectic to keep thoughts of Ataúlfo at bay. However, at the beginning of September 1940, she recalled the German invasion of Poland one year earlier when she had been at Sanlúcar. 'How miserable I was and how justified I was. I have not enjoyed myself for a single day since, and don't see that I shall again for a long time.' A year had passed but she was still not cured of her longing for him – 'I still feel just the same cold, empty feeling without the sod as I always did.' Life was made thoroughly difficult throughout the German bombing offensive on London during the autumn of 1940. Although inevitably appalled by the damage done by the Blitz, Pip's sense of humour did not desert her. She found it 'rather exhilarating being frightened like this all the time, it peps me up, but I do wish it would not give me diarrhoea. However, that at least is slimming.' She moved around between the homes of various friends and relatives after being forced out of her father's studio in Cadogan Lane by an unexploded bomb in the garden. Later, after she had got back into the studio, it was badly damaged by another bomb while she was sleeping. In the same air raid, across Belgrave Square, the façade was blown off Seaford House.[145]

A letter from Princess Bea expressing her anxiety that Franco might join the war alongside Hitler left Pip wondering if Ataúlfo would end up dropping bombs on London. The mid-September visit to Berlin of Franco's brother-in-law, Ramón Serrano Suñer, was assumed to herald Spanish belligerence. Her analysis of the strategic consequences if Spain went to war, in terms of the loss of Gibraltar and the closing of the Straits, was extremely acute. Her rhetorical question as to why Britain did not try to keep Spain neutral by offering to return Gibraltar after the war exactly echoed Churchill's own thinking. Her personal anguish at the implications of Spain at war with Britain could hardly have been more intense.

I can't imagine a greater hell than knowing that Ataúlfo is fighting against me and is bombing day after day. He will never live through a whole other war.

It just isn't possible. And I shan't even know if he is alive or not. I can't fight against a country I have fought with for two years, and I would rather die than fight against Ataúlfo. But still women don't fight and anyhow it is no good feeling that way because we have to win this war and if all the people I love best have to be my enemies meanwhile I will just have to put up with it ... For a year I have been miserable because I can't go back to Spain or see Ataúlfo, but at least I was happy to know that he was safe and enjoying himself and now even that consolation looks like being taken away.[146]

In the midst of her distress, she received an insouciant letter from Consuelo asking 'is London as destroyed as they say? What a shame, such a nice town, it is a great pity.' A philosophic Pip pondered, 'how very far we are from our fellow human beings, even great friends. It is funny to think how I worry about Spain joining in this war and how little they worry about us. And we are supposed to be the unfeeling, unemotional ones.' However, news of Franco's historic meeting with Hitler at Hendaye on 23 October 1940 renewed all of her anxieties. On that day, she had a terrifying attack of depression, – 'all of a sudden I began to feel utterly lonely and futile and within about two minutes was lying on the floor sobbing my heart out at the misery and beastliness of life ... I felt imprisoned by an impenetrable barrier of wickedness and pettiness and knew that I should never get out. I just lay in the middle of a circle of evil, wicked, mean things sobbing and exhausted with despair.' No doubt this was a delayed reaction to the terror that she was experiencing during the night-time bombing attacks. And further considerable anxiety was provoked by the fact that Franco, in whose cause she had given so much, was toadying up to Hitler, who was in the process of destroying London.[147]

Her reaction to another letter from Consuelo revealed a
Pip who was growing up fast. Consuelo wrote that Ataúlfo
was behaving very badly, was constantly drunk and deliberately
provoking rows with his mother and father. He had told her
that 'he did not care a damn any longer about pleasing his
parents as they had ruined his life by not letting him marry
the person he wanted to'. Pip's reaction was extraordinarily
mature and wise. 'What a fat head he is. Too weak to defy
his parents in anything important so he just drives them crazy
in small ways and no doubt makes himself miserable in the
attempt.' Her romantic longings of old seemed to be replaced,
consciously at least, by sadness that Ataúlfo was squandering
his talents. Some days later, she awoke in tears after a dream
about him: 'We were in a crowd of panic-stricken women
and swarms of babies. He kept trying to reach me and getting
swept away. I was terrified of something. At last he reached
me and just as he stretched out his hand to catch mine I woke
up simultaneously as he was swept away right out of sight.'[148]

That Pip's heart remained in Spain was revealed when Juan
Antonio Ansaldo made a visit to London prior to taking up
his duties as Air Attaché. When she was invited to have a
drink with him and some friends, she assumed that they would
have forgotten all about her 'the same as all my friends here
did while I was in Spain'. 'The only reason they were ever
so friendly was because they thought I was engaged to Ataúlfo,
but by now they will have forgotten that and I am just another
dim English girl who once went to Spain . . . Now maybe I
will wake up to the fact that I don't belong in Spain and no
one there cares two damns about me any longer outside of
Sanlúcar.' Her anxieties were totally misplaced. When they
met at the Dorchester, Ansaldo fell upon her effusively. She
was so moved by his affectionate response to her that she
wrote later: 'It was a feeling like coming home again after a
long exile. I felt as if someone had removed a ton weight off
me. Despite all my longing for Spain, I had not realised till

then just how much I loved it.' Her delight at being able to reminisce in Spanish was short-lived. As dawn was breaking on her way home from an extremely alcoholic dinner, she witnessed rescue squads trying to retrieve people trapped in the cellars of bombed houses. When she saw her Spanish friends again on the eve of their return to Madrid, she wept uncontrollably. 'I know this is my country but it does not feel like it. I feel like an exile from home and I can't go back.[149]

Nostalgia for Spain made it all the more difficult for Pip to throw herself into her Polish project. Having got embroiled in it so as not to be tempted to run back to Spain, she was now regretting the decision. She even began to wonder if she should not have accepted one of the several offers that she had had to go to Spain to work for British Intelligence. The visit of Ansaldo had left her feeling that her love for Spain was not just about Ataúlfo. 'I love that country and anything to do with it.'[150] Nevertheless, she put aside her distress and knuckled down to making a success of the Polish Hospital. In late October and early November 1940, all the preparatory work began to come together. Pip forged an alliance with Diana Napier, a minor film star and wife of the great Austrian tenor, Richard Tauber, who was in charge of organising ambulances for the Polish Army. A base was found at Dupplin Castle, between Perth and Dundee on the Firth of Tay. At first, Pip faced considerable difficulties in getting the hospital up and running: 'More and more I hate this Hospital and all the Poles . . . Loathe the Poles, loathe the Hospital and want to be back in Spain. Even without Spain I should still loathe the Poles.' Inevitably, as always happened, the more she threw herself into her work, the more engrossed and therefore the less unhappy she became.[151] The hospital was called SEFA – from the initials of Scott-Ellis, Marjorie Fielden and Dorothy Annesley.

There were occasional flashes of news from Ataúlfo, mainly when he was in Madrid, which convinced Pip that he was frightened of showing his feelings for her when he was at his parents' home. At the end of November, a brief stay in London was prolonged after a car crash in the blackout. She was recovering from minor facial surgery when she was visited by Peter Kemp. Her old comrade from the Nationalist ranks told her that he had seen Ataúlfo in Madrid just after he had received news of her flight from France. Pip was amused to be told that he had been furious to hear of her French adventure. He had said that he wished that she had been taken prisoner so that his family could have arranged for the Germans to send her to Spain. She was even more delighted to hear that while in Madrid liaising with the German military representatives, Ataúlfo had 'received a delegation from all the brothels of Madrid to ask him to ask the Germans to take their boots off!'[152]

In December 1940, Pip was given the title of honorary colonel in the Polish Army. She found it 'rather fun' being called '*Pani Pulkownik*' (Madame Colonel). Life settled down into a monotonous routine. Pip worked immensely hard and learned a lot of physiology and anatomy.[153] Her Polish became as fluent as her Spanish. Beyond her work, her main preoccupation regarding the outside world was that Spain did not enter the war on Hitler's side. She was as distressed as many of her Polish comrades by the idea of alliance with Soviet Russia. Her class prejudices, and her experiences in Spain, shone through in her remark that 'I should hate to fight with a lot of bloody Communists almost as much, though not quite, as I should hate to fight against Spain.'[154]

The next years are difficult to reconstruct. Her diary comes to an abrupt end in January 1941. Pressure of work is a possible explanation for the silence although she had managed to write daily under far more trying circumstances in Spain. The survival of a later fragment suggests that the diary was simply lost. Nevertheless, the value of her work can be deduced from the fact that, in 1943, she was awarded the Polish Golden Cross of Merit with the approval of the Foreign Office.[155] What is known is that the cold and damp of the Scottish climate intensified her tendency to very poor circulation. The chief surgeon at the hospital told her that smoking and drinking so much was exacerbating the problem. She seems to have tried sporadically to cut down but the daily stress of life at the hospital made abstention impossible for her. Life became unbearably difficult and she was diagnosed as having circulatory difficulties, known as Raynaud's disease. It was recommended that she go to live in a warm climate. Throughout her time at Dupplin Castle, she longed for the day when she would return to Spain although a lengthy affair with a Polish surgeon, Colonel Henryk Masarek, had helped her finally to put aside hopes of marrying Ataúlfo.

As a result of her experiences in Spain during the Civil War, the various informal approaches from the Secret Services in 1939 and 1940 were entirely understandable. Keeping Spain neutral was a major preoccupation and an upper-class English woman with Pip's impeccable political connections was an obvious target for recruitment. She was close to both the Orléans and Kindelán families, the two most important centres of the monarchist opposition to Franco within Spain itself. In mid-July 1941, the Special Operations Executive ran a security trace on her. The trace request to MI5 stated: 'It is our intention that the Honourable Miss Scott-Ellis should be employed in the investigation of the possibility of evacuating Polish prisoners-of-war from Spain. We would be glad to know, if you have any reason from the security point of view why this person should not be so employed.' The reply from MI5 cast doubt on her discretion citing a report that, at a dinner held at the Savoy for the Spanish Aid Mission in December 1940, she had blurted out that she had been asked to go to Spain as a spy, as she knew so many people there. She proudly stated that she had refused this request – probably the repeated approaches by Hugh Smyth made in the course of 1939. She had said that she would never work against Spain.[156] The reported remarks were entirely consistent with the heartfelt declarations in her diary.

Finally, in February 1943, the Continental Action Force of the Polish Government-in-Exile in Britain requested that Pip be sent to Spain to help in the evacuation of escaping prisoners-of-war. In the light of the earlier security report, the proposal was accepted only after some hesitation. It is difficult to reconstruct her work in Barcelona with the Special Operations Executive from the exiguous surviving files. However, she later hinted at what she did to her mother, her sister, to José Luis de Vilallonga and to her son, John. Her official position, or cover, was as a secretary working in the dissemination of pro-Allied information to counteract the domination of the Spanish media by the Third Reich. However, the Consulate in Barcelona was the main conduit for Allied personnel escaping across the Eastern Pyrenees. It would seem, therefore, that her role was to help in the safe passage of British and Polish pilots shot down over France and other escapees through Spain and into Portugal. Her language skills and her connections with the most prominent and influential pro-Allied monarchists make it eminently plausible that she was indeed organising their transit on to Lisbon.[157]

She had the perfect excuse for trips from Barcelona across Spain to a point relatively near the Portuguese border in her friendship with the Orléans Borbón family. In any case, her first port of call in Spain was the family's Montpensier Palace at Sanlúcar de Barrameda where she went to convalesce from the illness exacerbated by the Scottish climate. Thereafter, her visits to the family were as frequent and as lengthy as they had been during the Civil War. There is plentiful photographic evidence of Pip, looking thin but happy, riding with Ataúlfo in April at the Feria de Sevilla, helping Ataúlfo with his animals at the Botánico at Sanlúcar de Barrameda in May, then again riding with Ataúlfo at the Rocío in June, and then at a party

at Sanlúcar de Barrameda in August 1943. In the autumn of
1943, she went to Estoril to spend some time with her mother
who was there returning from Canada with her four granddaughters. She travelled to Estoril again in late January 1944
to see Gaenor who was returning from America with her
children. She had been with her husband Richard who had
been working in the economic warfare section of the British
Embassy in Washington.[158] By late 1944, with Allied forces
controlling the south of France, Pip's role was coming to an
end.

In any case, her life, both professional and personal, was
about to take a dramatic turn. At some point in late 1943 or
early 1944, she ran into José Luis de Vilallonga, the handsome
and dissolute playboy son of a rich Catalan aristocrat, the Barón
de Segur. There exists a photograph from January 1944 of
them together at a party. According to José Luis, they met at
a cocktail party at the home of the Catalan publisher Gustavo
Gili. Tall, elegant, with the pencil moustache fashionable at
the time, she found him irresistibly good-looking. He was also
seductively charming, as many other women were to discover
to their cost. José Luis wrote later: 'that evening, she would
have done better to have gone to the cinema or stayed at home
because I was going to make her miserable and humiliated for
the rest of her days ... I regret infinitely that I made a good
and loyal woman suffer so much for the dreadful error of
falling in love with me.'[159]

Perhaps José Luis's cruel treatment of Pip was connected
to the fact that she bore an uncanny resemblance to his mother,
Carmen Cabeza de Vaca y Carvajal. Pip's sister Gaenor was
once shown a photograph of the Baronesa, whom she had
never met, and asked to identify it. She thought it was Pip.
José Luis de Vilallonga later wrote of how his childhood was
marked by his mother's coldness and indifference. 'As a child,
I would have given anything for my mother to take me in
her arms and kiss me.' Oddly, in his memoirs, he denied that

any of his wives resembled his mother.[160] It is tempting to speculate that, in his systematically appalling treatment of Pip, he was somehow trying to punish his mother for the coldness that so scarred his childhood. He described himself as 'a hardened alcoholic who, without ever taking precautions of any kind, had slept with more whores than a porcupine has quills'. It is interesting that, when he boasts of his insatiable appetite for prostitutes, he admits always to having asked for women who were tall, blonde and blue-eyed, like Pip and like his mother.[161]

In his memoirs, Vilallonga portrays Pip as a self-possessed cynic when in reality she was nervously insecure. In his version of their first meeting in Barcelona, she offered to get him a job as a journalist if he will act as a propagandist for the Allies. In fact, as he writes elsewhere, he was already working as a journalist for the magazine *Destino* and she merely helped him with innocuous articles on English pipes, Virginia Woolf and the childhood of Winston Churchill.[162] They began to go out together and she soon fell in love with him and was to remain so throughout their long and unhappy marriage. That José Luis was utterly fascinated by her is revealed by the fact that, in his books, he romanticises her past in the most wildly colourful fashion. He places her in the Spanish Civil War in August 1936 at the massacre of Badajoz under threat of being shot as a spy by the Nationalist Colonel Juan Yagüe. Her time as a nurse in the Hadfield-Spears ambulance unit becomes a dark period in Paris during which it is insinuated that she was a secret agent. Her organisation of the Polish hospital in Scotland becomes service with General Anders' forces, despite the fact that Anders was imprisoned in Russia at the time and went into action in Italy only long after Pip had left the Poles. Most fanciful of all is the invention that Pip served as a lieutenant with the Spanish Republicans in the Free French forces that liberated Paris. Even more outrageous is a report of a conversation with Pip about her behaviour during the Spanish Civil

War. On learning that José Luis was seeing her, his father, the Barón de Segur, allegedly exploded that she had slept with – in one book, half the Spanish Army, in another, the entire Nationalist forces. It is clear from her diaries that Pip did not sleep with anyone in Spain. However, when asked about her sexual adventures, the fictionalised Pip – in an entirely uncharacteristic tone of pompous self-assurance and insouciance – tells her lover, 'Yes. I have had my adventures, just like everyone else. When death hovers over your head every day, certain moral values undergo changes about which it is useless to speak in peace-time.' The hard-nosed Pip of his various later accounts is unrecognisable as the vulnerable romantic of the diaries. Indeed, Vilallonga's fictionalised Pip has more in common with the coldly domineering Baronesa de Segur of his memoirs and novels.[163]

According to Vilallonga, they married because, with the war coming to an end, she was planning to return to London. It is possible that her position in the Consulate had been rendered difficult because of his indiscreet boasting about her work.[164] In one of his books, he claims that, faced with separation, she asked him to marry her. In another, when she announced that she had to go home, he begged her not to leave him. In one version, he responds by saying that he loved her but was not in love with her, and puts into her mouth the reply 'So what? That is no reason for us not to live together.' In another, he attributes virtually the same words to himself. What is absolutely clear is that he saw in Pip a way to facilitate his desire to escape Spain and his family to become a writer. He makes it clear that he was enticed by the idea. Moreover, Pip's open-minded and forthright conversation attracted him.[165]

It may well be that the idea for turning an affair into a marriage came from neither Pip nor José Luis. The romance caused sufficient gossip to provoke the concern of Princess Bea and Prince Ali who immediately set about rectifying the

situation. In the summer of 1945, Pip was summoned to Sanlúcar de Barrameda. The Infantes took charge of the relationship,
enveloped Pip in their protection and imposed a Spanish-style
engagement. This meant efforts to ensure that the couple never
met alone until their marriage and José Luis, to his intense
chagrin, was lodged for two weeks in a flea-ridden *pensión*.
On the eve of his wedding, the bridegroom was finally allowed
to sleep in the Palacio de Montpensier. However, he claims
that, on leaving his room en route to the bathroom, he found
Ataúlfo's elder brother Álvaro seated on the landing with a
shotgun to prevent him escaping – a story undermined by José
Luis's frequent remarks about his joy at marrying for money
and escape from Spain. To justify the claim that he was being
forced into marriage against his will, he alleges that Prince Ali
was desperate to see Pip married to anyone but his son because
she was really his illegitimate daughter. In fact, it is unlikely
that Prince Ali harboured any hopes of Ataúlfo ever marrying
at all and Tommy Howard de Walden's paternity of Pip is
not in doubt.

At the Catholic society wedding on 20 September 1945,
Pip, in white, was given away by Prince Ali. Photographic
evidence does not suggest that the radiantly beaming José Luis
was a pressed man. It is Pip who looks assailed by doubts.[166]
In the conditions prevailing at the end of the Second World
War, it was impossible for any of her family to travel to Spain
for the ceremony.[167] Hearing that Vilallonga's father, the Barón
de Segur, was fiercely opposed to the match, Tommy Howard
de Walden wrote him a stiff letter of protest and challenged
him to a duel. In a conciliatory reply, the Barón said that he
was not in any way opposed to Pip but was merely trying to
protect her, as he would any decent girl, from the martyrdom
of marriage to his wastrel of a son.[168]

In his brilliantly written, but otherwise deeply callous
memoirs, Vilallonga had the grace to write of Pip as 'a marvellous person whom, without a second thought, I made deeply

unhappy'.[169] The scale of egotistical irresponsibility portrayed in his own book makes it quite clear that Pip's life had just taken an irrevocably tragic turn. The wedding night was spent in an hotel in Cádiz. José Luis claims, equally revealingly whether it is true or false, that, after Pip fell asleep, he went out to spend the night in a brothel with some French prostitutes. From Cádiz the couple travelled to the Hotel Palace in Estoril in Portugal, where they spent a bizarre honeymoon. They arrived with little money and found that getting visas for London was not easy. Until eventually rescued by an emissary of Margot Howard de Walden, they were trapped in Lisbon for nearly six months. They were living in a luxurious hotel on credit which, given the family connections of both, was not as difficult as for some of the guests. Pip tried to eke out their finances at the casino having been given a system for playing roulette. Her occasional small successes were not enough to prevent her having to pawn her evening dresses. In the circumstances, it is difficult to believe José Luis's highly entertaining account of a life of high-society extravagance, in the frequent company of the exiled royalty of Europe.

José Luis alleges that he now began a poorly concealed affair with Magda Gabor, the sister of Eva and Zsa Zsa. The affair began with him, ever the gentleman, claiming to have demeaned his wife further by telling Magda that he found himself in the appalling situation of having to sleep with someone for whom he felt not the slightest attraction. At every opportunity, he says, he escaped to see his lover and a disconsolate Pip knew. Just as he was about to tell her that he planned to run away to New York with Magda Gabor, Pip announced that she was pregnant.[170] In José Luis's colourful account, making much of his great sacrifice in giving up Magda, he told Pip that 'the affair was over' but, as he wrote later, 'What stupidity! Everything had just begun. My alienation from her became ever greater.' Curiously, this did not deter him from staying with Pip for a further seventeen years. Nevertheless, he did, by his own account, engage in serial infidelities, with, amongst others, the same Magda Gabor he had just undertaken never to see again.[171]

Pip and José Luis left Lisbon in early April 1946, reaching England a few days later. When she finally reached home, Pip was already noticeably pregnant. The family was in Dean Castle, a small fortification at Kilmarnock in Ayrshire, Scotland, and, according to José Luis, had sent a car to collect them. This is strange given the total lack of petrol for private use in immediate postwar Britain. On the lengthy journey, (an improbable seventy-two hours in his memoirs) José Luis claims to have delighted himself reading about his father-in-law's properties in a copy of the Almanaque de Gotha which he conveniently found in the car along with other books. Apart from the fact that the properties of English aristocrats are not listed in that volume, the Howard de Walden car did not carry a copy. It may be, however, supposed that he faithfully reflects his feelings at the time when he writes of thinking: 'Mama could be proud of me. I had set myself up for life. At least so I thought.' He was enraptured by the magnificence of Dean Castle but astounded by what he perceived as the coldness of his hosts. He claims to have been greeted by Lord Howard de Walden dressed in a full suit of medieval armour, holding *The Times* with hands clad in iron gauntlets. In his account, an exaggeration of the anecdote told by Augustus John, his host wore different suits of armour all the time, even changing for dinner into an especially shiny one. His grotesquely amusing account presents the entire family frequently communing with ghosts.[172]

He was devastated to discover that, although her father was extremely rich, the bulk of his fortune would be inherited by Pip's brother John. That Pip was merely to inherit an amount of money that assured her what he bitterly dismissed as 'a mediocre comfort for life' led José Luis to comment revealingly in his memoirs that this was 'not at all part of my plans'. With a quite delicious lack of irony, he follows the bitter statement that 'it's one thing to marry a rich woman and quite another to marry the daughter of a rich family' with the assertion that he did not marry Pip for money. Forgetting his earlier story of the shotgun marriage in Sanlúcar de Barrameda, he asserted that he married her out of snobbery – the hope of annoying his father with photographs of Chirk Castle, alongside which the Barón de Segur's Palacio Falguera looked like a watchman's hut.[173] While at Dean Castle, according to José Luis, Lord Howard de Walden asked him point-blank if he had married Pip just for her money. He writes that, although fully aware that the dignified reply would have been to turn on his heel and leave the castle, 'the Spanish gentleman was in no position to burn his boats and leave himself on the beach with his feet in the water like any old ship-wrecked man'. He admitted to his father-in-law that he had indeed married his daughter for her money but also because they were good friends and she constituted an opportunity for him to break free from his family and from the asphyxiating atmosphere of the Spanish aristocracy.[174] Lord Howard de Walden was appalled by his son–in–law's ready admission that he was a gold-digger. He altered his will to prevent Pip, now twenty-nine, getting access to her money before she was forty.[175]

José Luis claims that, during a ball given at Dean Castle, while Pip was asleep on a sofa elsewhere, he passed a night of passion with Lady Audrey Fairfax, the wife of Admiral Sir Rupert Fairfax. Pip's sister Gaenor pointed out that there were no balls held in Dean Castle in 1946. After they left Scotland, the couple spent several weeks in London, staying at the Mandeville Hotel. While there, José Luis maintained the social life to which he was accustomed by accepting large sums of money from Pip. Given that this situation could not be sustained, that José Luis had no way of earning a living in Britain and that Pip's health required a warm climate, he proposed that they emigrate to Argentina.[176]

Tommy Howard de Walden owned a small shipping line, the South America Saint Line. In consequence, his son, Pip's brother John, was able to arrange a passage for Pip and José Luis to Argentina. He also arranged for there to be two medical men, Dr W. L. Roche and Dr W. D. Mulvey, and a nurse aboard. The ship, the SS *Saint-Merriel*, set sail from Liverpool for Buenos Aires via Las Palmas and Rio de Janeiro. Pip's labour started before the ship had reached the Canary Islands. The medical staff turned out to be of little help, since one doctor was in fact a dental specialist and the other an ophthalmologist. The nurse, who bore a remarkable resemblance to the young Margaret Rutherford, managed to break her leg just before Pip went into labour. Her son John was born at sea on 22 June 1946. It was a difficult birth and Pip was in danger of losing her life. An attractive fellow passenger, a fashion designer called Esterre 'Terry' Erland, helped with the labour. When the ship reached Las Palmas, there was a christening at which Terry Erland became John's godmother. His godfather was, thanks to Margot van Raalte and by the proxy of the ship's captain, Don Juan de Borbón. When the ship reached Bahia in Brazil, while Pip lay still convalescing on board, José Luis claims that he went ashore and slept with Terry Erland. José Luis made no secret of this and, for Pip, suffering a degree of postnatal depression, the effect was devastating. Even if she had not done so in Portugal, before reaching Argentina, she realised that she had made a dreadful mistake and that Prince and Princess Orléans-Borbón had been right about José Luis. However, with her boundless optimism, she determined to make the best of the marriage.[177]

During the sea voyage to Argentina, José Luis met a retired Hungarian cavalry officer, Count Laszlo Graffy, who was planning to breed and train horses on the pampas. He persuaded Pip that they should become the Count's partners in the enterprise. On reaching Argentina, at first their expenses were met by the agent of Lord Howard's shipping line. They acquired a flat in Buenos Aires, were able to buy land on the pampas for their stables and riding school, install a prefabricated house and buy a car. They suffered considerable privation since Pip could gain no immediate access to either her own funds or the help of her family since money could not be sent out of England until she had established herself as a British resident abroad. She had very little money and José Luis had none, since his family were outraged by the manner of his marriage and had effectively cut him off.

Since José Luis was repelled by the thought of childcare and Pip could not cope with John's crying, they left him with a series of nurses. Their own experience of parenting hardly prepared them for any other response. Moreover, their own relationship was in increasing difficulty.[178] José Luis, in his memoirs, asserts that when he made love to her, he could not disguise his indifference. Nevertheless, she was soon pregnant again. They hardly spoke to each other. José Luis claimed that he abhorred his son (although photographic evidence suggests otherwise) and spent ever more time in Buenos Aires.[179] Pip's skill with horses contributed greatly to the initial success of the business at Los Cardales where she worked with Graffy and the various Hungarian and Polish cavalry officers employed at the stables. However, money was so tight that, in an effort to make ends meet, Pip went into partnership with Terry Erland to open a fashion-design business and dress shop under the name Susan Scott Designs.[180]

Tommy Howard de Walden died on 6 November 1946. Because he had not made prior arrangements, the amounts that he left to his daughters were severely diminished by death duties.[181] Pip was to be left £50,000 – a considerable amount of money in 1946, about £1 million in 2001 terms – but it was tied up in the family estates. In any case, postwar austerity restrictions on capital movements prevented it being taken out of the country. Tommy did, moreover, leave Pip his studio in Cadogan Lane. Because, when the news arrived, Pip was suffering a difficult pregnancy and had been ordered by her gynaecologist to rest, José Luis went to London alone in the early summer of 1947 to wind up the estate. He stayed with Margot Howard de Walden at her house in Welbeck Street and soon established a warm friendship with a bisexual Austrian aristocrat called Count Boisy Rex. Boisy vaguely knew the family because his elder sister, Countess Marie Louise Rex, was married to the father-in-law of Pip's cousin, Charmian Russell (née van Raalte). José Luis used the impoverished Boisy as a cicerone to the gastronomic, sartorial and erotic delights of postwar London. Needless to say, he did not stint himself. After the reading of Tommy Howard de Walden's will, the cornucopia that was the studio in Cadogan Lane lay at the mercy of José Luis and Boisy. The house contained a wealth of modern art although some were fakes and the collection may not have included the Max Ernst, Braque, Otto Dix, Rothko and Jackson Pollock canvases, Hogarth and Picasso drawings and Rodin sculptures 'remembered' by José Luis. José Luis did not hesitate to move into the house with Count Rex nor, with his help, to sell off paintings in order to finance the rebuilding of his wardrobe. Given his vocation as a dandy, this proved to be a fabulously expensive endeavour.[182]

Since there was no detailed inventory of the contents of the Cadogan Lane house, there was little or no control over what José Luis was able to sell. He lived, as he put it, 'without restraint' ('*desenfrenadamente*'). Eagerly encouraged by Boisy, he escaped the austerity of postwar London and together they wallowed in delights available only to those with unlimited supplies of ready cash – restaurants supplied by the black market, clandestine gambling dens, nightclubs that never closed, and women. He claims that one of Lord Howard's drawings went to pay one year's rent on a furnished flat in Piccadilly for one of his lovers – a famous popular singer. Another paid for him to spend some time in Madrid and Barcelona where he stayed in the best hotels and replicated his

London hedonism. While in Barcelona, he received a telegram informing him that Pip had given birth tō a daughter. Born on 6 August 1947, she was called Susanna Carmen (for José Luis's mother), Margarita (for Pip's mother) and Beatriz (for Princess Bea). He returned to Buenos Aires via London. Before leaving, José Luis claims to have given Boisy Rex a priceless painting by Max Ernst the proceeds from which he used to establish himself in the world of greyhound racing. José Luis did give John Scott Ellis an umbrella which John immediately spotted as having belonged to Tommy. It was a small compensation for the fact that John had to meet the considerable debts left by José Luis.[183]

In José Luis's absence, Pip had tried to recapture his love by preparing an environment in which he could pursue his dream of writing. This took − he says − the form of three railway carriages − two sleeper cars and a restaurant car. One of the sleepers had two large rooms and a bathroom; the restaurant car became a kitchen and dining-room, the other sleeper was left as it was. To facilitate José Luis's writing, a magnificent study was prepared and a young Italian woman, Lucy Babacci, contracted to be his secretary. In no time at all, he says, she was his lover. He insinuates that this was with the complicity of Pip who, after her recent labour, had no desire for sexual relations. Little of this coincides with what Pip told her sister.[184] While José Luis philandered and wrote, Pip threw herself into looking after the horses, her dress shop and, to a lesser extent, the upbringing of the children. The dress and fashion business worked well until Terry Erland decided to return to Europe in 1949. The financial difficulties were exacerbated in 1950 by a decree that obliged companies to employ three Argentines for every foreigner. It signalled ruin for the stables. The business was sold to Colonel Graffy and, on the insistence of José Luis, they moved to Paris since neither he nor Pip wanted to live in London or Barcelona.[185]

Leaving Pip to wind up the estate, José Luis seized the

opportunity to go on ahead to Paris in April 1951. José Luis's attitude to his children had been at best lukewarm so John and Carmen were sent to England to live with Gaenor while Pip and José Luis tried to rebuild their fortunes, both emotional and financial, in Paris. There he wrote his first novel, *Les Ramblas finissent à la mer*. He claims that, realising that he did not want to share a life with Pip and their children in a Parisian apartment, he immediately persuaded her to live somewhere where he might visit them occasionally. The facts are that they separated only after seven years of deteriorating relations spent in different Parisian apartments. The relationship was doomed since José Luis was concerned only with establishing himself as an actor and a novelist – yet neither of them seemed prepared to bring it to an end. Along the way, he led a life of epicurean dissolution. According to his own accounts, he was taking money from a series of rich, older women, including someone called Kitty Lillaz and the actress Madeleine Robinson, whom he passed off as his wife. Pip knew but suffered in silence. Finally, on her fortieth birthday in 1956, she got access to her money and she bought a flat for them both in the rue Alsace Lorraine in the Bois de Boulogne. José Luis borrowed much of her remaining money and promised to return it when he inherited from his father. This he never did. To compensate for not seeing her children in school term time, Pip regularly indulged them with extravagant holidays skiing in Switzerland or Austria in winter, swimming at St Tropez or Monte Carlo in summer.[186] When she did have access to her own funds, according to José Luis, Pip frittered them away in acts of absurd generosity, of which he was often a beneficiary himself.[187]

José Luis also claims to have still possessed a large portfolio of drawings, watercolours and oils taken from his father-in-law's collection which facilitated his high-society existence. Once he had eventually found success as a novelist and journalist and insinuated himself into the world of cinema, divorce from Pip was inevitable. What is really astonishing – and suggests that there was more to the relationship than he admits – is that it took him so long to seek a divorce. In his memoirs, he depicts Pip's presence as an intolerable invasion of his privacy. If this is true, for a woman as insecure and as desperate to please as Pip, it must have been unbearable as, in the most adolescent fashion, he flaunted his many lovers. He claims that things reached a peak when, one night in Paris, no doubt driven by his own guilt, he tried to strangle her.[188] Again the truth about the end of the relationship was less dramatic. In 1958, he appeared in a very minor role in Louis Malle's *Les Amants* starring Jeanne Moreau. In 1961, he had an equally small role in Blake Edwards' *Breakfast at Tiffany's*.[189] José Luis was increasingly away on location or else with one of his many lovers. Pip had long since suggested that, given the needs of her health and the children's welfare, they should live in the South and there was no way that he would leave the capital.

Eventually, in 1958, Pip bought some land at Auribeau-sur-Siagne near Cannes. In a last effort to hold on to José Luis, and to make a home for her children, she created a splendid house out of two workmen's cottages knocked into one. The land had the small river Siagne running through it and, on the other side of the small valley from the main house, there were two small houses where the children stayed. José Luis did not live with the family at Auribeau although he visited frequently, having found another rich older woman, Countess Rosemarie Tchaikowska, with a house nearby. When he did visit, he would childishly challenge Pip by often disappearing in search of conquests in Cannes.[190] Increasingly alone with her children, Pip was not happy. There were occasional affairs but nothing could console her for the loss of her husband. Although a very competent mother, her son remembers Pip as sparing in her affections. His abiding memory is of her sitting at a desk and turning towards him, 'her knees like the double barrels of a shotgun'. He cannot remember her ever kissing him. His daughter recalled 'she was there, she was fun, but did not take part in the everyday nitty-gritty of life till much later on. All that was taken care of by the nuns at boarding school or the servants at home.' In that sense, Pip was following in the footsteps of her own mother. She really came into her own as a mother when her children grew older and were able to have a more 'adult' relationship. Both her daughter and her niece remember her to be 'loving and understanding' and a fount of boundless fun and someone with whom they could always talk about their troubles. The children were sent to boarding school in England and they would meet for spectacularly expensive holidays. Pip drank heavily, although never before 6.30 p.m., and never betraying the effects of alcohol. When she came to England to return the children to school after some holiday jaunt, they would stay at the Mandeville Hotel where she had once stayed with José Luis. She would leave them watching television while she went out in a desperate attempt to recreate the glittering social life of her youth.[191]

For much of the 1960s, José Luis was living with the actress Michelle Girardon – a relationship that ended when she committed suicide. In 1964, he sued for divorce in France and Pip challenged him for alimony. The court found in her favour but José Luis failed to pay the agreed settlement. In 1970, in Cuernavaca, Mexico, José Luis met a model called Ursula (Uschi) Dietrich. Believing her to be a wealthy Austrian aristocrat, he asked her to marry him. She was in fact a fortune-hunter who accepted his proposal because she in turn believed him to be fabulously rich. On the day that they wed, he was still technically married to Pip in Spanish law, given that there was no divorce in Spain. By chance, Pip's sister Gaenor happened to be passing through Cuernavaca and she rang Pip to tell her that her husband was about to marry. When José Luis reached Paris with Uschi and she was confronted by his small flat, she immediately left him and sued for divorce.[192] At that time, José Luis was living in Paris with his son John. That relationship came to an end in 1973, when John finally reached the conclusion that his father was incapable of an honest reciprocal relationship. Thereafter, John had no more to do with him.[193]

Pip never fully got over her passion for José Luis. She knew he was an outright cad but could not stop loving him. She would never allow her children to speak ill of him in her presence. Her greatest regret was that their marriage had effectively destroyed her friendship with Princess Bea and Prince Ali. She never contacted them again because she felt unable to lie about her unhappiness and unable to admit to them that they were right in warning her against José Luis. Indeed, so deep were her regrets that she never spoke about the Spanish Civil War again.[194] Ending the war as a colonel, Prince Ali had been made head of the Segunda Región Aérea. He was promoted successively to brigadier general and major general. He had become Don Juan's representative in Spain in 1943. To do so, he had to receive Franco's permission. On 19 March 1945, Don Juan published his Manifiesto de Lausanne and Prince Ali resigned his post in the air force. He was then placed under house arrest for a year at Sanlúcar de Barrameda. At the end of that time, he requested Don Juan to release him from his obligations. In 1955, he and Princess Bea sold the palace in Sanlúcar de Barrameda and moved into the houses at El Botánico.[195] Princess Bea died in Sanlúcar on 13 July 1966. Her funeral was attended by Prince Juan Carlos and Doña Sofía and the Condesa de Barcelona, Doña María de las Mercedes.[196] Ataúlfo who had become an agronomist, never married and had openly recognised the homosexuality that was the real reason for his inability to marry Pip. He died aged sixty-one on 8 October 1974 after a brief illness caused by pancreatic cancer.[197] Less than one year later, Prince Ali had a heart attack and died aged eighty-eight in Sanlúcar de Barrameda on 6 August 1975.[198]

After the French divorce, the unhappy Pip sold the big

house and half the land at Auribeau and returned to England with her daughter Carmen. There, the earlier closeness that had characterised her relationship with Gaenor was renewed. Determined to make it on her own and not to accept money from her wealthy brother John, Pip began to try to earn her own living. She took a job at the Inland Revenue and then at the British Tourist Office in St James's. Later she became a courier for the National Trust escorting groups. It paid badly but she was a great success. Commanding so many languages and being so affable, she was perfect for the job. She even took groups to India, Russia, the Seychelles and all over South America until her health rendered that impossible. In the 1970s, now virtually penniless, she sued José Luis in the French courts for unpaid alimony. Her claim was upheld but she never saw any money.

Pip and her daughter Carmen, lived in London, first in a seedy flat and then on a houseboat on the Thames near Cheyne Walk. Pip was still in love with José Luis but her life was changed in 1966 by meeting a tremendously good-looking opera singer from Manchester called Ian Hanson. Trying to build his career in London, he was a friend of another singer who lived in a house that belonged to Pip's sister Elizabeth. In consequence, he had become friendly with Pip's niece, the sculptress Tatiana Orloff-Davidoff, Elizabeth's daughter. This led to him going out with Carmen de Vilallonga and thus meeting Pip. She was entranced by his good looks – he was so handsome that Tatiana made a bust of him. Pip and Ian began an affair that would endure until her death. Ian, although a competent light tenor, never found the success that his earlier career had promised.[199] A man twenty years younger than her, and bisexual, he was fascinated by her aristocratic background and her boundless optimism. She had finally found a man with whom she could be happy. It is notable that the first and third of the great loves of her life were of ambiguous sexuality. In contrast, the second, José Luis, in his various memoirs, flaunts his alleged sexual triumphs to a remarkable extent. He even boasted that he earned a living testing out the prostitutes for the notorious Madame Claude.[200] Perhaps only in Ataúlfo, José Luis and Ian could Pip find men who could be as distant from her as her beloved father.

Pip sold the remainder of her land at Auribeau and went to America with Ian Hanson. In California, Pip had hopes of building a business. She and Ian Hanson settled in Los Angeles, and with her separation from José Luis now confirmed by a Spanish divorce, they married. She worked for Sotheby's in Los Angeles. With the proceeds from the sale of her land, she bought and planned to develop some property in California. It was a great miscalculation and came to nothing. Virtually penniless, she was diagnosed with lung cancer. Her family arranged for her to be taken to a decent hospital. After a long illness, during which she was nursed devotedly by Ian, she died in 1983. Ian Hanson died two years later, one of the first victims of AIDS. Pip was cremated in Los Angeles. Gaenor and Ian brought her ashes back to England and scattered them in the hills above Chirk Castle where Pip had played and ridden in her childhood.[201]

NAN
GREEN

NAN GREEN

—————— ❧ ——————

A Great Deal of Loneliness

O NE SATURDAY AFTERNOON IN JANUARY 1937, a young couple were shopping in the street market in Leather Lane in London. Near the great meat market of Smith-fields, Leather Lane was lined with butchers' stalls and green-grocers' carts – a good place to pick up cheap vegetables and cuts of meat at the end of the day. And George and Nan Green had very little money. They were both Communists and eked out a living as best they could by selling books from a stall and through George's exiguous earnings as a cellist in the Tottenham Court Road Corner House. George suddenly turned to his wife as if he had just found the solution to a problem that had been plaguing him for weeks. Without preamble, he blurted out: 'I've got to go to Spain.'

George Green was an activist in the Musicians' Union and Nan was the secretary of their branch of the Communist Party of Great Britain. The fact that they were out shopping together was an indication that, by the standards of the day, they had a good and fairly democratic relationship. They debated political issues, went together on marches to confront the fascist Black-shirts and shared responsibility for their two young children. Over recent months, their conversations were increasingly dominated by the inexorable rise of fascism and the struggle taking place in Spain against Franco, Hitler and Mussolini. They had talked at great length about the need to stop fascism.

They had raised money for medical aid for Spain. They had comrades who had already gone to join the International Brigades. But, on that particular Saturday afternoon, while her mind was on the search for food bargains, George's pronouncement was a bombshell. It came out of the blue, as much for him as for her. Aware of the enormity of what he had just said, he looked at her with trepidation. Without thinking, she just said 'Yes'.

She responded more like a Communist militant than a woman about to see her husband and the father of her children embark on a life-threatening venture. When she had time to think about what was being proposed, dousing her emotional reaction as a wife and mother, she consoled herself that, politically, it was the right thing to do. They had a six-year-old daughter and a son aged four and a half. How she and the children would manage alone had to matter much less than that fascism must be stopped. That was a prize for which it was worth fighting. And, if the Spanish Republic should be victorious, it might even open up the prospect of revolution. What victory might mean helped Nan make the conceptual leap to justify her family's inevitable privation. Within a month, George was on his way to Spain as an ambulance driver. Nan saw him off from the offices of Spanish Medical Aid in New Oxford Street. Within seven months, she would have made an even greater leap. Nan would go to Spain herself.

Nan Green's middle-class upbringing in an Anglican household was an unlikely beginning for the later heroine of the Spanish Civil War and stalwart of the Communist Party of Great Britain. Her early life was not in itself remarkable other than in the many clues it offers for her later courage and resourcefulness. The crumbling of both her family and its material well-being would be the basis of her later left-wing militancy. She was born Nancy Farrow on 19 November 1904, in Beeston, now a suburb of Nottingham, but at the time a small village on the outskirts. She was the third of five surviving children – a sixth died aged eighteen months. Her mother was Maria 'Polly' Kemp and her father was Edward Farrow. While Nan's grandfather was Chief Warder at Wandsworth Prison, Polly Kemp had been a 'bound apprentice' at the Arding and Hobbs department store in Clapham, where it still thrives. There she lived and worked in the same circumstances of near slavery described so vividly by H. G. Wells in *The History of Mr Polly*. When the family moved to Devizes, Polly pined for them and she was eventually 'bought out' of her apprenticeship. Nan's paternal grandfather was a guitar-maker and several of his seven children had some musical talent. Whenever they visited the Farrow home, there was much singing and laughter. The two families provided a strange mixture of characteristics. For Nan – in her own words, 'the solid, worthy, respectable and rather humourless Kemps and the "bohemian", singing, slightly seedy but jolly Farrows'. 'I incline to the Farrow side, both in temperament and sentiments.'[1]

Nan was born at home and she later described the birth.

> The delivery room had been made ready; the nurse (Nurse Marshall as I afterwards knew her) was in the house. But I wasn't expected that night and my mother, finding herself in labour, slipped out of bed to cross two landings with stairs between them, and I popped out before she got to the other bedroom. I never had a great deal of patience, and have always been a very quick mover ('like quicksilver' said Mem [Nan's younger sister, Emily Farrow]) until age and arthritis slowed me down.[2]

At the time of her birth, Edward Farrow was anxiously making his way up the social ladder. Before he was married, he had risen from being a mechanic in a small bicycle workshop which developed into the celebrated Raleigh Cycle company to become a chartered accountant and Company Secretary. He was earning £3.00 per week when he married, sufficient to afford a servant. The scale of his success could be measured by the fact that, in 1903, he moved his family to a splendid house, Surrey Cottage, in Glebe Street, Beeston. It consisted of two substantial semidetached cottages, and was considered of sufficient architectural significance to be the subject of a feature on domestic architecture in *The Studio*.[3] Half of the house was occupied by his wife's father. Nonetheless, the scale of the house somewhat belied Nan's later remarks to the effect that her father was 'a working man'. Edward Farrow had long since moved on from his working-class origins. Although not strictly untrue, her description perhaps owed less to historical accuracy than to a Communist's need for a politically acceptable past.[4]

Nan's principal memories of her early childhood were of being somewhat smothered by a neurotic mother. Her reaction to this goes some way to accounting for the later bravery and hardiness that she would manifest in both Spain and China. Polly Kemp had already had three children, Elizabeth, Charles and Edward, by the time that Nan was born. Although a large and robust woman, she was haunted by fear of the tuberculosis which had killed her younger sister, Emily Kemp. She was fearful for her own health, declaring herself to be 'delicate' and, like other middle-class women, spent much time reclining on a sofa. She was equally, if not more, anxious for her children. Her first son, Charles, died of diphtheria when not yet five years old. In consequence, she doted on her second son Edward and lived in constant fear for the welfare of her other children, dosing them with various potions and liquids to 'clear their bowels' and strengthen their chests. Nan's later dogged independence and headstrong nature were a rejection of a suffocating childhood, in which, as she put it, 'not only were we overdosed, we were over-clothed'. The children were heavily dressed in a manner conducive neither to mobility or personal hygiene.

Vests, woollen 'combinations' known with loathing as 'combies' and consisting of a one-piece vest and knickers were covered successively with a Liberty Bodice, thick wool, taped to give strength to the figure, white cotton knickers, blue or brown woollen knickers, a flannel petticoat, a white cotton petticoat, black or brown wool stockings, hitched with tape to the bodice, a jersey and a kilt or dress were topped indoors with a white cotton pinafore and out of doors, in winter, with boots and an overcoat, scarf, gloves and hat.[5]

Edward Farrow eventually became General Manager of Raleigh and the fortunes of the company were a topic that caused considerable anxiety within the family: 'Mother, who caused the entire working of the household to circulate round my father's interest and comfort (I think she was a little afraid of him), disciplined, hushed and hustled us out of the way with special rigour when it was Balance Sheet time.'[6] Her father's growing prosperity had made him a firm believer in the capitalist system. 'In my earlier childhood, we were all meant to be "rising in the world" with him and were sternly prevented from mixing with what were regarded as the lower classes.' She and her siblings were forbidden to 'play with anyone "rough" or socially inferior'. The children of the family were educated at the village's private school, which was unutterably snobbish. She was once severely chastised when she was caught playing in the main square of Beeston with some boys from the local Board School. Sending her to such a school was part of the quest for gentility by Nan's father. This quest also involved a move to High Anglicanism and sending his two oldest children to Anglo-Catholic Public Schools 'where they developed a kind of religious snobbery and looked down on Low Church people and Protestants with immense scorn'.[7]

Not only did Nan feel 'over-dosed and over-dressed', but also asphyxiated by religion and snobbery. Her childhood was not happy and she considered the main reason to be the lack of 'freedom and freedom from care'. In the style typical of the aspirant lower middle class, the Farrow children had their friends chosen for them. She did not like the friends considered suitable by her parents nor did she feel comfortable with rigid rules which required children to be 'good, clean, tidy, devout, quiet, incurious, well-mannered and obedient'. These rules were imposed rigidly, indeed cruelly. Transgressions were punished by severe beatings on the bare bottom administered by her father. She suffered a particularly harsh 'tanning' for riding her bicycle on the forbidden main road to Nottingham and another for protesting that her brother could go out and play immediately after tea while she had to help with the washing-up. Inevitably, Nan grew into a rebellious child, committing 'crimes' like paddling in the nearby River Trent. Her younger sister, Emily, wrote years later of 'Nan quick-thinking, independent, not afraid to defy or displease authority – God, teacher or parent'.[8] Yet Nan longed for approval and praise and was mortified when her efforts to win them met only with the ridicule of her parents.[9] Their unfeeling behaviour led to her writing in her memoirs: 'I cannot honestly say that I loved either of my parents.' In time, she came to understand and forgive them but she could never forgive the Christian Church for its imposition of guilt upon the faithful. She could never understand why her short-lived younger brother, Charlie, had been taken so young and was haunted by a picture of him in her bedroom. What little Christian faith she had garnered was lost when her desperate prayers for the relief of the suffering of the asthma-stricken Emily were left unanswered.[10]

The decorous standard of living enjoyed by the family until the First World War plummeted as her father faced both professional and health crises. A process of proletarianisation was about to begin and Nan would be the child most affected by it. Her mother never recovered from the labour after her last child, Richard, and slipped gradually into permanent illness. In the early days of the First World War, Polly suffered a stroke. Semiparalysed, she was confined to a wheelchair and the running of the house fell to her niece Marie Rice. A loving and kindly woman, Marie Rice (known in the family as Lela) became the surrogate mother for Nan's younger siblings.[11] In 1916, Edward Farrow lost his job because he had refused to falsify the firm's accounts in order to diminish its payments of taxes on war profits. With his wife seriously ill and five children to care for, he suffered a breakdown and became a patient in a mental hospital for a short time, although by 1917 he was working in London for the Ministry of Munitions.

Nan's childhood came to an abrupt end. In 1918, with her father in London, the entire family, except her, fell victim to the influenza epidemic. With neither antibiotics nor analgesics, the fourteen-year-old girl had to assume responsibility for nursing her mother, Marie Rice, and her brothers and younger sister. It was an experience that was to bring out Nan's ability to deal with crisis situations. She discovered a capacity for hard work, organisation and unflappability that would be the hallmark of her later life. Her patients all recovered but the family's position worsened rapidly thereafter. After the war, her father's job in the Ministry came to an end and he set up a small bicycle workshop. Hit by raw-materials shortages, it failed. Another step down the social ladder saw him obliged to go to Birmingham to work in the cycle factory of BSA. The family was now living in straitened circumstances in a small flat above a shop. Shortly after moving there in 1921, Nan's mother, Polly, died in hospital. Edward Farrow clung rather pathetically to his middle-class status, sending Nan to a mediocre private school that he could not afford. She attended night school and gained a free place at the Birmingham City School of Art. She attended for one year and, just as she won a scholarship for a further year, she was obliged to abandon her studies. To her intense chagrin, her father, who had lost his job and moved to Manchester, would not let her stay with relatives in Birmingham and continue her education.[12]

The four years between 1916 and 1920, during which she passed through her adolescence from twelve to sixteen, determined much of Nan's later life. In her later reflections, she summed it up as her falling between two sets of experience. Her two older siblings, Elizabeth and Edward, knew their mother when she was strong and healthy and when the family was prosperous. They had the benefit of an expensive Public School education and were out in the world, Edward as a bank clerk, Elizabeth as a teacher, by the time that poverty hit the family. The two younger siblings, Richard and Emily, remembered their mother less. In any case, they had the deeply caring mother-substitute of Marie Rice who eventually married Edward Farrow and became, in Nan's acute observation, 'his humble slave as my mother had been'. Because of the deterioration of the family's circumstances, both Richard and 'Mem' were sent to state schools with working-class children. In a rough and ready, but less poisonously snobbish, environment, they did relatively well. The situation for Nan was completely different on both the domestic and educational fronts. She remembered her relationship with her mother in these years with a touch of bitterness, recalling a fearful and demanding, wheelchair-bound invalid who needed help to dress, and expected each night to have the lights switched off and romantic novels read to her by candlelight. Edward and Elizabeth deeply resented their father's remarriage; Richard and Emily were delighted. Nan was indifferent – so locked in her own turbulent adolescence as to be unable to call on Marie for emotional support.[13]

It was hardly surprising that, by the time that she was sixteen, Nan had drawn far away from her father. The collapse of the family economy hit Nan hardest in terms of future career because, in her early teens, her dreams of going to Art School were shattered. She was obliged to abandon her scholarship and go out and seek work. As her father moved around looking for jobs, she had to move with the family, taking clerical posts. The instability made it difficult to make friends and her principal pleasure was reading – borrowing H. G. Wells, D. H. Lawrence, George Bernard Shaw and others from the public libraries of the family's various stopping points. The highlight of her existence was the visits of the touring opera company of Carl Rosa (the predecessor of English National Opera) and the Gilbert and Sullivan productions of the D'Oyly Carte Company. Eventually, she settled for a time in a job at a large wholesale drapery warehouse in Manchester and began to make friends. Through one of them, Marie Brown, she was introduced to the rambling association. They spent joyful Sundays walking in the rugged yet beautiful moors of the Peak District – to the horrified disapproval of Nan's father. On their walks, Marie Brown, an Irish Nationalist, explained the troubles in Ireland. Her account of the role of the British in Ireland was an important contribution to Nan's political education. Often they would arrive back in Manchester in time to attend a Sunday-night concert of the Hallé Orchestra. After the stultifying atmosphere of her family, a rambling holiday, striding over the hills and through bogs, with musical evenings, in which she sang, constituted an inspiring liberation. Fresh air, freedom and music were henceforth to be her formula for happiness.[14]

In the mid-1920s, the family moved back to Birmingham where the ramblers were less musical and more earnest. There she worked in a large insurance office and her experiences there pushed her further along the road to socialism. She was the head of a section of nine girls who worked out the figures for compensation in industrial accidents. She began to learn something of the conditions in which miners and other workers were injured. She was appalled by the fact that £300 (about £8,000 in 2001 terms) was the maximum a miner's family could get in compensation if he was killed. Even then the money would be paid only if he had been in consecutive work over the previous three years – which was unlikely given the instability of the mining industry. She was even more influenced by an incident in 1928, the year in which the voting age for women was reduced from thirty to twenty-one. The office manager asked her to use her influence over the girls in her office to ensure that they would not vote for the Labour Party. He argued that, since Labour intended to nationalise insurance, to vote Labour would be to vote themselves out of jobs. Nan was sufficiently incensed by this to march round to Labour Party offices to get the facts. There they explained to her that the clerks who did the work would be needed even more. Her report back at her office resulted in her colleagues voting Labour. She began to call herself a Fabian, read Fabian pamphlets and started to talk about organising a trade union in her office. When the management heard about this, they 'promoted' her away from fellow-workers to do statistical work in a separate office. However, her companion there was a charming old Irishman who enthused her with his own rebellious ideas.[15]

Another crucial step on the road to socialism was taken in the winter of 1928 as a result of an invitation by Marie Brown, her old friend from Manchester, to join her for a rambling weekend. Amongst the company was a musical family from Stockport called Green, consisting of two sons, the elder a pianist, the younger a cellist, two daughters and their mother. George Green, the twenty-four-year-old cellist, played in the orchestra on the Cunard liner *Aquitania*, which was in dry dock. Nan saw him as 'a rather bear-like figure over six feet tall with a broad face and kind, gentle grey eyes behind steel-rimmed spectacles'. They fell in love on that first night when, as Nan looked down the valley, George came out, put his arm around her and rubbed his cheek against her hair. Afterwards, she reflected that 'it wasn't romance that had come to me, it was *comfort*. I'd scampered around with young men before but had hated to be touched by them, and repelled their attempted kissing with a sort of loathing. But now here was a young man with whom I felt at home from the first moment, who hadn't tried to rush me but had gently shown his attraction.'

Since he was due back on the ship two weeks later, George moved fast. He invited her to go hill walking on the following weekend and she accepted. By the end of an extremely wet day, he had asked her to marry him and she had accepted. Despite her happiness, she could not tell anyone for fear of the heavy-handed ridicule of her father. She would get up early to collect George's letters before the rest of the family saw what the postman had delivered. George then gave up his job on the *Aquitania* and began to play at a cinema in Manchester. In economic terms, it would turn out to be a disastrous decision because silent films, and employment for the musicians who accompanied them, were about to be swept aside by the talkies. Unaware of this cloud on the horizon, the lovers began an idyllic courtship. Each weekend, she would go to Manchester and spend the Saturday evening in the cinema where he played. Then she would race with George to the railway station to catch the last train to Macclesfield, the gateway to the Peak District. They would head for a farm where they would spend the night before, early on the Sunday morning, setting out for the hills where they practised their growing devotion to rock climbing.[16] After some mountaineering in France, her love of adventure took the form of 'going to bed not by the stairs but up the outside of the house, from the back, from drainpipe to window sill and moulding to gutter, into my third-floor bedroom window'.[17]

Nan described the process of falling deeper in love with George in characteristically restrained terms:

it was never feverish or 'romantic' – I just felt more *at home*; there was nothing we could not say to one another and our enormous joy in expending our full strength, striding like giants over moor and fell in all weathers was totally satisfying. It will surprise young people, accustomed in these 'permissive' days to jump into bed at first or second sight that we did not sleep together and it will surprise Freudians, if there are any left, that I wasn't conscious of any wish to. George was by no means sexually inexperienced but he was possessed, in this as in other ways, of infinite patience and gentleness, and introduced me to sex very carefully and gradually and with a sort of whimsical matter-of-factness that made it seem perfectly natural.

They decided to get officially engaged which entailed a public announcement. Nan's father was livid that she should tie herself 'to a wandering musician'.[18] However, one benefit of the relationship with George that her father regarded as no compensation for penury was that it enabled Nan to develop her own innate musicality. As a result of undiagnosed mumps, she was deaf in her left ear. Nevertheless, after meeting George, she began to learn the viola and was thus able to take part in the concerts which took place at the Green home.

Another benefit for Nan was contact with the Green family, an altogether warmer and less complicated community than the Farrows. She was especially fond of George's father, William Alfred Green, a man she regarded as 'solid gold all through'. 'Flawlessly upright, wise, tolerant and astonishingly non-male-chauvinist (he instilled into his sons the absolute rule that no husband should allow his wife to wash a dirty nappy until the child was six weeks old and this is so much before his time that the time has not caught up with him yet).'[19] Throughout her life with George, her father-in-law would be an unstinting source of support and solidarity.

George inherited from his father a dry wit, his gentleness and his tolerance. He was a pacifist and a socialist.[20]

George and Nan were married on 9 November 1929. There was little work for cinema musicians in the depression, the more so since the advent of the talking pictures. They lived in Manchester, first in lodgings and then in an unfurnished flat. George still had a poorly-paid job accompanying the last silent films. To supplement his income, they opened a small business serving lunch-time sandwiches to offices in central Manchester. They made little money and towards the end of 1930, as the numbers of unemployed rose, orders were plummeting. This coincided with the fact that Nan was about six months pregnant. After initial difficulties because of high blood pressure, she had a normal pregnancy during which she and George drew ever closer. Their daughter Frances was born on 14 February 1931. Shortly afterwards they moved into a council house in Stockport. They lived austerely, not to say on the poverty line, managing largely by dint of growing their own vegetables and buying cheap meat on Saturday evenings when the butchers closed their stalls at the market.

George lost his job at the cinema and took short-term jobs playing the banjo in the Jack Hylton Dance Band and the guitar in a café. In the summer of 1931, he took a one-week summer job in a show at a seaside town. Away from the family, he had a brief affair, which seemed not to bother Nan at all.

> This was the first time he was 'unfaithful' to me, but he told me about it immediately on his return and it didn't seem to make any difference. It never did, for there were subsequent occasions, but since he always kept me informed, sometimes in advance, there was never any deceit. It is *deceit* which poisons a relationship and I was so absolutely confident in his love that the mere fact of his having gone to bed with someone else had no effect on me at all.[21]

Whether her later account reveals a suppression of her real feelings or was a genuine reflection of her cool rationality is impossible to say. Certainly, the incident seemed not to damage their relationship. After all, Nan was sufficiently independent-minded not to have stayed with him out of moral inhibition or because of the conventional aversion to separation and divorce. Nevertheless, when he acquired 'girlfriends', Nan's tactic was to invite them to tea. Meeting his wife and child was usually the prelude to their rapid departure from his life.[22]

Although she had been advised not to conceive for at least three years because of her blood pressure, by late 1931 she was pregnant again. With work ever scarcer and starvation looming, in the early summer of 1932, they split their last three pounds. She kept thirty shillings, George took the other thirty and set off to London in search of work. He got a job playing in the orchestra at the Lyon's Corner House in Coventry Street, near London's Piccadilly Circus. A week later, on 10 July 1932, she gave birth to a boy, Martin. It was the beginning of a deeply traumatic period for her. Perhaps as a consequence of the difficult circumstances and the separation from George, her pregnancy went on beyond the due date. Martin was a large baby, nine pounds at birth, so it was a long and painful labour. While Nan was recuperating, she was accidentally poisoned by a nurse with neat belladonna. She was in a coma, extremely ill, for some days and nearly died. Barely had she recovered from this trauma when Martin contracted whooping cough. When she was released from hospital in Birmingham, she was driven by her brother to London where George had found lodgings in Hampstead.

There, still exhausted from labour and the belladonna incident, she had to cope with two sick babies – since Frances had inevitably caught whooping cough as well. Awful days – poverty, a hostile landlady, boiling nappies, no detergents – were alternated with sleepless nights – no antibiotics, trying to feed a baby whose hacking cough was forcing him to vomit each time he was fed. She had no family or friends upon whom she might call for support. George was sharing the household and parenting tasks although his behaviour at the time can hardly have helped – for all Nan's benevolent recollections. George had found himself, as she put it, 'an additional preoccupation in the shape of a girlfriend he had acquired during our few weeks' separation'. It was either astonishing strength of character mixed with total devotion to George or else what is nowadays called denial that allowed her to tolerate this new transgression. Given Nan's circumstances, George's behaviour can only be described as, at worst, cruelly callous or, at best, selfishly irresponsible. Even she claimed later, that of the various occasions on which George did such things, this was the only time that she suffered jealousy. Nevertheless, she recounted the experience in terms that suggested an iron control over her feelings – 'I found the emotion so humiliating that I trod it down after a short struggle.'[23]

Finally, things improved. The children recovered their health, Nan got some occasional work reviewing books for the *News Chronicle*, and she and George began to take an interest in politics. They had a brief flirtation with the Independent Labour Party but were driven back with heavy losses by the patronisingly esoteric tone of the Hampstead branch. Their principal leisure activity was playing music, making up impromptu trios, quartets and quintets with George's friends. She also played the viola in some of the amateur orchestras conducted by Grandpa Green. Acutely aware of the inequalities of life in 1930s Britain, they were both deeply affected by John Strachey's *The Coming Struggle for Power*. In consequence, they decided that both would become members of the Communist Party. Nan's father who, despite his own proletarianisation, had remained a Tory, was appalled. To survive, given the precarious nature of George's income, Nan took a job in the advertising department of a wholesale chemist, having to pretend that she was single since, in those days, work for married women was frowned upon. They had moved to a flat in Heathcote Street off Gray's Inn Road, on the outskirts of Bloomsbury. The children spent weekdays at a day nursery in nearby Kingsway and were fortunate to have found one that they liked. Nan remembered their, and her own, happiness when she collected them each day. 'How many such moments', she asked rhetorically in her memoirs, 'would there have been if we had spent all day in each other's company with me performing exasperating chores and they getting under my feet?'[24] George spent as much time with the children as possible, as did Grandpa Green. They were thus brought up in an extremely musical household.

George and Nan embraced communism joyfully and with a degree of naïvety, common then, whether in terms of trying to revitalise the Musicians' Union, or avidly discussing the Russian revolution at cell meetings. Understandably, in a world in which the rise of fascism seemed inexorable, the existence of the Soviet Union was a beacon of hope for many on the left who knew nothing of the horrors of Stalinism. To the Greens and to many like them, the choice seemed clear: 'democracy and peace or fascism and war'. Militancy took various forms. They distributed leaflets, sold pro-Soviet pamphlets and the Communist newspaper, the *Daily Worker*, writing slogans on walls and making anti-fascist speeches on soap-boxes. Their conviction that history was on their side gave them an inner strength. Such was their faith that the Party dominated their social, political and cultural lives. It also dominated the lives of the children. They were taken to demonstrations, Martin later wrote of being 'An infant revolutionary wheeled in a pram/ Speakers' Corner meant more to me/ Than did the state of Peter Pan.' While Frances and Martin tried to get to sleep, political meetings would go on elsewhere in the house. As Martin remembered later, 'Lenin and Stalin were nursery gods.' By this time, Nan had given up her job and begun to run a second-hand bookstall at the Caledonian Road market.[25]

In July 1936, the Spanish Civil War broke out. After lengthy consideration, in early 1937, George decided to volunteer, convinced like so many others that if fascism were not stopped in Spain, it would soon affect the rest of Europe. He was out shopping with Nan in January when he said to her out of the blue: 'I've got to go to Spain.' She simply replied 'Yes' and there was no further discussion of the issue despite its momentous implications for the family. No doubt, as a faithful party member, Nan would have approved of his decision anyway. However, her identification with George's ideals and beliefs was absolute. Accordingly, when he asked, 'You'll be able to keep the home fires burning, won't you?' she did not hesitate to say 'Yes' without conditions. The difficulties for the family consequent upon his absence can easily be imagined. Yet, when her brother-in-law wrote her a letter abusing George for 'deserting' his wife and family, Nan wrote back proudly: 'Listen. George and I are thinking of more than our own children, we are thinking of the children of Europe, in danger of being killed in the coming war if we don't stop the Fascists in Spain.'[26] George told his friend Charles Kahn, a fellow member of the committee of the Musicians' Union, of his decision. Charles considered reminding him of his responsibilities to his wife, his children and the union but realised that there was no point. 'His hatred of the exploitation of humanity, his hatred of everything that was rotten in this world, and his love for everything that was fine were the guiding influences of his life. Peace, freedom, democracy and the right of everyone to a living were the incentives, but George knew that these ideals could not be attained by merely wishing for them; he knew they had to be fought for.'[27]

George left on or around 19 February 1937. His daughter Frances recalled being upset that he should leave just a few days after her sixth birthday.[28] The immediate problems for

Nan of running the family alone were resolved by the solidarity of Party members and other anti-fascists. The Jewish landlord slashed the rent for their flat by a third. Most crucial was the unstinting help with the children provided by Grandpa Green. Frances and Martin missed George but were proud of him.[29] The exact consequences of his absence are difficult to reconstruct because, unfortunately, Nan's many letters to George were lost at the front. It is, however, possible to deduce from his letters to her that she did everything possible to reassure him that the family was surviving economically. 'Are you really managing quite well about money and not worrying?', he wrote uncertainly in one of his earliest letters.[30] Whatever the problems, they would be greatly exacerbated when Nan herself also decided to go to Spain. Over the next nineteen months, Nan and George would see each other only about six times. It is not perhaps surprising that during this period, she had a short-lived affair with a Party comrade.[31]

George travelled out to, and served in, Spain with a wealthy English aristocratic eccentric, Wogan Philipps, the son of Lord Milford. Philipps was a painter (of 'wild, somewhat childish paintings'), a friend of several of the Bloomsbury Group and, at the time, husband of the novelist Rosamond Lehmann.[32] The lives of George and Nan would be changed because of the subsequent friendship between Wogan and George. Wogan Philipps already had some knowledge of the Spanish situation. While on holiday in Spain at the beginning of 1936, he had been much affected by the political turmoil surrounding the creation of the Popular Front and the electoral campaign of February. On his return to England, he had avidly followed the fortunes of the Popular Front Government. Inevitably, his sympathies were with the Republicans when the military uprising took place on 18 July 1936.

Wogan Philipps' opportunity to participate in the Civil War came about through an organisation called Spanish Medical Aid. In response to appeals from Spain for medical assistance,

Isabel Brown, secretary of the Relief Committee for the Victims of Fascism, had made contact with Dr Hyacinth Morgan, medical adviser to the Trades Union Congress. In turn, Dr Morgan approached Dr Charles Brook, a general practitioner who was also secretary of the Socialist Medical Association. In consequence, on 8 August 1936, Brook organised a meeting of sympathetic doctors, medical students and nurses at the National Trade Union Club in London to consider ways of sending urgent medical help to Spain. Out of the meeting came the Spanish Medical Aid Committee, of which Dr Morgan became chairman and Dr Brook secretary. A nation-wide appeal for funds was made immediately. Within days, enough money had been raised to permit the assembly of vehicles, supplies and medical personnel. The first unit left for Spain on 23 August. Philipps presented himself at the headquarters of the Spanish Medical Aid Committee at 24 New Oxford Street in London and offered to help in any way that he could. It was there that he met the woman who would be his second wife, Lady Cristina Hastings, Countess of Huntingdon, another left-wing aristocrat, who was joint treasurer of the committee along with Peter Spencer (Viscount Churchill, cousin to Winston) and J. R. Marrack, Professor of Biochemistry at Cambridge.[33]

Wogan Philipps bought a Ford van, packed it with medical supplies and, in convoy with other trucks and ambulances, drove across France to Barcelona. One of the other trucks, loaded with medical supplies and cigarettes, was driven by George Green. In Barcelona, they were met by Ewart Milne, a poet, who was horrified when their vehicles were hijacked by anarchists. They managed to recover them, although en route to Albacete in the south, their guide, a member of the quasi-Trostkyist Partido Obrero de Unificación Marxista (Workers' Marxist Unification Party), tried to divert them to his Party comrades on the Aragón front to the west. When they left the Catalan capital, they gave a lift to Stephen Spender, the poet, who was going to Albacete in search of his erstwhile companion and lover, Jimmy Younger, (nom de guerre of Tony Hyndman) who had volunteered for the International Brigades. Spender felt responsible for 'Jimmy' becoming a Communist and going to Spain.

In an article, entitled 'Heroes in Spain', written shortly afterwards, Spender described George as 'G—, fat, frank, bespectacled and intelligent'. In trying to explain what it was about the Spanish situation that seemed to justify leaving his wife and children, George told Spender that he had cried three times in his life, each occasion with a musical significance. Once was at the British Empire Exhibition at Wembley, 'when the whole crowd, hysterical with imperialist fervour', sang 'Land of Hope and Glory'. 'I cried then to think how they'd been fooled.' The second time was when, after playing musical trash, 'the usual slush', for months in the restaurant, he went to Sadler's Wells, and hearing Mozart's *The Marriage of Figaro* performed, 'realised what music might be'. 'The third time was yesterday in Barcelona, when I went to a meeting of the People's Front and heard the crowd sing the "Internationale". I cried for joy that time.' Spender commented: 'All the time I was in Spain I remembered these occasions on which G— had wept; they seem to me a monument of personal honesty, of the spirit in which the best men have joined the International Brigades.'[34] Remarkably, within a couple of weeks, George had heard of Spender's article in the *New Statesman*. He wrote to ask Nan if she had seen it, commenting dryly, 'I believe the word "fat" is used.'[35]

Fifteen years later, in his memoirs, Spender recalled the trip again. By then, he had become a committed anti-Communist but his admiration for George remained undimmed. 'George Green was firm and stolid, with bristly fair hair, brick-red complexion and spectacles, through which he looked out at the world with unwavering eyes. Behind the glasses and behind the blueness of his eyes a watchful, patient humorousness seemed waiting.' Spender repeated the remark about crying only three times which he remembered as 'a monument to the memory of George Green' whom he considered to be 'one of the few people who came to Spain with undivided hearts'.[36] Spender's spontaneous admiration for George's courage and moral stature was echoed by others who met him in Spain. 'A marvellous man', 'most gallant and selfless', was how he was described by a Scottish ambulance driver, Roderick MacFarquhar, who became a close friend.[37]

Although drivers with no medical training, George and Wogan were pitched straight into the inferno of the battle of Jarama in February 1937. After their crucial role in the defence of Madrid against the initial rebel assault in October and November 1936, in December and January, the International Brigades played a decisive part in fighting off the various efforts made by the Nationalists to cut the Madrid-La Coruña road to the northwest. Casualties among the International Brigades were particularly high. This was hardly surprising given the enormous advantages in training and equipment enjoyed by Franco's hardened colonial army, backed as it was by Hitler and Mussolini. After the fall of Málaga in February, Franco's military rebels launched a huge attack through the Jarama valley on the Madrid-Valencia highway to the east of the capital. This was defended fiercely by Republican troops reinforced by the International Brigades. As a result, the Nationalist front advanced a few miles, but made no strategic gain. The Republicans lost 25,000 including some of the most experienced British and American members of the Brigades, and the Nationalists about 20,000. The International Brigades bore the brunt of the fighting. The British Battalion of the International Brigades, lost four hundred dead and wounded in four days.

What George and Wogan Philipps experienced during the battle was horrendous. They found themselves having to carry out amputated limbs and corpses, mopping up blood and even, at times when casualties piled up, administering anaesthetics.[38] What they witnessed had dramatic effects. George was convinced that he would be of greater use as a soldier at the front and Wogan became obsessed with the need to improve medical services in Spain. The traumatic sense of helplessness that he suffered can be deduced from his later account of a Republican advance in the Sierra de Guadarrama near La Granja:

> my ambulance was very small. The heads of the wounded, as they lay on the stretchers, were level with me as I drove. I could talk to them, encourage them, or hear if they asked for anything. My ignorance was appalling. Sometimes a man would break down completely and scream he was dying. Another would cry for water. If it was a stomach wound, he could not have any, but the denying him seemed crueller than any death. Sometimes they died on the journey. Had my ignorance let them die? Am I even now responsible for the death of some of my friends? I know that once an unnecessary bump over a large shellhole helped a man to death.
>
> Wounded were everywhere . . . We couldn't move back from the front because that would have exposed the stretcher bearers to more risk, so we carried the whole dressing station to a deep sheltered ditch right in the lines. The sky was now full of enemy planes, cruising round and round, doing what they liked. Ours had had to go away to help hinder the Fascists at Bilbao. For three days and nights it went on. The nights were worse than the days. That black journey back to the hospital as quickly as possible without lights! It seemed as if one's mind was going to snap. Tears poured down one's face as one worked. What was the point of going on? Why couldn't they stop?[39]

At about the same time, George Green sent his wife a poem that he had written, 'Dressing Station, Casa de Campo. Madrid. March 1937'. In it, he managed to sublimate some of the horrors that he faced daily:

> Here the surgeon, unsterile, probes by candle-light the embedded bullet.
>
> Here the ambulance-driver waits the next journey: hand tremulous on the wheel, eye refusing to acknowledge fear of the bridge, of the barrage at the bad crossing.
>
> Here the stretcher-bearer walks dead on his feet, too tired now to wince at the whistle of death in the black air over the shallow trench: too tired now to calculate with each journey the diminishing chances of any return to his children, to meals eaten at a table, to music and the sound of feet in the jota.
>
> Here are ears tuned to the wail of shells: lips that say this, this one gets the whole bloody station: the reflex action that flings us into safer corners, to cover from the falling masonry and the hot tearing splinters at our guts.
>
> Here the sweet smell of blood, shit, iodine, the smoke-embittered air, the furtive odour of the dead.
>
> Here also the dead.

The meaning of the Spanish Civil War for George was carried in the last lines of his poem: 'This is the struggle that justifies the try-outs of history. This is the light that illuminates, the link that unites Wat Tyler and the Boxer rebellion. This is our difference, this our strength, this our manifesto, this our song that cannot be silenced by bullets.'[40]

Wogan Philipps was wounded in the late spring of 1937 on the Guadarrama front to the north of Madrid and was invalided back to Britain. On his return, he wrote the account from which the above passage is taken. In it, he arrived at a moving insight into the conflict between the sense of duty and commitment that drove people to volunteer and the human consequences of doing so.

> I was so moved by the calmness of these men, far from their own country, their families, of their own free choice, because they felt they had to go and help the people of Spain in the invasion of their country. Here they were, lying on the grass beside me, talking as if it weren't they who were going to meet that first hail of machine-gun bullets as they went into the attack. What did they really feel? What could their values be? How did they regard human relationships? – those they left behind? I felt terribly in love with my home, and showed photographs of my children. They were so pleased to see them and I felt happy. I saw that they felt just the same as any of us who think ourselves more sensitive, more human. Their proportions were different because first of all they had to fight to be allowed to live as loving humans. I seemed to see real values at last and knew that I would be different when I got home. I wrote to those I loved, just to talk to them because I felt so close, yet dared not tell them what I was doing, because I felt so guilty. Would anybody ever understand?[41]

Wogan Philipps's tortured reflections on the medical situation in Republican Spain make it possible to understand how, after he returned to England in early July 1937, he was able to persuade Nan Green to leave her children and go to Spain. In fact, the process of persuasion had already begun. Shortly before Philipps visited Nan, she had received an eloquent but heart-wrenching letter from George written probably during the Brunete offensive. In February at the Jarama and in March at Guadalajara, the Republicans had managed, at enormous cost, particularly to the International Brigades, to fight off two major attempts to encircle Madrid. Throughout the spring, however, Franco had concentrated his attacks on the Basque Country and in mid-June, Bilbao had fallen. With Franco's army now turning its sights to the rest of the northern industrial coast, the Republicans had tried to halt their seemingly unstoppable advance towards Santander and Asturias. Colonel Vicente Rojo, the Republican Chief of Staff, planned a diversionary offensive at Brunete, fifteen miles northwest of Madrid. Launched on 6 July, it achieved initial surprise but was over-ambitious. Nearly 50,000 Republican troops smashed through the Nationalist lines, but in conditions of extreme heat and great confusion Republican discipline broke down. By 9 July, the Nationalist General Varela was able to call up enough reinforcements to plug the gap. Although Brunete was strategically irrelevant, Franco delayed his northern campaign because he saw an opportunity to annihilate large numbers of Republican troops in a battle of attrition. Working in a field hospital near El Escorial, George Green bore witness to the Generalísimo's bloody purpose.

Referring to El Escorial (which he could not name because of the military censorship) as 'a town so famous that even the Fascists daren't offend culture by bombing the traditional resting place of half the El Grecos of the world,' he sent Nan a caustic account of its historic past and of the death agony of its builder Philip II: 'a royal madman as an unconscious symbol of Spain's decline from greatness searched for years for this site in the hills and for an architect worthy of the job – and was lucky enough to find them both – and retired permanently to the smallest room of the vastest palace in Europe, there to rot in piety until he stank himself to death of what the history books call a loathsome disease.' He was amused by the irony of the fact that part of El Escorial was in use as a Republican hospital. The field hospital in which he was working was located in an abandoned monastery building further down the hill from the royal palace in the direction of Brunete. His

description of the conditions under which he worked with
the brilliant surgeon Alexander Tudor Hart would have made
Nan more receptive – even more than her heart and head
must have made her already – to the arguments soon to be
put to her by Wogan Philipps.

George commented that

> as a hospital it's not bad except that the water supply
> is a bit inadequate until we get our own emergency
> dynamo working and the stairs are steep and bad for
> stretchers carried by the local boys whom we co-opt
> as *camilleros* [stretcher-bearers] with no time to train
> them properly. To make just four journeys – each time
> with a bed – to the top floor leaves me as distressed as
> if I'd run a mile, and I'm a good deal thinner and
> fitter than when I left England. We work dourly,
> saying hardly a word, cleaning out rooms, scrubbing,
> wiring, fixing lights in the theatres and in the triage
> downstairs (which has a bay window for reception,
> which again is a bad word, since it makes you think
> rather of a social function than a room where the first
> clean-up takes place, bloody trousers are ripped from
> quivering thighs, and the wounded are sorted into
> severe, not so severe – and dead), stealing labour
> from other departments and having labour stolen
> from our own ... We did not notice the coming of
> darkness except to be annoyed at the inconvenience
> and now it is light and nobody noticed the dawn ...
> Presently after a lot more work and the ambulances
> have all left for the front (and me with no vehicle still)
> I find myself doing all sorts of odd jobs, attached
> to nothing, putting tents up ... and then I found
> myself appointed as theatre orderly to Hart's theatre
> which may not sound very onerous but includes the
> duties of anaesthetist, all-in-wrestler, stage-manager,

settler of disputes between sister and surgeon, selector
of raw material from the triage, and secretary –
and occasionally assistant surgeon in a consultation
capacity when everybody else is too tired to use
common sense.

We worked for three days and nights with never
more than two hours sleep and you can't imagine the
tiredness of it and yet the feeling of being buoyed up
by the knowledge that the triage is full of wounded
men who depend on us and who may have already
waited for six or twelve hours before getting to hospital. And Nan, we have some *awful* wounds. Some of
them die on the operating table. One man had an
awful smashed leg. A piece of shell had cut through
slicing the bone and nerves and everything and we
worked like hell to save it and patched the holes. And
twice before he went under, as I was giving him the
anaesthetic, he asked whether he must lose his leg and
I said no he'd be walking around in a couple of months
time. And we mended it and cleaned it and took pieces
of metal out and put on a beautiful plaster cast – Hart
does some lovely plaster work – and spent altogether
about four hours on it and took him down in triumph
to the ward. And next day (he'd been out on the
hillside twelve hours before they brought him in) he'd
got gas gangrene and we had to have him up again
and the plaster was crawling with maggots and the
wound stank as only gangrene can stink and he was
dead as mutton from the hip down on his left side.
And on the table he was as patient and kind to us as
only Spaniards can be and just before he went under,
he asked me the same question again and I couldn't
answer him and I didn't need to because he already
knew and he closed his eyes. And then we fought to
get the leg off before the rot got any higher – and

Nan, you can see the stuff spread under your eyes –
and after I'd taken the stinking limb down to the fire
and got back to the theatre he came to before we got
him off the table although I'd been trying to get rid
of him before his eyes could see what we'd done to
him and he thanked us and said Salud as his stretcher
went out of the door. But he cried a little afterwards
in the ward they said because one gets fond of one's
legs. And that man lives.

He then told an even more distressing story of another man
who had gangrene in both legs whose 'body revolted at this
awful cutting and cutting and he just died'.

He wrote of the incredible strain of the work and recounted
a conversation in the early hours of the morning with a nursing
sister, Molly Murphy, who had served during the First World
War and 'during the last few hours has seen too many mothers'
sons carried with sheets over staring eyes down to the wash-
house at the bottom of the garden'. George tried to cheer her
up but the sheer horror of the situation and the inexorable
power of gangrene overcame her and suddenly she broke
down in tears. As she wept, saying over and over that 'It isn't
worth it', George tried again to rally her by saying

> the only possible things there are to say, the simple
> fundamentals that make us know with no blind faith,
> that if they kill every Communist and burn every book
> today and destroy the Soviet Union tomorrow that
> we shall still win, and the bargain made with the
> unborn sons of the sleepers in the wash-house will be
> kept, and we shall build a new world. And Murphy
> suddenly says, 'Have you got a son George?' And
> because I suddenly saw Martin's unwrinkled scrotum
> and the lacerated testicles round which I'd just been
> shaving in odd juxtaposition, I knew I couldn't speak
> because had I spoken I should have needed comforting

myself and here [there] is nobody who can comfort
me. So without answering I went out with my can
of coffee from the cook-house through this grey wind
that meant that dawn was almost here, and back to
the theatre.

George's letter provides horrific testimony to the reality of
the Battle of Brunete. In the midst of his stint in the hospital,
he spent eighteen hours driving an ambulance. 'The front-line
ambulance men – many of whom don't return to hospital
during the attack but feed a halfway dressing station – are all
suffering from lack of sleep and minor shell shock – and thirst.
They operate in a valley where there is no cover.' He described
having to drive a journey of nineteen miles without lights on
black nights. Tank tracks, shell holes and rebel air attacks meant
that the ambulances could go no faster than six or seven miles
per hour. Ambulances were often destroyed by bombing and
strafing attacks. At the battlefield itself, he experienced acute
thirst and the terror of being bombed in open country. Convinced that he would die, in his mind, he bade his bitter
farewells to Nan only to survive, getting up to see that the
shallow excavation into which he had burrowed was surrounded by still-smoking bomb craters. Despite his intense
fear, he then began to take the wounded to the dressing
stations. Recalled by Tudor Hart to the hospital, he wrote the
letter surrounded by photos from home sent to him by Nan
with her last letter. If she was not already considering joining
him to help alleviate the plight of the Republic, his last para-
graph must surely have put the idea into her mind. 'I want
you in the night and in the day to work with and to sleep
with and to wake with and to cry on and to comfort and be
comforted by and to hold your hand and to lean on me
sometimes at night if you feel like it and to love and to cherish.
Please write and say you want all these things too, or come
and tell me about them.'[42]

The message of George's letter was that the Republican medical services were acutely short of the medical staff necessary to provide the fast evacuation and swift treatment that would save lives. When Philipps visited Nan to try to persuade her that she could make a vital contribution, she was already thinking about it. What Philipps did was to convince her that, as a hospital administrator, she could help to get the best out of the volunteer nurses, doctors, ambulance drivers and stretcher-bearers. Wogan Philipps had posed an appalling dilemma for a young mother, even one who was a Communist. The practical – if not the emotional – problem of what to do with the young children was resolved by Philipps' munificence – he offered to pay the fees for them to go as boarders to the boarding school of her choice. She later described this as 'the most stupendous offer'. Nan would choose the progressive Summerhill School founded in 1924 at Leiston, Suffolk, by the child psychologist Alexander Sutherland Neill. George's father also offered to do as much as possible. Nevertheless, it was a difficult choice: 'I walked up and down for a *whole night* of turmoil, trying to decide what was best.' She would never have considered sending them to any school other than Summerhill. Neill was known to be a supporter of the Spanish Republic. Nan commented later 'It was the only place I could think of where having no father or mother around wouldn't matter.'[43] Nevertheless, at the time, she could not help agonising over the decision – 'Would the separation (however temporary) from both parents make them unhappy? Was I rationalising a desire to escape from the heavy responsibility I was burdened with?' For the rest of her life she wondered if she had been right to go although, as she later reflected, 'first of all it was a wonderful chance for my kids to get out of the poverty we were in and the filth of London'. She also thought 'if George has gone, he's gone because our children are no more important than the other children in Europe and we're trying to stop the war'. She

Actresses knitting and crocheting for the militia [© Museu de l'Historia de la Ciutat, Barcelona]

Anti-fascist guerillas [© Museu de l'Historia de la Ciutat, Barcelona]

Left: Priscilla Scott-Ellis (Pip) in Argentina, her equestrian skills and aristocratic bearing belying her insecurities.

Pip (centre in white) with the nurses of the Hadfield-Spears Mobile Hospital Unit in France, May 1940.

Top right: 'Pani Pulkownik' (Madame Colonel): Pip in Scotland in her uniform as honorary colonel of the Polish Army.

Pip with her beloved Prince Ataúlfo at the Feria de Sevilla, April 1943.

Below: Pip met José Luis de Vilallonga at a cocktail party in Barcelona in the winter of 1943-4.

20 September 1945: Pip marries
José Luis de Vilallonga in Sanlucar
de Barameda (Cadiz).

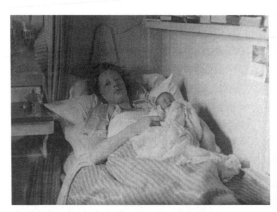

22 June 1946, Pip in her cabin shortly after
giving birth to her son John aboard the SS
Saint Merriel en route to Buenos Aires.

In Argentina (circa 1950), Pip with her
son John and daughter Carmen.

Pip in 1951, every inch the aristocrat.

Combatants on the Republican side in the Spanish Civil War:1936 [© Hulton Getty]

The twenty-one-year-old Nan Green in 1925.

Nan and George Green walking in the Peak District in 1929.

Left: Nan and Grandpa Green, with the children Frances and Martin, and a friend in London in mid-1937. George was already in Spain.

Above right: Nan, Frances and Martin in 1937 on the steps of their house in Heathcote Street, off Gray's Inn Road, London.

Below: George's improvised band at the International Brigades Hospital at Huete – George on cello, Nan with the accordion she learned to play in one evening.

Top left: In Spain, Nan brings a cup of tea to visiting Labour M.P., Leah Manning.

Top right: Nan on board the *Normandie*, returning from the Americas after taking Spanish refugees to Mexico.

Above: Nan joins in with a Chinese band in 1953.

Left: Nan in China in 1954 with her second husband, Ted Brake.

Overleaf: Militia men and women standing on a home-made tank in Barcelona: 28th August 1936 [© Hulton Getty]

convinced herself that she would be away for only six months but, in the event, she stayed in Spain for more than a year.[44]

Her decision may also have constituted a measure of both her blind loyalty to the Communist Party and her acceptance of progressive contemporary values regarding children. In her memoirs and other interviews she constantly reiterates how very difficult she found it to make the decision to leave the children and go to Spain. Many people at that time seem to have accepted as normal the idea of a period of separation from their children. Alfred and Norma Jacob, another couple who went to Spain together, also left their very young children behind. In 1930s Britain, boarding schools were widely regarded as both commendable and desirable. Moreover, children were routinely sent away for isolation in hospitals for infectious diseases for weeks at a time. Later, of course, there would be the mass evacuations of the Second World War when families were divided for months and sometimes years. Nan's decision was perhaps helped by the fact that a close friend and Party comrade, Winifred Bates, was also in Spain with her husband, Ralph. They had been walking on the Catalan side of the Pyrenees when the fighting began. They both worked for the Republican Government's propaganda and information services. Winifred worked as a writer and broadcaster for the Catalan Communist Party, (the Partit Socialista Unificat de Catalunya). Ralph was the first editor of *Volunteer for Liberty*, the journal of the 15th International Brigade.[45] The difference was that they had no children. In Spain, Nan would work in Spanish Medical Aid at the hospital of Valdeganga with another married couple, Lilian and Lou Kenton.[46]

At about the same time in September 1937 that Priscilla Scott-Ellis, complete with trunks and hampers, left England in a chauffeured limousine, Nan set off for Paris alone. She squeezed into two battered suitcases, loaded with medical supplies, the barest necessities for an indeterminate sojourn in Spain. She then travelled on by a series of trains to Puigcerdá and on to a hungry and shabby Barcelona. She arrived on a Sunday to find a power cut, no trams and no buses. Wearily, and not a little frightened, she dragged her heavy cases miles across the unfamiliar city and eventually reached the reception centre for Medical Aid. From there she was despatched on a crowded open lorry south towards Castellón. After stopping for the night at the convalescent hospital at Benicasim, she eventually reached her destination. The so-called 'English Hospital' was at Huete, in the province of Cuenca, approximately midway between Valencia and Madrid. It was in a twelfth-century monastery whose metre-thick walls surrounded an inner courtyard dominated by a large chapel. Once a seminary, its many rooms had been converted to wards for the wounded. Nan's post was to be assistant secretary in this hospital mainly staffed by Spanish, British and New Zealand personnel.

To her amazement and joy, there she encountered George whom she had not seen for eight months. His original intention had been to deliver the lorry that he had driven from London to Spain and then join the International Brigade. Since letters had to be extremely oblique, were censored anyway and replies sent to a coded address, Nan had not realised that he was still attached to the medical service. Shortly before she reached Spain, George had burned the skin of one arm with freezing petrol while trying to unblock the fuel feed of his ambulance on a mountain pass. He had originally been sent to the hospital as a patient then shortly after made acting political commissar there. Nan spent every moment that she could close to George, who faced indignant reproaches from other brigaders for 'monopolising this new woman', until he explained that she was his wife.[47] As commissar, George kept up morale there by his enthusiastic commitment to the Republican cause and by organising concerts. An American international brigader, Milt Felsen, who was a patient at Huete, recalled afternoons towards the end of George's convalescence.

He, George and another American 'would climb the hill back of the hospital and talk about politics, music, literature, the war and our hope for a future, hazily defined, that would see society develop free of war, poverty, and oppression'. Felsen remembered how George's music moved all those at the hospital: 'From somewhere he had obtained a cello, and he began to practice. Sitting in the center of the cavernous, empty church as the late afternoon sunlight filtered through the ancient stained-glass windows, he made sounds that were so unutterably sad and beautiful that anyone who heard would stop and not breathe or move until the last note was lost in the silent air.' For his concerts, George recruited Nan. To his impromptu ensemble of a German brigader from Bavaria, Willi Remmel, on violin, himself on cello, the local plumber on guitar, a Catalan playing the lute-like *bandurria*, he added Nan whom, in one afternoon, he taught to play an accordion left behind by a previous patient.[48]

The nursing staff of the hospital, largely British with three New Zealanders, was devoted and hard-working. Nevertheless, Nan was shocked to find that there were internal political tensions arising from the anti-communism of those who were 'non-political' or Labour Party supporters. She wondered if there were spies working on behalf of the Foreign Office and even suspected that there might have been some sabotage. George as commissar also had to persuade some of the nurses to relinquish their status symbols. Those who had reached the rank of sister wore a white triangular headpiece as a mark of distinction. Unfortunately, resembling a religious veil, it frightened many of the more poorly educated Spanish patients who had had experience of cruel treatment at the hands of nuns. Between them, George and Nan managed to overcome the nurses' reluctance to shed their signs of authority. Nan's own capacity for hard work quickly earned her the respect of both staff and patients. Milt Felsen recalled her as 'a brisk, efficient, dedicated no-nonsense woman of beauty and intellect'. Nan in her turn was inspired by the efficiency and care lavished by the nurses on their patients.

Despite the dirt and the political differences, she never heard any grumbling, 'I just saw a cheerful determination to do what had to be done and do the best for the patients. And sometimes they worked for three days and three nights without stopping as long as there were wounded to attend to.' She recalled Dorothy Low, 'a Sister who had served most of her nursing career in the British Army, who received in her ward three injured men who, because of negligence in another hospital, were near to death. Through sheer *nursing* she brought all three back to life and health, cleaning their disgraceful bedsores, tending their wounds, supervising their diet and scarcely leaving them day or night.' The conditions in the hospital were primitive. Nurses cleaned and dressed wounds and bedsores 'and all this, remember, before antibiotics had been heard of, before M and B had emerged from the laboratories' (a reference to May and Baker sulphonamides). There was a chronic shortage of medical supplies of all kinds, even of what was often the only antiseptic – plain soap. She was equally moved by the enthusiasm of the village girls eager to help in any way. One mother told her 'Before the Republic there wasn't a pencil in this village, and now all the children go to school. Yes, my daughter will come and help! Those wounded men are fighting so that our children can learn.' Many of the villagers learned nursing skills with a rapidity that derived from this powerful motivation. Nan herself set about learning Spanish with the help of one of her colleagues, a Catalan.[49] Unlike most British volunteers, she did so with great success. George too, with his musical ear, had picked up a good command of Spanish.

In December 1937, George was discharged from the hospital and permitted to go to the front and join the British Battalion. He had decided that working with the medical services was not enough and he felt that he had to take part in the fighting against fascism. His infectious optimism and faith in the cause ensured that, within three months, he would be promoted to infantry sergeant. He was sent to sub-officers' training school. It was not surprising that he became a leading member of what was called the Activist Movement in the Republican Army, aimed at creating exemplary soldiers who would become expert in the use of every weapon, in tactics and fortifications. The activists would then help their comrades to reach the same standard. He was often asked to help train Spanish recruits. The seriousness with which he took his duties, which was entirely shared by Nan, was reflected in a letter in which he wrote:

> it's a bit disheartening to have a bloc of about five Catalan anarchists with no knowledge of anything but Barcelona dance halls in one's section. They think it's funny to miss trench-digging practice or infiltration manoeuvres or cleaning the barracks: and it's very difficult – having seen SO many comrades with their mouths full of flies for lack of time to learn elementary strategy – it's very difficult to keep patience with them: but there are worse problems in the anti-fascist struggle and I expect you're having one of them now.[50]

His passionate conviction gleamed through all his letters to Nan. In the spring of 1938, he wrote:

> Will you tell the children why we came to Spain to meet trouble half-way and how important it was: they may not know. I know you will understand it was more than personal pride that made me come here from the Sanidad [medical services]. Nan, dear, whoever gets killed at Teruel or Aragón; or whatever gains the fascists may get today WE WILL WIN! And we, in our way, have helped the forces of progress to win. Don't ever forget that we are proud to be Bolsheviks.

That it is our faith in our ability to build a world where
people can lead decent lives, and our knowledge of
the forces that cause us to take up dynamite and
destruction; tho' loving peace & the growing of cab-
bages & the flight of kestrels; that it is this faith & this
knowledge that make a better world possible.[51]

Shortly after George left Huete, Nan was posted as Administrator to the nearby convalescent hospital at Valdeganga. Built
near thermal springs, in the past it had been a hydropathic
hotel. As befitted its former status as a health resort for the
rich, it was well-appointed, sporting marble baths with silver-
plated taps in the form of swans' heads.[52] At Valdeganga, Nan
encountered a very difficult situation. There was a poisonous
atmosphere arising from the tendency of some of the Communists on the staff to give vent to personal resentments
by accusing others of Trotskyism. Even Nan, a staunch and
uncomplicated Communist – would not go unscathed. Nevertheless, her memories of the hospital were good both socially
and in terms of the splendid medical work done there. Every
Saturday there was a dance for the patients and the villagers
at which she played her accordion – although fraternisation
was limited by the social constraints which forbade the village
girls to dance with strangers. They would lose their respect-
ability if they put their arms around any man to whom they
were not at least betrothed, if not married. Accordingly, they
would ignore Nan's impassioned weekly speech urging them
to dance with their 'brothers' of the International Brigades.[53]

However, Nan's time at Valdeganga was soured by a conflict
with the hospital's chief medical officer, Captain Kretzschmar.[54] Dr Carol Herbert Kretzschmar was a young German
Communist who had been arrested by the Nazis while still a
medical student at the University of Leipzig. He fled the Third
Reich and completed his medical studies in Graz in Austria.
Travelling from Austria, he joined the Eleventh Battalion,

the Thälmann, of the International Brigades in January 1937. According to a report written in Moscow in 1940, Herbert Kretzschmar was a good surgeon and a deeply committed Party worker. His blind loyalty to the Party was indicated by the fact that he was accepted for membership of the Spanish Communist Party, an honour reserved for particularly committed militants.[55] As far as Nan Green was concerned, however, he was an authoritarian who bullied the village girls who worked as maids in the wards and kitchens. There was also friction between them over the hospital's drug supplies. Nan believed that he was taking the hospital's morphine for his own use. To get more, he needed her signature for the requisition note, claiming that it was for addicts among the patients. She was convinced that the addicts were invented. He certainly tried to engage her in a sexual liaison. She rebuffed Herbert Kretzschmar and, largely in consequence, her time at Valdeganga ended badly.

Then, in March 1938, Nan made herself vulnerable to Kretzschmar's political fanaticism, if not outright malice, by having a short but passionate affair with an International Brigader who was a patient in the hospital. What happened was entirely understandable in the circumstances of the war. Surrounded by the dead and the dying, human beings often seek comfort in a life-affirming passion. She was alone and lonely – indeed, in his most recent letter, George had talked of death as inevitable: 'Have given up weighing up my chances of seeing you again as an unprofitable pastime: and we have made a decision to be carried out, haven't we?'[56] Despite these mitigating circumstances, Nan never forgave herself her moment of passion. She was infinitely harder on herself than she had ever been with George's frequent transgressions. In her memoirs, she wrote: 'I believe that due to altitude we were all infected with a touch of "mountain sickness" and lived in a permanent state of mild excitement.' She described her affair in terms that both expressed how badly she felt about it and her need to be distanced from it. 'In the last turbulent days of Valdeganga I had fallen victim to an ephemeral affair with a patient, a man much younger than myself, which in that over-charged atmosphere had exploded – and gone out like a rocket. The medical officer must have known about it, and probably a lot of others. I was feeling deeply guilty and wanted to put it behind me.' She also wrote of it as 'a stain on my conscience'.[57]

The 'younger' man was almost certainly William Day, from Canterbury, at thirty, hardly much younger than the thirty-three-year-old Nan. Shortly afterwards, he deserted – perhaps because Nan brought the short-lived affair to an abrupt end or maybe because he was worried about his pregnant wife back in England.[58] In Day's desertion, the spurned Dr Kretzschmar now saw his opportunity for revenge. The political commissar at Valdeganga, a Yorkshire railwayman named Frank Ayres, was obliged to return to England briefly to report to the Spanish Medical Aid Committee on the needs of the hospital service. He had been writing some notes that he had been taking on the functioning of the hospital and left them with Anita, the hospital's beautiful assistant housekeeper. The embittered senior housekeeper, in order to curry favour with Dr Kretzschmar, reported that Anita had a book hidden under her mattress. The medical officer then reported her to the police as a spy who had stolen the book to pass on to the enemy. Anita was arrested and taken to Cuenca. With considerable difficulty, Nan secured Anita's release and her return to the hospital. No sooner had they arrived than Kretzschmar immediately sacked her. Having got rid of Anita, the furious medical officer now turned on Nan. With the atmosphere in the hospital rapidly becoming more vicious by the day, at the beginning of April 1938, Kretzschmar drove to the International Brigades headquarters in Albacete. There he spoke with William Rust, ostensibly the *Daily Worker* correspondent, but a CPGB Central Committee member responsible for maintaining the political reliability of party members in Spain. He denounced William Day as a saboteur and made other wild accusations about Nan and Frank Ayres, inventing ludicrous charges of embezzlement of hospital funds.[59]

Although none of the charges were sustainable, they found their way into the files and followed Nan to her subsequent jobs in Spain. There is a reference to Nan's 'crime' in a lengthy document written in Spanish in the summer of 1938. Discovered in the recently opened Moscow archives, it carried the title 'List of Suspicious Individuals and Deserters from the XVth Brigade'. The inaccurate entry for Nan reads 'N. Green (English) – Was Hospital Administrator in Valdeganga. Arrested for defending an instigator. Expelled from Spain and is now in this area again. (NOTE: This is a female).' It is not clear if the 'instigator' was William Day or the entirely innocent Anita.[60] A more detailed report was filed by the ruthless William Rust who, as chief political commissar, was determined to eradicate any deviation from Stalinist orthodoxy within the British Battalion.[61] His report accused Nan of being an 'adventurer' (code for sexually promiscuous) and recommended that she be expelled from Spain. Her principal crime was deemed to be her sexual liaison with the hospitalised Brigader who had deserted. Reference was also made to Kretzschmar's denunciations of her work as administrator and to the alleged letter in her room 'full of criticisms of the Soviet Union'. The only allegation that Rust knew to be verifiable was the relationship with 'the very bad element' (William Day). His conclusion was, nevertheless, that 'In any case, it is clear that Nan Green should not be permitted to undertake any Party work. There is actually no work for this comrade in Spain and she should be advised to return to England.'[62]

In late April or early May 1938, using almost identical language, Rust also wrote a report on William Day to his superiors in the British Communist Party that was revealing of the paranoiac atmosphere in which Kretzschmar's accusations were given credence.

> William Day who recently deserted from here made remarks to me that indicated that he was either a Fascist or a Trotskyist. I was therefore surprised to find from letters that came into my hands that both Nan Green and Frank Ayres were extremely friendly with him. I therefore spoke to that young Austrian doctor who knew them all at Valdeganga and he was extremely critical of all three and declared that Day was nothing but a saboteur. He accused Nan Green of irresponsibility and said that both she and Ayres had been short in their accounts to the tune of several thousand pesetas. He added that a letter full of criticisms of the Soviet Union from a Trotskyist point of view had been found in Nan Green's room. He could not say who had written the letter but promised to bring it to me. On the other hand I remember that Ayres described the doctor to me as being a drug addict.[63]

It is reasonable to suppose that Kretzschmar was motivated by resentment at having been spurned by Nan and his reaction was of a piece with the bone-headed Stalinism current at the time. Dr Len Crome, who had been with George at El Escorial, and with whom Nan would work at the Ebro, wrote later:

> one of the least pleasant features of life in the International Brigades was frequent denunciation. To be sure, not among the English, who were as far as I know quite innocent of this, partly no doubt, because they were unfamiliar with illegal dangerous political work underground. No officer could retreat a yard without risking denunciation of being a secret Gestapo agent, or trotskyist, which at the time came to much

the same thing. Some of the reports were honestly believed in by the people who made them, but I have no doubt that many were inspired by personal animosity or envy, by a wish to prove one's own virtue, and often came from malicious, incompetent persons.[64]

Despite the flimsiness of the hysterical accusations against Nan, it was decided that a hospital could not function if its medical officer and its administrator were at war. Accordingly, she was ordered to resign. Having collected her things from Valdeganga, she managed to get back to Albacete and persuade the Commissar of the International Brigades to send her to the medical HQ in Barcelona in order that she could be reassigned. She got on a troop train heading for Catalonia. Shortly after leaving, it stopped and remained stationary for twenty-four hours.[65] This was the consequence of the fact that, on 7 March 1938, Franco had followed up his victory at Teruel in February with a massive offensive through Aragón and Castellón towards the sea. Up against Republican troops who were exhausted, short of guns and ammunition and generally unprepared, the Nationalist troops advanced rapidly. Demoralisation after the defeat of Teruel was compounded by organisational confusion. By the end of March, the River Ebro had been crossed. By early April, Franco's troops were moving down the Ebro valley progressively cutting off Catalonia from the rest of the Republic. By 15 April, they had reached the Mediterranean at the fishing village of Vinaroz. Nan's train was stopped because the territory ahead was now in Nationalist hands. Her own situation was resolved by the miraculous reappearance of Frank Ayres who had been put in charge of Spanish Medical Aid personnel. Frank got her off the train and took her back to another medical-aid reception centre in Valencia.

Nan's friend from London, Winifred Bates, had become a

propagandist and photographer for the Spanish Medical Aid Committee. However, she found herself resolving problems for the nurses that she met and she was made a kind of commissar for all British women personnel in the Republican medical services. Winifred had therefore been able to arrange for the Spanish Medical Aid Committee to appoint Nan to help reorganise a hospital at Uclés, on the Madrid-Valencia road south east of Tarancón.[66] Nan was delighted to join Frank and Anita there although she was appalled by the gory conditions that she found. Hygiene was abysmal, something that Nan believed to be a consequence of the secret Nationalist sympathies of the upper-class Spanish nurses and doctors. Soiled dressings and amputated limbs were simply thrown into a dry moat. Rats and lice abounded.[67] She remained at Uclés from mid-April to mid-May 1938. On 1 May, Nan had a significant emotional crisis. She had had no letters from George for a month and had no idea where he was or even if he was alive. The fact of it being May Day set her off thinking of previous such days spent with George and the children in London. Maybe she thought too about her betrayal of him with William Day. Whatever the case, she was weeping uncontrollably when found by Frank and Anita who rallied round with the customary 'nice cup of tea'. Years later, Frank told her that, until that moment, he had regarded her 'as admirably efficient but stony-hearted'. This was hardly surprising since, self-contained and never garrulous before, she had become a very reserved and tight-lipped woman since the accusations of Party disloyalty.

In early May, Winifred Bates, having reached the conclusion that Nan was swimming against the political tide at Uclés, recommended her for an important posting in the north. She was to replace the Australian, Aileen Palmer, as secretary to Dr Len Crome, the Chief Medical Officer of the 35th Army Corps.[68] However, the Republican zone was cut in two and communication was possible only by air or sea.

Frank Ayres found the solution. An English nurse, Penny Phelps, had been badly wounded when the surgical unit in which she was working was bombed during the Nationalist advance towards Valencia. Now, after being treated in the military hospital at Valencia, she was returning to England. Frank Ayres arranged for Nan to accompany Penny on a British battleship, HMS *Sussex*, from Valencia to Marseilles. There she bought a large amount of medical provisions, then presented herself at the British Consulate with a letter from Spanish Medical Aid requesting that she be returned to Spain. She was not admitted to see the Consul and she reached the conclusion that this was because she looked shabby in rope sandals and an old skirt and jumper. She bought a cheap outfit and a hat at a department store. She walked round to the Consulate and was admitted immediately to the Consul's office. He reprimanded her for using the Royal Navy as 'taxi service to get about the Mediterranean' but issued the necessary permit for her to return to Spain. She then flew to a hungrier-than-ever Barcelona.[69]

Nan started her new job hoping that the events at Valdeganga had been erased. The guilty reference in her memoirs to the 'stain' of her affair with William Day is deeply revealing, indeed startlingly so given her normal restraint. In part, it surely reflects her reaction to a moving letter from George sent in mid-May. Describing the privations of his unit in amusing terms, he made it quite clear that the ultimate deprivation was not seeing or hearing from his wife. He was 'desolate' when he had no news from her. The letter ended 'I've had a curious fancy. I know we don't give or extract promises, and all that, and I know that it was precisely when you were in *your* front line that I betrayed you, but whilst I am here, would you like to be faithful to me? Please love me.'[70]

It is difficult to calculate the effect on Nan of what must have made extremely upsetting reading. She already felt guilty about her affair with William Day before receiving George's uncannily prescient letter. However, that a transitory sexual transgression should then become the basis of accusations of Trotskyist deviation and even of consorting with fascists was altogether too much. Loyalty to the Communist Party was the *sine qua non* of Nan's existence. It had given her the solidity of both ideas and people that she had never found in the Farrow family. Moreover, loyalty to the Party and her relationship with George were indissolubly linked. To have her act of weakness turned into a major betrayal of both the Party and of her husband must have been devastating. The festering sense of guilt and the need to redeem her political and sexual 'sin' go some way to explaining the disappearance of the fun-loving Nan of earlier times and her transformation into a reserved and work-driven Party worker. She wrote later, with a shudder, of what happened to ex-International Brigaders in the Soviet Bloc tried as fascist or American agents just because they had been in Spain. In relation to her own experience, she noted with notable relief that 'I did not reap then or later the consequence of my folly (and cowardice?).'[71]

Whatever her personal regrets, aware of Frank Ayres's confidence in her, Nan believed that her appointment as secretary to Dr Crome, an extremely important and responsible post, meant that the Kretzschmar's accusations were a thing of the past. Accordingly, she did nothing when her friend Winifred Bates urged her to put the record straight because 'word was going round that I was an "adventuress"'. Although Winifred's advice was good, either through fear or guilt, Nan just ignored it. As Nan later discovered, Dr Kretzschmar's accusations had reached not her immediate superiors in the medical service 'but a much higher and more powerful authority, charged with the scrutiny of Communists from all countries'. Her typically cryptic reference was to André Marty, the walrus-moustached Frenchman who was secretary to the Comintern and ran the International Brigades' headquarters at Albacete. This hard-line Stalinist was fanatical in rooting out perceived

dissidence and brutal in his application of harsh discipline.[72]
There can be no doubt that the reports of William Rust
denouncing Nan's 'offence' of sleeping with an alleged Trotskyist and calling for her to be expelled from Spain had reached
Marty. Her name appears in a report from Marty's office on
another English volunteer, the medical secretary Rosaleen
Smythe, interrogated for having communication with *'éléments
mauvais'*. There were references to Nan Green as *'politiquement
très suspecte'*. *'Il y a des rapports spéciaux.'* It was noted that
Rosaleen Smythe's 'communication with Nan Green must be
investigated'.[73]

Interestingly, in 1976, in a pamphlet on the Spanish Civil
War written in collaboration with Alonso Elliott, Nan asserted

> Stories about 'NKVD agents' in Spain, especially in
> relation to the fight against Trotskyism, have been
> propagated so widely that one meets them almost
> everywhere, and this includes works by progressive
> historians. The authors of this article are inclined to
> think that most of them are apocryphal. One of us
> (Nan Green) was in Spain from September 1937 until
> the end of October 1938 and the other (A. M. Elliott)
> from May 1937 until February 1939, sometimes in
> circumstances in which we might reasonably have
> expected to hear of such activities by Soviet security
> agents if they had been at all widespread. We never
> did. This is not proof, of course, that they never
> existed[74]

Her memoirs, written later still, make it quite clear that she
did know about reports being made on her. Perhaps she did
not consider those reports to be anything to do with the
NKVD, which strictly speaking they were not. It is more
likely that she believed that to recount her own experience
would be to transgress the Party line.

In the early summer of 1938, the Republican Chief of Staff,

General Vicente Rojo, was preparing an attempt to restore contact between Catalonia and the rest of the Republican zone by means of an assault across the River Ebro. It would turn into the most hard-fought battle of the entire war. A special Army of the Ebro was formed for the offensive, which was placed under the command of General Juan Modesto, the domineering Communist. A huge concentration of men, numbering some 80,000, was secretly transported to the river banks and they crossed on the night and early morning of 24–5 July. By 1 August, they had reached Gandesa forty kilometres from their starting point but there they were bogged down when Franco poured reinforcements into the area. The Republicans would be pounded by artillery and aerial bombardment for the next four months.

While the preparations for the Ebro crossing were under way, Nan was reporting to the nearby HQ of the 35th Divisional Medical Corps which was commanded by Dr Len Crome, the Chief Medical Officer. The Russian-born Crome was an Edinburgh-trained doctor, whose brilliant improvisations saved many lives. It has been estimated that his innovations ensured that the wounded under his care received better treatment than they might have expected in the best teaching hospitals of the time in London.[75] Her job was to type Len's despatches in formal Spanish, to keep the divisional medical reports and convert them into useful statistical information and to stamp every official document which left the HQ. She took it upon herself to be a kind of welfare officer for the unit, making tea at all hours for doctors, ambulance drivers, mechanics, cooks and the patients. The ability to maintain the morale of those around her was always one of Nan's greatest qualities. When she first joined the 35th Division Medical Corps, its headquarters were an old farmhouse. One day, to her delight, a now-bearded George, who was serving with an anti-tank unit, came in briefly. They had no chance to be really alone but at least she knew that he was alive and they spent every minute together talking about the children. Shortly afterwards, Len Crome's medical unit moved to an emergency hospital in a huge cave in the side of a hill near the village of La Bisbal de Falset. The appalling state of primitive roads had obliged the Republican medical services to develop improvised hospitals as near as possible to the front to avoid the wounded being bumped and jostled en route to treatment.

A Spanish nurse who worked in the cave later recorded her memories of this time:

> There I met an extraordinary English woman; Nan Green. She looked so young and full of life and activity. I could not believe my ears when they told me she was the mother of two children ... She spoke beautiful Spanish and one day giving Ada (Hodson) and myself a cup of tea, she said, 'You in the ward are always full of work. I do nothing else but make cups of tea.' Even if it was in very good Spanish, I did not understand the meaning of the words. It was Joan Purser, the intelligent nurse always very kind to me ... who explained, 'You see Aurora, Nan also works very hard, she does all that grey unseen work without which we could not function as a hospital, but she is very modest.'[76]

The cave hospital was near the River Ebro which Nan crossed on the night of the second day, 25 July. The medical unit then set up headquarters in a farmhouse where emergency operations took place under the Nationalist artillery bombardments and air raids. In the wreckage, she found an English china teapot and a tea cosy to go with the bag of tea and the Primus stove that she took everywhere. She managed to create a kind of lounge with armchairs and a table where tea was served around the clock.[77] One of Nan's administrative tasks – as well as the morale-raising tea-production – was to analyse

the day's casualties from lists compiled by the doctors in charge
of the front-line dressing stations. She would classify them by
category (head wounds, leg wounds, amputations and so on)
and the weapons that had caused them (mortars, shells, bullets).
She then produced water-coloured graphs which greatly
assisted in identifying the crucial supplies most needed, ranging
from steel helmets to medicaments and also helped in the
prioritisation of treatment. Her system was taken over by
the distinguished New Zealand surgeon, Douglas Jolly, who
used it during the Second World War in North Africa and
Italy.[78]

Each day, as she compiled her statistics, Nan would frantically go through the lists hoping against hope that George's
name would not be among them. Early in the battle she
received a letter from George in which he complained of
being dirty and of being tired of corned beef but also revealed
his exhilaration at the crossing of the Ebro. Like every other
man at the front, he longed for a hot bath, clean clothes and
a hot meal, but, he added in Spanish, '*pero primero ganar la
guerra*' ('first let's win the war'). 'What do you think of the
Army of the Ebro eh? Losses very heavy. Major Attlee Column
crossed the river with 105 men and we've only got 32 left.
Everything missed me up to date. Have they bombed you
yet? I believe you're this side of the river . . . Crossing the
river itself was a beautiful operation.'[79] Perhaps the sense of
George being nearby and daily risking death gave an added
meaning to her duties. Perhaps not – her commitment could
hardly have been greater than it was. One duty, for which she
regularly volunteered, was to be a blood donor. It was an
unforgettable experience 'lying down beside a seriously
wounded man, on the point of death, I watched as the colour
came back into his lips, his breathing improved and he turned
back towards life'. At one point, she was able to visit the British
Battalion, 'a raggle-taggle bunch of weary men, scattered over
an arid hillside. George was there unharmed. We spent two

evenings together and one whole night, on a louse-infected sofa.'[80]

By all accounts, Nan was not one to complain, always finding the bright side of every situation. Nonetheless, she hated the dirt of her precarious existence near the front. 'Oh! How dirty I am', she wrote to her sister Mem, 'I have a cut-down pair of overall pants and a too-short shirt – neither of which have been off for five days except once when I took a bath in a pint of dirty water – my hair needs cutting – it has gone into tight dust curls like a Woolworths doll – the bandages round my infected feet are black – my one sandal goes flap-flap when I walk – everybody is dirty – cheerful – and the TEA does them good.' Despite, like George, missing the comforts of baths, sheets, decent food and sanitation, and above all, her children, she was sustained by an exhilaration that came from participation in a cause of universal importance,

> the indescribable feeling of comradeship this hectic life brings with it and the way you keep working, as long as there is something to do and then fall down on a mattress and think 'I'm tired.' They are going, one by one. 'Night, Nan. Thanks for the tea.' '*Salud y muchas gracias, camarada Nan.*' '*Salud, genosse!*' And so the work goes on.[81]

In August, George had been hit by a piece of shrapnel. The consequent head wound was minor. His head had been stitched and he was on the mend but the hospital insisted on keeping him in for treatment of suppurating sores on his legs – a common ailment at the front. Nan wrote to Mem, 'the principal thing I feel is relief that he is away back from that hell for a while and I don't suffer the tension of wondering if he is alive which, with every boom I hear, comes. He sends cheerful messages by the ambulance men to me.' One such messenger was his friend, the Scottish ambulance driver, Roderick MacFarquhar.[82] This mishap provided George with

a rare breathing space in which he wrote a long and moving
letter to his mother, Jessie. He began with heartfelt thanks for
the letters and parcels sent to them from home.

> It's difficult to say how much letters and parcels mean
> out here: more even than in the last war, because
> there, so much propaganda effort was put into the
> creation of the feeling that the whole people was
> united behind the soldier at the front. And here with
> British politics so hard to understand, with the feeling
> of fighting a lonely fight that our isolation can so easily
> give us, the man without letters or parcels from home
> can experience the bitterest sort of loneliness: and Nan
> and I are fortunate in having so many friends.

George tried to explain to her, and to the rest of his
extended family in Stockport, the reasons that had impelled
him and Nan to leave their home and children to go to Spain:

> 1. We came to war because we love peace and hate
> war. 2. Fascism, which is the maker of wars today,
> and which is threatening everybody's home and every-
> body's safety, this same Fascism can be decisively
> beaten in Spain and if it is beaten in Spain then it is
> beaten forever as a world force. 3. We are not pacifists
> because we believe that the pacifist line is a direct
> encouragement to the war-makers. Only the well-
> meaning but muddled thinking of the pacifists made
> it possible for Fascism's friends within the League of
> Nations to ensure that Fascism got away with the
> murders of Shanghai, of the people of Manchuria, of
> Abyssinia. With our help – and yours – they will not
> get away with the murder of Spain. Mother dear,
> we're not militarists, nor adventurers nor professional
> soldiers: but a few days ago on the hills the other side
> of the Ebro, I've seen a few unemployed from the

Clyde, and frightened clerks from Willesden stand up (without fortified positions) against an artillery barrage that professional soldiers could not stand up to. And they did it because to hold the line here and now means that we can prevent this battle been fought again later on Hampstead Heath or the hills of Derbyshire.[83]

Such sentiments were what inspired the volunteers to continue the fight against such overwhelming odds. George's faith in the worth of what was being done by the International Brigades and everyone who fought for the Republic, win or lose, was widespread. It was shared by Nan and by virtually all the volunteers. In the summer of the previous year, shortly before his death in battle, an American volunteer named Gene Wolman had written to his family in similar terms:

> For the first time in history, for the first time since Fascism began systematically throttling and rending all we hold dear, we are getting the opportunity to fight back. Mussolini rode unopposed . . . to Rome. Hitler boasts that he took power without bloodshed . . . In little Asturias the miners made a brave, but unsuccessful stand against the combined reactionaries of Spain. In Ethiopia the Fascist machine was again able to work its will without any unified opposition. Even in Democratic America the majority have had to undergo every sort of oppression without being able to fight back . . . Here finally the oppressed of the Earth are united, here finally we have weapons, here we can fight back. Here, even if we lose . . . in the fight itself, in the weakening of Fascism, we will have won.[84]

Gradually, under the incessant shelling, the Republicans were being pushed back towards the Ebro. At one point, the emergency hospital was ahead of the Republican lines. A rapid withdrawal saw medical headquarters set up in a derelict farmhouse near a railway tunnel that had been converted into a hospital. At this time, September 1938, the Republican Government decided to pull out the Brigades in the hope of facilitating international mediation. The International Brigaders were to be sent home – those who had homes, that is. For Italian, German and Austrian refugees from fascism and Nazism, the defence of the Spanish Republic had been their first real chance to fight back and eventually to go home. Now their future could hardly be bleaker. Volunteers from the democracies had something to look forward to but were in no hurry to abandon their Spanish comrades. After being wounded in August, George was still in hospital having treatment for the sores on his legs. However, when he heard about the proposed withdrawal, he courageously demanded to be allowed to return to his unit to take part in the final action with the rest of the British Battalion. In the letter to his mother four weeks earlier, he had written, 'For us, we shall be glad when it's all over. My idea of a good time is not being shot at, but is connected with growing lettuce and spring onions, and drinking beer in a country pub, and playing quartets with friends and having my children about me to educate me and keep me human.'[85]

On or about 18 September 1938, he went into the medical headquarters where Nan worked to hand in a document certifying that he had been discharged from the hospital at his own request. It was to be their last meeting. He was glad to be returning to the battalion and 'he was absolutely convinced that the French would now open the frontier and let the arms through which were waiting on the other side'. They spent a couple of hours eagerly talking about getting home and seeing the children. They decided that neither should go and see the children until both were back in England and thus able to do so together. 'When we last saw each other at the Ebro . . . we were expecting orders to return home. We knew we would have to make our way out separately so we made a pact that the first one to reach England would not see the children until the other arrived. We wanted to double the joy of reunion by sharing it with each other.'[86] The problem was that the withdrawal of International Brigaders was imminent but the medical staff were likely to be kept on for some weeks in order to train their successors. Originally 22 September was fixed as the date for the withdrawal. However, the severity of Nationalist attacks caused the British Battalion, which was in reserve just south of the Ebro river on the road to Gandesa between Ascó and Corbera, to be called back into the Republican front line. George had left for the front happy to be able to take 'a final swipe' at the Nationalists. On the evening of the 22nd, Nan studied the casualty list with dread and was relieved not to find George's name.

On the following night, however, two Brigaders came and wakened Nan with the news that George was missing. She was devastated but, as was her wont, showed little emotion. 'I pulled the sheets around my suddenly icy-cold shoulders and lay down, trying to grasp the thunderbolt. It must not, it could not be true.' Repeating a mantra of 'he might be alive, he might be dead', she determined not to weep in order to be able to cherish hope. 'He-might-be-alive-he-might-be-dead repeated itself with bewildering monotony in my waking thoughts for the rest of my stay in Spain and for the following months, gradually changing to despair.' Some weeks later, the medical unit withdrew. When they reached the village of Ascó, on the banks of the Ebro, Nan began frantically to telephone all the hospitals to which Republican wounded might have been sent. She got to a starving Barcelona which was now under bombardment. Hoping that George might still be alive, she began a desperate round of visiting hospitals in a forlorn search for him.[87]

George had in fact been killed in action on 23 September 1938. There is an account of his death in the memoirs of one of his comrades, Walter Gregory, the commander of his unit.

Gregory wrote, 'Of the 150 men of my Company who had crossed the Ebro on the night of 25th July, I had just under two dozen still with me. The rest were either dead, wounded or missing. I fear that many more were lying under the shallow, gravelly soil of the Sierras than were regaining their strength between the clean sheets of hospital beds.' On 18 September, the British Battalion was recalled to the front and it was at this time that George Green insisted on rejoining his unit. They were in a sector dominated by higher ground which was in Nationalist hands. To make matters worse, the stony soil made it difficult to dig trenches. Gregory stationed George in a defensive position with a Soviet-made machine-gun. For hour after hour on the morning of 23 September, they were pounded by a Nationalist artillery barrage. At midday, the waves of shells stopped and five tanks advanced at the head of the Nationalist infantry. Three of the five tanks were knocked out but the positions were encircled. 'On looking behind me I saw more Fascist troops advancing on my part of the trench. I shouted a warning to George on my left but before he and his crew had time to realign their machine-gun we were completely surrounded. There was nothing else for it but to accept the inevitability of my capture.' Gregory and his men were escorted under arms to enemy lines. 'I kept looking behind me in the hope of seeing George and his crew, but they never came. I doubt if they ever left the trench, since the Fascists had made it a policy to shoot machine-gunners on the spot.' At the beginning of that last day in action, there were 106 British Brigaders still in the Battalion. By the end of the day, there were only fifty-eight. The entire battalion consisted of 377 men, of whom 204 were killed, missing or taken prisoner.[88]

Still unsure of her husband's fate, Nan returned to London. By that time, her reputation within the Communist Party of Great Britain had been rebuilt, thanks to Winifred Bates. In a detailed report on the British women in Spain, Mrs Bates

countered the earlier damaging remarks by William Rust. She
wrote in September 1938, 'I believe she is a genuine and
sincere Communist and wants to give the best of her abilities.
She is brave and never seeks her own personal comfort. She
is the type of Communist who is always working to keep up
the morale of those around her.' In an oblique, not to say
coy, reference to the earlier difficulties, she wrote: 'She is not
the type of comrade to be in Spain for her own delectation.
I have heard irresponsible gossips say this. It is false and actuated
by jealousy.' Winifred Bates regularly visited the hospitals
where British nurses worked and she knew Huete and Valdeganga especially well. Her detailed knowledge thereby enabled
her to expose the sexual motivation behind Dr Herbert
Kretzschmar's accusations against Nan. She thereby went a
long way towards the rehabilitation that enabled Nan to go
on working in Spain and later in England for the Republican
cause.[89]

When Nan reached England, her first concern was how to
tell Grandpa Green that his son was missing. The next day,
they went to Summerhill accompanied by Nan's sister 'Mem'
and a friend called Noelle. They were met at the station by
A. S. Neill himself and the children. Martin remembers them
asking him to say 'which of the two sisters (they were very
much alike) was my mother'.[90] She told the children: 'Daddy
isn't coming just yet, we don't quite know where he is.'
However, one of Frances's classmates had overheard Nan telling Neill about George. Frances bounded up saying: 'Sally
says Daddy is missing. I don't want him to be missing!' Nan
was confronted with the dilemma of hating to lie to her children but wanting to give them some glimmer of hope.[91] She
stayed in London trying to trace him through British government channels. According to an interview in the *News Chronicle* in January 1939, 'Her final clue failed her last week and,
accepting the probability of her husband's death, she went to
the children's school in Suffolk alone. She could not bring

herself to tell them that she feared their father had been killed. They are still looking forward to his keeping another pact – not to shave off his beard, grown in Spain, until they had seen it.'⁹² In fact, she still refused to believe that George was dead.

Nan now faced the additional problem that Wogan Philipps was no longer paying for the children's school fees at Summerhill. She wanted to go on working for Spain since the Republic was not yet defeated. Food and medical supplies were needed more than ever. A. S. Neill came to her rescue by keeping the two children for the fees of one. Accordingly, she was able to join Winifred Bates in the National Joint Committee for Spanish Relief, the umbrella organisation founded in January 1937 to co-ordinate the work of the more than 150 welfare organisations and other groups dedicated to helping the Spanish Republic. The Committee worked with a total of 850 such groups in the course of the war.⁹³ Nan and Winifred persuaded nurses and doctors who had served in Spain to speak at fund-raising meetings. Nan worked frantically, trying to block out the dawning realisation that George must be dead. 'As the days wore on and there was no news I began to know in my heart that if George had been alive he would somehow by now have managed to communicate with me though I invented all sorts of fantasies to keep alive the fragile flame of hope. (Could he be a prisoner, seriously ill or blinded and unable to write . . . ?)' The lack of certainty made it impossible to grieve. She did not know if she was a widow or a wife.

Nan's long nightmare did not end until she got formal confirmation of George's death. Nevertheless, she seems to have accepted the inevitable earlier. An obituary for George which appeared in the *Musicians' Union Report* in March, and went to press some time before, began with the words 'I have just heard from Nan Green that the last hope of George being alive has gone.'⁹⁴ She received the official letter from the Republican Government in mid-March 1939. Winifred Bates, watching her open and read the letter, deduced the contents when she saw Nan's face go grey. The death certificate was signed by Colonel Antonio Cordón García, the Under Secretary at the Republican Ministry of Defence. It read as follows: 'This is to certify that George Green, nationality English, born in London (England) and volunteer combatant under the orders of the Government of the Spanish Republic in the XV Brigade, DIED in the Ebro-Gandesa sector, on 23 September of the present year, as a result of wounds sustained in action. This certificate is issued in Barcelona on 7 December 1938.'[95] 'What I built up in the next few hours was the determination not to show that I was shattered: for the sake of the children, who must discover that I could now cope with being both father and mother to them, and for the sake of George, upon whom no blame must fall. Pride, pride in his having given his life for the cause we all held dear must be the keynote.' This restrained retrospective comment was typical of her natural reserve. Only at this stage did she make the dreaded journey to Summerhill to face having to tell the children.[96]

In retrospect, Nan's comment about George's freedom from blame also suggests a struggle with an unconscious, and understandable, resentment at being left alone. It might also be speculated that her own sense of blame for her one, and entirely comprehensible, transgression in their marriage preyed on her mind. She had, by her own account, quickly forgiven George's extramarital adventures but there is a possibility that she could not forgive her own. Her lifelong loyalty to the Communist Party suggests a longing for a context of moral certainties. The 'original sin' of her affair with William Day, the weakness that had provoked the highly critical reports drawn up by her Party bosses, sat ill with that context. Although she would remarry, it was to be, by all accounts including her own, a passionless, possibly even a loveless, marriage. There can be no doubt that throughout her subsequent life, she grieved for George. Perhaps she experienced what has been called 'survivor guilt', the feeling of survivors that their own survival was somehow undeserved. Subconsciously, they want to punish themselves for having survived. However, it is difficult to conclude that, as she threw herself ever more determinedly into her party work, she was punishing herself for the past. Her commitment to Communism had a much more positive meaning for her. Rather, like Margarita Nelken, she used work to dull the pain of loss. Nevertheless, the warm and vibrant, open and fun-loving woman remembered by those who knew her in Spain gave way to a more serious and single-minded Party militant.[97]

Some years after, in her capacity as secretary of the International Brigades Association, in reply to a letter from a Mrs Fawcett, she wrote about George's death in a notably restrained manner. Mrs Fawcett was trying to get information about her son who had fought in the British Battalion under the name William Brent. He had been killed at the Ebro but his mother had kept on hoping that he might have survived and be in a Francoist prison. In giving Mrs Fawcett the sad facts of her son's death, perhaps trying to soften the blow, Nan recounted her own experience. Apart from the certificate sent by Colonel Cordón, she knew only that George had been killed. However, she wrote to Mrs Fawcett,

> In 1944 I had a letter from a seaman who heard of my name quite by accident, telling me how my husband died; but even then this man had not seen him killed – he was repeating the story of a Spaniard who had been with my husband at the time of his death, who was captured at the moment when my husband died and never even had the opportunity to make sure that he was not still alive.[98]

Despite, or perhaps because of, her personal loss, Nan was a fervent believer, as were most returning International Brigaders, that the fight in Spain must continue. The phrase used at the time to describe solidarity activities with Spain was 'We are merely changing the front and the weapons.' For her, the cause had a deeper personal significance. She wrote to George's friend, Charles Kahn,

> He didn't particularly want adventure, and looked forward most gladly to coming back and carrying on that dreary day-to-day struggle in the Union again, with the extra enthusiasm and the extra hatred of Fascism and the extra courage he had learned out of being a soldier. Fighting the same fight as hard as ever we can is the best way of showing our pride in him.[99]

There can be little doubt that, consciously or otherwise, Nan was trying to do the work that George would have done had he lived. All over Britain, fund-raising for the Spanish Republicans continued. Returning Brigaders spoke at meetings. After the Battle of the Ebro, most of the British doctors, nurses, ambulance drivers and hospital administrators had been working in Catalonia and were evacuated before the Francoist advance on Barcelona. They toured Britain collecting money and medical supplies. Nan threw herself back into work for Spain. She spoke at meetings and throughout February 1939 was active in the discussions that led to the creation of the International Brigades Association.

A conference was held on 5 March 1939, under the chairmanship of the British Battalion's one-time commander, Bill Alexander. The IBA's declared purpose was

> To carry on in Britain the spirit and traditions of the International Brigades as front-line fighters for the defence and advance of democracy against fascism, for the rapid development of common action and purpose among all anti-fascist people by spreading the truth about the struggle of the people, Army and

Government of Republican Spain and to win all necessary support for the Spanish Republic.

Although there were those who wished to confine membership of the IBA to fighting men, Nan Green fought successfully for the male and female medical personnel to be full
members of the Association. She also insisted on the importance of veterans being able to speak in public. Amongst the
principal concerns was the fate of those British and other
Brigaders held either in Franco's prisons and of the German
and Italian anti-fascists detained in French internment camps.
She was elected as the candidate for the London Committee
of the IBA by the highest number of votes cast. However,
Nan requested that she be allowed to withdraw and act only
as the fraternal delegate of Spanish Medical Aid. Nevertheless,
she was elected Vice-Chairman of the London Area Committee of the IBA.[100]

The Brigades Association also worked tirelessly on behalf
of the defeated Republicans, both separately and as part of
the wider Aid Spain movement through the National Joint
Committee for Spanish Relief. Franco's capture of Barcelona
and the drive to the French frontier had sent streams of refugees
fleeing from reprisals. Several hundred thousand Spaniards
made the hazardous crossing of the Pyrenees. The French
Government was totally unprepared for, and unsympathetic
to, the great mass of suffering humanity that flooded in.
Regarding the refugees as savages and murderers, they herded
them into improvised concentration camps of which the largest
and most notorious were to be found on the beaches of
southern France at St Cyprien, Argelès-sur-Mer and Barcarès.
Consisting largely of barbed-wire enclosures on the sand, without basic shelter or sanitary or cooking facilities, the living
conditions were appalling. In the first six months, 14,672
Spaniards died from malnutrition, dysentery and bronchial illnesses.[101]

The National Joint Committee for Spanish Relief began to raise funds to charter a ship to transport refugees to Mexico where they had been offered asylum. Accompanied by Sir Peter Chalmers Mitchell and the Earl of Listowel, Nan made speeches to audiences across the south of England and raised considerable amounts of money. A French ship, the SS *Sinaia*, hitherto used for taking pilgrims to Mecca, was chartered through the shipping connections of Wogan Philipps. The ship had a capacity of 2,000 – a substantial number but a drop in the ocean of stateless Spaniards. Observers from the Committee had to accompany the Spaniards but to ensure that they would not be wasting the place of a refugee, they had to have other functions. Accordingly, one of the leading figures in the Aid Spain Movement, the Labour MP Leah Manning, suggested that Nan be sent given her good Spanish and her medical experience. She wrote to Irene Grant, whom she had met through their mutual friendship with Dr Douglas Jolly, 'I am rather excited about this as there will only be me and a reporter who are not refugees (and even I have to be disguised as a nurse).'[102]

Nan went to the South of France and helped to reunite families that had been divided when scattered in different camps. It was hoped that, armed with what she learned on the trip, she could then go on tour again to appeal for more funds. The ship, one of the first two to take refugees to Mexico, left the French port of Sète on 25 May 1939. For the twenty-three-day voyage, a white-coated Nan spent virtually her entire time below decks organising the feeding every three hours of the many young children on board. When they reached the Mexican port of Veracruz, they were greeted by a rapturous crowd of thousands of Mexican workers holding aloft banners in favour of the Spanish Republic. The band of the famous Fifth Regiment played and Dr Juan Negrín, the Spanish Republican Prime Minister in exile, made a speech. It was a deeply moving moment for the defeated Republican refugees. Nan passed her charges on to the local committee but journeyed with them to Mexico City. She remained in the country for some weeks observing the warmth with which the refugees were received. Her observations of the practical planning which ensured that most of the Spaniards were found appropriate jobs as soon as possible provided her with ammunition for the fund-raising tour that she had to make on her return to Britain.[103] One of those fortunate enough to make the journey on the *Sinaia*, wrote years later 'once we were on board we received a thousand kindnesses from the British committee that accompanied us, looking after us until we reached Veracruz . . . We recovered once more our faith in humanity.'[104]

When she reached Britain via the United States, in late July 1939, there was little time to organise further fund-raising for Spain before the Second World War started. The National Joint Committee for Spanish Relief had started to set up a speaking tour but after a few meetings in the Home Counties, it had to be cancelled. Moreover, her Communist faith was somewhat dented by the announcement of the Nazi-Soviet Pact on 23 August 1939. She reconciled herself with the rationalisations made by the Communist Party, that in a hostile world, the Soviet Union needed to gain breathing space to prepare for the inevitable German assault. On 3 September, when Britain declared war on Germany, Nan was halfway between London and Summerhill, taking her children, Frances and Martin, back to school. If nothing else, it confirmed the view of Nan, and of all those who had gone to fight for the Spanish Republic, that the struggle in Spain had merely been a rehearsal for the war now beginning. The opportunity to continue the fight, and possibly reverse the defeat in Spain, was welcomed by the majority of veterans. However, the Nazi-Soviet Pact made that difficult – shortly after the outbreak of war, the executive of the British Communist Party, on instructions from the Comintern, declared the war to be an imperialist squabble. The General Secretary, Harry Pollitt, was so disgusted by this that he left the executive committee and returned to his old job as a boilermaker.[105]

During the bitter debates within the Communist Party that followed, Nan was in hospital with a suspected gastric ulcer, the consequence of the malnutrition, stress and traumas suffered in Spain and after. She emerged from St George's Hospital at Hyde Park Corner, 'entirely unconvinced as to the correctness of "the Party line" but lacking the moral courage to defy it openly (just as I had earlier suppressed my loss of Christian faith before the family)'. She therefore immersed herself in the task of aid to Spain to avoid confronting her own crisis of conscience. Prior to the Nazi–Soviet pact, her life as a Communist had been morally uncomplicated. She had thrived on the conviction that the world was divided between the forces of good and the forces of evil, at a crossroads between 'democracy and peace, or fascism and war'. About Spain, she had no doubts – 'Franco was a perjured rebel, assisted by those enemies of democracy, Hitler and Mussolini, who were hurtling Europe towards war.' She expressed concisely why the Spanish Civil War is so often considered to be 'the last great cause'. 'What a fortunate group we were,' she wrote in her memoirs, 'those who went to Spain, with a clear, uncomplicated cause that has remained untarnished to this day.'[106]

Nan threw herself into the work of helping Spanish and other veterans of the Republican cause who needed jobs in England. In this she was helped by Irene Grant who had had considerable experience in rescuing Jews from Germany and Austria. Nan and her flatmate, Ena Vassie, who had been a nurse in Spain, took in a Spanish refugee. Ironically, the man billeted with them turned out to be Nan's one-time commanding officer in the 35th Division, Enrique Bassadone. She helped him to resume his medical studies in England. Just before the Second World War broke out, they were joined by Frank Ayres and his beloved Anita, from Valdeganga, since married. In fact, the flat became a staging post for many returning volunteers. Aurora Fernández, who had worked with Nan in the cave hospital at La Bisbal de Falset, arrived in London with another Spanish nurse after a period at the French concentration camp at Argelès-sur-Mer. She recalled later, 'At Nan Green's flat there were so many nurses we already knew from Spain. They gave us a wonderful welcome after a "proper meal". We were taken to a room and Nan said, "It is for you. Choose what you want." There were clothes and shoes donated by the British workers.'[107] As the Spanish refugee problem diminished, Nan moved from the National Joint Committee for Spanish Relief to the Parliamentary Committee and eventually to the British Committee for Refugees from Spain where she helped find jobs for exiled Spaniards and some International Brigaders from fascist countries. As there was ever less to do, she looked for jobs in the country where she could take the children. There was no shortage of jobs but a dearth of accommodation for a mother with children. Since Summerhill had evacuated to the relative safety of Llan Ffestiniog in North Wales, she decided to leave Frances and Martin at school and work in London.[108]

To her astonishment, Nan became Invasion Defence Officer at Poplar Town Hall, at a time when there were doubts about the employment of Communists in the war effort and the Party itself was contemplating arrangements for going underground. In fact, British Civil Defence during the Second World War made the fullest use of those with Spanish experience. Central London, which came under the Holborn and St Pancras Civil Defence, was organised and staffed by men and women who had served with Spanish Medical Aid during the Civil War.[109] Nevertheless, although she didn't know it at the time, she was under sporadic surveillance from MI5.[110] She was living in a flat in the Temple near the Thames but one day while she was visiting a friend in North London, it was destroyed in a German bomb attack, in which George's cello was one of her few possessions to survive unscathed. She moved to lodgings near Baker Street which was sufficiently near to the major railway stations of Paddington, Marylebone and Euston to be extremely vulnerable. Not long after she arrived, the house was partially destroyed by fire during an air raid while she was sheltering in the basement. These disasters were mitigated somewhat by visits to North Wales to see the children and Grandpa Green who was living in Llandudno. He had managed to get a job at the Ministry of Food which had been evacuated there and he had been appointed conductor of the Ministry's amateur orchestra. Equally cheering was the news that, as a result of Hitler's invasion on 22 June 1941, the Soviet Union was now an ally of Britain. The agonising over the Communist Party's denunciation of the 'imperialist' war came to an end. Both Churchill and the reinstated Harry Pollitt declared that Britain and the Soviet Union were united in the struggle against Hitler.[111]

Until the end of 1942, Nan continued to work at Poplar, occupied principally by the task of rehousing bombed-out families. At that point, two things happened which brought as much happiness into her life as might be considered possible in wartime. She was asked by the International Brigades Association to become its secretary in succession to Jack Brent, a veteran who had been badly wounded at the Jarama. She also went to live in Battersea with Frank and Anita Ayres and a Basque girl named Laura whom they were looking after. Joining forces with two young men from the flat upstairs, they created a kind of commune. One of them, named Ted Brake, a sheet-metal worker who had been involved in a strike at the Austin Car Company, was an enthusiast for long country walks. It was not long before Nan was renewing her fondness for energetic country rambles. They spent more time together after he got a sliver of metal in his eye in a works accident. For nearly two weeks after an operation, he was almost blind and, in the evenings, she would read to him. Shortly afterwards he asked her to marry him. Aware of the need for security for herself and the children, and, for all that George's death had affected her, not inclined to devote her life brooding, after lengthy hesitation over a couple of months, she agreed.

Nan knew that there would be little warmth in the relationship. The love of her life would always be George but she admired Ted's honesty and reliability. In both his appearance and intellect, Ted was rather nondescript – something of a Communist Party hack. Nan described her feelings towards him in terms of notable coolness: 'I was fond of Ted as one is fond of someone to whom one has done a good turn (reading when he could not see). I did not love him, and he repelled demonstrative affection which was daunting.' Her final decision to say yes was taken when she was feeling particularly vulnerable and alone. She had come home late from a political meeting outside London. Leaving the darkened station in torrential rain, she had tripped over a railing in the blackout. 'Drenched, with scraped shins, tired and hungry', she went in and informed him that she would marry him. They went to Llan Ffestiniog to tell the children who seemed to accept the news in the most blasé manner. It would not be an easy relationship for the new stepfather. Nan tried to walk the line between keeping alive the memory of George and giving the children a real father. Neither Martin nor Frances ever came to like him. One of her friends later described him as 'a man without a personality'. Perhaps for that reason, Ted's inevitable jealousy of George was even stronger. In her memoirs, she gives little impression of it being much more than a marriage of convenience to provide herself with company and the children with a stand-in father. She made a point of maintaining her independence within the marriage, paying for the children's clothes and school fees out of her own earnings. Given their differing Civil Defence duties, they rarely coincided in their flat at night. Ted was in the Home Guard as a gunner in an anti-aircraft unit in Hyde Park three nights a week and Nan as a telephonist within the Poplar air-raid warning system.[112] It is difficult to reach any other conclusion than that it was a mistake.

Nan's activities with the IBA and her job in Civil Defence kept her more than busy. The role of the Soviet Union during the battle of Stalingrad and as the Red Army swept westwards renewed her faith in Communism. 'Our admiration and love for the heroic Soviet people grew and grew.' Any doubts that lingered from the purge trials of the 1930s and the Nazi-Soviet Pact were dispelled. Not that, as she made clear later, many doubts were entertained: 'The nasty taste left behind by the "confessions" faded: they confessed, right; so there must have been something, and anyway, the Soviet Union said so.' It was the reading, in the 1970s, of Artur London's *On Trial* that enabled her fully to realise how the trials were rigged. In 1945, however, she felt only 'exhilaration at the victories of the Red Army'. That joy did not distract her from her deep concern for the persecution of the left in Spain, for the fate of the Spanish exiles as well as for the European anti-fascists who had fought in the International Brigades and been forced into exile. The IBA, along with the British Trade Unions, continued to raise funds for them and seek the aid of members of parliament and other public figures. Nan was tireless, editing and physically producing a monthly magazine, *Spain Today*. She was also involved in translating and reproducing a regular information bulletin on the anti-Franco struggle that was issued by the Spanish club for exiles in London.[113]

Nan rejoiced at Labour's victory in the elections of the summer of 1945.

> There we were in the post-war world, a world filled with joy and relief at the defeat of fascism, but with no time to rest or to stop to mourn: the task all over Europe was to rebuild, to repair the wanton, senseless,

beastly damage that had been done to the work of man's hands, to economies, to agriculture and above all to men and women, to families, to homeless people.[114]

Her contribution to this process consisted of her work for Spain and Spanish refugees through the International Brigades Association. It was hard work. She wrote to Aileen Palmer (her Australian predecessor as secretary to Len Crome) 'We are in a whirl of activity now, trying to revive some of the feeling of what is called "the old Spain days". The so general feeling for Spanish freedom exists but it isn't mobilised.' As acting secretary, the job of trying to mobilise interest fell to her and, in consequence, 'I hardly know who I am by the end of the day'. She wrote to a Swedish comrade, 'There is some tendency here among our labour movement to take Spain for granted as it were, and to think that because everyone is in favour of breaking relations with Franco and freedom for the Spanish people, that nothing needs to be done.'[115] She and Ted now lived in a flat in Shipley House on the Larkhall Estate in Clapham where they organised political discussion groups among the residents. Her children were finally back at home and attending Battersea Polytechnic. The work of the IBA was an uphill struggle. The atmosphere of the Cold War quickly doused any hopes of the great powers turning on Franco.

In late 1945, the Polish Government invited the IBA to send a delegation to a ceremony for Polish International Brigaders. The Polish volunteers against fascism in Spain had been punished by the Pilsudski regime by being stripped of their nationality. Now they were to have it ceremonially restored and be decorated for their service in the anti-fascist struggle. As secretary of the IBA, Nan was selected, along with the Scottish veteran, Tom Murray, to travel to Warsaw. She was horrified by the destruction that she saw, with people living in the rubble from which the dead had yet to be retrieved.

She was also devastated by a visit to Auschwitz. Despite the horrors, she was greatly inspired to be reunited with many Polish comrades from the International Brigades and wrote afterwards to Aileen Palmer that the experience had been 'terrific'. The atmosphere in Poland reminded her 'of the tales told by delegates who went to the new Soviet Union in 1923 or so, who found impoverished conditions, destruction, hunger and so on but such an air of enthusiasm, energy and confidence that it made up for all the rest. It was like Madrid, if that explains it better.'[116] She left Poland on 24 November on a plane carrying some of the IB delegates from Western Europe. It landed in Berlin where bad weather forced a two-day stopover. After setting off for Paris on 26 November, one of the aircraft's engines caught fire and they had to make an emergency landing at an airfield near Magdeburg in the Soviet-occupied zone of Germany. At the time, the Red Army had only just begun removing the mines left by the Germans. It took two days for the necessary repairs and refuelling, but a further twelve days before the Soviet bureaucracy permitted them to leave and continue their journey. During the stay, in the Red Army barracks, she was shocked by the primitive behaviour of the Russian conscripts – 'extremely uncouth peasant types' incapable of using the German lavatories and bent on raping the women – but entranced by the exquisite courtesy of the officers.[117]

When she finally reached Paris, she went on to Toulouse where she arrived too late to attend the plenary session of the Central Committee of the Spanish Communist Party celebrated in the Salle Gaumont in Toulouse on 5 December 1945. To have been invited to that historic gathering was an enormous privilege and was a tribute both to her work with the IBA, her role during the Civil War and the fact that she was one of the few Party members available to go who spoke excellent Spanish. It was the first time since 23 May 1938 that the Spanish Party had been able to hold a plenum of the

Central Committee. The Party's Secretary-General, Dolores Ibárruri, Pasionaria, had returned from her Russian exile to take charge of the Party organisation in France in the conviction that the fall of Franco was imminent. At the plenum, the Party adopted a policy of promoting guerrilla war in the hope of sparking off a wider popular struggle to take advantage of the seeming international hostility to the regime. It was a great honour that Nan was invited as one of the foreign delegates – something that suggested that her work for the International Brigades Association had given her greater prominence within the British Communist Party than might be deduced from the rather oblique account in her memoirs. She had also been invited to the celebrations on 9 December of Dolores Ibárruri's fiftieth birthday. Although she arrived on the day after, she was able to give Pasionaria a beautiful hand-printed headscarf that she had brought from Mexico. She spent time with Dolores and with other Spanish Communist leaders including Santiago Carrillo in the freezing offices in which they worked in overcoats and wearing gloves. Enrique Líster, the politburo member in charge of the operations, offered to take Nan over the border to a guerrilla base. Although he guaranteed her safety, she felt that she had already been away too long and set off back to London where, after a bitterly cold journey, she arrived on 18 December.[118]

Nan's work with the IBA was focused ever more on efforts to save the lives and liberty of members of the anti-Franco opposition. Opposition to the regime was still deemed to be military rebellion and was tried by court martial. The IBA endeavoured to raise money in order to send British lawyers and interpreters to the trials as observers. Their presence at least served to inhibit some of the more appalling practices of trials in which large numbers of men were often accused, tried and sentenced collectively. In October 1946, Nan herself went into Spain and visited the women's prison at Ventas near the Madrid bullring. It was notorious for considerable overcrowding, deficient food, children and babies detained with the prisoners. Of the thousand or so prisoners, half were detained for political reasons. These women were often subjected to beatings and torture. Three women, a schoolteacher, Isabel Sanz Toledano, Consuelo Alonso, a typist, and María Teresa Toral, a scientist, had given food and clothing for prisoners. In consequence, they had been accused of creating an organisation to help political prisoners. The Labour Member of Parliament, Leah Manning, together with the Roman Catholic secretary of the Save the Children Fund, Monica Whately, decided to go and see the conditions in which they were held. Leah Manning, who had been a keen observer of events in Spain since the repression that followed the Asturian rising of October 1935, was testing Spanish Government declarations that there was nothing to hide about the prison regime.[119]

Nan was invited to be their interpreter. The Spanish security services would have prevented her receiving a visa had they known of her service for the Republic in the International Brigades. She avoided their scrutiny by travelling as Mrs Brake. Aurora Fernández wrote to her from Czechoslovakia:

> It was a great thrill to learn Mrs Brake is going to Spain or is probably over there by the time you get this. Of course, she is one of the best qualified to do it, not only for her magnificent record of continuing work towards Spain but because she is a very good speaker and possesses a lovely personality and all this goes a long way in the making of an able envoy. Please don't take this as an insult to her modesty. I mean every word of it; not without a certain nostalgia and envy that she is doing far more than me, a Spaniard.[120]

Nan was deeply affected by the return to Madrid. 'My heart became a clenched fist and began to hammer at my chest as we drove from the airport to the city.' She had known the

Spanish capital during the Civil War where, in shared austerity and collective hope, the besieged population had fought off Franco's columns. Now, she was shocked by the swastikas daubed on walls and by the wild inequalities of Franco's Spain, the women and children of the defeated begging for scraps while the well-dressed middle class frequented spectacularly expensive shops, restaurants and nightclubs. 'People are living in caves just outside Madrid. They are living in the basements of bombed-out buildings and even in the trenches which still exist around the Casa del Campo. And the beggars are begging for food, not money, while the rich eat every night meals which would make your eyes open wide, at prices which would stagger you.' Armed soldiers, Civil Guards and police patrolled the streets. The delegation met a member of the Socialist resistance, who said, 'We feel we have been abandoned by British democracy.' Nan felt 'bloody awful' when she had to translate Leah Manning's reply that Ernest Bevin was 'waiting for a sign from the Spanish people' and the Spaniard snapped, 'How can a man make a sign when he is tied hand and foot?' To the chagrin of the Spanish Embassy, Nan wrote an article on prison conditions on her return to Britain.[121]

Nan's home remained an open house for ex-International Brigaders. She maintained her faith in the cause of the Spanish Republic but in the Cold War that meant combating the efforts of those who wanted to defame it.

> The Spanish cause which was still my main responsibility within the Party, remained (and remains) untarnished despite the 'god-that-failed' desertion of those intellectuals who found that they could not sustain conviction and spent subsequent years justifying their weakness. And, later, the far Left all-or-nothingers who wrote books, articles, etc. on the 'betrayal' of the Spanish revolution by the Communist Party of Spain

and the USSR for having striven to build and maintain the Popular Front.

For her, Arthur Koestler, like George Orwell and others who reneged on their erstwhile support for the Spanish Republic, was 'one of the damned'.[122]

What Nan sensed, but could not know, was that an operation was being mounted by the CIA to promote the non-communist left as part of a cultural offensive – 'the theoretical foundation of the Agency's political operations against Communism over the next two decades'. Given that the struggle of the Spanish Republic remained a jewel in the Communist crown, a deliberate attempt was being mounted to besmirch it. A key element within that cultural war was the compilation of the collective book, *The God that Failed*. Inspired by Arthur Koestler, and edited by Richard Crossman, it was conceived as an operation of psychological warfare. In the book, six intellectuals confessed their Communist past and how they had been betrayed. Three of them, Arthur Koestler, Stephen Spender and Louis Fischer, had been in Spain.[123] If Nan read Spender's contribution, she can only have been appalled by what he had to say about the International Brigades. Amongst other things, he gave credence to the bizarre view of the British Conservative, Sir Arthur Bryant, that 'the Spaniards on either side hated the interventionists that rushed in to help them even more than they hated their Spanish opponents'. At least Spender, in his memoirs, published shortly afterwards, did have the grace to stand by the laudatory assessment of George Green that he had made in 1937.[124]

Alongside her commitment to Spain, Nan was also involved in the World Peace Movement, an organisation sponsored by the Soviet Union. She worked with the British Peace Committee, both collecting signatures for a petition against the atomic bomb and organising a world conference to be held in Sheffield. After a Herculean effort, in arranging everything from accommodation for the delegates, to traffic signposting throughout the city, to catering for the various ethnic groups represented, the Congress had to be cancelled because the Labour Government began to prevent delegates entering the country. It was shifted to Warsaw although, before the complex task of transferring it began, the meeting was symbolically opened for one day. Nan had the pleasure of greeting Pablo Picasso who had reached Sheffield. His speech was short: 'My father was a painter of animals and birds and as I grew up he let me help in painting the legs of birds. How proud he would be to know that my two modest doves have circled the world.'[125]

At around the same time, she began to have tiny splinters of doubt about her Communist faith. In retrospect, unconsciously echoing one of George's letters, she wrote of 'unlearning blind faith' in 'fits and starts until 1953'. She was deeply perplexed by the issue of the so-called 'Russian brides'. She could not understand why the Soviet Union would not let Russian women who had married British and foreigners during the Second World War accompany their husbands back to their home countries. Even more distressing because it involved her personally was an issue that arose out of the Soviet Union's hostility to Tito's regime in Yugoslavia. She was ordered to disband a broad-front Committee of Friends of Yugoslavia that was largely run by its Communist members. With regret, she obeyed, persuading herself that this was merely a temporary response to a temporary disagreement within the committee. Her friend Leah Manning 'saw through me with unerring clarity' and told her that she was being 'disingenuous'. It was not until many years later, with typical rectitude, she felt obliged to write to Leah Manning to acknowledge that she had been dishonest. At the time, whatever her misgivings, she kept them to herself. She was able to cling on to her Communist convictions because she was involved in such self-evidently worthwhile work in the peace movement. After the success of the World Peace Council Congress in Warsaw, Nan was appointed organiser of the London Peace Council. Her role at the IBA was taken over by Alec Digges.

As a result of this, in 1952 she ended up going to China. This was because the Chinese Communist Party had asked the British Communist Party (CPGB) to provide technical helpers for a Peace Congress of the Asian and Pacific Regions. She travelled through the Soviet Union and reached Beijing where she was utterly entranced by the sights, the smells and, above all, by the people. The Chinese authorities were sufficiently impressed by her work to request her to return to help create a permanent Peace Centre in Beijing.[126] Since Martin was now doing his National Service in the army and Frances by now married, she was inclined to accept. She was, in any case, keen to get out of the conflictive atmosphere of the London Peace Council. The implications of leaving her husband are brushed over with striking rapidity in memoirs that are marked throughout by their cursory coverage of emotional issues – especially where Ted Brake is concerned. Her only comment was, 'Ted would not say yes or no.' In the event, he stayed in London at his job in the sheet-metal works. However, when she got back to China, there was no real job for her and she spent most of 1953 doing sporadic translating work.

When she finally gave up hope of the work in Beijing materialising, she returned to London only to discover that she was in demand back in China to work on English and Spanish-language publications of the Foreign Languages Press. She did not want to live alone in China and wanted to try and salvage a marriage that was dying of the attrition of boredom. Accordingly, she had made it clear that she would not go back unless Ted could go with her. Having long since decided that he did not want to spend the rest of his life as a sheet-metal worker, he eventually agreed to accompany her. In China, he found a new career, editing in Beijing the English-language journal of the All-China Federation of Trade Unions. After a battle for Nan's services between two organisations, she worked with the journal *China Reconstructs*. Now aged forty-eight, she achieved the near impossible and learned the language well, travelled widely and became an enthusiast for the way in which the Chinese revolution had massively improved living standards for ordinary people.[127] She was still there in 1956 when the Communist world was shaken by Nikita Khruschev's revelations of the crimes of Stalin in his speech to the 20th Congress of the Communist Party of the Soviet Union. For Nan, like so many other Communists, it provoked a devastating re-examination of everything that she had believed and sustained her in her political activism. 'For me, but slowly, slowly, it was like the lifting of a stone from my heart.' Another blow to her faith in the Communist vision came on a journey far to the northwest. When she reached the Sino-Soviet border, she was horrified to see armed sentries facing each other in manifest hostility.[128]

In 1958, she had accumulated enough funds to permit a visit to Mauritius where her daughter Frances lived with her Mauritian husband Noel and their three children. At the invitation of the anti-apartheid campaigner, Cecil Williams, the journey was also to include a further trip on to South Africa. She travelled in stages to Mauritius, with stops at Rangoon, Calcutta, Bombay, Karachi, Aden, Nairobi, Madagascar and Reunion. 'Calcutta and Bombay were shattering. I had never seen such poverty, misery and suffering. The pavements were thronged by camping people, gathered round stand-pipes for access to water: people lay sleeping – alive or dead?' She remembered 'the agony of the dark bony hands which stretched into the car windows whenever the car stopped at traffic lights, accompanied by soft cries for charity'.[129] In Mauritius, as photographic evidence shows, she was 'much in demand in the Chinese community'. That same evidence reveals that, at fifty-five, Nan was still recognisable as the trim crop-haired brunette who had worked in Spain twenty years earlier – still a remarkably attractive woman. In January 1959, she went to Johannesburg and began a clandestine tour. She addressed twenty-seven meetings in two weeks, all arranged with astonishing efficiency under the noses of the secret police. She spoke in the townships and in factories and managed to attend a trial in Pretoria. She met the Chairman of the African National Congress, Chief Albert Lutuli, Joe Slovo of the South African Communist Party, Winnie Mandela and many anti-apartheid militants. It was a deeply moving experience for her. She wrote later: 'The humiliation of having to use whites-only doors, lifts, post-office counters and park benches burnt me up. But with the help of our friends I was able to cock a final snook at the government.' She gave an interview to the progressive *Rand Daily Mail* on condition that it was not published until after she was safely out of the country. The authorities were furious when an article appeared beginning 'A British Communist woman has been touring South Africa.' She returned to Mauritius and spent time with Frances and her family.[130]

On her return to Beijing, Nan discovered that she had hepatitis. She was ill for nearly two years. Her convalescence gave her time to reflect on the growing Sino-Soviet conflict. Chinese admiration for the Russian Revolution was now giving way to a growing hostility to all things Russian. She was nonplussed by the scale of the anti-Soviet propaganda that became the norm. An amazingly less dramatic crisis occupied her too. Although she remained friends with Ted Brake, their marriage had never been especially close and now their relationship was nearing its end. He was already talking about a return to London. While she was hesitating about whether to stay or go, pressure was put on her to renounce the pro-Soviet CPGB and take Chinese nationality. This decided her to return home. She may have had doubts about the international Communist movement, but she was not prepared to renounce everything that underpinned her past. In the event, she went to London first and Ted stayed in China for another year. When he finally returned to England, they separated and were eventually divorced in 1973.

On her return from China at the end of 1960, she resumed her job as secretary of the International Brigades Association and she also began to work in an editorial capacity with the Communist Party publishing house, Lawrence & Wishart. There she prepared manuscripts for publication and also did some translation. In 1963, she translated a book by two Spanish Communists, José Sandoval and Manuel Azcárate, *986 días de lucha* which was published in Britain as *Spain 1936–1939* (London: Lawrence & Wishart, 1963). In 1962, during the great strike wave in the mining valleys of Asturias, she returned to Spain to act as interpreter to a delegation of the National Union of Mineworkers that gave financial aid to the strikers. The IBA was active in this period raising money for observers to be sent to attend the trials of political prisoners threatened with the death sentence, most notably Julián Grimau and Marcos Ana.[131] Also in late 1963 and early 1964, Nan collected material and money for an exhibition on the Spanish Civil War under the title Spain Fights for Freedom. Initially intended to be small, mobile and portable, it became a large-scale enterprise given the wealth of photographs, posters, documents and other relics with which the IBA was inundated.[132]

Now a grey-haired, but trim as ever, sixty-eight year-old, in 1972, she retired from Lawrence and Wishart and increasingly her thoughts turned back to Spain. In 1970, she had published a substantial article in the Communist Party's theoretical journal. Vividly written, it was a lucid account of the British role in the Spanish Civil War from a Communist point of view.[133] On 15 May 1974, Nan Green was appointed Caballero de la Orden de la Lealtad a la República Española by the President of the Republic in exile.[134] In 1976, the History Group of the Communist Party commissioned her to write, with Alonso Elliott, the pamphlet *Spain against Fascism 1936–39. Some Questions Answered.*[135] Her work with the IBA went on until the very end. The events of Czechoslovakia in 1968 and the Soviet invasion of Afghanistan were elements that further undermined her 'blind faith' but she never broke with the British Communist Party. Indeed, she never gave any public indication of her doubts. She devoted considerable time to the initial cataloguing of the considerable archive materials of the British Battalion and of the IBA.[136] In a letter written in 1971 she commented: 'I have now got over 1,000 items catalogued for the archive but there are still cupboards full to be done and I've had to stop for the moment because my granddaughter who is living with me for the present has got a new baby (making me a great-grandmother).'[137] Eventually donated to the Marx Memorial Library, where the full indexing was done by Tony Atienza, those well-ordered files and documents are, in a real sense, her monument – a testimony both to her commitment to the cause of the Spanish Republicans and also to her organisational skills and capacity for hard work.

In her later years, she began to write memoirs and give interviews about her life. She wrote that she had 'unlearned blind faith', a reference to the toll taken on her convictions by the Nazi-Soviet Pact, the Stalinist purges, the Sino-Soviet conflict and other revelations about the Soviet system. However, her basic commitment to the Communist ideal never wavered and she never lost her faith in the anti-fascist struggle in Spain. She had spent her life cherishing the memory of George. Now she talked much more openly about him and her belief that his death was justified by the cause for which they both fought. In August 1976, she gave a long interview.

I've never felt able to be sorry for him because he was doing the right thing. We all feel that. We had this privilege of being . . . right straight down the high road of history in the right cause. And there hasn't been anything quite like it since, so flawless and so black and white and so good and so wholesome. And he was doing that. And he was sure that we would win. And he was sure that the French were going to send the things over. And he was with the battalion. That's how he died. I'm sorry he didn't see the children. I think about that still when I see the grandchildren. I'm sorry for myself because I've suffered a great deal of loneliness for him. But I can't feel sorry for him. I can't feel sorry for any of them because they died in the confidence that it was going to be . . . you know, that they were doing the right thing and it was going to save the world from war.[138]

Throughout her life, she had tried to be a good Communist and a good friend to those around her. She was a dedicated and hard worker in whatever she did. Those who worked with her remembered her as always composed, always serene, always helpful, although, as arthritis took its toll, she could be rather prickly. In the late 1960s, she had broken one of her hips. It was not set properly and, in consequence, one of her legs was left shorter than the other. Thereafter, she was in great discomfort. Typically she refused to take painkillers. In consequence, she was a little more short-tempered than before. In 1973, she wrote a sharp letter to Fredericka Martin, who was compiling information on the American contribution to the International Brigades medical services. After a series of warm and helpful letters in response to the queries of her American comrade, the final one in the series was brusque and territorial: 'Your list of English nurses is both incomplete and incorrect. We sent 44 nurses, 120 ambulance drivers and 17 or more doctors to Spain. But as I understand you are writing a history of the *American* medical service, I can't see what you want with English ones. We'll be writing our own

history in due course.' It ended 'Yours sincerely, Nan Green',
whereas she had usually ended its predecessors with '¡Salud!'
or some other reference to Spain, and just 'Nan'.[139]

There can be little doubt that her work in China, in the
peace movement and in the IBA was always inspired by what
had happened in Spain and by memories of George. Her time
in Spain and her love for George were the peaks in a full life.
In 1978, she told the journalist Judith Cook,

> I like to think he died full of confidence. I think it
> was a good way to die. He believed it must come
> right. He was doing what he knew he had to do and
> he believed the Republic would be victorious. So I've
> not felt sorry for him as a young man, dying at the
> age of thirty-four, doing what he wanted and feeling
> that they were bound to win. So there's a young man
> forever confident. I'll never regret it. As for George
> – well, he died like a bird who dies in flight – it just
> keeps on flying.[140]

Nan herself had increasing difficulty in walking and suffered
from poor circulation related to smoking. She caught pneumonia and died aged seventy-nine on 6 April 1984.[141] In 1986,
her son Martin took her ashes to Spain and scattered them
near the position where her husband had been killed.

MERCEDES
SANZ-BACHILLER

MERCEDES
SANZ-BACHILLER

So Easy to Judge

I N THE CASTILIAN CATHEDRAL CITY of Valladolid, on 17 July 1936, a young mother of three children celebrated her twenty-fifth birthday. Mercedes Sanz-Bachiller had many reasons to be happy. She was in love with her husband, a handsome virile man who loved her passionately in return. Her three children, two daughters aged four and two, and one year-old baby son, were healthy and strong, and she was four months pregnant again. She was economically secure, owning some fertile agricultural land near the prosperous village of Montemayor, in the province of Valladolid. However, her birthday was not a joyous occasion. Anxiety pervaded her home. Her husband was Onésimo Redondo, one of the principal figures of Spanish fascism, and he had been imprisoned four months earlier for his political activities. Now, he was in the jail at Ávila, nearly eighty miles (125 kilometres) away, and she feared for his safety. Four nights earlier, on 13 July, the monarchist leader, José Calvo Sotelo, had been murdered by a squad of Republican Assault Guards on a revenge mission for the shooting of a comrade by Falangist gunmen.

It was hardly surprising then that Mercedes Sanz-Bachiller should be eaten up with worry about the fate of her husband. Moreover, the streets outside her home pulsed with fear. After months of rising political violence in the city, both left and right were anticipating a military uprising and bloodshed on the streets. The right in Valladolid was confident since important elements of the Army, the Civil Guard and the Assault Guards were implicated in the local preparations for the coup.[1] There was electric tension as both sides in the city awaited the outbreak of violence. By the evening of 17 July, news was filtering through that garrisons had rebelled in Spanish Morocco. By the following day, the right was in control in Valladolid and the main provincial capitals of Old Castile. In Ávila, Onésimo Redondo was released and he raced home to Valladolid, desperate to see his wife and children. After a passionate reunion with Mercedes, he resumed command of the local Falange. Five days later, he was dead, killed near the front, at the village of Labajos far to the north of Madrid. When she heard the news, brutally conveyed in a telephone call from military headquarters, Mercedes Sanz-Bachiller collapsed. She lost her baby and her life was in tatters.

Six months later, Mercedes Sanz-Bachiller would be one of the two most important women in the rebel zone of war-torn Spain. She was at the head of a massive welfare organisation, which she had created literally out of nothing. She oversaw a huge daily logistical operation feeding hundreds of thousands of people and had many thousands of women under her orders. The woman whose strength of character, will-power and dynamism had enabled her to recover from the shock of bereavement and launch herself from obscurity to political pre-eminence was born on 17 July 1911 in Madrid. Her parents were from Valladolid and happened by chance to be passing through the capital when her mother went into labour. Both her parents came from Montemayor, to the southeast of Valladolid. Mercedes Bachiller Fernández came from a comfortable rural family of the provincial bourgeoisie that possessed numerous farms and estates. From her mother, Mercedes Sanz-Bachiller inherited a sense of the crucial importance of the land. Her father, Moisés Sanz Izquierdo, was not from a wealthy family and had no more than the most basic education. However, he was a man of great intelligence and drive. He had been to Latin America three times on business. Mercedes Sanz-Bachiller claims that it was he who discovered roast chicory as a coffee substitute.[2]

Despite the advantages enjoyed by her parents, Mercedes would have a harsh and lonely childhood. They had had two previous children but both had died in infancy. Moreover, the marriage did not long survive Mercedes's birth. Two years after giving birth to her daughter, the couple separated. Moisés had clashed with his wife because of her reluctance to sell any of her property to invest in his various business schemes. Mercedes Bachiller returned home to her widowed mother's house in Montemayor and broke off all relations with her husband and his family. According to Mercedes Sanz-Bachiller, her mother was a strong-minded and inflexible woman. To take the initiative in separating from her husband in the fervently Catholic area of northern Castille was an indication of her fierce independence. The consequence for Mercedes was that she was brought up in the oppressive atmosphere of her grandmother's house. The house was shared by her mother and one of her two sisters, who was subnormal and required constant vigilance. According to Mercedes Sanz-Bachiller, her aunt was 'abnormal, illiterate, aggressive and always after men. Since workers and farm labourers came into the house, she would chase after them'. The fear of scandal was such that visitors were not made welcome. Mercedes was brought up by two widows, her mother and her grandmother, and her bizarre aunt in 'what was a gloomy household'. After separating from her mother, her father died in 1914 before he was forty and when Mercedes was barely three. She saw her father only twice, once when she was three years old and again when he was laid out in his coffin.[3]

Montemayor was an unusually prosperous village. As a

consequence of the common ownership of some land rich in resin-producing pines, the local school was free to the villagers and of a high standard. The pharmacy was also free for the inhabitants who, thanks to the common lands, enjoyed a small-scale social security system within a mini-welfare state. Nevertheless, Mercedes's mother was intensely sensitive to social differences and thus never allowed her daughter to play with other children from the village. Mercedes went to the village school until the age of nine but was allowed no local friends. She longed to play with the other children and would sneak out to play with the son and daughter of a neighbouring smallholder who rented land from the Bachiller family. Her mother was unyieldingly strict and not given to any verbal or physical demonstrations of affection. Mercedes Bachiller rarely hugged or cuddled her daughter. Despite their affluence, she never bought her toys or dolls or what she considered to be frivolously pretty clothes. On the other hand, to mark the differences from the village children, Mercedes was the only one in the village made to wear a hat to Sunday mass. Perhaps because of the loss of two earlier babies, Mercedes Bachiller Fernández had only one preoccupation regarding her daughter – that she would grow up strong and independent. She was particularly concerned to ensure that she ate well. Living on a wealthy estate, there was never any shortage of eggs, chicken, lamb, cheese and vegetables. Brought up in a high altitude, surrounded by pine forests, the young Mercedes grew strong. Her mother was also insistent – for health reasons rather than as a holiday – that every year the young Mercedes spent time on the coast at the fashionable resorts of Santander or San Sebastián in order to swim. The consequence was the extraordinary physical robustness that she was to enjoy throughout her life.[4]

When Mercedes was nine, she was sent to a boarding school in Valladolid – the College of the French Dominican Nuns. It was a relatively progressive school and, in comparison with the narrow rigidity of her mother, represented a liberation. Mercedes Bachiller was so tough that she used to leave her daughter in the boarding school at Christmas. Mercedes Bachiller Fernández died in 1925 when Mercedes Sanz-Bachiller was fourteen. She felt little sense of loss. 'When my mother died, I was fourteen and had a guardian. The very first thing that I did was to buy a doll.' It was a small harbinger of the future, an act of independence, yet far from being subversive. Aged fourteen, Mercedes was alone in the enormous house in which she had been brought up. Her grandmother was dead and, such was her mother's relationship with her aunts that as guardian for Mercedes, she had chosen a cousin, a doctor, Aurelio Bachiller. Her guardian, who effectively administered her substantial inheritance – principally land – was her only family. He looked after her property honestly but was so coldly distant that he never once invited her to his house. From the rents on her land, he paid her school fees, gave her a small allowance and invested the rest. She remained at the French College in Valladolid until 1928. At that point she wanted to transfer to the school run in Paris by the same order of nuns. She sought legal permission to administer her own patrimony and her guardian thought that she was sufficiently mature to grant her wish. After a pleasant year in Paris, Mercedes returned and was allowed to live in rooms within her old College in Valladolid. In retrospect, she felt that the dark seclusion of her childhood had left her with a positive determination to get the most out of life.[5]

In 1929, the now eighteen-year-old Mercedes met the man who would effectively mark out the rest of her life – Onésimo Redondo Ortega, a future leader of the Spanish fascist movement. Onésimo Redondo was born on 16 February 1905 in Quintanilla de Abajo, a small but prosperous village in the province of Valladolid. Brought up in a deeply Catholic family, Onésimo was a brilliant student who, despite his modest background, won the scholarships which enabled him to climb the educational ladder. After a conventional rural schooling, he went on to secondary school in the provincial capital. In 1923, he took competitive civil-service examinations for the Ministry of Finance and accepted a posting in Salamanca in order that he could also study law at the University there. There, through his confessor, Father Enrique Herrera Oria, he entered into contact with the Asociación Católica Nacional de Propagandistas. Founded by Enrique's brother, Ángel, the ACNP was an elite Jesuit-influenced organisation of about five hundred prominent and talented Catholic rightists that endeavoured to exercise influence in the press, the judiciary and the professions. During this period, the sincerely pious Onésimo was an enthusiast for the dictatorship of General Miguel Primo de Rivera. After obtaining his degree in law, he returned to Valladolid in early 1926 to prepare for the competitive examinations to join the elite Corps of State Lawyers. He was unsuccessful when he presented himself the first time in 1927 and shortly afterwards he took a job teaching Spanish in the college of commerce at the University of Mannheim.[6] During the 1927–1928 academic year in Germany, he developed an admiration for the Catholic Zentrum party about which he corresponded with Ángel Herrera Oria, the founder of the ACNP. He later told Mercedes that he had been shocked by the sexual and social freedom of the Weimar Republic. For that reason, despite a deep-seated hostility to the application to Spain of foreign models, he was interested by the declared aim of the nascent Nazi Party to reimpose traditional values.[7]

On his return from Germany in the autumn of 1928, Onésimo Redondo began to work as administrator and legal adviser of the recently founded small Syndicate of Sugar-Beet Producers of Old Castille. The central problem facing the growers was the concentration in very few hands of facilities for sugar-refining. Onésimo successfully began a major reorganisation of a previously inactive union, recruiting new members through propaganda tours and began the process of collecting funds for the union to build its own refinery. Onésimo Redondo's elder brother, Andrés, lived in the same building as the president of the beet-growers union, Millán Alonso de Las Heras. One of Mercedes's closest friends was Don Millán's daughter, Sarita Alonso Pimenter. One day, 11 June 1930, Mercedes was going up in the lift with Don Millán and they coincided with the twenty-five-year-old Onésimo. With dark curly hair, penetrating eyes and an engaging smile, he was a handsome man. The petite, rosy-cheeked Mercedes entranced him and, on the following day, he eagerly interrogated Don Millán as to her identity. 'Come and have coffee after lunch tomorrow and I'll introduce you,' replied his boss. Having been introduced the next day, Onésimo, a daily communicant, produced a killer chat-up line: 'Which mass do you usually go to?' 'Nine o'clock at the Jesuit Church,' she replied without a trace of coyness. 'Well, I'll see you there.' On the following day, after mass, since they had both fasted before communion, he had the perfect excuse to invite her to a café for breakfast. They met again on the third day and went for a long walk in the gardens known as the Campo Grande. He was already dazzled by her charming directness and independence. Without preamble, he asked her if she wanted to marry him and, equally swiftly, she said yes. 'I said yes, suddenly, without thinking. I had no house or home, and he was a very attractive man.' Her principal doubt concerned his name: 'the word Onésimo gave me the creeps.' 'I said to myself I'm saying yes because there'll be plenty of time to say no.' Later he told her that, if she had turned him down, his pride would never have permitted him to ask her again.[8]

It was typical of Mercedes's impetuous nature but it was also an instinctive response that she never regretted. Their eight months of courtship was carried out in large part by letter since Onésimo was busy travelling in an effort to build up the Beet-Growers' Union. He wrote extremely romantic letters that quickly turned her few doubts into passionate love.

They married on 12 February 1931 in the chapel of the Arch-
bishop's Palace in Valladolid. They spent their wedding night
and the first few days of their honeymoon in Madrid before
setting off on a planned tour of Andalusia. However, after
a couple of days, in Seville, Onésimo received a telegram
summoning him back to Valladolid to act as lawyer for his
father in a civil case.[9] During the campaign for the municipal
elections of 12 April 1931, which were universally regarded
as a referendum on the fate of King Alfonso XIII, Onésimo
campaigned on behalf of the monarchist candidates in Valladolid. The results showed that a majority of Spaniards did not
forgive the King his betrayal of the constitution in accepting
the military dictatorship in 1923. The sweeping victory for
Republican candidates saw the royal family abandon Spain and
the King head south, accompanied by his cousin Alfonso de
Orléans Borbón. When the Queen, Victoria Eugenia, travelling north by train, passed through Valladolid, Onésimo
Redondo was amongst those who went to pay their respects.[10]

From the very first, Mercedes took an interest in the political
activities of her husband. As a Catholic and a landowner, it
seemed natural to her that, in the early days of the Republic,
Onésimo should be linked to Acción Nacional (later Acción
Popular), the Catholic political group founded on 26 April by
Ángel Herrera and principally supported by Castilian farmers.
On 5 May 1931, he created the provincial organisation in
Valladolid and headed its propaganda campaign for the parliamentary elections of 28 June 1931. On 13 June, Onésimo
founded in Valladolid the fortnightly, and later weekly, anti-
Republican newspaper *Libertad*. It was launched with money
donated by a conservative upper middle-class lady of the city,
but it was soon facing financial difficulty. Among the paper's
contributors was a seventeen-year-old disciple of Onésimo
Redondo, the baby-faced Javier Martínez de Bedoya, who
would eventually become Mercedes Sanz-Bachiller's second
husband. The highly intelligent Martínez de Bedoya was the

son of a notary from Guernica and had studied law at the University of Valladolid. He had met Onésimo Redondo at a meeting of the Casa Social Católica in Valladolid on 16 April 1931, two days after the foundation of the Second Republic. They became close friends. After the elections had given a huge majority to the Republican-Socialist coalition, Onésimo severed his formal ties with Acción Nacional. On 9 August, along with his older brother Andrés and a medical student, Jesús Ercilla, Onésimo founded the Juntas Castellanas de Actuación Hispánica (the Castilian Hispanic Action Groups). The bulk of the new organisation's militants followed him from the Valladolid branch of Acción Nacional, which was left virtually without members.[11]

Onésimo had little difficulty enthusing Mercedes with his quest for a more radical line than that offered by the conservative Catholicism of Acción Nacional. His combination of a rhetoric of social justice with a fiery commitment to traditional values appealed to her. After all, her experience in Montemayor — far from representative though it was — seemed to suggest that a rural community could achieve a collective prosperity without conflictive expropriations. On 10 August, *Libertad* published a fiery proclamation by Onésimo. It revealed his passionate commitment to the traditional rural values of Old Castile, to social justice and to violence. He wrote:

> The historic moment, young countrymen, obliges us to take up arms. May we know how to use them in defence of what is ours and not at the service of politicians. Out of Castille may the voice of racial good sense emerge and impose itself upon the great chaos of the moment: let it use its unifying force to establish justice and order in the new Spain.

His official biography, published anonymously but written by Javier Martínez de Bedoya, describes the article as the bugle call that attracted members to the new organisation. Its advocacy of violence set the tone for the organisation.[12] Certainly, it brought an element of brutal confrontation to a city previously notable for the tranquillity of its labour relations.[13] The new recruits quickly armed themselves for street fights with the predominantly Socialist working class of Valladolid: 'On the outskirts of the Puente Mayor (across the River Pisuerga) bulls' pizzles were bought in order to assert our permanent faith in violence.' The JCAH's meetings were held in virtual clandestinity and, as they could afford to do so, they began to buy pistols. Over time, Onésimo Redondo's advocacy of violence would become even more strident.

Given the numerical weakness of the JCAH, Onésimo was also quick to seek links with similar groups. Accordingly, his gaze fell upon the first overtly fascist group in Spain, the miniscule *La Conquista del Estado* (the Conquest of the State) founded in February 1931 in Madrid by Ramiro Ledesma Ramos, a post office functionary from Zamora and enthusiastic disseminator of German philosophy.[14] In the first number of *Libertad*, Onésimo Redondo had referred favourably to Ramiro Ledesma Ramos's newspaper: 'We approve of the combative ardour and the eagerness of *La Conquista del Estado*, but we do miss the anti-Semitic activity which that movement needs in order to be efficacious and to go in the right direction. We will not tire of reminding it of this.'[15] Anti-Semitism – not a Nazi import but derived from fifteenth-century Castilian nationalism – would recur again in Redondo's writings. In late 1931, for instance, he wrote of coeducational schools as an example of 'Jewish action against free nations. A crime against the health of the people for which the traitors responsible must be pay with their heads.'[16] It is hardly surprising that Ramiro Ledesma Ramos himself later wrote of *Libertad* as 'finding itself in an unequivocally ultra-rightist position'. In October 1931, Jesús Ercilla introduced Onésimo to Ramiro Ledesma Ramos in Madrid. It was the first of several meetings in Madrid and Valladolid that would culminate in the loose fusion of the two groups as the Juntas de Ofensiva Nacional Sindicalista (the Groups of National-Syndicalist Offensive) on 30 November 1931. The new group adopted the red and black colours of the anarcho-syndicalist CNT and took as its badge the emblem of the Catholic Kings, the yoke and arrows. It was anti-democratic and imperialist, demanding Gibraltar, Morocco and Algeria for Spain and aspiring to 'the extermination, the dissolution of the Marxist parties'. To bring about its ambitions, national-syndicalist militias were to be created 'in order to oppose red violence with nationalist violence'. Onésimo's philosophical links to Ángel Herrera and political Catholicism, and his own sincere piety, sat ill with the more radical fascism of Ramiro Ledesma Ramos.[17]

In the meanwhile, for all that she sympathised with her husband's views, the emotional situation for Mercedes can only be imagined. A girl of respectable upper middle-class origins, she now found herself married to a man who was sacrificing his promising career as a lawyer by involvement with a tiny and penurious party that lived on the edges of the law. According to Mercedes, the relationship was warm and physically passionate but marriage to Onésimo would also bring with it, among other things, bouts of sorrow, loneliness and financial difficulty. On 13 November 1931, her first child, a boy, was stillborn. Onésimo was away at a political meeting in Plasencia, as was the gynaecologist who was supposed to assist at the labour and so, completely alone, she gave birth in their apartment in Valladolid.[18] Typically resilient, she refused to let herself be overwhelmed with depression and got on with supporting her husband. She had land and some income from it but Onésimo was earning very little because of his political commitments. The JONS was behind with the 100 pesetas per month rent on their modest Madrid HQ and could barely afford to produce propaganda leaflets.[19] In Valladolid, Onésimo was devoting ever more time to the conversion of his forty or fifty followers into warriors of what he now called '*milicias regulares anticomunistas*'. Soon they would be involved in bloody clashes with left-wing students and workers in the University and in the streets of Valladolid. At considerable expense, pistols were being bought and considerable time was spent on training. Already by the spring of 1932, Onésimo Redondo was writing about the inevitable civil war to come –

> The war is getting nearer; the situation of violence is inevitable. There is no point in refusing to accept it. It is stupid to flee from making war when they are going to make war on us. The important thing is to make preparations so as to win, and, to win, it will be necessary to take the initiative and go onto the attack.

Propaganda became more virulent in response to the proposed statute of Catalan autonomy. On 3 May 1932, a pitched battle was fought with the left in the Plaza Mayor of Valladolid which saw more than twenty people hospitalised. Onésimo himself was sentenced to two months in prison for the excesses of *Libertad*.[20]

As street violence became more common, Onésimo's rhetoric became more radical. Mercedes does not remember remonstrating with her husband other than to urge him to be careful. As a twenty-one-year-old recently out of her convent, it is doubtful that she fully understood Onésimo's political position. She sympathised broadly because he was her husband, because of their shared Catholicism and basic right-wing views. The increasing polarisation between right and left in the city of Valladolid was a reflection of social tension throughout the province. As a landowner herself, Mercedes reacted to the new Republic's agrarian legislation like many small to medium Castilian farmers, some of whom were members of the Beet-Growers' Union that he was trying to build up. On 29 April 1931, a Ministry of Justice decree had frozen all leases, automatically renewed any which fell due, and prevented eviction other than for failure to pay rent or lack of cultivation. Its object was to prevent hitherto-absentee landlords from taking possession of their land to avoid the consequences of the proposed agrarian reform. As of 11 July, tenants were allowed to petition local courts for reduction of rents. Those who rented out land – such as Mercedes Sanz-Bachiller – saw their income and their property rights diminished. Several other measures had been introduced by the Republican Government in order to alleviate the penury of the landless labourers at the expense of the big landlords. The great estates or *latifundios* were predominantly a Southern phenomenon. In northern and central areas of mainly small and medium-sized holdings, such as Valladolid, the effects on many small farmers were extremely damaging. The Law of Municipal Boundaries prevented labourers from outside a given municipality being hired while there were still local workers unemployed. It was intended to prevent the import of cheap blackleg labour to break strikes or permit the slashing of wages. However, it also sometimes prevented essential skilled labour from a nearby village being used. Similarly, the introduction of Jurados Mixtos (arbitration committees) to set wages and working conditions was opposed by many owners as an offence against property rights. The imposition of the eight-hour day, instead of the previous sunrise to sunset working (de sol a sol) dramatically increased costs to farmers. In summer, this used to mean sixteen-hour days. Now, the smaller owners had to undertake considerably more work themselves because they could not afford to hire more men or pay overtime.

All of these measures, which had been intended merely to alleviate the misery of the rural poor, were perceived by the owners as a provocative revolutionary challenge. Many Valladolid farmers who produced wheat were mobilised by a campaign for an increase in the minimum price for wheat. The increase was made necessary, it was argued, because the arbitration committees had pushed up agricultural wages and therefore the cost of producing wheat. The Government was not prepared to raise bread prices at a time of high unemployment, so the bigger owners refused to release supplies onto the market. Faced by shortages, the Government authorised wheat imports from the Americas. When prices reached their highest figure ever, in July 1932, 250,000 tonnes of wheat miraculously appeared on the market just as 175,000 tonnes of foreign wheat was delivered. There followed a bumper harvest and by the autumn of 1932, wheat prices plummeted to their lowest since 1924. A crisis caused by the speculation of the bigger landowners was presented to the smallholders as part of a deliberate Republican-Socialist plan to destroy Spanish agriculture. In Valladolid province, these various issues inevitably led to an intensification of hatred between farmers and labourers. Many of the sons of farmers joined the JONS.[21] Mercedes's own origins in a prosperous rural family go a long way to explaining her identification with her husband's politics.

In June 1932, Onésimo organised an excursion to visit Dr José María Albiñana, an eccentric neurologist, who, in 1930, had founded a small ultranationalist anti-Semitic group, the Partido Nacionalista Español (Spanish Nationalist Party), complete with blue-shirted, fascist-saluting Legionarios de Espâna (Legionaries of Spain). Albiñana's party occupied in the province of Burgos a position analogous to the JONS in Valladolid. For his persistent attacks on the Republic, he had been condemned in May to forced exile in the inhospitable area of Las Hurdes in Extremadura near the Portuguese border. A carload of Jonsistas reached Martilandrán, the remote hamlet where Albiñana was confined. The voluble doctor indiscreetly related to them what he knew of the preparations for the military coup being planned by General José Sanjurjo.[22] The visit and the information gleaned perhaps lay behind an editorial Onésimo wrote in *Libertad* on 18 July 1932. It was an incitement to a coup. 'Against the foul provocation of the Marxists, the nation must reply with an armed action.'[23] Ramiro Ledesma Ramos later suggested that Onésimo was involved in the gestation of the coup. Certainly, in the wake of its failure on 23 August 1932, *Libertad* was banned. Onésimo was tipped off that the police were about to arrest him, and, already facing the earlier prison sentence, he went into hiding before making his way into exile in Portugal.

In September, he was joined there by Mercedes who was about six months pregnant. They lived first in a small coastal resort, Curía, and later in Porto. During his time in Portugal, living mainly on the income from his wife's properties, Onésimo studied and wrote. He also remained in contact with the Beet-Growers' Syndicate and did some small tasks for his brother's bank. The twenty-one-year-old Mercedes suffered considerably because of the circumstances of her husband. Her pregnancy was reaching its culmination and, because it was difficult to get money out of Spain, they were living in a rather squalid boarding house. Accordingly, Onésimo suggested that they went to a nearby clinic run by nuns to see if the child could be born there. The nuns treated them with patronising contempt as if they were unmarried runaways. A furious Onésimo took Mercedes by the hand, slammed the door and stormed back to the *pensión*. Their daughter, christened Mercedes, was born in their room in the *pensión* on 13 November 1932. Onésimo managed to find a doctor but it was an excruciatingly painful delivery, with forceps and without anaesthetic.[24] Exile was a wretched experience as can be deduced from a number of letters by Ramiro Ledesma Ramos to Onésimo reproaching him for his lack of letters and the pessimism of those that he did write.[25]

After the birth of their daughter, their financial situation worsened. Mercedes was obliged to sell some of her land in Montemayor and, as soon as she was able to travel, she returned to Valladolid with the infant Merche to make the arrangements. In June 1933, Mercedes went back to Portugal where

she and Onésimo lived out the remainder of his exile.[26] Back
in Valladolid, in Onésimo's absence, his young friend, Javier
Martínez de Bedoya, and other Jonsistas had bypassed the ban
on *Libertad* by bringing it out under the name *Igualdad*
(Equality). Onésimo was a frequent, if anonymous, contribu-
tor, writing on 3 March 1933 'Hitler is the oath that marxism
will be exterminated.'[27] On 16 October 1933, with the opening of the campaign for the elections of November 1933,
Onésimo returned to Spain. He was arrested shortly after arriving but was freed after two days. He hoped to stand as candidate for the elections as part of the ticket dominated by the
legalist Catholic party associated with Acción Popular, the
Confederación Española de Derechas Autónomas (the Spanish
Confederation of Autonomous Right-Wing Groups, or the
CEDA). However, after the failure of the military coup of
August 1932, the CEDA leader, José María Gil Robles, wanted
to dissociate his party from the violent ultrarightists known as
'catastrophists'. Onésimo briefly campaigned as an independent JONS candidate but withdrew shortly before the elections took place, concerned that he might split the right-wing
vote.[28]

Exile had not mellowed him. In January 1934, he wrote

Get your weapons ready. Learn to love the metallic
clunk of the pistol. Caress your dagger. Never be
parted from your vengeful cudgel!
Wherever there is an antimarxist group with cudgel,
fist and pistol or with higher instruments, there is a
JONS.
Youth should be trained in physical struggle, must
love violence as a way of life, must arm itself with
whatever it can and finish off by any means the few
dozen Marxist swindlers who don't let us live.[29]

The weakness of the Juntas de Ofensiva Nacional Sindicalista
impelled Onésimo amd Ramiro Ledesma Ramos to seek like-

minded partners. This led, in mid–February 1934, to the fusion of the JONS with the Falange Española, the small fascist party led by the aristocratic José Antonio Primo de Rivera.[30] The new party, with its interminable name of Falange Española de las Juntas de Ofensiva Nacional Sindicalista, was to be led by a triumvirate of José Antonio Primo de Rivera, the aviator Julio Ruiz de Alda and Ramiro Ledesma Ramos. Onésimo was simply a member of the executive known as the Command Council (Junta de Mando). He was not especially bothered by this demotion, being altogether more concerned with fears of left-wing revolutionary preparations.

FE de las JONS was launched in Valladolid, on 4 March 1934. Onésimo Redondo's speech at the Teatro Calderón was not as good as he normally expected of himself because he was utterly exhausted. Just before midnight on 3 March, Mercedes had given birth to her second child in their house in Valladolid. Onésimo, although not present at the birth – which would have been extremely unusual at the time – had spent the entire previous night accompanying Mercedes in the earlier stages of her labour and the hours thereafter holding his new daughter, Pilar.[31] The meeting was the biggest public event of his political career. Coachloads of Falangists from Madrid and the other Castilian provinces had converged on Valladolid. The local left had declared a general strike and the meeting went ahead in an atmosphere of barely contained violence. There were mounted police in the streets outside, holding back hostile workers. Inside the theatre, bedecked with the black and red flags of FE de las JONS, a forest of stiffly outstretched arms greeted the orators with the fascist salute. Despite his exhaustion, the speech delivered by Onésimo, along with that by José Antonio Primo de Rivera, was sufficiently provocative to fire up the audience to rush out and engage in a bloody street battle with the workers outside. Shots were fired and, at the end of the day, with many broken heads on both sides, there was one Falangist dead. Those leftists involved who could be identified would be shot by the Nationalists during the Civil War.[32] As the enmity between right and left intensified, Onésimo was trying to build up an arsenal of small arms. He also hired a sports ground on the banks of the Río Pisuerga where he would drill and train the local party militia. On Sundays, he would lead military parades through Valladolid itself or other towns of the province. During the miners' insurrection in Asturias and the Catalan federalist rebellion of October 1934, there were bloody clashes in Valladolid between Falangists and picketing railway workers. In the aftermath of these events, Onésimo Redondo distributed a pamphlet in which he advocated that the Republican leader Manuel Azaña, the Socialists Francisco Largo Caballero and Indalecio Prieto, and the Catalan president Lluis Companys be hanged.[33]

Mercedes was fully aware of Onésimo's developing ideas. When his comrades and collaborators – Ramiro Ledesma Ramos, José Antonio Primo de Rivera and others – visited Valladolid to discuss policy with him, she would accompany them at meals and have her say. She got on particularly well with the charming José Antonio Primo de Rivera but the fusion of the Falange with the JONS would eventually have negative consequences for both groups. José Antonio's Falange had enjoyed a degree of financial support from upper-class monarchists impressed by his credentials as a Southern landowner, a *grande de España*, an eligible socialite, and above all as the eldest son of the late lamented military dictator. Now the merger with the altogether more radical and proletarian JONS hinted at a danger of Spanish fascism getting out of establishment control in the way of its German and Italian equivalents. Financial contributions began to dry up. At the same time, some of the more militant members of the JONS, notably Ramiro Ledesma Ramos, and including Javier Martínez de Bedoya, resented the fact that their organisation's radicalism was being vitiated by the link with the Falange. Like Ledesma,

Javier Martínez de Bedoya was disillusioned by the petty bureaucracy of Party life and was especially opposed to the personality cult surrounding José Antonio Primo de Rivera. Tensions between Ledesma Ramos and José Antonio intensified during 1934 over the use of terror squads. The leader of the Falange's student section, Alejandro Salazar, wrote in his diary in the summer. 'For some time now Ramiro Ledesma is no longer one of ours.' Ramiro had told him that 'we' (that is to say, the Jonsistas) 'are the true ones, not the children of Primo de Rivera'.[34] Ledesma Ramos had long resented José Antonio's wealth and aristocratic style. His bitterness was intensified because of the speech defect that prevented him from ever matching José Antonio as a fascist orator – a shrill voice and an inability to pronounce the letter 'r' other than as 'w', an affliction later cruelly ridiculed by José Antonio.[35]

The inevitable clash between José Antonio's conservative inclinations and Ramiro Ledesma Ramos's radical anticapitalism was provoked by the elaboration of the programme of the new party. The radical draft drawn up by the journalist Francisco Bravo and Ramiro Ledesma Ramos was watered down by José Antonio. The consequent friction over the programme developed into a struggle for power.[36] On 14 January 1935, a press note, apparently signed by Ledesma, Alvarez de Sotomayor and Onésimo Redondo, announced that they planned to reorganise the JONS outside the Falange. Onésimo had not actually signed the communiqué but Ledesma had included his name on the assumption that he would join him. To pre-empt the potential split, two days later José Antonio announced to the executive committee (the Junta Política) that Ledesma Ramos had been expelled because of persistent factionalism. An elegantly attired José Antonio had addressed a hostile group of blue-shirted syndicalists and been sufficiently convincing for the bulk of the Jonsistas, including Onésimo, to opt to remain within FE de las JONS. Javier Martínez de Bedoya – who spoke years later of 'the sickening snobbery' of José Antonio Primo de Rivera and his group of friends – sided with Ramiro Ledesma Ramos.[37] Ledesma denied that he had been expelled and claimed that he had left of his own initiative because of José Antonio's dilution of the 27-point programme. Javier Martínez de Bedoya also wrote four witheringly critical articles in Ledesma Ramos's new, and short-lived, newspaper, *La Patria Libre* (The Fatherland Free) – for which he would be made to pay a heavy price in the future.[38] The hostility between the erstwhile partners was so intense that José Antonio needed all his authority to forestall a Falangist assassination attempt on Ledesma Ramos who subsequently dwindled into political obscurity. He returned to his post-office job and, early in the Civil War, on 1 August 1936 was arrested and, on 29 October, shot.[39]

Javier Martínez de Bedoya now slipped out of the lives of Onésimo and Mercedes. He withdrew from politics after the schism and returned to the university to start studying for a doctorate in law. As part of his studies, he went to Germany in July 1935 in order to work for a term at Tübingen and later for another in Heidelberg, not returning to Spain until June 1936. For Onésimo, the consequences of the split were also notable. There was a state of some unease within the Valladolid Falange Española de las JONS. A number of disagreeable incidents reflected the FE/JONS division. That perhaps explains why increasingly he had thrown himself into his work with the Beet-Growers' Syndicate and as a lawyer – although he was also delighted to be able to spend more time with his wife and children. In May 1935, Mercedes gave birth to a son, Onésimo.[40] In the campaign for the elections of 19 February 1936, Onésimo tried to make a deal whereby he could run on a united right-wing ticket. He wrote to the President of Acción Popular in Valladolid – the group he had himself founded and later split. Now, he offered to collaborate, without conditions about either the possible number of Falangist candidates or their position in possible joint lists. It was to no avail. In Valladolid, as in the rest of the country, this was not possible and the Falangist candidacy was obliged to stand in isolation. Nevertheless, he put enormous energy into the propaganda campaign, taking part in thirty-five meetings.[41]

In December 1935, José María de Areilza, a Jonsista from Bilbao, visited Valladolid. They discussed the possibilities for an armed insurrection against the Republic for which Onésimo was training his small para-military groups. Redondo told his friend that he was pessimistic about the likely outcome of the elections and that, in the course of the campaign, he was facing intense hostility from both the left and the right. On the platform of Valladolid station, while waiting for his train to return to the Basque Country, Areilza asked after Onésimo's wife and children. Like most men who met her, Areilza – himself a notorious ladies' man – had been deeply struck by the vivacious Mercedes. The severity of her tightly drawn-back black hair was belied by her mischievously sparkling eyes. Areilza recalled 'the serene and extraordinary beauty of her dignified Castilian demeanour'. He commented that 'Onésimo was an affectionate man, who loved his family, his home and especially his little daughters who figured often in his conversation.' Before the train drew out of the station, Onésimo made a sombre prediction, telling Areilza, 'if the Popular Front wins, by the next day, we will all be in jail'.[42]

The Popular Front was victorious in the elections of 16 February 1936. Immediately, there was a big increase in recruitment for FE de las JONS in Valladolid. Young men from more moderate right-wing groupings, especially the youth movement of the CEDA, the Juventud de Acción Popular (The Youth of Popular Action), began to move into the Falange. On 7 March, at a meeting of the JONS, Onésimo Redondo promised that 'the decisive moment' would soon be announced. After a bomb attack on the main police station in Valladolid, on 19 March, Onésimo and the principal leaders of the local Falange were arrested. Mercedes was alone again yet did not complain to Onésimo since she believed firmly in his political principles. She remained as supportive as always, never reproaching him for endangering himself and his family. And shortly after Onésimo went into prison, she discovered that she was pregnant. In jail, her husband's time was mainly devoted to the three dominant themes of his life, his family, religion, and above all, the role that his militias would play in the forthcoming uprising. He wrote frequent, passionate and poetic letters to Mercedes, organised daily gymnastic sessions for his cellmates and also oversaw the fulfilment of their religious practice. He also liaised, through a Falangist prison warder, with the conspirators on the outside. He was fully involved in the preparation of the Falange's participation in the rising in Valladolid, smuggling out messages and instructions through one of the prison guards, Conrado Sabugo. Onésimo was also in constant correspondence with José Antonio Primo de Rivera and was fully apprised of the preparations for the military coup in the rest of Spain.[43]

On a daily basis, Falangists were involved in violent con-frontations with the left in both the provincial capital and other small towns. A cycle of provocation and reprisal created a climate of terror. In mid-June, Falangists armed with machine pistols assaulted several taverns where left-wingers were known to congregate. Bombs were placed at the homes of prominent members of the Popular Front and in various workers' clubs (Casas del Pueblo). Leftist reprisals were swift: Falangists were attacked and the Carlist Tradicionalist Centre sacked. Onésimo and other Jonsistas clashed violently with left-wing prisoners, for which the Inspector of Prisons held him responsible. On 25 June, to prevent the possibility of a Falangist attack to free him from the prison at Valladolid, he was transferred to Ávila.[44] Mercedes visited him there as often as she could. According to the official biography of her husband, Mercedes herself began to play a role in the Falange: 'she was a source of encouragement, she transmitted orders, and resolutely assisted in the preparation of the movement. Every week, accompanied by a comrade, she visited Onésimo in his prison in Ávila.' She also played a token part in Falangist subversion. Like a naughty schoolgirl, she went with four young Falangists and broke a plate-glass window in the house of a local leftist. Simply because she was Onésimo Redondo's wife, she believed that her own home was in danger of attack. So she sent the three children to stay with Onésimo's parents in Quintanilla de Abajo and moved out of her apartment.[45]

On the eve of the military uprising of 18 July 1936, Valladolid was a city already seething with hatred. The Republican Civil Governor, Luis Lavín Gautier, faced enormous difficulty in containing street clashes between right and left. The local FE de las JONS was increasingly unrestrained in its violence. In this, they were encouraged by the marked Falangist sympathies of the local police, Assault Guards, Civil Guard and Army units all of which joined them in the rising. That was one of the reasons why the rebellion was quickly successful in Valladolid, even before the arrival of General Andrés Saliquet, the conspirator chosen to lead the coup in the city. Despite later Francoist claims, leftist resistance was minimal. Against troops, Assault Guards and armed Falangists, the left had little chance. Lavín's orders that the workers be armed were disobeyed and guns were distributed to the Falange instead. The general strike declared by the left-wing unions was quickly and brutally smashed. Hundreds of Socialists took refuge with their families in the cellars of their headquarters in the Casa del Pueblo. After the building was briefly shelled by artillery, they surrendered.[46] Most of the women and all of the children were allowed to go free but 448 men were arrested. According to official figures, nearly one thousand Republicans, Socialists and anarcho-syndicalists were arrested in the city, including the Civil Governor Luis Lavín, the city's Socialist mayor, Antonio García Quintana, and the province's only Socialist deputy, Federico Landrove López, all three of whom would be shot.

Over the next few months, anyone who had held a position in a Socialist municipality, in a trade union or a left-wing or Republican party was subject to arrest and court martial. A further 642 would be detained in August and 410 in September. General Saliquet's declaration of martial law published in the early hours of the morning of 19 July, effectively issued a death threat against all those who had not actively supported the uprising. 'Crimes' that would be met with summary trials and immediate execution included 'rebellion' (which signified defence of the Republic against the military rebels) and extended to disobedience, disrespect, insult or calumny towards both the military and those who had been militarised (thus including Falangists). Men were arrested on suspicion of having their radio dials set to a station broadcasting from Madrid. Court martials were set up and firing squads began to function.[47]

On Sunday 19 July, within twenty-four hours of the coup, Onésimo was freed and returned to Valladolid, hungry to see Mercedes and to slake the passion pent up during three months in prison.[48] He was also raring to lead his militias. He made contact with General Saliquet and then set up headquarters in the Academia de Caballería, directing squads of armed Falangists all over the province to crush left-wing resistance. Now he was tireless in putting into practice his oft-repeated declaration of the need to exterminate Marxism. In his first radio broadcast, on 19 July, he spoke of the need to 'redeem the proletariat' through social justice. Declaring that the economic life of the city should go on as normal, he threatened that 'the lives of workers and shop assistants will depend on their conduct. And hidden subversives, if there are any left, will be hunted down by the vigilant eyes of our Falanges and *centurias*.'[49]

Onésimo had barely got back to his wife and taken up the reins of his political role when he was killed on 24 July at the village of Labajos in Segovia. He was travelling from Valladolid to visit Falangist comrades fighting with the Nationalist forces advancing on Madrid through the mountain pass at the Alto del León in the Sierra de Guadarrama to the northwest of the capital. Mercedes was at home when she received a stark telephone call from General Saliquet himself with the news. Before she had time to react, the house was full of Falangist militiamen. The shock completely knocked her out. Shortly afterwards she miscarried and, for the rest of her life, she remained convinced that her unborn child had died when she heard the news.[50]

The ambush in which Onésimo lost his life took place within the Nationalist zone. Accordingly, there have been rumours, both at the time and since, that he was killed, deliberately or otherwise, by partisans of his own side. Mercedes believed that Onésimo had been murdered – 'The death of Onésimo was not an act of war, it was a vile murder perfectly planned – since he was the most important politician who was in Nationalist Spain, his elimination was important – for whom?' On the basis that Onésimo was the only remaining senior Falangist, she feared that elements from a group of fanatical supporters of José Antonio Primo de Rivera might have been involved, having already, in 1935, sent a squad to assassinate him.[51] In the absence of incontrovertible proof, the speculation that Onésimo was killed by Falangists has to be weighed against the more plausible theory that, with the front far from stabilised, his group had run into a truckload of Republican militiamen from the column commanded by the famous Colonel Julio Mangada known to have been in the area.[52]

The death of Onésimo Redondo would eventually project both his wife and ambitious older brother, Andrés, into political prominence. In the short term, Mercedes was bedridden and too ill even to visit the chapel of repose that had been set up in the Town Hall of Valladolid. Mercedes thus did not attend the requiem mass celebrated on 24 July at the Cathedral with the pomp normally reserved for national heroes. All shops in the city were closed during Onésimo's funeral. His coffin, covered by a Monarchist flag, was carried on a carriage pulled by six white horses. The procession was led by Falangist squads and followed by girls carrying huge wreaths of flowers and a military band. According to an eye-witness, the prominent local journalist, Francisco de Cossío, the atmosphere at the funeral was imbued with a barely contained desire for rapid revenge. After the ceremony, Andrés Redondo had been elected by the acclamation of an emotional crowd Jefe Territorial of León and Old Castile.[53] It was indicative of the personalism of the Falange that political pre-eminence could thus be 'inherited'. In a radio broadcast on the night of 25 July, Andrés Redondo declared that 'all Falangists have sworn to avenge his death'.[54]

Andrés Redondo's words were gratuitous. A savage process of revenge against the left in Valladolid was already under way and would intensify over the next few months. Large numbers of Socialist workers from the railway engineering works were herded into the tram company garages. Those who, having obeyed the union order to strike on Saturday 18 July, and had not returned to work by Tuesday 21 July were shot accused of 'abetting rebellion'. Estimates of the scale of the repression in Valladolid have varied wildly, as high as 15,000 but none lower than 1,303.[55] Exact figures are impossible since many deaths were not recorded. There were 1,300 men and women tried between July and December 1936 often in groups of more than one accused. Such 'trials' consisted of little more than the reading of the names of the accused, the charge and passing of sentence. Although most of those accused of military rebellion were likely to face the death penalty or prison sentences of thirty years, they were given no chance to defend themselves and were not even permitted to speak. On most weekdays, several courts martial were held. All 448 men detained after the surrender of the Casa del Pueblo were tried together, accused of the crime of military rebellion. Forty were sentenced to death, 362 to thirty years' imprisonment, 26 to twenty years' imprisonment, and nineteen were found not guilty. The selection of the forty to be executed was made on the basis of their having held some position of responsibility in the local Socialist organisations. There were other cases in which 53, 77 and 87 accused were 'tried' at once. In some cases, the 'crime' was simply to be a Socialist member of parliament as was the case with Federico Landrove and also José Maesto San José (deputy for Ciudad Real) and Juan Lozano Ruiz (Jaén) who were captured on the outskirts of Valladolid.

Prisoners condemned by court martial were taken out in the early hours of the morning and driven in trucks to the Campo de San Isidro on the outskirts of the city. This became such a regular occurrence that coffee and *churro* (doughnut) stalls were set up as the killings were turned into a public spectacle attended by educated members of the middle classes. Guards had to be assigned to hold back the crowds that thronged to watch and shout insults at the condemned. So shocking did this seem that the newly appointed Civil Governor of the province, Lieutenant Colonel Joaquín García de Diego, issued a reprimand to those who took their wives and children to the executions. The terror became 'normal' and no one dared condemn it for fear of being denounced as a Red.[56]

At least the 394 executions carried out in Valladolid as a result of summary wartime courts martial were registered. In contrast, the unofficial murders carried out by the so-called Falangist 'dawn patrols' are impossible to quantify. These killings were significantly more widespread if rather less public. Corpses were sometimes just left by the roadside, at other times buried in shallow common graves. The sacas or paseos of prisoners were often carried out quite arbitrarily by Falangists who would arrive at the tram sheds or the bullring just before dawn. An inhuman and macabre humour might see a victim selected simply because it was his saint's day. On the basis of those towns and villages in the province for which it is possible to reconstruct what happened, it has been calculated that at least 928 people were murdered by the patrols. The total number is likely to be significantly higher. The random killings caused public-health scares for fear that rotting corpses might be affecting the water supply.[57] Certainly, by any standards, the scale of the repression was totally disproportionate to the fighting in the city on 18 and 19 July.[58]

In the weeks immediately following the death of her husband, Mercedes was too overwhelmed with grief and concern for her children to take very much notice of the repression. Nevertheless, the loss of Onésimo combined with the imprisonment of José Antonio Primo de Rivera meant that, through her brother-in-law, her isolation from politics would not continue very much longer. On 2 September, Andrés Redondo hosted in Valladolid a meeting of the remaining Falange leadership to discuss the problem arising from José Antonio's continued absence in the Republican prison of Alicante. The most powerful elements were worried about the ambitions of others. Agustín Aznar, the thuggish chief of the Falangist militias, wanted nothing to happen before José Antonio Primo de Rivera returned. Andrés Redondo and Joaquín Miranda, the interim Jefe Territorial of Andalusia were regarded as having leadership ambitions. Accordingly, a compromise solution was adopted. A provisional command council (Junta de Mando) was set up under the leadership of Manuel Hedilla Larrey, once Jefe Provincial of Santander and currently Inspector Nacional for the northern provinces. It consisted of Aznar, Andrés Redondo, José Moreno, Jefe Provincial de Navarra, Jesús Muro, Jefe Provincial de Zaragoza, and José Sainz Nothnagel, Jefe Territorial of the New Castile, comprising the Provinces of Cuenca, Toledo and Ciudad Real. Hedilla was chosen as a man not perceived as a threat to the ambitions of the big players. It was widely felt that he could easily be removed when the occasion arose. In fact, as the various component members returned to their provinces, Hedilla was left alone in his office in Burgos.[59]

Mercedes was given little time to grieve for the loss of her husband whose death was to have an unexpected political impact on her life. The Valladolid Falange looked to her to adopt his mantle in some way. In fact, her way of coping with her grief was to throw herself into political activity. Leaving her three small children in the care of nannies, she installed herself in the Cavalry Academy, where the local Falange had established its headquarters. She undertook to collect blankets, jerseys, and other warm clothing for the Nationalist volunteers at the front. In the Castilian sierras, even in summer, the nights could be bitterly cold.[60] In an ironic conflict of mentalities, while Mercedes set out to assert her independence, her brother-in-law hoped to resolve her future with a paternalist gesture, finding her an *estanco* (an outlet for the National Tobacco Monopoly) that would guarantee her a splendid income.[61] Neither the prospect of running a kiosk nor collecting jerseys for the front seemed adequate outlets for the energy of women as dynamic as Mercedes Sanz-Bachiller.

The death of Onésimo Redondo was not the only event that thrust Mercedes into the political limelight in Valladolid. The outbreak of war had caught the Provincial Delegate of the Sección Femenina of Valladolid, Rosario Pereda, on holiday in Santander. She was thus trapped in the Republican zone, where she would remain for the next thirteen months. Accordingly, Andrés Redondo, on his own authority, named Mercedes as head of the Sección Femenina of Valladolid, an organisation with fewer than forty members. Mercedes had previously never had any contact with the Sección Femenina –

> They called me territorial chief but they might just as well have appointed me Bishop of Madrid or of

Valladolid. I hadn't the faintest idea what was going on. I didn't know Pilar Primo de Rivera and I'd never even seen her in my life. I had met José Antonio Primo de Rivera through Onésimo but I had never met Pilar and I had nothing to do with the Sección Femenina.[62]

In fact, Andrés Redondo's grounds for naming Mercedes as Provincial Delegate had no more substance than those that lay behind his own assumption of power – in a power vacuum, he simply asserted 'rights' of inheritance. Moreover, there was a problem in that Mercedes's views on the role of women in politics were diametrically opposed to those that prevailed within the Sección Femenina.

The founder of the Sección Femenina, the austerely beautiful but entirely assexual Pilar Primo de Rivera, had enthusiastically taken her cue from her brother José Antonio. The watchword was to be female subordination. Pilar Primo de Rivera would faithfully impose upon the organisation the spirit of her brother's words to thirty-odd female followers on 28 April 1935 in the town of Don Benito (Badajoz). His patronising declaration about the subordinate position of women within the Falange was swiftly printed as a fly sheet and distributed to the Jefes Provinciales with instructions for it to be adopted as the party line and disseminated as widely as possible. At Badajoz, José Antonio told his awestruck listeners that the Falange had a particular affinity with women because it rejected both flattery and feminism. He then elaborated the sophistry that would encapsulate the mission of the Sección Femenina: 'we are not feminists. We do not believe that the way to respect women is by diverting them from their magnificent destiny and giving them manly functions. Man is a torrent of egoism; woman almost always accepts a life of submission, service and abnegation.'[63]

Mercedes never believed in an exclusively feminine organisation and even less in one dedicated to propagating the submission of women.[64] In this regard, Mercedes was nearer to Margarita Nelken than to Pilar Primo de Rivera. Instead of waiting to be told what to do, she took her own initiative. In the streets of Valladolid, it was virtually impossible not to notice large numbers of apparently abandoned children. This was the consequence of numerous factors. To begin with, the poor of Valladolid were adversely affected by the collapse of what little welfare machinery existed before the war. There was notable social dislocation consequent upon the war, with people unable to return to Valladolid because they were trapped in the Republican zone. Many men were away fighting and many were dying at the front. All of these factors help account for some of the street children. However, the biggest single reason was almost certainly the savage repression that had been unleashed in the city by the triumphant military rebels and their Falangist allies. Indeed, the unauthorised detentions and killings being carried out by the Falange impelled the Civil Governor, Joaquín García de Diego, to make various feeble attempts to impose military control over the repression. As early as 28 July, he issued an order that 'detentions, searches, interrogations and everything related to public order may be carried out only by agents under my authority'. Nothing having been done to impose this order, it was reissued on 4 August and again one month later, 'recommending' that it be respected. Valladolid's two prisons, the old and the new, were overflowing. Excess prisoners had to be kept not only in the tram company's garages but also in the city slaughterhouse. By the autumn, there were also three detention camps in the province, at Santa Espina, Villagodio and Canal, where the harsh conditions accounted for an extremely high mortality rate.[65]

Mercedes was made aware of the social problem by her own observations and because many women had been to see her to beg for help. Her early notions about welfare work began to take shape in the autumn of 1936. The need for welfare organisations was acute given the shortages of many goods. However, it was intense in the case of the victims of the repression. The wives and children of Republicans who had been killed or of the thousands more in prison faced total destitution. An American Quaker relief mission in 1937 spoke of 9,000 destitute children, most of them fatherless as a result of the war.[66] State welfare was nonexistent and, for ideological reasons, religious organisations provided little succour for the children of the despised 'Reds'. The autumn cold was already biting when Mercedes determined to do something to put in place some form of welfare for the helpless. The idea of how to go about the task had partly come from Javier Martínez de Bedoya, the young Jonsista friend of Onésimo Redondo who had abandoned the Falange in 1935 along with Ramiro Ledesma Ramos. Having returned from Germany for the summer holidays, the outbreak of war had caught him in his family home in Guernica. The Secretary of the town Popular Front Committee gave him a safe-conduct to Bilbao. There, he was able to use papers showing that he was returning to the University of Heidelberg to get aboard a German ship heading for Bordeaux. After considerable difficulty, he had managed to cross the frontier back into Spain at Irún and reached Pamplona on 16 September. The local Jefe Territorial, José Moreno, sent him to San Sebastián where he began to work on the Falangist newspaper *Unidad* and to help establish the Central Obrera Nacional Sindicalista. However, within a week, he was invited to Valladolid by Onésimo Redondo's brother Andrés, who had seen his articles in *Unidad*. He wanted Bedoya to take over the organisation of worker syndicates in the province.[67]

Javier Martínez de Bedoya was astonished to receive such an invitation from, of all people, the pompous Andrés Redondo, whom he remembered as a pious bank manager. He wrote in his diary, 'I can't just forget the constant arguments with

Onésimo in which Andrés represented Jesuitical conformism against what he called the "lunacies" of Onésimo.' Having been away from Valladolid for over a year, he was baffled by the apparent change. 'Andrés', he wrote, 'never had a drop of national-syndicalism in his blood.' When they met, Andrés claimed that he had little desire to continue as Jefe Territorial and was anxious to return to his work at the Banco Hispano-Americano in Valladolid. On a journey to Ávila with Bedoya, Andrés recounted his brother's death at Labajos, giving it a particularly religious spin: 'Onésimo had reached such a level of perfection in his spiritual life that Our Lord God had taken him to his side. While as far as I was concerned, seeing that I was not prepared for a good death, he mercifully left me alive.' More alarming than this bizarre way of thinking was the fact that Andrés made a point of driving around in a huge Buick at 130 kilometres an hour as proof of his personal bravery. Javier concluded that Andrés Redondo's notion of the appropriate qualities for a Falangist chief were the same as those shown by the average prince in a Viennese operetta.[68] And this was the man who, completely off his own bat, had made Mercedes Provincial Chief of the Sección Femenina of Valladolid. Clearly, she would need more substantial support than Andrés could ever provide.

For some days after his arrival in late September, the twenty-two-year-old Javier dithered about visiting Mercedes Sanz-Bachiller to convey his condolences for the death of her husband. He had met her only once before, shortly after she and Onésimo had returned from Portugal. 'At that time', he wrote later, 'she had seemed to me to be just a very young mother, interested mainly in the funny things done and said by her little daughter, Merche. She had a kind of beauty that seemed very new to me – very serene and luminous.' Now, afraid of not finding adequate words of sympathy, he had delayed the visit for a week. When he finally plucked up the courage to go to her offices in the Cavalry Academy on

1 October, he was deeply affected by the encounter. 'I found that beauty now enhanced by a marble pallor, her face made childlike by an expression of surprise at everything that had happened; her cheekbones and her chin emphasised by the suffering of seeing two young lives shattered, Onésimo's and her own.' When she reproached him for not coming sooner, pointing out that Onésimo often spoke of him, he was entranced by the delicate softness of her voice. He had intended to do no more than give her his condolences for the death of Onésimo and to avoid the painful subject as much as possible, they had talked mainly of the social problems caused by the war.[69]

During their conversation, Mercedes spoke both of her anguish at the distress to be seen in the streets and her desire to do something that would enable her to 'be a human being in my own right once more'. Their conversation turned to the plight of the many mothers who had suddenly and unexpectedly become widows because of the deaths of their husbands at the front or in the repression behind the lines. Out of this conversation, Mercedes Sanz-Bachiller precipitately determined to throw herself into social welfare. What she vaguely outlined reminded him of the Nazi Winterhilfe (Winter Help) relief organisation. During the time that he had spent as a student in Heidelberg, Martínez de Bedoya had been impressed by what he saw of its workings.[70] With a typical burst of energy, Mercedes immediately decided to borrow the money necessary to get the operation started. With Javier still in her office, she immediately telephoned the secretary of the Town Council of Valladolid, Teodoro Giménez Cendón, an old Jonsista friend of Onésimo. In response to her request for a loan, he offered the not inconsiderable sum of 5,000 pesetas for three months. While she spoke to Giménez Cendón, Javier made a list of things that needed to be acquired and done to get the operation off the ground. Her next stop was the office of her brother-in-law, Andrés, who, in addition to being Provincial Chief, was also the manager of the Banco Hispano-Americano in Valladolid. He offered a credit of 50,000 pesetas. According to Javier, from that moment, Mercedes stopped presenting herself as 'the widow of Onésimo Redondo' and started to sign documents and introduce herself as 'Mercedes Sanz-Bachiller'.[71]

However, in the tense atmosphere of wartime Valladolid, to launch a welfare organisation that aimed to attend to the needs of the poor and helpless irrespective of ideology was not without risk. The greatest numbers of the poor were victims of the repression and there were many middle-class inhabitants of Valladolid who believed, and proclaimed loudly, that they deserved their fate as 'Reds'. Years later, the Falangist intellectual, Dionisio Ridruejo, who, as Provincial Chief first in Segovia and later in Valladolid, had done what he could to save lives, lamented that 'I lived with, tolerated, gave my indirect approval to the terror with my public silence and by remaining a militant of the Falange.' It is all the more significant then that Ridruejo regarded the launching of Auxilio de Invierno as 'an act of courage because, to begin with, it was founded on the basis of a recognition, and implicit denunciation, of the scale of the repressive purges in Valladolid'.[72] Sympathy for the victims could easily be mistaken for, or distorted as, sympathy for the Republic or lack of enthusiasm for the Nationalist cause. From the very first moment, Mercedes Sanz-Bachiller made it clear that there would be no political discrimination in the help given. In contrast to Onésimo's vengeful attitude towards the left, Mercedes was altogether more compassionate: 'For me, a child was a Spanish child and that was all there was to it. And a woman was a Spanish woman and no more. Nothing about Reds or bandits or the like.' This suggests that she had not fully understood the implications of her husband's violent rhetoric.[73]

The simple translation of the Nazi Winterhilfe as Auxilio de Invierno was, according to Mercedes, an effective way of neutralising opposition within the Falange. The inclusion of the word Invierno (winter) was a declaration that this was an entirely temporary or provisional response to an immediate problem and thus implicitly renounced any ambition to challenge the existing power structures and relationships within the Falange. Charitable help for those worst hit by the rigours of the season was altogether less likely to meet opposition than the establishment of another permanent organisation. Moreover, the Nazi connotations helped mitigate suspicions that the operation was tainted by solidarity with the Republican victims of the repression.[74]

The idea of calling the organisation Auxilio de Invierno has often been attributed to Clarita Stauffer, daughter of a German chemist at the famous Mahou brewery. This has no basis other than the coincidence of the German origins both of her family name and of Winterhilfe. What little influence Clarita had came from her closeness to Hitler's emissary to Spain, the retired General Wilhelm Faupel, a one-time organiser of the Freikorps. A staunch Nazi, Faupel presented his credentials to Franco on 30 November 1936. Thereafter, Clarita Stauffer, in her capacity as deputy chief of the Sección Femenina's Press and Propaganda Department did some liaison work between his headquarters and General José Millán Astray but her involvement in Auxilio de Invierno was negligible.[75] It was Javier Martínez de Bedoya who advocated the adoption of similar emblems, lapel badges, collecting boxes and rubber stamps to those used by the German organisation. Certainly he received considerable help and advice from General Faupel's propaganda attaché, Kroeger.[76] The organisation's shield consisted of a male forearm whose fist was thrusting the point of a spear into the jaws of a wolf. Designs were provided by a young German named Frank.[77]

With the money collected from Teodoro Giménez Cendón and Andrés Redondo, Mercedes and the rather short and plump Javier set to work with manic energy. They arranged for the badges and collecting boxes to be manufactured. Uniforms were made for the canteen staff. Mercedes had the idea of offering jobs in the kitchens to women whose husbands were in prison or had been shot, so that they could at least eat, feed their children and maybe even earn a small wage. They found premises for the first ten canteens and arranged for supplies of food. Mercedes threw her not inconsiderable powers of persuasion into recruiting volunteers. The people that she approached were swept along by the example of her own tireless efforts combined with an overwhelming charm that brooked no contradiction. Volunteers were found to staff the canteen, to collect money and to start a census of the needy. In this, she was helped by a doctor friend of Onésimo, Cipriano Pérez Delgado, who lived in the same apartment block and by a lawyer, Manuel Martínez Tena, who was the private secretary of Andrés Redondo.[78]

Even before Auxilio de Invierno was off the ground in Valladolid, Mercedes and Javier were thinking about the logistics of its extension to other cities within the Nationalist zone. The main military authority in the North was General Mola, whose headquarters were in the Town Hall of Valladolid. Mola was aware that the repression alone could not secure the future of the regime that the military hoped to establish and he was thus interested in the possibilities for such a social welfare apparatus. He told Javier Martínez de Bedoya: 'the war today has a direct impact on the civilian masses in the big cities and the military quartermaster's administration does not have the organisation, the means or the time to take on responsibility for these masses until there is a return to normal civilian existence.' Mola's notion was to try out the notion of Auxilio de Invierno in Bilbao. He told Javier that he would be attached to his headquarters as a simple private and that his aide, Colonel Luis Calderón, would give him facilities to try out the idea. Javier was puzzled since, at the time, all Nationalist eyes were on Madrid. Indeed, the military operation against the Basque Country would not begin for another five months, at the end of March 1937, and Bilbao itself would not fall into Nationalist hands until early June 1937. Nevertheless, Javier took Mola's words as a broad overarching military authorisation for the scheme. On 28 October 1936, the first collection for Auxilio de Invierno was held in the streets and squares of Valladolid. Forty-six thousand pesetas was collected which seemed a fortune. On that same day, Mola transferred his headquarters to Ávila in order to be nearer to Madrid. However, Colonel Calderón instructed Javier to report to him once a month and to plan ahead for the launching of Auxilio de Invierno in Bilbao, once captured.[79]

By 30 October, the first canteen for one hundred orphans was opened in an old cafeteria in the Calle Angustias in Valladolid. Over the following weeks, other canteens were established elsewhere in the city and in other towns of the province. Given the scale of distress to be found in the streets of virtually all the towns and villages of Castille, the idea quickly spread to neighbouring provinces. On 17 November, the second collection was held. Donors were given a small metal badge consisting of an imperial eagle holding the word PAN (bread) in its claws.[80] Auxilio de Invierno would make a major contribution to social welfare in the form of soup kitchens, orphanages and literacy programmes as well as eventually providing laundry services and medical support for the Nationalist forces. The first task was to help the large number of orphans that had been created by the war and the repression. Money was raised by public collections, the publicity for which caused considerable hostility in certain circles. The first canteens, where clothes, medicines and money were distributed as well as food, were highly public and the object of critical commentary. Nevertheless, the idea also provoked sympathy among many who were appalled by the repression. Contributing to Auxilio de Invierno was an acceptable way, in some cases, of expressing disapproval and, in others, of salving consciences.[81]

At the beginning of November, a delegation including Mercedes and Javier went to Seville to see Pilar Primo de Rivera who had managed to escape from Republican Madrid and had reached the Nationalist zone in early September.[82] The purpose of their visit was to explain the functioning of Auxilio de Invierno and to request the collaboration of the Sección Femenina in order to extend it all over Spain. They were not putting themselves under Pilar's orders but rather requesting that the militants of Sección Femenina be allowed to help with Auxilio de Invierno. The meeting was cordial but Pilar's suspicions were aroused. If the bulk of Sección Femenina members were to undertake to work with Auxilio Social, then her organisation would have little function beyond producing file-card indexes of women available to work in the Nationalist zone.[83] In mid-November, an aristocratic Falangist writer from Seville, Manuel Halcón, visited Valladolid. He was enthused by what he saw of Mercedes's organisation and wrote an appreciative article in the principal Falangist newspaper FE in Andalusia. This provoked local demand for Mercedes to establish Auxilio de Invierno in Seville, where the social problem caused by the repression carried out by the bloodthirsty General Gonzalo Queipo de Llano was, if anything, worse than that in Valladolid. At the time, it was widely believed in the Nationalist zone that Madrid would soon fall to the combined forces of Mola's northern army and Franco's African columns and that the end of the war was in sight.

On 20 November 1936, José Antonio Primo de Rivera was executed in Alicante. A vicious power struggle within the Falange was now virtually inevitable and that would inevitably have implications for the nascent Auxilio de Invierno. At a meeting of the Junta de Mando in Salamanca on 22 November, it was decided to keep the news secret. That night Hedilla visited Valladolid. Mercedes and Javier Martínez de Bedoya buttonholed him to persuade him that he had nothing to fear from them: 'We grabbed the opportunity to let him know that our position is one of simple fidelity to the Falange, without being tied to any one person, and to stimulate his interest in what we've done so far with Auxilio de Invierno.'[84] Within the Falange, as in other political formations of the Nationalist coalition, thoughts were turning to the future. Mercedes Sanz-Bachiller had been carried along by her own dynamism into a territory regarded as her own by Pilar Primo de Rivera, the National Chief of the Sección Femenina.

In late November, Pilar Primo de Rivera established the national headquarters of the Sección Femenina in Salamanca. Now, with a view to asserting her authority over the woman she regarded as an upstart rival, Pilar accompanied by Hedilla and an official of the German Embassy, visited Valladolid on 7 December. Mercedes and Javier took them to see an Auxilio de Invierno canteen in Medina de Rioseco and spent their time together reiterating to both their visitors that they were standing aside from any power struggle within the Falange.[85] That Pilar was impressed could be seen in the rapid appearance of large advertisements for Auxilio de Invierno in the Falangist press of Andalusia in mid-December. Appeals for new and unwanted clothing, along the lines of what was being done in Valladolid, were now interspersed with a wider propagandistic message. 'Falange is beginning to carry desires for brotherhood among all Spaniards into the National Conscience – such zeal for brotherhood and for justice will bring joy to forgotten homes.' Pilar announced her own higher authority by appearing at the inauguration of the first Auxilio de Invierno canteen in Seville on Christmas Eve 1936 along with civic authorities and senior figures of the Falange. There was no way in which Pilar Primo de Rivera was going to let her authority be challenged in the very area that she regarded as a family fief. Her point was made even more strongly in her home town of Jérez when the next canteen to be opened, on 5 January, carried the name of the Comedor Pilar Primo de Rivera.[86]

Pilar's sudden interest in Auxilio de Invierno was sending

a message that she had no intention of contemplating a serious rival. She was determined to bring the new organisation into her own orbit. Pilar's ambitions in this regard and her suspicions about the emergence of Mercedes Sanz-Bachiller as a challenger to her position were understandable. Auxilio de Invierno had a quite staggering success. On 19 December, the first so-called 'brotherhood kitchen' (Cocina de Hermandad) had been opened in Valladolid. It prepared food for adults, principally the widows and the aged parents of men killed in the repression or at the front. To avoid the shame associated with charitable canteens, the Cocina prepared meals that could be collected or even, in some cases, delivered to the homes of those fortunate, or unfortunate, enough to be on Auxilio de Invierno's books.[87] Within a year of its creation, it would have 711 canteens and 158 Cocinas de Hermandad throughout the Nationalist zone. By 1939, it would have 2,847 canteens and 1,561 'brotherhood kitchens', 3000 centres providing soup kitchens, maternity and child care and stores of clothing for the destitute.[88] Auxilio de Invierno was soon spreading to other parts of the Nationalist zone. Therein lay the seeds of the future conflict.

At first, Auxilio de Invierno operated rather ambiguously both with the authority of General Mola and also, rather vaguely, under the umbrella of the executive of Falange Española de las JONS, the Command Council or Junta de Mando. Because Mercedes was a local official of the Sección Femenina, Pilar Primo de Rivera felt able to fight to subject the new organisation to her authority. Mercedes did not, of course, consider Auxilio de Invierno to have been an initiative solely of the Sección Femenina. She was in some demand as her idea found sympathetic echoes in other cities. Despite the difficulties of wartime travel, she took her idea to other provinces in the northern zone. In this, Mercedes operated with very considerable independence given that she believed that she was under the protection of General Mola and also enjoyed the support of the overall provisional chief of the Falange, Manuel Hedilla. However, her success was attracting suspicious glances. Given the chaos of competing authorities within the Nationalist zone and Hedilla's lackadaisical management style, a clash was inevitable.[89]

The shy, childlike, appearance of Pilar Primo de Rivera belied her dogged stubbornness. In her memoirs, she refers to her rivalry with Mercedes only as 'that problem'. Nevertheless, her outrage at being challenged and her determination to prevail may be read between the lines of her remarks about Mercedes. On arrival in Salamanca, says Pilar, she became aware of the presence in Valladolid of Mercedes Sanz-Bachiller, 'a woman gifted with very good qualities. Very sure of herself, she had, to a certain extent, begun to take over the Sección Femenina.' The unmistakable insinuation is that Mercedes had been driven by an ambitious determination to take advantage of Pilar's confinement in the Republican zone: 'She had had the advantage of being in the Nationalist zone all along which had allowed her to organise the Sección Femenina in Valladolid and establish her influence in other neighbouring provinces.'[90]

There were two reasons why Pilar Primo de Rivera had reason to fear the influence of Mercedes Sanz-Bachiller. In the first place, Mercedes opposed the very essence of the Sección Femenina as conceived by Pilar – an entirely female organisation at the submissive service of superior males. Secondly, many of the women being recruited by Mercedes to work for Auxilio de Invierno were already members of the Sección Femenina. Pilar thus regarded them as falling under her command. Accordingly, she set about re-asserting her authority. As she put it, 'All of this posed some difficulties for the Sección Femenina, and it was necessary to employ much diplomacy, but, at the same time, an unswerving tenacity in restoring the natural order and in putting everyone in their correct place.'[91]

A further source of future difficulties for Mercedes lay in Javier Martínez de Bedoya's past frictions with, and present views about, the so-called 'legitimists' – a close circle of friends and relatives of José Antonio Primo de Rivera who gathered around Pilar. In early November 1936, Javier was confiding to his diary his view that the Falange was 'headless' and being badly run by a number of 'bad heads' irresponsibly appointed by José Antonio Primo de Rivera in the organisation's early days: 'This ruling group of nouveaux riches totally lacks any political sense.' His views on the legitimistas could hardly have been more contemptuous and hardly boded well for his, and Mercedes's, future relations with them:

> Sancho Dávilo (a rich fop and a lousy leader), Rafael Garcerán (an articled clerk in José Antonio's chambers, totally lacking in political experience), Andrés Redondo (who has never understood the Falange and has a Jesuitical temperament), José Moreno (just about up to being a Jefe Provincial, miserable wretch), Agustín Aznar (decent enough as head of an action squad, but without the slightest possibility of commanding a militia of 200,000 men, uncouth and overexcitable), Manuel Hedilla (a poor workman who believed in the social content of the Falange – he might just about be able to run the local branch of a metalworkers' union), Francisco Bravo (a journalist, politically mediocre and pretentious), Muro (a simple soul, a decent Provincial Chief), Sainz (a good centurion).

According to Javier, they behaved like medieval feudal lords, constantly conspired against one another and went everywhere accompanied by an escort armed with machine guns: 'Take for example the fact that Andrés Redondo thinks he's the new Philip II.'[92]

Over the next three years, there would follow a lengthy, sporadic, and undeclared, power struggle. In the last resort, the power of Pilar's family connections, combined with her own stubborn determination, would guarantee her eventual victory. Mercedes's weakness, in terms of political struggles, was also her greatest strength – she was simply not interested in petty bureaucratic squabbles and was devoted to getting on with her welfare work. Two more different rivals could hardly be imagined. The wife of one of the founders of the JONS was feisty, energetic and outspoken, a mother and a warm-hearted woman at ease in the company of men. The sister of the founder of the Falange was, in contrast, timid in public, cold and introspective, a childless celibate, shy in the company of men. Moreover, there was a deeper hostility. Beyond any personal jealousy, there was a profound ideological enmity. Pilar's determination to bring Mercedes Sanz's Auxilio de Invierno into the orbit of the Sección Femenina paralleled the efforts by the followers of José Antonio within the wider Falange to tame the radical followers of Onésimo Redondo in Valladolid. The outbreak of the Civil War and the influence of the German and Italian allies of the Nationalists had revived the JONS radicalism which had been suffocated by José Antonio Primo de Rivera in February 1935.

Several of the friends and relatives of José Antonio Primo de Rivera dismissed so contemptuously in Bedoya's diary made up the powerful band of 'legitimists' led by Pilar. The most aggressively determined of the group was the twenty-four year-old Agustín Aznar, who was the fiancé of José Antonio's cousin, Dolores Primo de Rivera y Cobo de Guzmán. They were determined both to subjugate the Jonsistas and, eventually, to see off the leadership aspirations of Manuel Hedilla, whom they regarded as a proletarian upstart. In late December 1936, that struggle saw the defenestration of Andrés Redondo as Territorial Chief of Castilla. The emotional fervour that had seen him acclaimed as Jefe at Onésimo's funeral had by now dissipated and the militia groups were keen to remove him.[93] The head of the Valladolid militias was José Antonio

Girón de Velasco, a one-time Jonsista and collaborator of Onésimo Redondo who had thrown in his lot with the 'legitimists'. The loutish Girón claimed, rather implausibly given his own notorious bellicosity, that Andrés Redondo had tried to have him murdered and forced him to seek the protection of Hedilla. In early December 1936, there was a theatrical struggle in Hedilla's office in Salamanca, during which Redondo made to draw a revolver but was restrained by Hedilla. The schism was resolved when Hedilla came down on Girón's side. Andrés Redondo was officially removed as Jefe Territorial de Castilla at a meeting of the Provisional Command Council on 8 January 1937. He accepted the decision with a dignified docility, withdrawing from politics and returning to his career in banking, as he had told Javier he would.[94] He was replaced by José Antonio Girón de Velasco with the somewhat different title of Territorial Inspector of Castilla, and Dionisio Ridruejo, a close friend of José Antonio Primo de Rivera, became Provincial Chief of Valladolid.[95] At this point Mercedes and Javier were careful not to get involved in these internal divisions within the wider Falange. Nevertheless, the gulf between Falangists and Jonsistas was encapsulated within the women's movement by Mercedes's comment that 'I simply do not feel the Sección Femenina's notion of their political activities being only for women.'[96]

The opening move in the power struggle was made by Pilar. At the first national assembly (Consejo Nacional) of the Sección Femenina held in Salamanca and Valladolid between 6 and 9 January 1937, she announced the formal incorporation of Auxilio de Invierno into the Falange. That she was able to do so reflected both her own prestige as the sister of José Antonio Primo de Rivera and the chaotic weakness that characterised Hedilla's stewardship of the Command Council. Pilar was throwing down the gauntlet with a massive assertion of her authority. Pilar herself was chief, or Delegada Nacional, of the Sección Femenina which was, in Falangist jargon, a 'delegation' or section of the Falange. Auxilio de Invierno was, in turn, now deemed to be a subsection, or Delegación, of the Sección Femenina. All the provincial chiefs of the Sección Femenina were to become provincial delegates of Auxilio de Invierno. This left Mercedes Sanz-Bachiller as no more than the provincial chief of the Sección Femenina and provincial delegate of Auxilio de Invierno for Valladolid. It was apparently a massive triumph for Pilar.[97]

However, one thing was the issuing of statements at a meeting and another was the reality on the ground. The decisions of the Consejo Nacional reflected the fact that Pilar had used her authority to influence Hedilla. However, Hedilla was not very bright and was easily manipulable. Moreover, although now deemed administratively to be under the jurisdiction of the Sección Femenina, Auxilio de Invierno was, in practical terms, independent. Unlike the Sección Femenina, Auxilio de Invierno was not the exclusive terrain of women and prominent roles were being played by men. The most important of them, Javier Martínez de Bedoya, had a relationship with Mercedes that was deepening into something more than political collaboration. Given his friendship with Onésimo Redondo, and his early prominence in the Juntas de Ofensiva Nacional Sindalista, Javier was the object of considerable suspicion from the 'legitimists' in general and Pilar in particular. After all, in their eyes, he was a traitor who had left the Falange in January 1935 along with the other JONS founder, Ramiro Ledesma Ramos, in protest at the growing power of José Antonio Primo de Rivera.[98]

Mercedes and Javier moved quickly to counter Pilar's influence over Hedilla. On 10 January 1937, the day after the national assembly of the Sección Femenina closed, they visited Hedilla at his headquarters in Salamanca. Javier argued that Pilar should be replaced by Mercedes as Delegada Nacional and the Auxilio de Invierno transferred from the jurisdiction of the Sección Feminina to become a separate branch or Delegación of Falange Española de las JONS. Aware of the latent hostility of the Primo de Rivera clan towards himself, Hedilla was quickly persuaded that the new movement could be of great value if controlled directly by the Falange's Command Council (Junta de Mando). On 14 January 1937, Hedilla, in his capacity as Chief of the Provisional Command Council of the Falange, issued a decree naming Comrade Javier Martínez de Bedoya as national secretary of Auxilio de Invierno. Pilar could not prevent this but, on seeing the document, under Hedilla's signature, she had added by hand 'As chief of the Sección Femenina, in charge of Auxilio de Invierno, Pilar Primo de Rivera'. She had not been able to block formal recognition of Mercedes Sanz-Bachiller's position as head of Auxilio de Invierno but at least she ensured that the organisa-tion remained, theoretically at least, under the jurisdiction of the Sección Femenina.[99]

Pilar's imposition of her authority at the Sección Femenina's national assembly coincided with the defenestration of Andrés Redondo and the victory of the 'legitimists' over the Jonsistas in Valladolid. The fact that Pilar belonged to one clique within the complex struggle for control of the Falange was a weakness in terms of her rivalry with Mercedes Sanz-Bachiller. Mercedes and Javier did not aspire to run a national party, merely to get on with running – as independently as possible – their welfare organisation. They had distanced themselves from the coming struggle for power within the Falange. It was therefore possible that Pilar's involvement in the wider Falangist ambitions of her group might be used in their favour. In the internal div-isions within the Falange deriving from the arrest of José Antonio and intensified by his execution, Pilar was at the head of one of the two principal factions. Officially, leadership lay with the radical fascist group led by Manuel Hedilla, who was close to the German Chargé d'Affaires in Spain, the enthusi-astically Nazi, General Wilhelm Faupel. The Falangist intellec-tual, Pedro Lain Entralgo, saw a copy of Hitler's *Mein Kampf* on Hedilla's desk which he assumed to be both unread and a gift from Faupel.[100] However, Hedilla's enjoyment of German support was countered by the considerable influence wielded by Pilar's patrician group of 'legitimists' who regarded Hedilla with a snobbish contempt for his proletarian origins and his thuggish style. They had acquiesced in his election as Provisional Chief only to keep open the leadership issue while they had still hoped that it might be possible to get José Antonio Primo de Rivera back to the Nationalist zone via a prisoner exchange. Shattered by the news that their founder had been executed, and aware of the ever-present threat of being taken over by General Franco, the 'legitimists' aimed to keep the post of National Chief open until the arrival of José Antonio's friend, executor and Secretary-General of the Falange, Raimundo Fernández Cuesta, at the time imprisoned in Madrid. In this context, with two Primo de Rivera brothers, Fernando and José Antonio, dead and another, Miguel, still in a Republican prison, Pilar became the key card in the 'legitimist' hand as the principal living link with the founder of the Falange.

Pilar was described by Ramón Serrano Suñer, Franco's brother-in-law and closest political adviser, as the 'priestess' of the 'legitimist' group. Closely watched by Franco's spies, they used to meet in her house in the Plazuela de San Julián in Salamanca. Falangists from all over the Nationalist zone would stop by to receive their instructions from her or to pass on their complaints about Franco's failure to fulfil the legacy of José Antonio.[101] Pilar had not endeared herself to Franco by opposing the adoption of the Royalist yellow and red flag and anthem (the Marcha Real), and by distributing a leaflet advocating the red and black flag of the Falange and its hymn 'Cara al Sol' as the national anthem. When some of the things said about him in Pilar's apartment were reported back to the Caudillo, he was furious.[102] Javier and Mercedes claimed consistently that they stood aside from these inner party rivalries and concentrated on their work in Auxilio de Invierno.[103] Nonetheless, the *tertulia* or salon held in Mercedes's apartment in Valladolid became a kind of headquarters for the one-time Jonsistas who opposed the 'legitimists'.[104]

The cause of Auxilio de Invierno was fortunate in that, at the end of 1936, Dionisio Ridruejo had been named by Hedilla as Provincial Chief of the Valladolid Falange to replace Andrés Redondo.[105] There was a special bond between Dionisio Ridruejo and Mercedes Sanz-Bachiller. When Mercedes had been a student at the French convent in Valladolid, one of her best friends had been Ridruejo's girlfriend. That personal link was always to tie them. According to Ridruejo,

> Mercedes was direct, vehement, and both bodily and spiritually, was the very image of fresh natural drive and energy. She was a brunette, with a voice and gestures that were rather poignant, strong, with a beauty that was accentuated by the rather old-fashioned mourning and the austerity of her dress. She had a wide face, a firm body, very expressive hands that seemed to grasp and give shape to her thoughts.[106]

Javier was very much the opposite – quiet and reticent, with a soft, round appearance. His innate caution was often mistaken for cowardice. Unlike Mercedes, Javier fitted ill with the aggressive and impetuous tone that was fashionable in the early Falange. She inspired an enthusiasm bordering on adoration; he provoked a puzzled suspicion. For Ridruejo, they complemented each other perfectly – 'we could speak of impetuosity and reflection, of impulsiveness and patience, of a capacity for quick decisions and a capacity for painstaking organisation'.[107]

A situation of outright hostility between Pilar and Mercedes did not develop in part because of the conciliatory efforts of the new Provincial Chief. Dionisio Ridruejo was not really interested in the internal wranglings and he thought highly of what Mercedes and Javier were trying to do through their new organisation. As a good friend of Mercedes, he extended his friendship to Javier. Almost every night in the early days of 1937, they would both spend the evenings chatting with Mercedes about the progress of the war and the future role of the Falange. During these conversations, Mercedes, with typical impetuousness, declared that it was a scandalous waste of money that Ridruejo, Javier and other Falangist leaders should be spending money living separately in pensions. She found them a house and a woman to cook for them. The friendship was not without its tensions since Javier remained a Jonsista at heart. In lengthy discussions, he would counter the Falangist notions of Ridruejo with the ideas of Onésimo Redondo and Ramiro Ledesma Ramos. Nevertheless, the link with Ridruejo was enormously useful for Auxilio de Invierno. As Provincial Chief, Ridruejo was able to provide substantial funds for the enterprise. More importantly, he accompanied them to Salamanca whenever it was necessary to negotiate with the Command Council and the leadership of the Sección Femenina. Ridruejo was the perfect intermediary since he had considerable influence with Pilar Primo de Rivera. That was partly because of his friendship with her brother José Antonio. In turn, Pilar relied on Ridruejo for political advice and for help in drafting her speeches.[108]

A series of Machiavellian manoeuvrings in April 1937 saw Franco take over all the political forces of the Nationalist zone and forcibly unite Falangists, Carlists and monarchists into a single party known as Falange Española Tradicionalista y de las JONS. Fortuitously, Mercedes and Javier took little active part in the machinations surrounding the so-called *Unification*. They were, understandably, given the rivalry with Pilar Primo de Rivera, more sympathetic to Hedilla, and Mercedes certainly enjoyed the strong support of the Chief of the Provisional Command Council.[109] However, because they were too busy following the orders of General Mola to prepare, in anticipation of the fall of the Basque Country, for the extension of Auxilio de Invierno to Bilbao, they were simply unable to get involved in the events in Salamanca. Nevertheless, Javier had made no secret of the fact that he and Mercedes were hoping for the success of Hedilla.[110] It was a tactical error for which they would pay dearly, not immediately but in the years to come. For the moment, they were saved by the fact that, during the actual power struggle in Salamanca, Pilar Primo de Rivera played an ambiguous game. It was only the tactical ineptitude of Hedilla, together with the residual prestige of her name, that rescued Pilar from the consequences of her failure to side with Franco from the first. Eventually, she was able, by dint of enthusiastic and submissive collaboration, to rebuild her position within the Francoist regime. However, that would take time and, in the meanwhile, she would lose vital ground to Mercedes Sanz-Bachiller.

In the wake of the first national assembly of the Sección Femenina and until the April 1937 decree of unification, there were five delegations or sections of the Sección Femenina – Press and Propaganda, Administration, Nurses and Soldiers' Welfare, Auxilio de Invierno and Flechas ('Arrows' or Youth). On 30 April 1937, Captain Ladislao López Bassa, the new secretary of FET y de las JONS, issued a document that ran as follows: 'In the name of the Caudillo, I issue this provisional appointment as National Female Delegate of the Movement of FET y de las JONS of Pilar Primo de Rivera y Sáenz de Heredia, in order that she proceed with the greatest urgency to the organisation and integration within the Movement of the old feminine organisations of Falange Española de las JONS, the Traditionalist Communion (the Carlist organisation) and Auxilio de Invierno.'[111] Armed with this commission, Pilar Primo de Rivera set about trying to unify and impose her authority upon the three principal female organisations of the Nationalist zone. It was the beginning of years of friction. The two organisations with which there were the greatest difficulties were Auxilio de Invierno because of its identification with the JONS and with Hedilla and the Carlist 'Fronts and Hospitals' led by María Rosa Urraca Pastor because of its patrician and monarchist connections.

In the short term, however, Mercedes and Javier were quick to see that Pilar's position had been severely weakened in Franco's eyes. They sped to Salamanca where they secured an interview with López Bassa, an obscure and mediocre soldier from Mallorca, who had been imposed as Secretary of FET y de las JONS by Franco with the task of maintaining a vigilant control over internal Falangist politics. Barely had they shaken off the dust of the road from Valladolid than his visitors proposed to him that the name of Auxilio de Invierno be changed to Auxilio Social and that the organisation be not a dependency of the Sección Femenina but a separate entity within the new single party. The jettisoning of a name originally adopted to imply objectives limited in time and scale was a barely masked declaration of ambition. López Bassa replied that it was a good moment to do what they wanted.

Within hours, they were received by Franco's immensely powerful brother-in-law, Ramón Serrano Suñer, at the Caudillo's headquarters in the Episcopal Palace of Salamanca. Javier recalled Serrano Suñer afterwards as 'a vision from beyond the grave: pallid, white-haired, in pain, anguished, dressed in strict mourning. He was a suffering soul who spoke to us of his two brothers sacrificed in the Red zone and whose memory would always be with him.' He too was sympathetic and undertook to pass on their request to Franco. Given his virtual autonomy in political matters, it is unlikely that Serrano Suñer needed much time in order to convince a Franco more concerned with military problems. The change of name was successfully implemented on 24 May 1937 together with the transfer of massive power to Mercedes Sanz-Bachiller. In an altogether astonishing document, López Bassa wrote to Mercedes:

In the name of the Caudillo, and at the suggestion of the Delegada Nacional of the Feminine Movement of Falange Española Tradicionalista y de las JONS, I issue this appointment of Mercedes Sanz-Bachiller, widow of Redondo, as National Delegate of Auxilio Social, which includes 'Auxilio de Invierno', the organisation known as 'Good Works for the Protection of Mother and Child', 'Relief for the Sick' and other similar welfare initiatives of the old organisations of Falange and Requeté. She is authorised to unify, within the organisation of 'Auxilio Social', in accord at all times with the General Government of the Spanish State, all the welfare organisations which receive official funding.[112]

These changes regarding Auxilio Social made political and administrative sense. After all, Auxilio de Invierno was never meant to be an entirely female initiative. There was also a case for consolidating all of the various welfare activities of the Nationalist Government. However, granting such sweeping responsibilities to Mercedes Sanz-Bachiller as part of the Falange Española Tradicionalista y de las JONS, parallel to and not subordinate to Sección Femenina, was also Franco's punitive reaction to Pilar's role during the murky intrigues of the unification process. A singularly malicious touch could be noted in the inclusion of the patently absurd statement that the entire thing came about as a result of a suggestion from Pilar. The knife was driven home further by the reference to the Sección Femenina as 'the Feminine Movement of FET y de las JONS', which may be taken as the consequence of more than López Bassa's clumsiness. Pilar was castigated by Auxilio Social being granted its independence and, in a move typical of Franco's cunning, given a rival, Mercedes Sanz-Bachiller, as a reminder that she could be cast into the darkness at any moment. The punishment went no further since the Caudillo needed the endorsement of the Primo de Rivera name for his regime. For the moment, a furious Pilar shelved thoughts of reasserting her control of Auxilio Social and occupied herself with the immediate task of incorporating the Carlist feminine organisation, the Margaritas, into the Sección Femenina. There can be no doubt, however, that she harboured thoughts of retaliation and revenge.

Mercedes was now able to undertake far more ambitious tasks than before. Nurseries for the children of working mothers, centres for the prevention of child disease and homes for orphans were opened. It became apparent that the money gathered in the occasional collections was not enough to meet these needs. In its new guise, Auxilio Social was looking to run medical centres with laboratory facilities, ambulances and its own transport operation for the distribution of food. Mercedes came up with an idea that not only helped resolve the economic problem but also brought enormous propaganda benefit for the incipient Franco regime. She proposed the constitution of an international network of Amigos de Auxilio Social. She travelled to Lisbon, Paris and Biarritz where she established links with socially prominent Spaniards. Soon the Friends of Auxilio Social in France had a committee whose honorary president was Marshal Pétain. Committees were established in New York, Buenos Aires, Manila and London, where its patrons included the ex-Queen of Spain, Victoria Eugenia. Mercedes herself would make propaganda visits to Germany, Italy, France and Britain. Shortly after her organisation's conversion into Auxilio Social, General Mola had ordered that six gigantic military transports were to be made available to it when Bilbao finally fell. The capture of the Basque capital on 19 June 1937 saw Auxilio Social make its first entry into a previously Republican-held city. This enabled the press coverage of Mercedes's fund-raising initiative to give the impression that the social work being undertaken was aimed at alleviating the atrocities of the Reds.[113]

Within hours of the fall of Bilbao, Auxilio Social's six huge military trucks, heavily laden with food, were rumbling in. They did the journey back and forth from Vitoria and some days later an Auxilio Social train entered the city. The scale of the operation was such that, perhaps inevitably, jealous glances were cast from elsewhere in the Nationalist coalition. In addition to the festering determination of the leader of the Sección Femenina to bring Auxilio Social back under her authority, now the Catholic Church began to move. The principal ecclesiastical complaints were that Auxilio Social's rhetoric of justice obviated the need for the traditional virtue of charity and that the organisation's facilities for children were contrary to the Catholic exaltation of the family. Mercedes Sanz-Bachiller and Javier Martínez de Bedoya responded quickly with their customary shrewdness. They set up an advisory office for moral and religious questions under a young priest from Valladolid, Andrés María Mateo. Father Mateo was encharged with creating a network of religious advisers for each province.[114]

These moves went some way to neutralising religious qualms about Auxilio Social but they could not diminish the advantage given Sección Femenina by the similarity of its ideology to traditional Catholic views on women and the family. In any case, the ecclesiastical authorities were outraged that a simple priest should be given nationwide responsibilities in the area of moral questions without being subject to the authority of each diocese.[115] In general, the Catholic Church was highly suspicious of the Falange. On 24 April 1937, the Primate Cardinal Gomá had written to the Vatican about the 'Hitlerian tendency' of the Falange towards 'the exaltation of material strength and of the omnipotence of the State'.[116] In this regard, the veteran Jonsistas were more outspoken in support of a 'statism' that seemed inimical to Catholic values. In contrast, the piously Catholic Pilar Primo de Rivera, in the context of her submissiveness to male authority, was especially compliant, indeed subservient, where the Church was concerned. This would be a significant advantage for her after the Civil War was over.

For the moment, the rivalry between Pilar and Mercedes would remain latent, ready to burst to the surface at the first sign of weakness on the part of the organisers of Auxilio Social. It was fed not only by personal jealousy but also by a serious conflict of ideals. Mercedes Sanz's concept of Auxilio Social aimed to mobilise women along the lines of a rather fanciful and idealised notion of the role of women in Nazi Germany. Pilar's ideas were a faithful reflection of her brother's Badajoz speech on the role of women. She was influenced more by Italian fascism than by Nazism, and even more by Catholic traditions of patrician charity work than by any foreign models. Pilar's life's work had as its principal objective the demobilis-ation of women to prepare homes and provide children for Falangist warriors. In 1937, however, the circumstances of the war favoured Mercedes Sanz. As major Republican cities were being captured, occupied and savagely purged, there was a need for a logistical operation of social welfare much larger than the original canteens of Auxilio de Invierno. In the wake of wartime casualties and the repression, the enormity of the consequent social dislocation was beyond the capacity of the Sección Femenina. To the chagrin of Pilar, the range of the responsibilities entrusted to Auxilio Social grew ever larger.

As the war in the North moved westwards into Cantabria, Auxilio Social was warned that it would not be able to count on military transport for its materials. Moreover, the nascent government had set up a Welfare Delegation under José María Martínez Ortega, the Conde de Argillo (the future father-in-law of Franco's daughter). It immediately competed with Auxilio Social, requisitioning vehicles and collecting mass donations in kind via the Civil Governors of each province. It was typical of the decisiveness and determination of Mer-cedes that she immediately mobilised her foreign Committees of Friends of Auxilio Social to raise money to buy lorries. So successful was her initiative that Auxilio Social soon had its own road haulage fleet. At the same time, Javier Martínez de Bedoya, with Mercedes's agreement, worked on an alliance with the Quakers. The New York Committee of Friends of Auxilio Social had suggested the connection but both Javier and Mercedes had been reluctant to act upon it. They were worried about the suspicions of the Catholic Church and of the hostility of pro-German Falangists and Army officers to the idea of Quaker delegations wandering around the front. In the event, Javier was able to generate enthusiastic support for the idea in Franco's acting Foreign Minister, General Francisco Gómez Jordana. The Conde de Jordana supplied the necessary safe-conducts for the Quaker representatives. Soon the aid of the Quakers was being channelled through Auxilio Social. Within hours of the fall of Santander on 26 August 1937, a ship loaded with food arrived from Southampton.[117]

It was an indication of Mercedes's growing status within the Nationalist zone that she was increasingly called upon to play a prominent role in official functions. She had become an important part of the Nationalist establishment, her presence required for the inauguration of new institutions. She inspected units of Falangist militia at major occasions. Particularly significant in this regard was her official visit to Germany on a lengthy fact-finding and fund-raising tour at the beginning of August 1937. According to Javier Martínez de Bedoya, whose professional and political admiration of Mercedes was developing into something much deeper, 'she received a tremendous reception'. She was received by Hermann Göring and by Dr Robert Ley, head of the Nazi Labour Organisation, the German Workers' Front. Interviewed by the correspondents of the Falangist press, she expressed her interest in comparing Auxilio Social with the work being done by the Nazi Party. Among the many sources of charitable donations to Auxilio Social, substantial sums were raised in Germany along with large gifts of food, clothing and machinery. She returned in 1938 and also visited Fascist Italy.[118] That she could absent herself in this way was an indication both of Mercedes's genuine commitment to improving her organisation and also to the pleasure that she derived from her public presence. However, it also suggested a degree of naïveté or perhaps insouciance about the pettiness of Falange politics. To a large extent, she lacked the malice and narrow-mindedness required for success in the internal struggle for power.

This was revealed at the end of August 1937 when the previous Jefe of the Sección Femenina of Valladolid, Rosario Pereda, was enabled by the Francoist capture of Santander to return home. During her absence, the number of women belonging to the organisation had risen from thirty-six to twelve thousand. Nevertheless, Mercedes was delighted by the reappearance of Rosario and, already overburdened with her work as National Delegate of Auxilio Social, happily issued a statement to the press announcing her own withdrawal and the appointment of Rosario Pereda to replace her. She would later regret her rash generosity in relinquishing her power base in the Valladolid Sección Femenina. Rosario Pereda had once been in love with Onésimo Redondo and always held a grudge against Mercedes which was exacerbated by seeing her now enjoy such power and prestige. Within two months of taking over the local Sección Femenina, she would be working to turn its affiliates against Mercedes. It was a betrayal that hurt greatly: 'What she made me suffer!' exclaimed Mercedes later but, typically, she did not bear a grudge and soon forgave her rival.[119] Rosario died young and, on her deathbed, begged her husband Anselmo de la Iglesia to convey her apologies to Mercedes which he did in a moving letter.[120]

For the moment, however, the political fortunes of both Mercedes and Javier were still in the ascendant. From 6 to 10 September 1937, Javier attended the Nazi Party Congress at Nuremberg at the special invitation of the German Government. He took advantage of the trip to get closer to Ramón

Serrano Suñer, with whom he achieved the use of the intimate 'tu' form of address. They returned via Rome, and Javier was struck by the contrast between Serrano Suñer's enormous enthusiasm for Italian fascism and the 'physical repugance' that he felt for German National-Socialism. Javier arrived back in Spain in time to speak at the first Congress of Auxilio Social held from 13 to 18 September. As he expected, the Congress was a great public acclamation of the work of Auxilio Social and particularly of Mercedes Sanz-Bachiller.[121] On 19 October 1937, Franco created the first Consejo Nacional de Falange Española Tradicionalista y de las Juntas de Ofensiva Nacional Sindicalista. It was to be the supreme consultative body of the regime with theoretical responsibility for helping the Caudillo decide on the broad lines of policy. It had to meet at least once a year. Mercedes Sanz-Bachiller was named as number ten of the first forty-seven *consejeros*. Pilar Primo de Rivera was number one. The relatively high position accorded Mercedes Sanz-Bachiller was a symbolic recognition of her position as the widow of Onésimo Redondo as much as of the importance of her work in Auxilio Social. Javier Martínez de Bedoya, the only other Jonsista in addition to Mercedes Sanz, occupied the twenty-eighth place – a reflection of his burgeoning relationship with Ramón Serrano Suñer. The balance of forces was revealed in the fact that there were seventeen Falangists, of whom thirteen could be considered 'legitimists'.[122] Mercedes's designation would be repeated on 9 September 1940 when the Second Consejo Nacional de Falange Española Tradiciona-lista y de las Juntas de Ofensiva Nacional Sindicalista was named and she was promoted to number six out of sixty-four *consejeros*.

The scale of the task undertaken by Auxilio Social gave rise to fears about maintaining the volunteer labour force necessary, particularly once the war was over and the survivors would want to return to some kind of normality. There were forty thousand women working in Auxilio Social and already the numbers of volunteers was drying up – as Javier noted in his diary, 'the women comrades of the Sección Femenina are rather losing heart'. Accordingly, working on an idea from Jesús Ercilla, Javier and Mercedes began to work on a draft project for a female equivalent of military conscription to provide the necessary labour to keep Auxilio Social's services runnning. On 29 September 1937, they visited Ramón Serrano Suñer to discuss the idea with him. He was so enthusiastic that he asked them to wait while he went to speak with Franco. Within half an hour, they were in the presence of the Caudillo. Javier noted that evening in his diary, 'He is extraordinarily small, a soft face, with big eyes that dart about constantly. His voice is smooth, sweet, and at times a speech defect is discernible.' They were nonplussed when he treated them to a lengthy eulogy of the work of Auxilio Social. Unusually, using the 'tu' form, he invited them to join him in armchairs in his darkened office and, in a voice quivering with emotion, said, 'You are the apostles of a social mysticism. The Falange and Spain will thank you for this.'

His enthusiasm, as he made clear, was because of the importance that he attributed to the rearguard in the war. The purges in the rearguard were a reflection of Franco's obsession with the need for the long-term 'redemption' of the Spanish people from their leftist errors. In that context, he was quick to see the relevance of the welfare work of Auxilio Social. With regard to the specifics of the Servicio Social project, however, they had to work hard to persuade him of the need for such a service. He put objection after objection, concerned that the project would break with the traditional role of Spanish women. They tried to convince him that welfare activities had always been carried out by Spanish women 'either out of charity or good taste'. Finally, he cut off the discussion saying laconically only, 'Well, go and draw up a draft decree and I will study it article by article.' They left his office convinced that the project would not prosper.[123]

Refusing to be downhearted, they did everything possible to create a favourable climate for his reception of the draft project. On 5 October 1937, Ramón Serrano Suñer telephoned Javier to congratulate him on the special issue of *Libertad* that he had prepared to commemorate the first anniversary of the Caudillo's elevation to power.[124] In fact, Franco reacted favourably to the draft and gave orders for the creation, on 9 October 1937, of Women's Social Service (Servicio Social de la Mujer) under the auspices of Auxilio Social. The possible implications of this were outlined by Javier in terms that were redolent of his profound Catholicism and yet would not have been out of place in the Nazi Party. He published an article on 29 November 1937, seven weeks after the decree was issued:

> Let it be perfectly clear that a premise of the National Syndicalist freedom that we are offering must be the rigorous taming of any trace of arrogance and impurity, of envy and of anger, of avarice and slander. For all these things, Falange does not request discipline: Falange will impose discipline harshly and all resources to do so will not be enough. The militia life, labour service, the 'Servicio Social' rigidly and strictly imposed for women, the tightest syndical organisation and propaganda will be the natural means that we must use to this end. But we should not forget the efficacy of violence and of the total expulsion from the bosom of the national community of those who who resist the discipline of our Movement.[125]

The reference to the 'national community' was redolent of the *Volksgemeinschaft* with which, no doubt, Javier had become familiarised during his time in Germany.

Franco's intention was to establish a permanent regime from which all traces of leftism and liberalism had been eliminated. Considerable cruelty was visited upon women under the rhetorical Francoist umbrella of 'redemption' – rape, confiscation of goods, imprisonment as retribution for the behaviour of a son or husband. Widows and the wives of prisoners were raped. Many were forced to live in total poverty and often, out of desperation, to sell themselves on the streets. The increase in prostitution both benefited Francoist men who thereby satisfied their lust and also reassured them that 'Red' women were a fount of dirt and corruption. If the repression was the stick of 'redemption', Auxilio Social was the carrot, a crucial source of food and shelter for those left hungry and homeless by the war. Nevertheless, as Sheelagh Ellwood has noted, there was a 'bitter irony' in such aid being given by an organisation that was part of the very forces responsible for the devastation and bloodshed.[126] Inevitably, although it was certainly not the intention of Mercedes Sanz-Bachiller, the distribution of charity carried with it a price for the recipients.

That is often the way with charity. Just as the recipients of handouts from the Church were expected to stay for mass, so too those who ate in the Auxilio Social canteens were expected to sit under portraits of Franco and José Antonio Primo de Rivera, to say grace before they ate, to give the fascist salute and to sing the Falangist hymn 'Cara al Sol' (Face to the Sun). For those who were of the left, this signified being patronised and humiliated. In the words of one witness,

> widows and orphans still alive and free have to hide their grief for fear of being killed. They begged secretly, because anyone who helped the widows or orphans of a 'Red' exposed him or herself to being shadowed. Only the Social Assistance which has been organised is able to allay material suffering, but even then it is by imposing moral suffering: obliging orphans to sing the songs of the murderers of their father; to wear the uniform of those who have executed him, and to curse the dead and to blaspheme his memory.[127]

Franco perceived that, in addition to its humanitarian value, the work of Mercedes Sanz-Bachiller had enormous propaganda potential for the Nationalists both inside and outside Spain. Florence Farmborough, a British propagandist for Franco who broadcast regularly from Burgos, was a great enthusiast of the work of Auxilio Social and wrote an idealised account of its work.

> The young girls, all enthusiastic volunteers, all staunch followers of the Phalanx, are standing about in groups; white aprons over their dark dresses, their badge of red yoke and arrows showing up plainly against the navy-blue of their blouses; they are ready to begin their work of serving. The doors are opened and men and women enter. In their hands are pots and large muglike receptacles. Food is given to all in abundance; no documents are required, no personal questions are asked. What does it matter if they are White or Red! What *does* matter is that they are hungering – that is sufficient for the Phalangists. And, if they are Reds, all the better! Let them learn the great lesson that although they clench their fist in hatred – to take by force – the Phalanx opens its hand to give – with love.

Clearly oblivious to the fact that any adult who was considered to have left or liberal sympathies was in prison, executed or in hiding, Miss Farmborough went on to extol the work for children done by Auxilio Social. 'And here the Social Aid workers demonstrate their womanly tenderness in all its beauty, for these children of humble origin, ignorant and accustomed to the harsh blows of an unkind world, must first be *won*! Many of them have the seeds of class hatred sown by the hands of their own parents; and it is this hereditary malice that the workers have to disperse.' The children in question were hungry because their parents were either dead or in prison or, at best, deprived of work. Miss Farmborough seemed unaware of this background.

> For them, this spacious dining room, with its white-aproned attendants and its abundance of good things to eat, is a revelation! They had been told that the 'Fascists' carried daggers in their hands; but, instead of a dagger, it was bread! . . . White bread! And the heart of the child eagerly responds with intuitive ardour and reasoning, for what so quick as a child's instinct to sense sympathy?

Her paean of praise to the white-aproned women of Auxilio Social ended with the claim, 'The children are healthier in body and soul for having come into personal contact with them; they come to these Social Aid centres as wild woodland creatures; they leave them as rational human beings.'[128]

In less romanticised terms, an American pro-Franco propagandist, Merwin K. Hart, wrote of the 'vision and courage' in the welfare work carried out by Auxilio Social. In his version this work was necessitated because, in recently occupied villages and cities, 'crimes had been committed. Civilians, men, women and children, had been murdered. The whole population had been terrified for weeks, possibly for months, and had been undernourished; many had become emaciated; food was the first requisite.' The Nationalist repression that made Auxilio de Invierno necessary in the first place was conveniently forgotten. Hart recounted an interview with a senior figure of Auxilio Social. He asked, 'Is the work of the Auxilio Social done for Nationalists only, or do those who have sympathised with the enemy benefit too?' She replied, 'No distinction whatever is made. The only qualification for relief at the hands of our organisation is to be Spanish and to be in want. No questions are asked.'[129]

The Francoist propagandist, the bewildered surrealist Ernesto Giménez Caballero, commented on the other touch of simplicity and formidable charm of our girls of Auxilio Social is to be found in the white apron worn over their uniforms. How many times, while at one or another front, has one gone to visit the children of the 'Auxilios' and help the helpers, not so much in a burst of combative charity as rather carried away by enthusiasm and envy of those children whose servers and cooks were the most beautiful girls in white aprons and blue frocks. The Spanish soldier never felt so soldierly as when he was alongside these little kitchen workers of Auxilio Social.[130]

If not all had as idyllically fragrant roles as those described by such enthusiasts, women by the thousands were recruited for war work by the Auxilio Social. Originally all volunteers, since the creation of conscription for women in October 1937, a period in the Women's Social Service (Servicio Social) was obligatory for any female who aspired to a job in the civil service or as a teacher, to acquire a professional qualification in any educational establishment, and to obtain a passport or a driving licence. There were very few exceptions. They included nuns, widows or married women with children, the eldest of eight unmarried siblings or girls who had lost their family at the hands of the left in the Spanish Civil War. These conditions ensured that a high degree of social control could be exercised through the Servicio Social. To have persuaded Franco to create the Women's Social Service was a remarkable triumph for Mercedes and, inevitably, it was perceived as an affront to the Sección Femenina. As Javier Martínez de Bedoya himself recognised later, 'This was our first political error, because, obviously, we were invading a terrain that was not exclusive to us as a result of which from that very day we faced the obstinate and continuous hostility of Pilar Primo de Rivera, of all her political allies and of all her pressure groups.'[131] Mercedes herself commented, 'Well, of course,

Pilar was furious. We organised a social service that was the absolute tops . . . I can understand . . . I know I was invading the territory of the Sección Femenina.'[132]

Javier was mistaken if he thought that the hostility of Pilar dated only from September 1937. It went back to a year earlier. However, in the immediate wake of the unification of the Nationalist political groupings in April, the 'legitimists' had lost vast areas of ground and a seething Pilar had had to bide her time. Now, bitterly resentful at this new interference, as she perceived it, by Mercedes Sanz-Bachiller in her own sphere of power, she was determined to recoup the ground lost. Pilar was far from being without power or influence. In the last resort, by offering her name to Franco in his quest to impose his authority on the Falange, she acquired considerable political leverage. If Mercedes Sanz-Bachiller and Javier Martínez de Bedoya played their cards badly, they would find her ready to pounce.

In early 1938, Javier was summoned to Burgos by the newly appointed Minister of Syndical Action and Organisation, Pedro González Bueno, who offered him the post of Undersecretary. He refused, on the grounds that he did not believe in vertical syndicates. So outraged was the Minister that he insisted that Javier personally explain his refusal to Franco. In the event, the Caudillo seemed unconcerned. However, the intensity of Javier's relief at not having to move from Valladolid to Burgos made him acknowledge that his feelings for Mercedes Sanz-Bachiller were changing. He reflected later

> I realised for the first time that my days would become interminable and my work hateful if I didn't have the certainty of having Mercedes, in some way, alongside me, even if it was only in the broadest sense of knowing that she was involved in the same task. I was frightened to think that this feeling might be love.

He endeavoured to allay his own fears by reflecting that he was not alone in feeling that there was somehow something special about working with Mercedes.

> I tried to calm myself by thinking about the fact that, in all the men who worked under Mercedes's orders, I had noticed something similar: a special delight in obeying her, a pleasure in working without a break just for her and a belief that to have a one-to-one meeting with her was a real reward. And this was not just among those of us who surrounded her in Valladolid, but also among those from other provinces, for whom a telephone call from Mercedes was always decisive and a private meeting with her something really special.[133]

Shortly after spurning Pedro González Bueno's offer of an undersecretaryship, Javier was summoned once more to Burgos to see the new Minister of the Interior, Ramón Serrano Suñer. He offered him the job of directing the newly reorganised Office of Welfare Services. It was an offer that could not be refused. It meant taking over the operation of a rival, the Conde de Argillo, and it meant that Auxilio Social would become a charge on the finances of the State. Instead of being financed by charity and street collections, Auxilio Social would now receive a subvention for each person dependent on its services. This opened the way to massive expansion. Based in Valladolid, the principal function of the Office of Welfare Services was to rebuild some kind of social infrastructure in towns that had been in the Republican zone, been captured and subjected to purges. The appointment of Javier thus significantly strengthened the position of Mercedes.[134]

When the Nationalist forces entered a starving Barcelona on 26 January 1939, Mercedes arrived at the head of the Auxilio Social team. She established herself in the Ritz along with much of the top brass of the regime. Seeing her surrounded

by men, Javier felt twinges of jealousy which confirmed that
he had indeed fallen in love with her. If not quite the great
beauty that she seemed in Javier's eyes, Mercedes was sensuously attractive and had a tremendous vitality. She was also
gifted with a great facility – bordering on flirtatiousness – for
putting men at their ease. Javier was struck by 'the enormous
success that she had as a beautiful, intelligent woman with a
youthfulness that seemed the more remarkable because of her
special serenity'. He was alerted to his feelings by seeing
admirers hanging on her every word. 'I was able to see how
soldiers, politicians, diplomats, doctors, architects, businessmen
fluttered around her, dazzled by the charms of such a complete
personality, whose smile and whose conversation managed to
transport her interlocutor onto a plane of trust and mutual
interest that made the minutes or the hours pass unnoticed.'

These reflections made him begin to fear that, as soon as
the Civil War was over, he would lose her. He assumed that
she would rebuild her life without him. Alarmed by the prospect, he could no longer deceive himself as to the real nature
of his feelings. At the first opportunity to speak to her alone,
he asked her to marry him. Although she was not unaware of
his affections, his proposal came as a shock. She replied calmly,
'What you suggest, Javier, is madness: first, because I already
have three children; secondly, because of the political com-
motion that would be caused by the marriage of the widow
of a hero of the Cruzada with the war hardly over.' It was
an astute comment. He responded with an assurance of his
commitment to her children and of his conviction that any
political scandal would blow over quickly. She promised to
think over his proposal. Not unattractive, the round-faced
Javier was yet very different from Onésimo Redondo. Where
Mercedes's first husband was more conventionally handsome,
intense and brutally direct in his political ideas, Javier was
altogether more complex. His face shone with intelligence,
he was sensitive, an intellectual of considerable sophistication.

Shortly afterwards, Mercedes gave him her answer saying, 'I think you will be able to enjoy a house by the sea when we are married.' It was a reference to his childhood dream of living by the sea and the fact that she had just bought a house in Torremolinos called La Aldea. It would be their home for many of the next fifty years.[135]

At the end of the war, the Office of Welfare Services and Auxilio Social moved together to Madrid. The task facing Auxilio Social in the capital was monumental. It was necessary to deal with mass hunger, refugees from other parts of Spain, homelessness, broken families, orphaned children. In the early weeks after the capture of the capital, Auxilio Social distributed around 900,000 food rations each day. In Valencia, over two hundred thousand rations were distributed daily.[136] The scale of hunger throughout the recently captured Republican zone was a powerful argument for Mercedes Sanz-Bachiller to use against those who suggested that Auxilio Social was superfluous now that the war was over. In consequence, Auxilio Social and its budget grew, while jealousies within the Falange intensified. Pilar Primo de Rivera's resentment of Mercedes had simmered throughout the war and continued beyond the end of hostilities. Given Spain's social problems in the immediate postwar period, Auxilio Social grew substantially but was brought down by a number of unexpected political errors. At the end of the Civil War, for instance, Pilar's friend and ally, Raimundo Fernández Cuesta, the Minister-Secretary of the Falange, humiliated Mercedes Sanz-Bachiller when he hijacked her plans to move Auxilio Social into splendid offices in Madrid at Alcalá 44, requisitioning the building as headquarters of FET y de las JONS.[137]

Throughout 1939, the rivalries within the Falange became ever more embittered. Javier Martínez de Bedoya threw away the advantages of his position by a quixotic gesture that deeply offended Serrano Suñer. On 26 July, Serrano Suñer had suggested that Javier be made Minister of Labour in the forthcoming cabinet reshuffle. This was to come about as a result of his having persuaded his brother-in-law Franco that the composition of the Government should reflect those who carried the greatest weight in the war. However, Javier's nomination was opposed by both monarchists and the 'legitimist' group of the Falange, led by Pilar and Miguel Primo de Rivera. When Javier had left the Falange along with Ramiro Ledesma Ramos in January 1935, he had burned his bridges with harshly critical parting words about José Antonio Primo de Rivera. The 'legitimists' had almost certainly not forgotten but their memories were now jogged by a best-selling biography of the Falangist leader. Felipe Ximénex de Sándoval's book reminded them that, in an article in Ledesma Ramos's newspaper, *Patria Libre*, Javier had spoken of 'the dead weight of the Falange', claiming that the elitism of José Antonio and obsessive bureaucracy had stifled any element of popular participation. He had ridiculed José Antonio as putting no effort into the Falange – 'he went only from twelve o'clock to two, before lunch, because, with ridiculous punctuality, he spent his afternoons showing off in parliament'. In his own account, the life of Onésimo Redondo published in 1937, Javier had massaged his own role out of the story and now it was exposed in embarrassing clarity.[138]

Since Raimundo Fernández Cuesta was being replaced as Minister-Secretary of the Falange Española y de las JONS by General Agustín Muñoz Grandes, the 'legitimists' complained to Serrano Suñer about the prospect of seeing a Jonsista as the only representative of the old Falange in the Government. At the same time, Franco asked his Chief of the General Staff, General Juan Vigón, for his opinion of the proposed 'victory government'. Vigón replied, 'this will be the first government of combatants and this lad has neither set foot at the front nor heard a shot. Don't you think that it would be a slap in the face for those who have risked their lives?' Accordingly, believing that Javier Martínez de Bedoya, at twenty-five years old, had plenty of time for preferment in the future, Franco struck him from the proposed cabinet list. On 7 August, Javier was told that he would therefore not be given the expected Ministry but would instead be made Undersecretary with the possibility in the future of becoming Minister. Mercedes was delighted. However, in extremely complex circumstances, internal intrigues within the regime saw the undersecretaryship given to one of the 'legitimists', Manuel Valdés Larrañaga. A furious Javier gave vent to his radical Jonsista instincts. Against the urgings of Mercedes, he wrote to Serrano Suñer, resigning his posts as Director General of Welfare Services and as member of the Consejo Nacional of FET y de las JONS. He also rashly denounced the new cabinet as 'a triumph of the CEDA', that is to say a triumph for the old conservative, Catholic establishment – a great insult to Serrano Suñer, who had been a parliamentary deputy for the CEDA and left it for the Falange. Furthermore, he encouraged other Falangists from Valladolid and from within Auxilio Social to write similar letters to the Minister. Serrano Suñer was livid.[139] It was hardly surprising when Javier was removed as Secretary of Auxilio Social by the Secretary General of FET y de las JONS, General Agustín Muñoz Grandes.[140]

This was the opportunity for which the group around Pilar Primo de Rivera had been waiting since May 1937. Javier Martínez de Bedoya had thereby played into their hands at a particularly difficult moment. The climate was changing rapidly in relation to welfare and the position of women. The relatively progressive stances that had been possible because of the wartime necessity for female labour were giving way to the reimposition of the most conservative traditional social values. With men returning from the front and looking for jobs, it was always inevitable that there would be postwar pressure on women to stay in their homes as wives and mothers. However, in the gender politics of the Franco regime, this economic rationale combined with a patriarchal ideology to reinforce a sweepingly passive role for women. Seeing which way the wind was blowing, Mercedes Sanz-Bachiller authorised the publication of a series of short practical manuals on motherhood, child-rearing, dressmaking, domestic science and the family.[141] They were readable, approachable and not weighed down with a sententious religious veneer. As an attempt to pre-empt a takeover bid by the Sección Femenina, they made sense but it was too little too late.

Javier had already given a hostage to fortune with his proposal of marriage to Mercedes at the end of the war. For the moment, oblivious to the gathering storm, they made preparations for a quiet wedding. Javier had taken a job as commercial director with the Valladolid publishing company Afrodisio Aguado. However, he was offered a generous olive branch by Serrano Suñer. As chairman of the executive committee (Junta Política) of the FET y de las JONS, Serrano Suñer had created the Institute of Political Studies under the chairmanship of Alfonso García Valdecasas, an old friend of José Antonio Primo de Rivera. With Serrano Suñer's agreement, García Valdecasas offered Javier the headship of the social policy section. He accepted but did not use the opportunity to build bridges to the Minister of the Interior. It was another serious error and deprived him and Mercedes of a valuable ally in the struggles to come. Javier and Mercedes married quietly on 3 November 1939. The wedding was considered by many extreme Falangist 'old shirts' as, in the words of Dionisio Ridruejo, 'the violation of a myth'. With typical humanity, Ridruejo commented that the undermining of her image as a heroine restored to Mercedes her human status.[142]

Mercedes herself was fully aware of the implications of what she was doing. Looking back in later life, she commented:

How easy it is to judge and to judge thoughtlessly! To try to rebuild a life when you are twenty-six years old. The dilemma is that either you live in the most absolute loneliness of soul and of body – yes, that too – or break with that loneliness. I knew that meant the renunciation and the loss of the esteem and the halo that surrounded me because I still carried with me socially the memory and the love of the myth, of the hero. But for me, he wasn't a myth, he was a man, the husband, the being who showed me the first essential things about life. The man with whom I suffered and underwent dreadful political persecution, exile, the incomprehension of many of his comrades and everything that a woman united with and in love with her husband suffers when she sees him suffer. To get married again did not mean forgetting him, if anything the opposite. It meant being able to find myself again, with serenity, with tranquillity in the soul, dignity and certainty in my actions and in my behaviour. It meant, at the end of the day, following the advice of Onésimo himself. How often during our five years of marriage did I say to him, 'Onésimo, they're going to kill you!' He would reply, 'You must remarry.' I would say, 'Who is going to want me?' Putting his hands together and linking his fingers, he would say, 'Like this. That's what you must do.' And so I followed his instructions.[143]

Within the value system of the time, much political capital could be made out of the contrast between the virginal dedication of the sister of José Antonio Primo de Rivera and the carnal weakness of the widow of Onésimo Redondo. The timing could not have been more unfortunate for Javier and Mercedes. The news of their wedding became public knowledge as preparations reached their height for the massive commemoration of the third anniversary of the execution of José Antonio Primo de Rivera by the Republicans on 20 November 1936. In an elaborately choreographed and widely publicised operation, for ten days and ten nights, a torchlit procession escorted José Antonio's mortal remains, exhumed in Alicante, in a five-hundred-kilometre journey for reburial with full military honours at El Escorial, the resting place of the Kings and Queens of Spain. An atmosphere of reverential hero worship which had revived many of the passions of the Civil War provided the perfect context for a campaign of gossip and innuendo against Mercedes Sanz. It bore fruit in the Teatro Español in Madrid on 21 December 1939. Serrano Suñer, keen to secure his own endorsement by the Primo de Rivera clan as legitimate successor to José Antonio, took up their case, criticising the entire basis of Auxilio Social in his closing words at its third National Congress.

In a speech whose aggressive intent was scarcely masked, he emphasised that the organisation was merely a temporary response to wartime problems – 'the work of Auxilio Social, in many of its facets, should not be considered a permanent institution'. He implied that canteens and day nurseries were left-wing ideas that encouraged indigence, citing José Antonio Primo de Rivera's criticisms of Soviet soup kitchens. The insinuation that Auxilio Social was somehow betraying the legacy of the founder of the Falange, coming so shortly after his burial in El Escorial, was a difficult blow to parry. In this regard, Serrano Suñer spoke of Auxilio Social as 'a lesser evil' and stated that 'we must ensure with all urgency that we avoid the danger of stimulating the begging spirit in Spaniards, fomenting rather the spirit of work'. Finally, he asserted that the principal concern of Auxilio Social should not be nurseries and child-minding facilities (which would permit women to work) but the organisation of orphanages. In typically Francoist rhetoric, he declared that Auxilio Social, 'by using traditional welfare structures instead of creating unnecessary new ones, could avoid hitting the reef, and escape the temptation to hold onto the trenches and maintain pedestals from which to distribute prebends and organise personality cults'. Mercedes immediately understood the devastating implications of the speech and escorted Serrano Suñer to the door in the midst of the glacial silence that had greeted his words.[144]

Serrano Suñer's speech reflected the fact that the wide-ranging radical pretensions of Auxilio Social – and particularly its aim to provide nursery facilities to help working mothers – had provoked the jealousy not only of Pilar Primo de Rivera and the Sección Femenina but also of the traditional charitable establishment, including the Catholic hierarchy. Moreover, the progressive humanitarian dimension of Auxilio Social sat ill with the ambience of repressive, regressive, postwar Francoism. Even more indicative of the enmity that Mercedes now faced were remarks made by Ramón Serrano Suñer in his speech about the financial probity of Auxilio Social. Amongst 'the guidelines for the new stage of Auxilio Social', he included 'austerity and rigour in its financial management; an implacable rigour that will be applied at all costs'. Referring to the need to avoid damaging rumours, he declared, 'Where there is an abuse, where an immoral situation is produced, it matters to us more than to anyone to cut them short and punish them with Falangist efficacy and swiftness.' In a totalitarian regime, where public statements were usually triumphalist, such comments carried the darkest implications.[145]

The unmistakable insinuation was that there had been a corrupt use of the massive funds of Auxilio Social. There were plenty of Falangists happy to add a gloss to the Minister's ambiguous statement. Soon there were rumours that Mercedes had embezzled several hundred thousand pesetas, among other things in order to buy La Aldea in Torremolinos. The allegations could not be proved, but, as is the way with malicious rumours, her name would remain besmirched.[146] Nevertheless, Mercedes began to fight back immediately. She sought an audience with the Minister-Secretary General of FET y de las JONS, General Agustín Muñoz Grandes. She made an eloquent case in favour of Auxilio Social and persuaded him to undertake a full-scale inspection of the organisation and its accounts. He was sufficiently impressed with the results of his investigation to undertake Mercedes's defence and went, on the morning of 28 December 1939, to speak to Franco on her behalf. He told her at lunchtime of that day, quite plausibly, that Franco had replied to his energetic defence of her work with Auxilio Social by saying only, 'I have a high regard for Mercedes for her qualities and for what she does. Nevertheless, she has made a lot of enemies all at once. Let us try to gain time.' It was typical of Franco's opacity. What he meant was that he was prepared to try to save Mercedes Sanz-Bachiller from the shipwreck of her new husband's political career.

The Caudillo had already been persuaded by Serrano Suñer of the political benefits of subordinating Women's Social Service to the Sección Femenina. Later the same afternoon, Franco signed the decree handing over the necessary powers. A mini civil war within the Falange started although the result was a foregone conclusion. Mercedes, now two months pregnant, briefly contacted political friends to see if there was any possibility of mounting a defence. It was too late. The 'legitimists' wanted to see Mercedes deposed as head of Auxilio Social and removed from the Consejo Nacional del Movimiento. The all-powerful Serrano Suñer was now their ally and he was still smarting from Javier's tactless reaction to failure to gain promotion. On 12 January 1940, Mercedes offered Franco her resignation from Auxilio Social. Through General Muñoz Grandes, he gave her a chance to reconsider but she replied that the dismantling of Auxilio Social together with Serrano Suñer's public attack on the organisation obliged her to stand firm.[147] It was typical of her essential rectitude and the fact that she was commited to the social work carried out by the organisation and had no desire to become embroiled in political squabbling.

The triumphalist attitude of the 'legitimists' was quickly manifested in the crowing of the official Falangist daily, *Arriba*.

Controlled by Serrano Suñer's Delegation of Press and Propaganda, the paper began in mid-January 1940 to attack the work of Mercedes. An editorial of 17 January 1940 accused Auxilio Social of being 'an institution for scroungers' providing a 'food distribution system for scroungers'. She was appalled that all the work she had invested in Auxilio Social could end in such a way – 'I was deeply upset for a few days, so I just resigned, went home and never went back.' The official acceptance of her resignation could not have been more coldly dismissive. She received a letter signed by Pedro Gamero del Castillo, the Vice-Secretary General of FET y de las JONS, the man through whom Ramón Serrano Suñer controlled the Movimiento. It simply thanked her for 'the collaboration given' and passed on the text of a note dated 16 April 1940 from Serrano Suñer recommending that her resignation be accepted 'since it is not convenient that the present situation in the leadership of Auxilio Social be prolonged' and because of the 'need to cut disproportionate expenses and salaries'. She also received from José Lorente Sanz, the under-secretary, and Serrano Suñer's man, in the Ministry of the Interior, a peremptory request to account for all the foreign donations that had been given to Auxilio Social.[148]

On 9 May 1940, Mercedes was replaced as National Delegate of Auxilio Social by a man, Manuel Martínez de Tena – Andrés Redondo's one-time secretary. She was especially hurt by what she saw as a betrayal by Martínez de Tena and Carmen de Icaza, who now became National Secretary of Auxilio Social. Both were her one-time friends and collaborators, who had achieved prominence in the organisation through her. Certainly, in order to gain their new positions they would have to have ingratiated themselves with Pilar Primo de Rivera and the 'legitimists'. Mercedes retained her position in the Consejo Nacional and, given her remarkably energy and resilience, would soon be playing a role in public life.[149] Nevertheless, her removal from the leadership of Auxilio Social constituted a resounding victory for Pilar and the Falange 'legitimists'. Franco's central motivation in thus favouring the Sección Femenina was entirely practical and in accordance with his conservative instincts. Women were to be demobilised and returned to the home after the emancipation implicit in their participation in the war. The move away from that glimpse of equality and back towards a submissive, homemaking role also fitted better with the predilections of Pilar – and her spiritual advisor, Fray Justo Pérez de Urbel – than with the rhetorical social radicalism of Mercedes Sanz-Bachiller.[150]

For the moment, Mercedes was principally concerned with the imminent arrival of her new baby. Both she and Javier turned their main efforts to building their private life. Mercedes had found them a spacious apartment in the (then) Calle Abascal in the capital. On 22 August 1940, in the sweltering heat of Madrid, Mercedes went into labour. She gave birth to a girl, Ana María. The next day, while Mercedes recovered from her exertions and Javier doted on his daughter, the long arm of Falangist rivalry reached into their home. They were visited by the publisher, Afrodisio Aguado, the owner of the company for which Javier worked. He informed them that irrestible pressures obliged him to insist on Javier's immediate resignation. Aguado was more than satisfied with Javier's work, but he had been threatened that the business would be shut down if he did not obey some, unnamed, higher authority. All Spanish publishing and printing houses depended for their survival on the quota of paper allowed them – and in wartime, paper was short in blockaded Europe. Accordingly, Javier and Mercedes reached the unavoidable conclusion that the political persecution to which they were being subjected was now extended into a campaign to deprive them of their livelihood. Their telephone was bugged and they were subjected to police surveillance.[151]

Nevertheless, Mercedes still retained the ultimate protection of Franco and thus remained a member of the Consejo Nacional which gave her considerable prestige. Javier had been offered and accepted the post of Commercial Director of a small film company, the Compañía Española de Propaganda e Industria Cinematográfica (CEPICSA). This was a period of near-famine for much of Spain. However, Mercedes owned farms in the province of Valladolid which provided lentils, flour, garbanzos and honey. Mercedes had also placed the one-time bodyguard of Onésimo Redondo, Tomás García, as foreman of the house and land near Torremolinos (La Aldea) that she had acquired towards the end of the Civil War. Under his stewardship, it began to produce some batatas (sweet potatoes), peanuts, white beans and charcuterie. At Christmas 1940, the family took possession of La Aldea. Javier was so delighted with the house that he began to think in terms of moving there permanently. This required finding a way of making the land profitable. Much effort went into doing so by dint of irrigation and fertiliser. He also opened a law office which brought considerable economic success. He also, in early 1941, began the process of rebuilding bridges to Serrano Suñer, writing him a letter of congratulation for his push for greater power for the Falange. He referred later to this as 'a letter to exorcise the evil fates'.[152]

Just as Mercedes fell from grace as a victim of the power struggle within the Falange, her return to prominence was the result of another squabble. During the Second World War, there was intense friction between the traditional patrician and monarchist right, represented by the generals, and the more radical and proletarian Falange. Senior officers believed that callow uneducated Falangists were getting inflated salaries simply for being part of a useless bureaucracy. There was also a foreign-policy dimension to the conflict. Falangists were predominantly pro-Axis. Irrespective of their preferences, numerous senior officers inclined to the view that the Allies would eventually win and that, in consequence, Spain should refrain from getting too close to Hitler. Military resentment focused on Serrano Suñer who, in turn, sought to build his popularity within the Falange and seek Axis support for his domestic position. Tension reached such a peak that there were rumours of the Army planning a coup against Franco in order to get rid of Serrano Suñer.[153] The Portuguese Ambassador described Serrano Suñer as 'the most hated man in Spain'.[154]

Since 17 October 1940, when he had become Minister of Foreign Affairs, Serrano Suñer had accumulated massive power. He was only notionally replaced at his previous post of Minister of the Interior, by Franco himself. In practice, this left Serrano in control since the time-consuming task of administering the Ministry's machinery was carried out on a day-to-day basis by his friend and collaborator, the Under-secretary, José Lorente Sanz. The entire press and propaganda machinery remained at his disposal. Serrano Suñer also had considerable authority in the Falange both through his position as president of its executive committee, the Junta Política, and through his influence over Pedro Gamero del Castillo, Minister without Portfolio and Vice-Secretary General of the FET y de las JONS. Although the official Minister for the Falange was General Agustín Muñoz Grandes, real day-to-day authority in the Falange was wielded by Gamero who took orders from Ramón Serrano Suñer.

The crisis in the rivalry between the military and Falangist camps came to a head on 2 May 1941 when Serrano Suñer made a radical speech at Mota del Cuervo in Cuenca. He attacked England, spoke of the need for fulfilling commitments to Germany and Italy and implied that the victory in the Civil War was being squandered. It was widely interpreted as a call for the Falange to assume the monopoly of power.[155] It had been followed quickly by a suggestion to the Caudillo that Falangist representation in the cabinet should be increased by creating a Ministry of Labour for the young Valladolid fanatic

José Antonio Girón de Velasco. As part of the orchestrated pressure, on 3 May, Franco received a letter from Miguel Primo de Rivera resigning from his posts in the Falange in protest at the weakness of various Falangist organisations.[156] These indications that Serrano Suñer was trying to elevate the Falange over the military persuaded Franco to take action. He agreed to the promotion of Girón but also took other measures to counter the surge of Falangist power.[157]

On 5 May 1941, in a mini-reshuffle, the Caudillo appointed as Minister of the Interior a faithful soldier, Colonel Valentín Galarza, and made Girón Minister of Labour. Two days later, he replaced Galarza as undersecretary to the Presidency with the dourly devoted Chief of Operations of the Naval General Staff, Captain Luis Carrero Blanco. These were decisive moves in the war between the Falange and the military High Command. The Caudillo had decided to clip Serrano Suñer's wings. The fiercely anti-Falangist Galarza made a series of moves – possible only with the agreement of Franco – immediately replacing Serrano Suñer's man, José Lorente Sanz, with the traditionalist lawyer from Bilbao, Antonio Iturmendi. His anti-Serrano Suñer offensive at the Ministry of the Interior was crowned when a soldier was appointed to replace another of his henchmen, José Finat y Escrivá de Romaní, the Conde de Mayalde, as Director General de Seguridad. Moreover, a number of Civil Governors were replaced including Miguel Primo de Rivera in Madrid.[158]

There ensued a battle in the press fought out with passionate but arcane articles on both sides. Galarza dismissed from the Ministry of the Interior those Falangists in charge of Press and Propaganda, including Dionisio Ridruejo and Antonio Tovar. The tension between the military and the Falange reached new heights with Serrano Suñer, as Minister of Foreign Affairs, José Luis de Arrese, as Civil Governor of Malaga, and José Antonio Girón de Velasco, as Minister of Labour, resigning their posts. Franco dealt separately with Arrese, Girón and

Miguel Primo de Rivera. They could not resist the temptations put before them and a much-weakened Serrano Suñer hurriedly withdrew his own resignation. There was an intervention by the German and Italian Ambassadors expressing concern at the apparent assault on pro-Axis elements. Franco assured them that nothing could be further from the truth and that he was merely engaged on adjustments of domestic policy. His reassurances were backed up by the transfer of the Press and Propaganda department from the Ministry of the Interior to a new Vice-Secretariat of Popular Education within the Falange. Then, in the ensuing cabinet reshuffle of 19 May, two additional Falangist ministers were appointed, Miguel Primo de Rivera as Minister of Agriculture and José Luis de Arrese as Minister-Secretary of the FET y de las JONS, while Girón remained as Minister of Labour. The elevation of Arrese and the other Falangists was taken, at the time, to represent a victory for Serrano Suñer. In fact, they were being rewarded for their loyalty to Franco and their betrayal of Serrano Suñer. Those who lost their posts were Serrano Suñer's most faithful friends – Ridruejo and Tovar in the Press and Propaganda section of the Ministry of the Interior, José Lorente Sanz as Undersecretary of the Ministry, the Conde de Mayalde as Director General de Seguridad and Pedro Gamero del Castillo as acting Minister-Secretary of the Falange.[159] From May 1941 onwards, Serrano Suñer's position was ever more precarious. While he put his faith in rallying Falangists to the battle cry of the unfinished revolution, the Generalísimo was happily going about the business of domesticating them by the distribution of preferment.[160]

Franco had consolidated his power and a large section of the Falange had revealed itself to be docile. The failure of the threatened mass resignations had inadvertently revealed that Serrano Suñer did not control the Falange. Now, he had more powerful enemies than ever before in the cabinet. The dour Francoist Luis Carrero Blanco was in the powerful position of the Caudillo's Undersecretary or Cabinet Secretary. José Luis de Arrese, who was a clever manipulator of Franco's ego, was the leader of the so-called Franco-Falangists. There was also the Minister for the Army, General José Varela, as the visible head of military opposition to Serrano Suñer.[161] In a three-week period, Serrano Suñer had lost control of the Ministry of the Interior, the department of Press and Propaganda and of the Falange itself. This situation was to have favourable repercussions for Mercedes Sanz-Bachiller and Javier Martínez de Bedoya. José Antonio Girón de Velasco, it will be recalled, was a Jonsista from Valladolid. As soon as he took possession of the Ministry of Labour, he ordered a large portrait of Onésimo Redondo to be hung on the wall. He also sent a message to Mercedes informing her of his determination to put right the injustices that had been committed against her.[162]

In consequence, when Girón spoke of this to Serrano Suñer, he, with his customary elegance and shrewdness, undertook to reinstate her in politics. In early June 1941, Serrano Suñer invited Mercedes to visit him at the Ministry of Foreign Affairs in the Plaza de Santa Cruz. While an anxious Javier waited for her in the nearby Plaza Mayor, the interview took place in an atmosphere of exquisite cordiality. Mercedes was delighted by Serrano Suñer's amicability and even more so by his offer to appoint her to the board of the Instituto Nacional de Previsión, the body responsible for what little provision of social security was provided by the Franco regime. At the beginning of July 1941, she received a letter from Gerardo Salvador y Merino, the Falange's National Delegate for the official trade unions, naming her head of the union section of the Social Security organisation. She was delighted to be welcomed back into the political arena, as the Falange's representative on the Instituto Nacional de Previsión.[163] She threw herself into the work with her customary enthusiasm, undertaking to make more welfare reach the peasantry. This would involve a massive investment of time and energy, first in drawing up accurate lists of those employed in agriculture and then in setting up offices of the Instituto de Previsión Social in rural towns and villages. In the event, she managed to go some way towards this ambition by using her influence within the syndical organisation of the Falange and by recruiting thousands of members, past and present, of Auxilio Social. It was a remarkable tribute to her capacity to motivate people with her own infectious enthusiasm that she persuaded over five thousand of them to give their labour free for one year to carry out the necessary rural census.

Mercedes commented later with a degree of pride, 'Pilar was always fond of what she called transmitting the spirit of José Antonio but I often ask myself if the spirit of José Antonio ever changed anything important.'[164] With her work in Social Security achieving remarkable success, she was less distressed than she might have been when, in November 1942, Franco succumbed to pressure from the 'legitimists' and removed her from the Consejo Nacional. In any case, both she and Javier were made *procuradores* (unelected deputies) in the newly fabricated pseudo-parliament, the Cortes, that Franco inaugurated on 17 March 1943.[165]

In October 1943, Javier was asked by Franco's Foreign Minister, the Conde de Jordana, to go to the Spanish Embassy in Lisbon as press attaché. Jordana realised that the Allies were likely to win the war and he wanted to start counteracting Spain's clear links with the Axis ahead of time. He asked Javier to establish contacts with Jewish refugee organisations. When he discussed the offer with Mercedes, her reaction suggested that she gave a higher priority to her political life than to her family. She told him that if he wanted to sacrifice his lawyer's practice for something that he considered to be a patriotic duty, she understood perfectly. However, by the same token, she was not prepared to sacrifice her project within the Instituto Nacional de Previsión to extend social security to the countryside. Accordingly, she suggested that, while establishing a home in Lisbon, they would both have to travel to and from Madrid where they would maintain their household. Mercedes accompanied him and spent much time setting up a splendid establishment in the Portuguese capital. When he went to Lisbon in February 1944, he went alone. His work was facilitated by the fact that the Jewish representatives with whom he negotiated took it for granted that Franco was a Jew. In the event, Javier was part of a chain involved in rescuing Sephardic Jews with Spanish passports from occupied Germany. Finally, from September 1944, Mercedes and Pilar, her eldest children by Onésimo Redondo, were sent to a boarding school in Lisbon.[166]

After the Second World War, Javier's hopes that he would be relieved of his post in Lisbon were not fulfilled – yet resignation was simply not contemplated. In December 1945, Mercedes was confirmed for another period as a member of the board of the Instituto Nacional de Previsión. There had been some efforts to unseat her but Franco himself had made it clear that she was to be prejudiced no further as a result of the internal power struggles of the Falange. It happened again in February 1947. Using the excuse that there were problems arising from her frequent absences in Lisbon, the National Delegate for the Falangist vertical syndicates, Fermín Sanz Orrio, requested her resignation. Remembering the vicious campaign unleashed at the time of her resignation from Auxilio Social, she was less innocent than she had been in 1940. She insisted on public recognition of her six years of hard work in the Instituto Nacional de Previsión and that Franco be given a full account of why she was being removed. On receiving Sanz Orrio's explanation, Franco replied, 'Don't be ridiculous! Leave her alone.' Mercedes continued to work in the Instituto Nacional de Previsión until the late 1960s.[167] In mid-June 1947, in a recognition of her pre-eminence in the field of social welfare, Mercedes was called upon to receive Evita Duarte de Perón during her official visit to Spain.[168]

Political triumphs were, however, darkly overshadowed by another personal tragedy. In 1946, her son Onésimo had a bad fall. One year later, he was suffering intense pain in his right leg. At first, he limped, then he was confined to bed. He was diagnosed as suffering from spinal cancer. Javier kept the news from Mercedes in the hope that, not knowing, she might better infuse the boy with the will to live. It was decided to take Onésimo from the clinic in Madrid to the family home in Malaga, Aldeamar. The prestige enjoyed by Mercedes within regime circles was revealed in a gesture by the ex-Minister of Public Works, Alfonso Peña Boeuf. For the night-long journey, he arranged for the special railway carriage belonging to the Ministry to be put at her disposal. Known as the 'break de Obras Públicas', this was the aged wagon once used by Alfonso XIII, and in which water had leaked onto Franco while he travelled to Hendaye for his historic meeting with Hitler on 23 October 1940. Javier bought a Fiat Topolino convertible in order to be able to take Onésimo around the estate and the local area. However, he soon found the pain provoked by the bumps intolerable and retired to the terrace. Shortly afterwards, he could not even bear to move from bed to the terrace and he was confined to his room. He died on 5 July 1948. Mercedes was beside herself with grief.[169]

In the late summer of 1948, to help deal with her sorrow, she decided to accompany Javier to Paris. He was to form part of a Spanish delegation which hoped to influence the deliberations of the United Nations Assembly meeting there from 21 September. It was believed that his contacts with Jewish relief organisations could be used to seek support for the Spanish case for entry into the United Nations. Mercedes arranged for her two daughters, Mercedes and Pilar, to be accepted at a French boarding school. When they returned, the major preoccupation of the family was the extension of Aldeamar, planting more trees, expanding the irrigation system and increasing the production of sugar cane and of livestock.

In fact, Javier was still, theoretically at least, press attaché in Lisbon. During Franco's state visit to Portugal in late October 1949, the Caudillo made a special point of seeking out Mercedes and spending time talking to her. At the beginning of January 1951, Javier was finally relieved of his position, it having been insinuated to him that, finally, he would be given a Ministry. He discovered that his promotion had been opposed by Girón, the Minister of Labour, on behalf of Luis Carrero Blanco, the Falange 'legitimists' and General Fidel Dávila, the Minister for the Army. Javier was convinced that this was their revenge for his years of co-operation with Jewish organisations. Instead, he was offered the post of press attaché in Paris. Despite his inclination to refuse out of hand, Mercedes persuaded him to accept. Her reasoning was that to leave Franco's service in such circumstances would be to confirm the hostility of those who opposed him.[170]

They had barely had time to set up an apartment in Paris when Javier was offered the job of Undersecretary at the Ministry of Agriculture. Rafael Cavestany, who had been named Minister in Franco's new cabinet of 18 July 1951, had read an article by Javier and decided that he was just the man to help him in his projects. However, Franco vetoed the appointment. Accordingly, the family was established in a magnificent apartment in the Avenue Raymond Poincaré. Mercedes herself would spend a few days in Madrid each month carrying on her work with the Instituto Nacional de Previsión. In fact, as Javier conceived the post, he required substantial funds for entertaining, and thus influencing, the French press. To carry out his job at the level he believed necessary, he requested the upgrading of his post to the level of Counsellor of Embassy but was told that this was impossible. Accordingly, in April 1952, with the permission of Franco, he resigned. To his astonishment, his successor was given the rank of Counsellor. With the agreement of Mercedes, he decided to take over the day-to-day running of Aldeamar and dedicate much of his time to writing. His first novel, *El torero* (the bullfighter), was a huge success, being broadcast on national radio and also made into a film. With the profits, he built a petrol station which, for long being the only one on the busy road from Malaga to Gibraltar, was the source of substantial income. With the profits from his second novel, *Falta una gaviota* (a seagull is missing), he built an hotel, Los Álamos, one of the first in Torremolinos.[171]

Despite material prosperity, Mercedes Sanz-Bachiller retained an interest in social and political issues. In 1967, she wrote an article in the daily newspaper, *Ya*, which appeared under the headline 'No Women in the Cortes seats for representatives of the Falange Syndicates'. She believed that it was absurd that she personally be excluded but equally absurd that there should be no other women at all. It was an indication of her enduring prestige within Francoist Spain that, within a matter of hours, her article had stung the Syndical authorities into writing a comically hurt reply.[172] Mercedes gave an example of her essential magnanimity when Pilar Primo de Rivera died on 17 March 1991. Within two days, she published a generous appreciation of her rival, recognising their many disagreements but principally paying tribute to her austerity and dedication to her ideals.[173] She and Javier lived happily between Madrid and Torremolinos until his death in 1991. With typical resilience, the eighty-year-old Mercedes overcame her grief and set about arranging her affairs in time for her own demise. She distributed her fortune among her three daughters yet, ten years later, she was still pursuing a vigorous existence, devouring the daily newspapers, taking a close interest in the lives of her grandchildren and great-grandchildren and leading a busy social life.

The many satisfactions of her life could not entirely hide a residual discomfort with regard to the major achievement of her life. Rather like Trotsky in Stalinist histories of communism, Mercedes Sanz-Bachiller was effectively written out of the history of the Sección Femenina. Indeed, the period of independence, during which Auxilio Social was responsible directly to the Government rather than a mere branch of the Sección Femenina, disappeared altogether. In the many official publications of the organisation, Mercedes's role in the creation of Auxilio de Invierno and Auxilio Social was reduced in various ways. She was described as simply one among many who had the idea, albeit an outstanding one.

> It arose simultaneously in many provinces: each one interpreted in their own way under the initiative of the local Jefe Provincial de la Sección Femenina. But it was the Jefe Provincial of Valladolid, Mercedes Sanz-Bachiller, who stood out within this service, and gave it tone and form and unlimited horizons.

It was stated that the positions of responsibility held by Mercedes Sanz-Bachiller as head of Auxilio de Invierno and of Auxilio Social had been graciously given her at the suggestion of Pilar Primo de Rivera.[174] In the organisation's official history, the creation of Auxilio de Invierno is baldly stated as 'a birth under the discipline of the Sección Femenina'. In this version, the provincial delegates of the Sección Femenina were named immediately as provincial delegates of Auxilio de Invierno and 'ordered all members to volunteer to work for that new undertaking of the Falange'.[175] In the various magazines and journals of the Sección Femenina, *Y, Medina, Consigna* and *Teresa*, the annual *Sección Femenina, Anuario* and its official history, photographs of Pilar Primo de Rivera abounded. Of Mercedes, there were virtually none.

MARGARITA
NELKEN

MARGARITA NELKEN

A Full Measure of Pain

AT THE BEGINNING OF 1939, Barcelona was a city bursting at the seams with hungry refugees from all over Spain.
Their respite from the relentless pursuit by the troops of General Franco was short-lived. Purgatory was about to turn into
hell. When news came on 23 January that the Nationalists had
reached the Llobregat river a few miles to the south of the
city, a colossal exodus began. Hundreds of thousands of terrified women, children, old men and defeated soldiers began to
trek towards France. Through bitterly cold sleet and snow,
on roads bombed and strafed by Nationalist aircraft, many
walked, wrapped in blankets and clutching a few possessions,
some carrying infants. Those who could squeezed into every
kind of transport imaginable. From 28 January, a reluctant
French Government allowed the first refugees across the
border. The retreat of the wretched human mass moving
slowly north was covered by the desperate heroism of the
remnants of the Republican army. Among the last to leave on
10 February was one of the Republic's youngest officers, Santiago de Paúl Nelken. He did not know that crawling along
in the stream of refugees his men had been trying to protect
was a car carrying his mother and sister.

On crossing the border, the defeated Republicans were
received by the French Garde Mobile as if they were criminals.
The women, children and the old were shepherded into transit

camps. The soldiers were disarmed and escorted to insanitary camps on the coast, rapidly improvised by marking out sections of beach with barbed wire. Under the empty gaze of Senegalese guards, Santiago de Paúl Nelken and his unit improvised shelters by burrowing into the wet sand of the camp at St Cyprien a few kilometres to the southeast of Perpignan. By this time, his mother and sister Magda, a nurse, were at the Spanish Consulate in Perpignan trying to help the refugees who arrived there. They had avoided the camps because Margarita Nelken was a parliamentary deputy, a famous writer and spoke perfect French. Their situation was infinitely better than that suffered by most of those who had trudged north. Nonetheless, as she helped the refugees, Margarita Nelken faced myriad anxieties. She had responsibility for her daughter who was ill. She had just collected her own sixty-six-year-old mother and her three-year-old granddaughter, both of whom had been waiting for her near Perpignan. Moreover, she had endured agonies of worry about her son since she had last seen him several weeks earlier.

The surge of relief that she felt on managing to find out, on 12 February, that Santiago was still alive would live with her for the rest of her life. It would always be linked in her mind with a touching encounter that took place shortly afterwards. Her friend, the great cellist Pau Casals who was forming a relief organisation for the refugees, visited the Consulate. Even as they embraced, his first words were 'And what of your son? Did he get out?' It was a glimmer of humanity that illuminated the desolation all around. A few days later, she was able to secure the release of her son. She was one of the lucky ones. Yet, she had lost everything except her family. Her home in Madrid, with her library and art collection, was at the mercy of Falangist looters. Her life as a distinguished art critic and writer and as an influential politician seemed to be over. At the age of forty-five, she faced having to rebuild what she could in an uncertain exile.

The glittering career that now lay in ruins had been hard won. In the first third of the twentieth century, Spanish men did not take kindly to being challenged by independent women who provoked their political and sexual fears as Margarita Nelken did. Accordingly, a bizarre measure of the scale of her achievements may be found in the vilification to which she was subjected by the victorious right. The abuse heaped upon her was equalled only in the case of Pasionaria, Dolores Ibárruri. Margarita Nelken's crime in the eyes of the right was twofold. She had used her remarkable gifts, artistic, literary and political, to crusade both for women to be liberated from the male oppression of Spanish society and for the landless peasantry to be freed from the daily brutality of lives often little better than those of slaves. The tenor of the rightist response may be summed up by the remark 'she was not a woman, but a repulsive mixture, an almost androgynous item'. Needless to say, the attack on her as 'not a woman' went hand-in-hand with the contradictory accusation that she was a whore: 'one of those women with an easy smile and easy access who exploit their femininity for remunerative affections'. Her speeches were seen as vehicles for 'the most immoral theories, the concepts of greatest aberration, the teachings of the most corrosive immorality. It is in these demagogic speeches that blasphemy, fiercely appearing on the lips of a self-proclaimed woman, alternated with apologetic descriptions of free love and boastful accounts of her own personal cultivation of the doctrine.'[1]

Political hostility to Margarita Nelken drenched in sexual innuendo was astonishingly widespread. Even before the Civil War unleashed the worst abuse, the sexist opprobrium was echoed by the extreme right-wing poet Roy Campbell, a man hardly well informed about Spanish politics. He remarked to the Socialist mayor of Toledo who was under attack from the local anarchists, 'Why don't they give you a guard of a couple of bastard sons of the Nelken or the Pasionaria, seeing you

are the Mayor?'[2] Her ethnic origin was also the basis of insult:
'Nelken's nationality is a mystery. German? Polish? Certainly
Jewish. That is the fundamental origin which defines her.'
'Unlike so many other presumed intellectuals, who are whores
in their own imaginations more than in their real sexual adven-
tures, she is fortunately not Spanish. She is not even a woman.'[3]
Another Francoist referred to her as 'the Jewish Amazon'.[4]

A salacious and avid interest in her sex life was hardly less
common on the left.[5] That is hardly surprising. She predicated
female independence through her writings and her lectures.
In a repressive and moralistic society, her ideas on the subject
were caricatured as the advocacy of 'free love'. She practised
her independence to the extent of having a child out of wedlock and living with a married man. She defended it in terms
so robust as to seem to her prudish contemporaries as boasting
of promiscuity. Of course, an equally independent sex life in
the case of a man would simply not have occasioned comment.
The attitude to sex of both the Socialist and Communist Parties, to which she belonged at different times, ranged, behind
a rhetoric of liberality, from harsh puritanism to lubricious
prurience. Accusations of being a whore, along with stirring
revolutionary oratory, prominence in the defence of Madrid,
exile in Moscow, ensured that the career of Margarita Nelken
was often compared with that of Dolores Ibárruri. In fact, the
resemblance was superficial. Margarita never attained a similar
degree of political pre-eminence but far outstripped Pasionaria
in intellectual achievement. She was a highly educated and
cosmopolitan intellectual whereas Dolores was closely tied to
her proletarian origins. Margarita Nelken was dismissed maliciously as someone desperately trying to emulate Pasionaria, yet
in politics, as in every other aspect of her life, she simply went
her own way.

Margarita and her sister, Carmen Eva, were the daughters
of a Jewish family. Their parents were Julius Nelken Waldberg,
a German jeweller from Breslau, who had emigrated to Spain

in 1889, and Jeanne Esther Mansberger, a Frenchwoman born in Anglet, Bayonne. Jeanne's father, Enrique Mansberger Klein, was a Hungarian Jew who, after settling in Madrid in 1866, had become court watchmaker to Alfonso XII. Julius and Enrique ran a flourishing watch and jewel business in the Puerta del Sol No.15. In July 1893, Julius married his partner's daughter in the synagogue of Bayonne. Margarita was born María Teresa Lea Nelken y Mansberger in Madrid on 5 July 1894. Carmen Eva was born in 1898.[6]

The two girls were brought up in a deeply cultured house-hold. They learned French from their mother, German from their father, Spanish at school and English from their nanny. In the stultifying and puritanical atmosphere of late-nineteenth, and early twentieth-century Spain, their school life was extremely difficult. Margarita and her sister were taken for foreigners, because of their origins, the fact that they were not Catholics and their cosmopolitan education. They were both subjected to taunts by their peers for not joining in the religious rituals that took place at various points in the school day. Their budding friendships were curtailed by Catholic parents scandalised because the Nelken girls did not attend mass. The stigma of being Jewish and atheists ensured that they were both marginalised. Accordingly, Margarita left school and studied the French curriculum at home with private tutors. In compensation, the prosperity of their parents meant that they were as well travelled as they were well read. The consequence was that they were both self-confident and cultured, the very antithesis of the contemporary norm of submissive and ignorant women. In the case of Margarita, that confidence was inflated by the fact that she was the object of the obsessive admiration of her mother. In later life, Carmen Eva was to lament bitterly that Jeanne Mansberger divided the world into Margarita and the rest.[7]

In an effort to distance herself from her mother, Carmen Eva later wrote under the pseudonym Magda Donato and had considerable success as a journalist, translator and writer of children's theatre. In exile in Mexico after the Civil War, she achieved great celebrity as an actress.[8] She was intelligent and attractive but less so than her sister. The consequent sense of envy and rivalry between them led to considerable hostility.[9] It is also likely that they became rivals for the affections of the artist, Salvador Bartolozzi, whose illustrations had introduced Pinocchio into Spain.[10] Certainly, Margarita's admiration for Bartolozzi, as revealed in a chapter of her book, *Glosario*, was sufficiently enthusiastic as to suggest considerable partiality. She referred to him as 'the most complex, the most refined, and yet the most simple and the most pure of all of today's draftsmen; pure with that wise and ecstatic purity which receives all sensations'. Margarita Nelken's writing on Bartolozzi is suffused with outrage against the neglect of his work in Spain which obliged him to work as an illustrator.[11] The fact that Bartolozzi eventually settled with Magda could account for the intensification of the enmity between the sisters.

Margarita was even more of an achiever than 'Magda'. As a very young girl, she had already manifested considerable artistic and musical talent. She could draw competently before she could read. Having ambitions of being a painter, she was sent at the age of thirteen to Paris. There she studied painting with the Spanish Cubist María Blanchard and with Eduardo Chicharro. Among her fellow students was Diego Rivera, the Mexican muralist with whom she would later be associated in exile. She also studied composition, harmony and piano. She became friendly with the expressionist painter Ignacio Zuloaga y Zabaleta, the sculptor Auguste Rodin and with the composer Manuel de Falla.[12] Her work was shown in several exhibitions and she mounted her own shows in Vienna in 1914 and in the Parés Gallery in Barcelona in 1916. However, she was forced to abandon her career as an artist as a result of losing a high degree of sight in one eye while still a young woman.

Threatened with blindness, she could not risk long hours of close work. The decision caused her great sadness. Nevertheless, her characteristic response was to throw herself into a career in art criticism.

Already, aged only seventeen, she had published in 1911 notable articles in international journals, including one on El Greco in *Le Mercure de France* in Paris. She abandoned her bohemian existence on the Parisian Left Bank and returned to Madrid. Thereafter, she gave painting courses at the Prado and the Louvre. She frequently wrote essays on art which were published in journals in Spain, France, Germany, Italy, England and Latin America. As a vibrant lecturer on art, she was a much sought-after speaker.[13] Years later, she recalled her embarrassing initiation into regular journalistic collaborations with newspapers in Spain.

> The first place where I wrote in Spain was in *La Ilustración Española y Americana*, whose editor at the time was my illustrious friend Wenceslao Fernández Flórez. I had never set foot in a newspaper office nor even seen a newspaper editor. In the foreign magazines where I had been writing for years, [and signing M. Nelken] they just assumed that I was a man. Well, the mere fact of going to hand in an article had me so nervous that I handed the sheets to Flórez with my eyes glued to the ground, and totally flustered, I ran out without saying a word. Afterwards, I heard that Flórez had said, 'That girl must be stupid; an upper-class twit who writes poetry for her canary, I can just see it.' But he read the article, and to his, and my, surprise, he soon commissioned another.[14]

Around about 1914, Margarita fell deeply in love with the reclusive sculptor Julio Antonio, who was born in Mora de Ebro, Tarragona, in 1889. She wrote about him in the book *Glosario* in which she dealt with Gauguin, Rodin, El Greco,

Zuloaga, Klimt, Bartolozzi and others about whose work she felt zealous enthusiasm. *Glosario*, published in 1917, was a typically emotional book – 'it is not a work of criticism; it is a book of intimacy with some intimacies which just had to be chosen and praised to the skies'. Without ever losing her acute critical sense, her chapter on Julio Antonio reflected her heartfelt commitment to his work. She admired the life, the sadness and the aggression with which he imbued his sculptures.[15] On 26 March 1915, Margarita gave birth to an illegitimate daughter, Magda. There can be little doubting that Julio Antonio was the father.[16] It is not known why they chose not to live together. The most probable reason is that, as a penniless artist, he was too egocentrically obsessed with his work to be prepared to come to terms with the distractions of family life. She herself wrote later of his 'years of severe struggling and poverty' and of his 'unremitting toil and privation' during these years.[17]

Although not living with the man she loved, Margarita took on the role of single mother with pride and courage. Her attitude may be deduced from her 1923 novel *La trampa del arenal* (Trapped in the Quicksand). One of its central characters, Libertad, an independent, free-thinking woman, clearly represents the views of Margarita Nelken herself. Luis, the man trapped in a loveless marriage who is falling for Libertad, asks about her previous relationship, 'Don't you miss anything?' 'Yes, I would like to have had a child.' Luis misunderstands and assumes that she wanted a child in order to hang on to her erstwhile partner: 'If you had had a child, you would still be with the father.' 'In no way,' replies Libertad vehemently, 'I don't know how to play-act and it would be play-acting, with or without a child, to live with a man to whom I was not tied by love or mutual respect. Don't you agree?' Luis finds this difficult to assimilate. 'Surely, but what would people say?' 'What people?' she interrupted heatedly. 'Those people who turn their backs on a mother alone and will tolerate any vile injustice as long as there is a flag of convenience with which to legalise the contraband. If I had a child, I would not need such people who could not begin to despise me as much as I despise them.' 'How brave you are!' replies Luis admiringly. 'I've never been short of courage for anything, it's true, and, especially to be true to myself. But if I had a child, a child that was *mine alone*, I believe that I would have the strength to face anything the world could throw at me.'[18]

Whatever reasons lay behind the fact that Margarita lived as a single parent, she got on with her life, as a mother, as an art critic and, increasingly, as a campaigner for women's rights. She needed all her resilience to cope with an unexpected blow. On 15 February 1919, Julio Antonio died prematurely in Madrid, at the age of twenty-nine. Margarita was plunged into a dark despair. It has even been suggested, albeit without any evidence, that she contemplated suicide.[19] Given her grit and resolution, this seems highly unlikely. Despite the strength of her feelings for Julio, Margarita had long since come to terms with the fact that they were unlikely to live together. Already, in the autumn of 1917, she had started another relationship. In mid-1920, she became pregnant again. In her unpublished memoirs, she speaks of lecturing while in an advanced state of pregnancy in early 1921.[20] Enormous joy was brought into her life by the birth of her son, Santiago, on 11 March 1921. Her new partner was Martín de Paúl y de Martín Barbadillo, a businessman from Seville. Nevertheless, in 1922, a Madrid exhibition of Julio Antonio's work rekindled her enthusiasm for his work and her sadness at his early death. A touch of bitterness may be discerned in her comment that 'it was not till he reached the very threshold of the grave that Julio Antonio attained a fame which has without doubt placed him amongst the great names of his country'. She compared his work with that of Donatello and described it as 'an oeuvre which ranks amongst the most important not only of modern Spain but of all periods'.[21]

Now the mother of two children, Margarita Nelken was reaching the peak of her literary fecundity. She wrote prodigiously yet without repetition. Her books and articles were always written with lucidity and intelligence, with grace and wit, with passion and energy.[22] Indeed, her literary production was just one index of her remarkable vitality. She would produce a novel and seven novellas. She wrote a fluid, agile prose, like an impressionist painting, in its depiction of landscape, urbanely witty in its dialogue. Amusing satires on high society, her novels and stories helped her earn a living but were considerably lesser achievements than her non-fiction. She wrote widely on literature, including a classic study of Spanish female writers and a biography of Goethe.[23] She published two substantial works on feminism as well as a pamphlet on maternity and childcare.[24] In her twenties, and again in her postwar exile, she wrote extensively on painting and sculpture. Throughout the 1930s, when her principal activity was political, she wrote a significant analysis of the development of the Second Republic and many of her speeches were published.[25] In addition, she translated numerous books from French, English and German into Spanish. Indeed, she was the first translator of Kafka into Spanish.[26]

Vivacious, attractive, cultured and witty, Margarita made many friends in the literary and artistic worlds. She was a favourite of the great novelist Benito Pérez Galdós who kept on his writing desk a photograph of her with her daughter. By dint of her independent turn of mind, she was one of the few women to enjoy the respect and friendship of the abrasive philosopher Miguel de Unamuno. She was a friend of the great Spanish scientist, Ramón y Cajal. She did much of the research for, and drafting of, his famous anthology on women. She had warm friendships with the Chilean Nobel Prize-winning poet, Gabriela Mistral, and the Spanish poets Manuel and Antonio Machado and Federico García Lorca. In her unpublished essays, she recalled Lorca playing the piano and singing flamenco in her house in Madrid.[27]

And it was in Madrid that the income from writing and teaching gave Margarita a proudly guarded independence. It enabled her to pay for childcare although her mother Jeanne also helped to look after her children. She was thus able to keep up her prodigious work rate. She was belligerently proud of her ability to earn a living by hard work, telling an interviewer: 'I am one of the very few Spanish writers who lives exclusively from their pen, without some related official salary.'[28] However, she soon began to feel the social constraints that limited the range of action of a young unmarried mother of her energies and ambitions. She widened her repertoire of lectures to include social and political subjects, speaking at the Madrid Socialist headquarters, the Casa del Pueblo.[29] She began organising art classes for the poor children of the working-class neighbourhoods of the capital. The experience of leaving her middle-class world to encounter the 'silent' world of hunger, ignorance and neglect affected her profoundly. In 1918, she established, at Calle Bocángel near the Ventas bullring in Madrid, *La Casa de los Niños de España* – a small orphanage for illegitimate children and care centre for the children of working mothers. It was the first non-religious children's nursery in Madrid. Needless to say, the Church was deeply hostile to an initiative that was perceived as a challenge to its monopoly of charitable activities. Moreover, in the narrow world of Madrid, such adverse and malicious comment was generated by Margarita's outspoken feminism that charitable donations dried up. By 1920, she was obliged to close the centre. This depressing experience pushed her into the orbit of the Socialist Party on which she began to pin her hopes of social reform.[30]

Infuriated by the undermining of her orphanage, she gave impassioned lectures on social problems at the Madrid intellectual club, the Ateneo, and at the Socialist Casa del Pueblo.

She set out to expose the extent to which the Catholic Church
and upper-class do-gooders monopolised social welfare for
women and used their charitable activities to control, patronise
and humiliate the women who turned to them. Unmarried
mothers were excluded from such 'charity'. A price in terms
of ostentatious religiosity was exacted from the *humildes* (the
'humble' as their benefactors called them). She was also concerned about the inappropriate treatment given to the few
children who were taken in by Church schools. She took a
leading role in a campaign to expose the unsanitary conditions
of a Catholic refuge at Vallehermoso in Madrid where children
were fed badly, often expected to share beds and not educated
at all. What infuriated her was the notion underlying patrician
and religious charity that the poor had no rights and should
be glad of anything that they got.[31] She believed that the
Catholic Church's monopoly of education and social welfare
was misused. Throughout her life, she would maintain a highly
critical stance towards the Church. One of the consequences
was that, in right-wing and Catholic circles and in their influential press networks, she was portrayed as an evil harridan.

Her experiences in investigating the situation of working-
class women and children impelled her to write the book that
would bring her to public prominence, *La condición social de
la mujer en España*. Despite the speed of its composition and
the indignation that inspires every page, it was a substantial
piece of work, thoroughly researched as well as trenchantly
written. In it, and in her lectures, she argued powerfully and
lucidly for social and sexual equality for women. In this, she
was courageously outpacing her few contemporaries in the
Spanish feminist movement. Her bleak examination of the
many areas in which women were subordinate in Spanish
society led her to conclude that the full achievement of
women's rights would require the success of a revolutionary movement. Her concerns and indignation ranged from
the appalling conditions of unskilled women in factories to

the institutional and social obstacles to women's progress
in the liberal professions. She urged the Socialist Party to accept
its duty of mounting educational programmes for women. Her
break with the genteel charity-based approach then prevalent
was considered truly scandalous. Issues ranging from prostitution to a lack of maternity provisions would be remedied,
she claimed, only when socialism triumphed. Feminism faced
larger tasks than could be fulfilled by what she called, in a
caustic side-swipe at the literary feminism of Madrid intellectuals, 'the feminist with short hair, a brandy-pickled voice and
a butch walk'. She expected a strong woman to be a 'true
companion for a man'.[32]

La condición social de la mujer provoked enormous scandal
and was condemned by the Bishop of Lérida, Dr Miralles.
This led, in turn, to the Minister of Education (Ministro de
Instrucción Pública), César Silios, dismissing a lecturer at a
teacher-training college who had recommended the book to
her students. Margarita Nelken claimed jokingly some time
later that the Bishop had protested merely out of kindness in
order to create publicity, rescue her from neglect and make
sure that her book was a bestseller. The furore over the book
and the sacking of the lecturer was such that the incident was
debated in the Cortes. Margarita Nelken was in the public
gallery when Indalecio Prieto demanded that the offending
passage be read out. The Minister, unaware that he was referring to the author, refused on the grounds that 'there are ladies
present and they might hear it'.[33]

The success of the book and the publicity given to her
outspoken views saw the beginning of right-wing hostility and
accusations of being a foreigner. The Catholic newspaper, *El
Debate*, regularly attacked her.[34] The power of her arguments
made numerous enemies. She was scathing, for instance, in
her criticisms of the do-gooders who worked to 'control'
prostitution without any understanding of the social context
that kept it alive. The middle-class men who took sexual

advantage of their domestic servants effectively condemned them to prostitution. For such women, or others driven by poverty to sell themselves on the streets, society offered little help, criminalising and stigmatising them.[35] The vehemence with which Margarita Nelken wrote of the problems of female life and work was born of a deep empathy with those condemned to suffer hardship. Although she came from a well-to-do background and had the talent to earn a comfortable living as a writer, her experiences as an unmarried mother and an independent woman had marked her profoundly. An underlying theme of her book is the compatibility of motherhood and feminism. The way in which she had responded to her own situation was also summed up in her book:

> Now that social progress has taken the Spanish woman out of her secular culture, it is time to start considering the cultivation of her brain and the development of her physical energies. Out with the child-woman incapable of looking after herself capable only of being either the courtesan or the servant of the man. But also out with the pallid, anaemic, narrow-shouldered girl, whose poetry glimpsed through the windows of a country-house is not enough to compensate for the sickliness that she will transmit to her children. Mothers who want their children to be robust and healthy men and women must be strong and they must know how to win respect for their own strength.[36]

The last sentence of that passage could have been the axiom by which she lived her own life.

The notoriety earned by the book ensured that Margarita Nelken was in great demand as a lecturer on feminism and women's rights. In consequence, she was simplistically accused of merely propagating free love. Irene Falcón, the feminist intellectual, regarded Margarita as a crucial influence on her

A group of middle-class women enthusiastically give the fascist salute to Franco's troops as they enter Barcelona: January 1939. [© Hulton Getty]

Above: Mercedes Sanz-Bachiller (left) failing to share the triumphalist mood with Franco's wife, Carmen Polo, in Burgos 1938.

Below: Mercedes Sanz-Bachiller and Pilar Primo de Rivera, despite their youth and apparent innocence, the two most powerful women in the wartime Nationalist zone.

Above: Mercedes (centre) uncomfortable with the fascist trappings given to her welfare organisation.

Below: A happier Mercedes surrounded by children being cared for by Auxilio Social.

Above: Mercedes Sanz–Bachiller in August 1938 in Hamburg as the guest of the Nazi welfare organisation, Winterhilfe.

Above right: Mercedes visits Fascist Italy, here in Rome 1938.

Right: Carmen Polo, Mercedes Sanz–Bachiller and Evita Duarte de Perón during the latter's visit to Spain in June 1947.

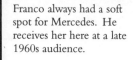

Franco always had a soft spot for Mercedes. He receives her here at a late 1960s audience.

The twenty-nine-year-old Margarita Nelken in 1923, at the height of her literary fame, her mischievous good humour to the fore.

A rare posed 'glamour' shot of Margarita from 1926.

Left: Margarita revelled in motherhood. Here, with her daughter Magda and son Santiago in Madrid, in the mid-1920s.

Forced to flee Spain after the
failed revolutionary movement
of October 1934, Margarita in
exile in Russia in 1935.

Left: Margarita with Santiago in
their Madrid home in 1932.

Below: Margarita in 1937 with the officers of the
Margarita Nelken battalion of the Republican
Army.

Margarita in August 1938 at the Ebro front.

Right: In exile in Mexico City, Margarita's husband Martín de Paúl with her daughter Magda in 1940.

In Mexico in 1941, Margarita with her granddaughter Cuqui who was born in Russia in 1936. At the registration of her birth, one of the guests said prophetically, 'this beautiful girl one day will be Mexican, whether you like it or not. You'll see.'

In exile in Mexico, Margarita, separated from her husband, kept a family consisting of her mother, her daughter and her granddaughter, by her own efforts as a writer and art critic. Here, she is pictured in her study in Mexico City in 1941.

Devastated when her son Santiago was killed in the Second World War, Margarita never recovered from the death of her daughter Magda, from cancer in June 1954. This is the recently engaged Magda, six months previously.

This is probably the last ever photo of Margarita, aged seventy-four, and seriously ill. She died in Mexico City on 9 March 1968.

own thinking. Irene attended her lectures in the Madrid Ateneo in the early 1920s and wrote many years later:

> She had a bad reputation, especially among the more macho of her journalistic colleagues who malevolently called her the 'copy room mattress' because she boasted of having many children each by a different father. I admired the audacity, the freedom and the good judgement with which she proclaimed her promiscuity and prolific maternity. The truth is that it was all bravado because years later I got to know her really well when she worked for the AIMA news agency. She was in a stable marriage with one son and one daughter.[37]

The ironic bragging with which Margarita chose to justify her way of life and her independence marked the way in which she was perceived in a puritanical society. By vehemently defending her right to use her body as she wished and to have children with whomsoever she wished, she inadvertently nourished the widespread assumption that she was a whore.[38] In fact, in this, as in every other aspect of her life, she acted according to a strict ethical code. Whether there were other men in her life before Julio Antonio is simply not known. After him, there was only Martín de Paúl, the man she was eventually to marry. She remained faithful to him from the time that they began to live together in 1920 until they ultimately separated after the Spanish Civil War. If they did not marry yet, it was simply because Martín was already married (to Concepción García Pelayo) and there was no divorce in Catholic Spain. When Margarita knew that she was pregnant, she gave Martín an ultimatum – either they would live together as a functioning family or else she would prefer to bring up her child alone and not see him again. Her alter ego, Libertad in her novel *La trampa del arenal*, explains that she is leaving the married man, Luis, because 'you know that

I cannot be a mistress'. Martín gave in and left his wife. At the time, Concepción was also pregnant. Since Martín travelled a lot in his business with homes in both Sevilla and Madrid, it is likely Margarita did not know all the facts until later. As a mother herself, and given her views on such female solidarity, she can only have felt great unease about taking another woman's husband. Certainly, the subject matter of *La trampa del arenal* – unwanted pregnancy, a man trapped in a loveless marriage, the dilemma of the independent woman who loves him – suggest that Margarita Nelken suffered a degree of guilt.[39]

Throughout the 1920s, Margarita and Martin shared an apartment with Magda and Santiago in the elegant Avenida de Menéndez Pelayo, overlooking Madrid's elegant park, the Retiro. They lived in No. 29 and her parents in No. 31. Martín was a typical Andalusian *señorito*, handsome and by nature a philanderer. He had shown that by leaving his wife and family. However, in the first years of their relationship, Margarita was enough for him. She was not a conventionally beautiful woman but she was powerfully, sensuously attractive, with an irresistibly mischievous smile, myopic eyes that still gleamed with provocative curiosity and unruly wavy hair. Full of life and energy, she was deeply in love with Martín but was a strong enough personality not to put up with any infidelities. Capable of earning her own living, experienced as a single mother and sure of the help of her parents, she would not have tolerated his antics out of fear of losing a breadwinner. If anything, the boot was on the other foot – it was fear of losing her that restrained his wandering impulses at this time.[40]

Now settled, in addition to her feminist proselytism, Margarita wrote widely on art and literature and was the art correspondent of the influential Madrid daily, *El Sol*. She also wrote for the conservative weekly magazine, *Blanco y Negro* with an amusing regular column entitled 'La vida y nosotras' (life and us women).[41] Throughout the early 1920s, she earned money writing the short stories and novellas which, while fashionably frivolous, often contained a subtle feminist message.[42] In the middle to late 1920s, she was a consultant for the great Exposición de Barcelona. Intelligent and attractive, her determined feminist views on domestic servants earned her the resentment of many middle-class women. At the same time, her perceived colourful sexual past also caused her problems even, or perhaps especially, with women of the left. She was mortified when she was refused membership of the rather prim women's club in Madrid, the Lyceum. Founded in 1926, the Lyceum quickly became a centre for literary and scientific discussion. In a society in which women were expected to gather in public only for prayer or dancing, this 'rebellion of the skirts' provoked misogynistic fears. Its general blue-stocking ambience, together with the preciousness and eccentricity of some of its regulars, were used as an excuse for considerable male ribaldry.[43] Yet this club which frightened liberal males was too genteel to be able to accept Margarita Nelken. Some members regarded her as unsuitable because of her presumed promiscuity while others resented her particularly robust version of feminism. Her sharp wit was also the cause of some problems in such a fragrantly polite milieu.[44]

In 1929, Margarita Nelken published an intriguing short book called *Tres tipos de Vírgenes*. It was a measure of her standing that she was invited to publish in a prestigious series called *Cuadernos Literarios* every one of whose titles had been contributed by a major literary or intellectual figure. Other works had been contributed by the many novelists and essayists including Pío Baroja and Azorín, the surrealist Ernesto Giménez Caballero, the Republican leader Manuel Azaña, and the historian Ramón Menéndez Pidal, as well as by the expressionist painter José Gutiérrez Solana. Margarita's book was based on lectures that she had given at the Prado. It was typically original in its conception, learned in its wide-ranging references, immediate and direct in its language. Her object was to examine the way in which Christian art had represented the idea of the Mother of God. She compared the representations of the Virgin Mary in the various Annunciations by the fifteenth-century Dominican, Fra Angelico, in the numerous Madonnas by the sixteenth-century master Rafael and in the canvases in the Cathedral of Granada by the seventeenth-century Andalusian painter, Alonso Cano.

Her approach was down-to-earth and unpretentious, with the emotional and the sensual taking priority. The Virgin of Fra Angelico represented 'the most unearthly mysticism, the Virgin Mother considered, not as a lofty woman but rather, despite the tenderness of her real appearance, one might say, as intangible divinity'. She saw in the Virgins of Rafael 'the bland sensuality that impels the artist, in order to adore María, to identify her with his feminine and amorous ideal'. In the representation of the Virgin by Alonso Cano she perceived 'the realist impulse, which sees in Mary the woman that the artist sees at all hours, the sublimation, not of his internal feelings, not even of his earthly ideal, but rather what was before him most directly every day'. Margarita wrote about the paintings vibrantly, with fervent enthusiasm and warmth. She was able, through her empathy with the artists, to give a vivid sense of how they worked and the obstacles that they had to overcome. Similarly, in a book without illustrations, she was able to bring alive the very figures represented in the paintings, in particular rhapsodising over the emotions portrayed on the Virgin's face. She identified with the mother in the paintings and this gave rise to her vividly tactile appreciation of Rafael's Virgin – 'how she rejoiced feeding him at her breast! What sweetness that other women could not know.'[45]

In 1930, Margarita Nelken published an equally committed book which was even more representative of her passionate nature and her lucidity as a critic. An historical survey of Spanish women writers of quite remarkable erudition, *Las escritoras españolas* must have been some years in the making.

Unlike almost all Spanish books of the time, it included scholarly footnotes, a substantial bibliography and an alphabetical index. It was both extremely learned yet compellingly readable, in large part because of the militant way in which her views shone through the scholarship. It was dedicated to her daughter Magda, now fifteen years old. The book was an affirmation, with unmistakable autobiographical overtones, of the immense literary achievements of Spanish women writers. The opening remarks had a clear relevance to her own life: 'it is not abroad but right here, and even in the most cultured circles, that it is regarded as an unheard-of novelty that a Spanish woman might frequent university lecture rooms or express her personality through the pen'. In it, as in her art criticism, her enthusiasm for the works under review was linked to a deep empathy with those she wrote about. She took particular care in emphasising not only the literary achievements of her chosen authors, but also the obstacles that they had had to overcome to publish and be taken seriously in a male-dominated society. In particular, she related to the sixteenth-century mystic, St Teresa of Avila. The warmth, spontaneity and emotional honesty of Teresa were, in their different ways and different context, akin to those of Margarita Nelken herself. It was the combination of sensuality and learning with which Santa Teresa expressed her love for God that stimulated Margarita's admiration. She defended Teresa from the facile charge of hysteria with which her religious ecstasy was often dismissed by her male commentators. It would not be going too far to suggest that Margarita identified her own zeal and erudition with those of the saint.[46]

Margarita Nelken had an insatiable *joie de vivre*. She was equally passionate about everything that she did. She was also articulate about it. She believed in what she called 'a more widely human feminism' and she rejoiced in femininity.[47] She lived all of her experiences to the full, rejoicing in her relationships with men, in motherhood, in her writing, in her lecturing, in her politics. Her boundless energy and enthusiasm constantly pushed her past boundaries of decorum and the social and sexual expectations of the day. Her vivacity was such that her feminism did not stand in the way of her fibbing about her age. This may account for the frequency with which scholars have given her date of birth incorrectly. In an unsuccessful application for a grant to write a book on the painter Rosales, made in February 1919, she gave her age as 23, when she was in fact 24. In an interview in 1923, the journalist Artemio Precioso asked her age point-blank. At the time, still six months short of her twenty-ninth birthday, she rather engagingly hesitated and replied, with apparent reluctance, 'Well, without suppressing anything, I will tell you, although it doesn't please me one bit to do so, that I am going on – and it is contrary to all my wishes – for twenty-six.' The entire interview sparkled with humour. Asked what she thought of the Spanish male, she replied, 'Given that there are Spanish men among my readers, it is naturally my opinion that the Spanish male is a superman par excellence. I'm hardly likely to upset the customers.'

Asked whether men should stand to give their seat to a woman on the tram, she quipped, 'Of course. When I get on a full tram, I always go from one end to the other to see if someone feels sufficiently gallant for me not to have to suffer from my high heels. Unfortunately, there are some very preoccupied men.' On a serious note, Precioso asked her if she was in favour of divorce. She replied, 'I cannot understand matrimony without that safety valve.' Pressed to name the most intelligent woman who had ever lived, she laughed. 'Me, of course! Make sure you say that but as if it was your own opinion, because, like every interviewee, I am the soul of modesty and discretion.' Elsewhere in the same interview, she was quoted as claiming that, at the age of fifteen, she had published an article on the Frescoes of Goya in San Antonio de la Florida in *The Studio* (London). In fact, that article was published when she was twenty-five. This may have been an error of transcription by the journalist or she may have been carried away by the momentum of the interview to exaggerate her achievements as a child prodigy.[48]

The anarcho-syndicalist Federica Montseny felt that Margarita Nelken's outspoken views on feminism and on sex led to her being shunned in her lifetime and ignored after her death: 'Margarita Nelken led a very free life, which clashed with all the prejudices of that time ... She had a free sexual life, and that bothered people profoundly.' She made the male establishment uncomfortable and they responded by ignoring her. As Montseny put it, 'both when she wrote and when she spoke, if she had to attack, she attacked, and that made her many enemies'.[49] In fact, her speeches and articles, while often impassioned, were always lucid and often graceful. If her public appearances were stigmatised as incendiary and provocative, her fury was a response to the context of injustice in which they were delivered.[50] Her political writings could be acerbic but that came from the open way in which she engaged with the issues. Unable to dismiss her intellectually, the male establishment tried to diminish her because of her sexuality. The other major political women of the day – Pasionaria and Federica Montseny herself – played down their sexuality and played up their maternal side to make themselves more acceptable within the Spanish establishment.[51]

Having lectured widely and powerfully on the subject of her 1921 book, Margarita Nelken was drawn even more into politics as a result of following the situation in Germany after the First World War. In 1920, in the Ateneo de Madrid, along with a number of writers and university professors, she had formed part of a committee set up to help the starving children of postwar Germany and Austria. Because of her fluent German, she was elected by the committee to visit Berlin and she was shocked to find a level of cold, hunger and misery that seemed to her to be 'almost from another planet'.[52] During the dictatorship of General Primo de Rivera, she gave lectures to the miners of Asturias which led to her being expelled from the province by the Governor, Fuentes Pila.[53] Considered a member of the opposition to the regime, her mail was subjected to censorship.[54] Those inconveniences aside, by this time, her life was extremely comfortable. Her companion, Martín de Paúl, was a prosperous businessman and she was a successful writer and lecturer. By 1930, they had moved from Menéndez Pelayo to the altogether grander Avenida de la Castellana (No. 51). They had two maids and a car, although Margarita never learned to drive.[55]

However, material success in no way diminished her social concerns. Shortly after the establishment of the Second Republic, she was invited by Julián Zugazagoitia, the editor of *El Socialista*, to write the 'Tribuna Parlamentaria' section for the paper which she was to do throughout the period 1931–1933. Zugazagoitia commissioned her articles under the mistaken impression that she was already a card-carrying member of the Party although she and her companion, Martín de Paúl, joined the Socialist Party together very soon after.[56] She was swiftly to leap to prominence within the party.

In the poverty-stricken southern province of Badajoz, one of the successful Socialist candidates in the elections of 28 June, Juan Morán Bayo, had renounced his seat because he had also been elected for Cordoba where he was a professor in the University. There was considerable acrimony within the local party organisation (Agrupación Socialista de Badajoz) over the selection of a candidate for the consequent by-election called for 4 October 1931. The local group was pushing the candidacy of Juan Miranda Flores, a radical landless labourer who was in jail for a common crime. The choice of Miranda reflected the radicalisation of a local rank-and-file in the face of the brutality of the landowners of Extremadura. However, the other Socialist deputies, all senior members of the Badajoz group of the party, were alarmed by this choice. Accordingly, using the excuse that even if he were elected, Miranda would not be let out of jail to take up his seat, they managed to get his name dropped. Then, to avoid a divisive debate over a replacement, a woman candidate was suggested.

Since the PSOE had no female deputies, the proposal met with the approval of the Madrid hierarchy. When two of the PSOE deputies for Badajoz, Narciso Vázquez Torres and Juan Simeón Vidarte, began to canvass for names, Antonio Fabra Ribas, the Under-Secretary at the Ministry of Labour, suggested his friend Margarita Nelken on the grounds that she was highly educated and a born fighter. Given her solid reputation as a writer in Spain, and the fact that she had done so well writing the parliamentary reports for *El Socialista*, it never occurred to any of them that she had formally to apply for Spanish nationality. Margarita herself seemed unaware of the fact that technically she was German. It was only after Vázquez and Vidarte had declared her candidacy that this obstacle to her election came out and the Badajoz group was subjected to some ribaldry within the party. The fact that she was a woman and also such a new recruit to the party were additional causes of considerable friction. That she could be a candidate for parliament without years in the trenches of trade unionism and the administrative slog of local party *agrupaciones* annoyed many senior Socialists. Trifón Gómez, the railway workers' leader, commented, 'It's the first I've heard of this woman being a Socialist.' In fact, her membership card was so recent that many were unaware that she had already joined the party. It was thus later alleged, incorrectly, that she joined merely to permit her to stand in the Badajoz by-election. She campaigned vigorously, appealing to the local landless labourers with speeches critical of the repressive role of the Civil Guard. However, during the campaign, she was subjected to considerable racist and sexist abuse for her fame as a feminist and for her German-Jewish origins. The influential Socialist intellectual Luis Araquistain jokingly – and prophetically – reproached a deeply embarrassed Fabra Ribas, 'what a load of trouble you've landed those good people in!'[57] She was elected easily, by 59,783 votes against the 23,656 of her nearest opponent, José Manuel Pedregal.[58]

Many years later, it was claimed by her fellow Socialist deputy for Badajoz, Juan Simeón Vidarte, that at this time she married Martín de Paúl merely in order to secure Spanish nationality in a hurry to validate her parliamentary candidacy.[59] Vidarte's normally good memory failed him here. Margarita did not need any stratagems to prove her Spanish nationality. Having been born and brought up in Spain, she believed that she was of Spanish nationality and she did not marry until more than two years later. She presented her parliamentary candidacy in October 1931 as Margarita Nelken Mansberger, not as Señora Nelken de Paúl. There has been some confusion about her marital status, not all inspired by malice. In 1932, she told the French journalists, Germaine Picard-Moch and Jules Moch, that she was married to a businessman who was a member of the Socialist Party and had a daughter aged seventeen and a son aged ten. The part about her marriage was a white lie – she had lived with Martín de Paúl out of wedlock but in a stable and monogamous relationship since 1920.[60] They married formally in early 1933 as soon as the introduction of divorce in December 1932 by the Second Republic freed him from his first marriage. There is no doubting their continued commitment to each other. Moreover, now in a hostile political spotlight, the issue of legitimising her children meant rather a lot to Margarita. Shortly after the ceremony, Martín de Paúl recognised Magda as his own daughter.[61] In the elections of both November 1933 and February 1936, she did present herself as Señora Margarita Nelken Mansberger de Paúl, having married the man she loved, not for political convenience. In 1947, when Margarita was exiled in Mexico, a journalist wrote bizarrely that she had been married to the German Ambassador in Madrid during the First

World War. She wrote a letter to the newspaper to set the record straight. She pointed out that she had never had any husband other than Señor Martín de Paúl, a native of Seville, the son of Señor Pedro de Paúl and Señora María de los Dolores de Martín-Barbadillo, born in Cádiz, of totally Spanish descent (Andalusian and Basque).[62]

Once installed as deputy for Badajoz, Margarita's intense empathy with the plight of the landless peasantry would quickly push her to adopt extreme positions on the great social problems of the province. Far from soothing spirits within the Badajoz Socialist group, her increasing radicalism intensified conflict to an unprecedented level.[63] Indeed, her parliamentary career met controversy even before she had taken her seat. One week after the by-election, the Secretary of the Cortes, coincidentally Juan Simeón Vidarte, presented the results for parliamentary approval. A formal protest was made on 16 October by the Radical deputy, Diego Hidalgo Durán, on the grounds that she was not Spanish. Her statement in her own defence was characteristically direct and energetic, pointing out her birth and uninterrupted residence in Madrid, apart from short stays abroad for her education, the fact that she travelled on a Spanish passport and had undertaken important work on government commissions on both social and artistic issues. Despite having seen the statement, Hidalgo, backed by a number of right-wing deputies, pursued his efforts to have her election nullified. On 18 November 1931, there was an acrimonious parliamentary debate which reflected the embittered relations between the Radical and Socialist deputies for the province. In the event, her candidacy was approved and she was granted Spanish nationality on the grounds of being born in Spain and resident there for thirty-seven years. Despite what Vidarte remembered thirty-five years later, the question of her marriage did not arise.[64]

Margarita Nelken quickly became a prominent, if less than popular, figure within the PSOE. Despite its commitment to sweeping agrarian and social reforms, the Socialist leadership was quite conservative in its attitudes. Moreover, the leadership of the party – a rather puritanical and hierarchical patriarchy – did not take easily to women. The writer Matilde de la Torre, from 1933 deputy for Asturias, wrecked her health in the service of the Socialist Party. A far less abrasive figure than Margarita, she was equally undervalued, not to say ignored, by the male leadership.[65] Nelken's feisty directness did not coincide with their expectations of a woman. Even less did their basically reformist attitudes permit them to sympathise with her often rash and precipitate enthusiasm for causes which they perceived as dangerously revolutionary. The PSOE was a party in which reverence for tradition, procedure and seniority were paramount. Margarita Nelken had little interest in any of that. Still maintaining a steady output of journalism and an active involvement in the art world, she had no time or patience for the minutiae of Party bureaucracy. She sidestepped Party life at its epicentre, the Agrupación Socialista Madrileña, and soon got involved in what she considered to be the burning issues of the day in Badajoz. What she saw as the higher priority of the agrarian problem led her to shelve her feminist evangelism. Indeed, she opposed female suffrage on the grounds that the reactionary influence of the clergy would impel the majority of Catholic women to vote for the right.[66] However, since her own election as a deputy was not confirmed until 18 November, she was unable to participate in the constitutional debate on the vote for women. Nor could she attend the Cortes sessions of 30 September and 1 October 1931 at which female suffrage was approved by 141 votes to 106.[67]

The same reasons that saw Margarita eschew Party bureaucracy probably had an impact on her married life. In many respects, she was an overwhelming force of nature bursting with vitality and creativity. Family legend has it that Martín was the weaker partner in the relationship. This would eventually be revealed in a series of infidelities with submissive women whom he felt he could dominate. However, this would not happen until growing political commitments – and eventually exile – obliged her to spend less time with him. Her myriad activities, and particularly, her superhuman efforts on behalf of her peasant constituents, took their toll. As she neared her fortieth decade, her looks began to fade and, without her imposing presence to inhibit him, the eye of Martín the Andalusian ladies' man began to rove once more.

As deputy for a conflictive agrarian province, Margarita Nelken quickly became involved in the struggle of landless labourers for better conditions and for agrarian reform.[68] Badajoz was one of the provinces where the Republic's efforts to introduce better conditions for the landless labourers or *braceros* was meeting the most brutal resistance from the local landowners. Their plight particularly engaged Margarita Nelken who responded with belligerent oratory and calls for radical solutions. On 26 November 1931, the PSOE parliamentary group created a party commission to collect evidence of abuses by the Civil Guard. It was hoped to be able thereby to build a case for the reform of the Civil Guard. Margarita Nelken was nominated, along with three other PSOE deputies – Antonio Fernández-Bolaños Mora (Málaga), Hermenegildo Casas Jiménez (Seville) and Enrique Esbrí y Fernández (Jaén). With her characteristic impetus and energy, she took the lead and threw herself into the task.[69]

In December 1931, there took place a series of events in her constituency that would definitively turn her into a *bête noire* of the right. The Socialist landworkers' union, the Federación Nacional de Trabajadores de la Tierra, had called a strike against the landowners' constant infractions of the Republic's social legislation. On 31 December, in the remote and impoverished village of Castilblanco, a peaceful demonstration of strikers was fired upon by the Civil Guard. One man was killed and two others wounded. The outraged villagers rounded on the four Civil Guards and beat them to death. The Socialists interpreted the events of Castilblanco in terms of the long history of appalling social deprivation and brutality of the area. Margarita Nelken was alleged to have described the events as a necessary outlet for oppressed spirits and asked what had happened in the village before this incident.[70] This infuriated the right and Margarita Nelken was blamed for the entire incident by General José Sanjurjo, at the time, Director General of the Civil Guard. Sanjurjo was especially furious because he had had to miss a big society banquet in Zaragoza to go to Castilblanco. He had been scheduled to appear at the wedding of the daughter of the Vizconde de Escoriaza as one of the bride's witnesses.[71] Speaking to journalists, Sanjurjo compared the workers of Castilblanco to the Moorish tribesmen that he had fought in Morocco, claiming – mendaciously – that even after the colonial disaster of Annual in 1921, 'even in Monte Arruit, when the Melilla command collapsed, the corpses of Christians were not mutilated with such savagery'. In a tendentious reference to Margarita Nelken's participation in the Party commission on the Civil Guard, Sanjurjo claimed that 'an information office has been created against the Civil Guard and it is directed by Margarita Nelken who is not even a Spanish citizen'.[72]

The Cortes returned from its Christmas recess on 5 January 1932. On the morning of that day, the Socialist parliamentary group (*la minoría socialista*) met to consider the issues raised by Castilblanco. Margarita Nelken gave a deeply emotional account of the lives of the peasants of Castilblanco, condemned to year-long hunger and subjected to the physical abuse of the Civil Guard. The bulk of her party was convinced by her call for the events to be put in the context of 'black history' of the Civil Guard and by her demand that the long-term origins of the incident be taken into account in any investigation. However, she was mortified when she was accused by her fellow deputy for Badajoz, the cautious Besteirista Manuel

Muiño, of helping to cause the tragedy by dint of 'predicating excesses and dangerously inciting the workers of Badajoz'. Passions were running so high that it was agreed that none of the deputies for Badajoz should intervene in the imminent parliamentary debate. The PSOE view was to be expressed by the moderate Andrés Saborit.[73] The Minister of the Interior, Santiago Casares Quiroga, dismissed talk of Socialist provocation and attributed the incident to 'a reek of primitive instinct, to popular impulse'.[74] However, later that day, in the Cortes, Margarita Nelken was directly accused of responsibility by the Carlist deputy for Pamplona, Joaquín Beunza. The Radical deputies for Badajoz, with Diego Hidalgo at their head, echoed Sanjurjo and tried to pin the blame on the left. After praising the moderate Narciso Vázquez, Hidalgo blamed the strike on 'two or three people who provoked it as a pedestal for their own political career'. He mentioned by name Margarita, Nicolás de Pablo and Pedro Rubio Heredia, both members of the local Landworkers' Federation. Incensed by this, Margarita forgot party discipline and became involved in an unseemly screaming match with the Radicals. This tendency occasionally to let her political passion override her better judgement made it easier for right-wing caricature to dismiss her as a wild haridan.[75]

Azaña made a statesmanlike speech that went some way to calming the situation. However, he was furious at Margarita's intervention. Later that night, he wrote in his diary:

> Nelken having opinions on political matters drives me mad. She is the personification of indiscretion. She has spent her life writing about painting and I could never have imagined that she had political ambitions. I was amazed when I saw that she was a candidate for Badajoz. She won with Socialist votes . . . but the Socialist Party took its time about admitting her to its bosom and the Cortes also delayed before accepting

her as a deputy. You need vanity and ambition to go through everything Nelken has gone through to be able to sit in the Congress.[76]

Given Azaña's predilection for women less independent and outspoken than Margarita Nelken, it was hardly surprising that he would be especially irritated by the fact that she was making things more difficult for him.[77] In fact, his remarks revealed more about himself than about her. On another occasion, on 28 February 1933, he sneered at one of her parliamentary speeches as being twee and pretentious (*cursi*) 'like those one used to hear in the Ateneo', on the grounds that it dealt with the Popes, prostitution, women's wages, maternity, etcetera, etcetera'.[78]

Margarita Nelken had certainly been active in Badajoz province as a speaker at the meetings of the Socialist landworkers' union, the Federación Nacional de Trabajadores de la Tierra (FNTT). However, she had not actually set foot in Castilblanco, which could be reached only by car to Herrera del Duque and then along a narrow track by foot or mule.[79] Another Socialist feminist, Regina García, who later reneged on her own early beliefs and sought redemption by embracing Francoism, ingratiated herself with her new masters by portraying Margarita as part of the 'Jewish-Bolshevik conspiracy'. She claimed that Nelken, 'Jewish by family and by religion, hated the Civil Guard for we don't know what dark complex of corrupt greed typical of her race'.[80] Within a week, the Civil Guard had taken a terrible revenge which saw eighteen people killed: three days after Castilblanco, there were two killed and three wounded in Zalamea de la Serena (Badajoz). Two days later, a striker was shot dead and another wounded in Calzada de Calatrava and one striker was shot in Puertollano (both villages in Ciudad Real) while two strikers were killed and eleven wounded in Épila (Zaragoza), and two strikers killed and ten wounded in Jeresa (Valencia). On 5 January, six were killed and fifty wounded in Arnedo (Logroño). Margarita Nelken pronounced a deeply moving oration at the burial ceremony on 7 January. Over the next few days, a further four died of their wounds and many had to have limbs amputated.[81]

Margarita Nelken had expressed her growing frustration with the government's inability to protect the landless peasantry from officially sanctioned violence in articles in *El Socialista* and *La Verdad Social* (Badajoz) published both on the eve of Castilblanco and in its aftermath. For three of her articles, 'Caza Mayor' (big game) on 24 December, 'Carta abierta al Ministro de la Gobernación' (open letter to the Minister of the Interior) on 26 December, and 'Después de la huelga de Badajoz' (after the Badajoz strike) 3 January 1932, she was taken to the Supreme Court, accused of insulting the Civil Guard. The words that caused problems were as follows:

> but what is the worth of any testimony, of any proof, no matter how weighty, up against the declaration of an individual who, as soon as he wears his uniform and his tricorn hat, takes possession of an infallibility higher even than that of the Pope? . . . Those of us who have never believed in the infallibility of the Supreme Pontiff find it difficult to believe in that of the tricorn hats, and even more difficult to accept that the big game for which the institution of the Civil Guard was created in other times now has to be replaced in our times by the hunting down of unarmed workers. Perhaps you remember how I informed you that this violent attitude of the Civil Guard, sabre charges, women held at gunpoint, often having gun barrels pushed into their breasts, workers thrown to the ground, etc, was fomented in the most shamelessly provocative manner by certain elements of the old regime . . . There should be a proclamation to inform

us that the supreme authority in Spain, above even the representatives of the Government and above all the clauses of the Constitution, is the Civil Guard. Accordingly, the Civil Guard can then unleash one of its ill-timed shows of forces whenever it fancies in order to provoke those mournful events which give so much satisfaction to the declared and hidden enemies of the Republic.

She appeared before a military investigating judge on 23 February 1932 and openly accepted that she was the author of the offending articles. She was called before another military investigator on 31 December 1932. She declared that 'she had no other intention than to draw attention to certain excesses of some members of the Civil Guard which, if not severely curtailed, would lamentably undermine the prestige of the institution and would show that within it there are activities contrary to the spirit of the Republic'. She refused to withdraw a phrase or a letter of the articles in question since she had made the same denunciations both verbally and in writing to the Director General of the Civil Guard who had received them with the necessary consideration for a representative of the nation. She was astonished that these denunciations, all specific, and with the signature of a parliamentary deputy, had produced no result other than these proceedings. In her opinion, the natural outcome would have been that an investigation would have been launched to examine the relevant responsibilities. She declared that

it seemed to her intolerable that the Civil Guard when it wants to look out for its own prestige, instead of correcting the faults committed by some of its members which is what undermines that prestige, thinks only of declaring its own inviolability which is something that only parliamentary deputies possess.

The case was finally dropped in April 1933 because the Cortes refused to waive her parliamentary immunity.[82]

The slowness of reform and the success of right-wing deputies in blocking reform further undermined Margarita Nelken's faith in parliamentary democracy. Along with other Socialist deputies for the rural South, she was infuriated by the apparent incapacity of the Republican-Socialist Government to control the brutality of the Civil Guard. In particular, she was outraged by the supine attitude of the Minister of the Interior, Santiago Casares Quiroga, when it came to selecting the appropriate senior officers for command in sensitive provinces such as Badajoz.[83] As she lost faith in the Government, she threw herself into the job of persuading the landless labourers that it was possible to change their fate. Her empathy with the suffering of her constituents found voice in a hitherto undiscovered oratorical skill: 'She is an orator with a mystic tone who knows how to stir an audience with emotive descriptions of the human pain of those who hunger and thirst for justice.'[84] She became so popular as a speaker in the most bitterly divided rural areas that the Executive Committee of the PSOE could barely cope with the dozen or more per week requests for her presence. Working-class women's societies in New Castile took her name. In Talavera de la Reina in the province of Toledo, there was the Sociedad Agrícola de Mujeres Margarita Nelken. In El Bonillo (Albacete), there was the Grupo Femenino Sindical Socialista Margarita Nelken. A street was named after her in Almendralejo in the province of Badajoz.[85]

Badajoz was a province on the verge of civil war. During the first two years of the Republic, there were more than two hundred clashes between right and left, between peasants and the armed guards of the landowners, or between peasants and the Civil Guards. There were assaults on estates and on town halls. At least twenty deaths were recorded in consequence.[86] Margarita Nelken made a number of dramatic and moving parliamentary speeches denouncing the rural lockout which was condemning the day labourers to starvation. She was incensed by frequent incidents of starving peasants being beaten by the Civil Guard for collecting windfall olives and stealing acorns (a pig food) or arrested for collecting firewood. Her eloquent and well-informed speeches showed that, as with everything that she did, she had thrown herself fully into being the champion of the landless peasants that she represented.[87] In parliament, she was always well prepared, demonstrating a considerable mastery of the agrarian problem. Despite the fact that she was widely regarded as an electrifying orator, her speeches were ridiculed in the right-wing press as the pitiful efforts of a German trying haltingly to speak Spanish.[88] The effectiveness of her public speaking can be deduced not only from her immense popularity in Badajoz, but also from the response of right-wing critics. For the Francoist propagandist Francisco Casares, she spoke 'with a spiteful smile, arrogant and disdainful . . . her words scratch more because of their strident sound than because of their content'.[89]

The abrasive and incendiary style of Margarita Nelken was like a spark to petrol. There was an incident on 1 May 1932 at an estate called Monte Porrino near the village of Salvaleón in Badajoz, in which she was involved. Together with the local FNTT leader, Nicolás de Pablo, she had called a meeting of Socialists from Badajoz, Barcarrota, Salvaleón and other villages in the province. At the meeting, the speeches of Margarita and Nicolás de Pablo so fired up the crowd that they set off for Salvaleón with the intention of attacking the Civil Guard barracks there. When a shot was fired from the crowd, the Civil Guard opened fire and three people were killed. Arrests were made, including Nicolás de Pablo and the Mayor (Alcalde) of Salvaleón, '*Tío Juan el de los pollos*' (Uncle John the Chicken Man). Margarita simply disappeared before she could be arrested. On other occasions, the local right would impede meetings planned for Margarita Nelken.

Margarita's work with the landless labourers brought her

into contact with Ricardo Zabalza, the leader of the Federación Nacional de Trabajadores de la Tierra. They worked together closely because of their shared involvement in the agrarian struggle. Through his visits to her home in the Avenida de la Castellana in Madrid, he met and fell in love with her maid, Obdulia Bermejo Oviedo. His increasingly frequent visits to the house to court Obdulia fed malicious, and totally unfounded, slanders that Margarita was having a love affair with him. Along with Zabalza, she became one of the most prominent Socialists pushing the PSOE Secretary General Francisco Largo Caballero to adopt ever more radical tactics. Indeed, at one point, she was sending virulent articles attacking the PSOE's centrists to the newspaper of the Socialist Youth, *Renovación*. This heightened her profile as a rabble-rouser.[90]

Despite all her political activity, with her remarkable capacity for work, she maintained a significant presence in the art world. In March 1933, she visited Paris to give a lecture about the political situation in Spain and also to carry forward a project for two major art exhibitions. The first, of modern French painting, was to be held in Madrid; the second, of modern Spanish painting, was to be held in Paris.[91]

By the time that the elections of November 1933 were on the cards, the indignation felt by Margarita about the plight of the local peasantry had dramatically pushed her political views further to the left. She was coming to believe, along with many supporters of Largo Caballero, that the Republic had betrayed the workers. Accordingly, they had pushed for the abandonment of the electoral alliance with the Republicans. The Badajoz group of the PSOE was deeply divided between the older moderates and those, like Margarita, who felt that revolutionary action was the only answer. She was active in the Socialist election campaign at both national and provincial level. In a speech at the Madrid Casa del Pueblo on 27 October, she drew upon the themes of her book *La condición social de la mujer*. Referring to the right-wing propaganda directed at women under the slogan '*Patria, Familia, Religión*', she gave a coruscating reply:

> *¡Patria!* Of what fatherland dare speak those who sent your sons to fight overseas in defence of capitalist interests, who have neglected the education of our children and deprived the villages of Spain of the most basic schools? *Religión!* What do they know of religion those fine ladies who offer alms to those who have the right to demand justice? *Familia!* They say that divorce is destroying the family as if Spain was not the country of *tornos* at the foundlings hospital (the device whereby unwanted babies were left on a revolving table in the wall) and of children with no name. What family are they talking about? They say it to us who know that the bourgeois family is one of the greatest farces and hypocrisies.[92]

Given the scale of unemployment in the province of Badajoz, nearly 40 per cent, and the consequent near-starvation of many of its inhabitants, the radical line struck a chord. The election campaign was marked by considerable violence. Margarita's deeply felt concern for the land-workers and their families, expressed in ringing speeches, had made her genuinely popular. In consequence, she became a target for right-wing hatred. A local thug known as Bocanegra was released from prison expressly in order that he might attack her.[93] Her speeches at meetings in Badajoz were passionate and drew loud applause. However, they were often suspended by the local authorities or, if they went ahead, interrupted by hecklers. On several occasions, in villages without microphones, the orchestrated interruptions were so overwhelming as to force her to give up, her voice exhausted by the effort of trying to be heard over the din. When she spoke in Madrid, she drew large and enthusiastic crowds.[94]

On the morrow of the election, Margarita Nelken telegrammed the Minister of Labour, Carles Pi Sunyer:

> My fears were sadly confirmed yesterday when the vote had to be suspended. A group of thugs led by the Radical Mayor (Alcalde) of Aljucén opened fire on groups of workers, killing one, seriously wounding two and wounding four or six more. The day of the elections constitutes a disgrace for the Republic given the pressures of the forces of Law and order, scaring the people and permitting electoral falsification by religious fanatics, playboys and thugs crowing that they could do so with impunity. Spanish democracy has definitively gone wrong[95]

There was significant falsification by the right – votes bought with food and/or blankets, intimidation of voters, repeat voting by truckloads of right-wing sympathisers. Margarita was herself manhandled at gunpoint after a speech in the Casa de Pueblo of Aljucén. The consequence was that the PSOE won only the three seats of the minority block for the province – Margarita Nelken, along with fellow radical Socialists, Pedro Rubio Heredia and Nicolás de Pablo. However, because of an error in the count, the moderate Juan-Simeón Vidarte was re-elected at the top of the Badajoz Socialist list, and Nicolás de Pablo dropped out.[96]

Margarita had begun her association with the peasants of Badajoz in a spirit of optimism. In a speech in Plasencia in May 1932, she had declared 'Socialism is the caravan that advances with steady steps across the desert and will reach its destination whether others want it to or not and unaffected by the howling of the jackals.'[97] She had been deeply affected by what she had seen since in terms of the ruthless way in which powerful landlords had ignored the Republic and set about crushing the landless labourers. During the election campaign, she was appalled to see upper-class women, escorted by machine-gun toting Civil Guards, buying votes in brothels and, at the voting stations, local bosses (*caciques*) buying votes from starving peasants with chunks of chorizo and bread. Villages that were known to have a majority of Socialist votes but had no telegraph, telephone or railway line, like Siruela and Villarta de los Montes, nonetheless saw right-wing victories declared and registered in the provincial capital minutes after the 'count' ended. Queues of labourers waiting to vote had their voting slips torn from their hands at gunpoint and were obliged to take replacements already made out for right-wing candidates.[98] Angered and frustrated by the powerlessness of the Republic to prevent the bullying arrogance of the Southern landowners, she had lost faith in legal democratic means to alter the injustices of the countryside. Henceforth she would line up with those who believed that only revolution could solve the problems of the landless peasantry.

Nationally, the elections of November 1933 saw a triumph for the right. The defeat affected Margarita greatly and she became convinced that the principal cause was the pro-rightist vote by so many women. She was appalled by the speed and savagery with which the landowners of southern Spain in general, and Badajoz in particular, took advantage of the shift in power. She spoke eloquently in the Cortes on 25 January 1934 about abuses of the law by the landowners: the use of cheap outside labour, the evictions of sharecroppers (*aparceros*) and the systematic exclusion of workers known to belong to the Socialist Unión General de Trabajadores (General Union of Workers). The increase in unemployment, sharp reductions in wages, and the consequent hunger was reflected in the spread of anaemia and tuberculosis among the children of the region. When the landless labourers protested or tried to collect windfall acorns or olives, they were beaten by the Civil Guard. An impassioned, but reasoned and factually detailed, speech ended with a terrible warning about the tragic situation being provoked in the south.

Those men go to collect acorns like wild beasts; they live like wild beasts. If one day in the not too distant future, you have to face them in a struggle which I hope will be fair, do not be surprised if those men whom you oblige to live like beasts, to seek food for their children like beasts, fighting for food with animals, risking their lives as the beasts do, do not be surprised, I say, if these men are left with no human sentiments when it comes to fighting.[99]

The battling conclusion to the speech was typical of Margarita Nelken's emotional involvement in the problems of the rural South. After a speech based on appalling facts, lucid and with little rhetoric, she ended giving vent to her anger at the inhuman treatment to which her constituents were being subjected. She was wrong in her prophecy, however. When the clash that she predicted came to pass in 1936, the hungry peasants would not be the perpetrators but the victims of bestial violence at the hands of the forces of 'order'.

Margarita Nelken's increasingly revolutionary reactions were the fruit of the heart-rending letters that she received from her constituents. In the spring of 1934, she had written in the landworkers' newspaper: 'Do we have to wait until the peasants eat one another before we are moved? Do we have to face the shame of the rest of the world organising a charity campaign to bring succour to the starving of Spain?' Her article ended with words that once more led to the courts taking an interest. 'Those who sow the wind reap the whirlwind ... Seeds of tragedy are being sown by the handful. Let nobody be surprised, let nobody complain, let nobody be scandalised and protest tomorrow, if these winds provoke a storm of blood.' Her words again saw her dragged before the courts but an amnesty law in April saw the case shelved.[100]

Her sense of impotence as a parliamentary deputy and her

indignation were intensified when her heartfelt litanies of rural brutality were greeted by the flippant responses of right-wing deputies and the radical Minister of the Interior, Rafael Salazar Alonso. Her frustration sometimes led her into rancorous skirmishes as tempers frayed.[101] Her articles and speeches saw her taken to court accused of inciting unrest. A biting article in the May Day 1934 issue of *Socorro Obrero Español* spoke of 'the tyranny of the putrid, shameless bourgeois who want to pull all of us down to the ground with imprisonment and intolerable injustices'.[102] She believed that the landless peasantry was being forced by starvation to see violence as the only escape. This inclined her to lend a sympathetic ear to the blandishments of Víctor Codovila, the Argentinian agent of the Comintern. She introduced him to Largo Caballero and thereby facilitated the entry of the Communist Party into the wide labour front known as the Alianzas Obreras.[103] There have been accusations that she was one of a number of members of the Socialist Party who remained inside despite having already pledged their loyalty to Moscow.[104] There is no evidence to suggest that this was the case. However, in the context of the urgency with which she viewed the revolutionary agenda, it would not have been the horrendous betrayal that it has been made out to be. Nevertheless, her concerns at this stage were about the rising tide of right-wing violence, and not about inter-party rivalries. She certainly had begun to feel that the moderate reformist social-democrat line of the older PSOE leadership was sterile and counterproductive. However, in her enthusiasm for a more radical line, she drastically overestimated the possibilities for revolution in Spain.

Given her ties to Badajoz and her friendship and ideological affinity with Ricardo Zabalza, it was hardly surprising that Margarita was involved in the organisation of the national peasant strike of the summer of 1934. It was a strike that had been provoked by the consistent flouting of labour legislation by the owners of the big estates who enjoyed the unstinting support of the Government. Legal procedure for the declaration of the strike had been scrupulously observed by the Federación Nacional de Trabajadores de la Tierra (the Landworkers' Federation of the UGT). Ten days' notice had been given that the strike would start on 5 June. Salazar Alonso used the time to prepare his repressive measures. He declared the harvest to be a 'national public service' – a device to make the strike illegal and justify the use of force. It militarised the labourers and thus put strikers in a mutinous situation. Thousands of peasants were arrested and the harvest brought in, under Civil Guard protection, by machines and cheap imported labour.[105] According to Salazar Alonso, Margarita Nelken, along with fellow PSOE deputy Pablo Rubio Heredia, was in Badajoz organising the strike.[106] Certainly, she was back in Madrid by 7 June 1934, where she spoke vehemently in parliament about the large numbers of landless labourers detained in inhuman conditions despite Government assurances that the strike was a total failure.

Her indignation got the better of her. 'Where landowners in Jaén or Seville have dared bring out their machines into the fields and the machines have been burned, or where landowners have been killed . . .' At this point, the Radical deputy for Jaén, Nicolás Alcalá Espinosa, interjected: 'Murdered!' 'Very well,' she continued, 'murdered; just as the Civil Guard murders . . . So, despite the fact that we are told that nothing is happening, there are many deaths . . .' Alcalá Espinosa again interrupted, shouting, 'Murders!' 'Call them what you like,' she snapped back.

> At the end of the day you are not going to frighten me! If you are going to frighten anyone, it will be the bosses! There are workers dead, and where a landowner was, as the right honourable gentleman says, murdered, it was because the father of that landowner opened fire with shotguns on peaceful workers. Let it

go on record that the peasants' strike, contrary to what
the Government says, is general.[107]

The tactless outrage of her speech reflected the extent to which
the abuses committed by the forces of order during the
repression of the strike appalled her.

Peaceful strikers were savagely beaten, their families terror-
ised and those arrested taken on open trucks hundreds of
kilometres from their homes, then left to make their own way
back home on foot. Her indignation was expressed in a series
of powerful newspaper articles and speeches that constitute
further milestones on her road to revolutionary radicalism.[108]
On 15 July, she spoke at a meeting in Asturias, denouncing
the conduct of the Ministry of the Interior (Gobernación) as
immoral giving examples of the repression in Extremadura.
She also claimed that the Minister himself, Rafael Salazar
Alonso, had offered 15,000 pesetas, a substantial sum at the
time, to have her murdered. The Government delegate present
reported on the speech and trial proceedings against her were
opened. Before the case could be heard in 1935, she would
be in exile in Russia and, by the time that she returned to
Spain in 1936, the case was covered by an amnesty.[109]

In the midst of the peasants' strike, she courageously
denounced the role of a Falangist, Alfonso Merry del Val,
in the murder of the young Socialist Juanita Rico who was
assassinated on 10 June 1934 in retaliation for the death of a
Falangist earlier the same day. She claimed that the five-person
hit squad, which was transported in Merry del Val's car,
included his wife and Pilar Primo de Rivera. Although publication of the article in which she made her allegations was
prevented by the right-wing censorship, its contents were the
object of widespread comment in Madrid. Given the readiness
with which the Falangist death squad, the Falange de Sangre,
was beginning to function, it was a brave act.[110] On 4 July
1934, she made a speech accusing the Minister of the Interior,

Salazar Alonso, of covering up the murder, and that of another Socialist, in the knowledge that they were carried out by fascist terror squads. Once more, the case was discussed by the Supreme Court (Tribunal Supremo) and once more, she was saved by her parliamentary immunity.[111]

On 29 August 1934, Madrid witnessed a massive working-class demonstration as the Communist and Socialist Youth movements escorted the coffin of Joaquín del Grado, a young member of the Communist Party assassinated by Falangists. Speeches were made by Pasionaria (Dolores Ibárruri) and by Margarita Nelken.[112] By this time, carried away by anger at the behaviour of the Government and the landowners, she was a fervent advocate of a united front of the Socialist and Communist parties and also of armed insurrection.[113] She was now only too ready to exchange her sense of impotence for the heady revolutionary exhilaration offered by the so-called 'radicalisers' or 'bolshevisers' of the Socialist Youth (Federación de Juventudes Socialistas). Nothing came of the plans by their leaders, Santiago Carrillo, secretary-general of the FJS, Amaro del Rosal of the bank workers' union and Carlos Hernández Zancajo of the urban transport workers, to create an armed Socialist Youth militia.[114] Their loud advocacy of 'armed insurrection' without real preparation merely exacerbated political tension and alerted the Government and the right to the need to make the appropriate defensive preparations. Like the other young Socialists, Margarita Nelken was almost certainly unaware of the extent to which she and her fellow 'radicalisers' were falling into a trap being set by the right. Both the Radical Minister of the Interior, Rafael Salazar Alonso, and the leader of the CEDA, José María Gil Robles, were anxious to see a revolutionary coup in order to smash it and set up strong counterrevolutionary barriers against the left.[115] In September 1934, she implied in one article that Salazar Alonso was a fascist. In another, when another Socialist was killed, she accused the Minister of 'hatred of the working class in his joyful sadism'. The Minister tried to have her prosecuted on both counts but the cases were refused by the Supreme Court.[116]

After the defeat of the peasants' strike in the summer, the possibilities for revolutionary success were dramatically diminished.[117] During the preparation for the miners' uprising of October 1934, Margarita Nelken was on the fringes of plans being made by Amaro del Rosal, one of the most prominent 'bolshevisers' of the Socialist Youth. In the course of her work in Badajoz in defence of the landless peasants, she had come into contact with a few dissident Civil Guards sickened by the repressive role they were called upon to play. In the hope of securing their collaboration in the forthcoming revolutionary movement, she introduced Rosal to a Corporal Panero at her flat in the Avenida de la Castellana in Madrid. A few days later, she presented Rosal, again in her home, to her husband and her friend, Lieutenant Fernando Condés Romero of the Civil Guard.[118] Her principal task during the October rising was to carry the instructions of Largo Caballero's revolutionary committee to the peasants of Badajoz.

She arrived in the town on 4 October where she met with the opposition of the moderate Besteirista leader of the Badajoz Socialist group, Narciso Vázquez. He claimed, plausibly, that it was too soon after the summer harvest strike. Margarita also visited a number of prisoners who had been detained after the summer incidents. According to police reports, she spoke to various soldiers and Civil Guards in the hope of getting them to join in the revolutionary general strike that had been called. Her efforts came to nought. The strike was swiftly put down in Extremadura by the Civil Guard. Given that martial law had been declared, warrants were issued for the arrest of Margarita on charges of military rebellion ('*delito de rebelión militar cometido en la plaza de Badajoz*').[119] She went into hiding in the Cuban Embassy in Madrid under the protection of the Ambassador, Alfonso Hernández Catá. Her parliamentary immunity was lifted and she was condemned to twenty years' imprisonment in her absence. She remained in hiding for two months and established a life-long friendship with the ambassador's daughters, Uvaldina and Sara. Heavily disguised in theatrical make-up by Uvaldina and Sara and her friend, the actress Margarita Xirgu, she was provided with a Cuban passport and managed to get into France masquerading as the wife of her daughter's boyfriend, Adalberto Salas. She was later joined there first by Magda and later by her fourteen-year-old son, Santiago ('Taguín'). She stayed in Paris for some months, establishing in the process a friendship with Henri Barbusse who played chess with Santiago.[120]

While in exile, Margarita Nelken toured several European countries to raise funds for the victims of the repression that followed the October insurrection. She also joined with several Northern European Communist parties in denouncing the failure of Social Democratic parties to support the Spanish revolutionary action of October 1934. The nature of her visit to Denmark at the beginning of March 1935 led to a protest to the PSOE executive from Alsin Andersen, the Secretary of the Danish Socialdemokratisk Forbund. In a letter of 7 March to the Socialist International, he complained that, on 21 February, the Danish Communist Party newspaper, *Arbejderbladet*, had published 'a sensationalist article by Margarita Nelken containing hymns of praise for the Soviet Union and calumnies for the Socialists'. In the section of her article quoted in his protest, Margarita Nelken had drawn unfavourable comparisons between the outrage expressed by European Socialists at the trials following the assassination of Kirov and their muted reaction to the atrocities committed in the post-Asturias repression. *Arbejderbladet* had then advertised a public meeting of Red Aid at which Margarita Nelken would speak. On 2 March, she visited the Danish Social Democratic Party headquarters and spoke to Alsin Andersen and, allegedly, claimed to be unaware that Red Aid was a Communist organisation.

Nevertheless, she spoke (in German) at the advertised meeting.

The PSOE Executive Committee informed her of the complaint. She replied from Paris on 1 April. She asserted categorically that she had not presented herself as an official delegate of the PSOE and commented on the rude and contemptuous way in which she had been received by Andersen. Her visit to Denmark formed part of a tour which included Sweden and Norway and her sole intention was to give lectures about the situation of the Spanish working class after Asturias, help in the creation of solidarity committees and raise funds for the relief of the victims of the repression. Although aware of Communist involvement in Red Aid, she pointed out that many Socialists collaborated in its work. She denied sending any article to *Arbejderbladet* or any other Communist newspaper, noting that the piece in question had been written for a newspaper in Switzerland. Nevertheless, she reasserted her disgust with the Social Democrats who made more fuss about 'the horrors of Russia' than the right-wing atrocities in Spain.

> I do not seek the collaboration of the Communists. I follow the line of my Party which, in the struggle, both before and after, has shown that it does not consider them to be enemies. I do not insult Socialists but I cannot conceal the fact that I and many other Socialists consider the conduct of Alsin Andersen and his ilk in opposing the movement to be deplorable.

As vice-secretary of the PSOE, Juan-Simeón Vidarte replied to the Socialist International in such a way as to make it clear that he believed Margarita Nelken's account of the events. He knew her well enough to know that she might occasionally be carried away by her political commitment, but she always told the truth.[121]

After her visits to Scandinavia, with the help of Red Aid, she made her way to the Soviet Union accompanied as always by her son Santiago, her daughter Magda and Magda's fiancé,

Adalberto Salas. During her time in Russia, Margarita was feted as Spain's most prominent female politician and as an important writer. She travelled all over the Soviet Union and was introduced to many prominent writers, artists and musicians, both Russian and European. In particular, she became friends with Elena Stasova, one-time secretary of Lenin.[122] Inevitably, given her commitment to the revolution of October 1934 and the supportive response of the Soviet Union, she went further down the path that would eventually lead her to join the Communist Party. While in Moscow, she was a signatory, along with a number of Spanish refugees, both Socialists and Communists, to a letter sent on 16 May 1935 to the PSOE executive. The letter echoed the Communist interpretation of the events of October 1934 as proof of the efficacy of a wide class-based workers' alliance. Effectively rejecting the PSOE executive's call for a much wider Popular Front with the middle-class liberal Republicans, this letter faithfully reflected the PCE's line of unity of action between the Socialists and the Communists.[123]

In June, she sent an open letter to 'the Socialist Workers of Badajoz'. It was the fruit of her reflections on what had happened nationally and in Extremadura during the revolutionary events of October. Substantial extracts of the letter were published by the Communist monthly *Frente Rojo*. The complete letter, which was circulated clandestinely in Badajoz, goes some way to explain the ideological trajectory of Margarita at this time. Her indignation at the impunity with which the landowners of the South had flouted the labour laws of the Republic had led her to lose faith in democratic legality. For that reason, she had collaborated in the revolutionary movement of October. Now, in retrospect, it seemed to her that the revolution had failed in Badajoz because the Besteirista leadership of the provincial Socialist group had prevented detailed instructions being delivered to the local organisations in the outlying towns and villages. She openly accused the reformist leadership, without actually specifying names, of squandering the revolutionary élan of the masses. 'Is it not the case', she asked rhetorically, 'that in Badajoz, if instructions for the insurrection had been received in time, the workers of each village could have taken over the town halls, the sparsely defended Civil Guard barracks and the houses of the owners?'

She placed the blame firmly on those who boycotted the revolution and were now free to move around with the approval of the Government. She ended with a call for adoption of the revolutionary line associated with Largo Caballero. The line being advocated by both Indalecio Prieto and Azaña for an electoral front to work for the legal conquest of the apparatus of the state seemed to her to be playing into the hands of the bourgeoisie.

> A return to legality! Can any of you be satisfied by the idea of once more being ridiculed and machine-gunned by bourgeois governors? Were not Barcarrota, Salvaleón, Villanueva de la Serena, Arroyo de San Serván and so many, many of the names of proletarian martyrdom written 'within legality'? I remember, comrade harvesters, when, two years ago, hundreds of you clamoured your misery to me at the gates of Badajoz, when three of your number died of hunger, despite that legality and that democracy which now is portrayed by some as if it were a paradise.[124]

It is not difficult to see how Margarita had been brought to this point by the impotence of the Republic to mitigate the harsh brutality of daily social relations in the South. However, the more pragmatic line of Prieto had far greater possibilities of success while the revolutionary line was fraught with danger not least because its practitioners were occupied with provocative rhetoric rather than with practical planning.

During her time in Russia, Margarita wrote *Porqué hicimos*

la revolución, a passionate and vivid book about the experiences of the left during the Second Republic. In what it had to say about the run-up to the social conflict of 1934, the peasants' strike and the October insurrection, and about the events in Asturias, it was well informed, perspicacious and written with her habitual clarity and passion. In its analysis of the failure of revolution in 1934 and its advocacy of a further commitment to armed struggle, it represented a triumph of a political line over her own experience. She seemed oblivious to the un-even battle facing those who proposed to confront the state apparatus. She believed that there was a 'perfectly elaborated revolutionary plan' in place, when the reality was that the revolution was ill prepared and hesitantly executed in most places. In consequence, she blamed defeat on Catalan betrayal and a lack of truly revolutionary leadership.[125] She was target-ing the moderates in the party. However, her criticisms rebounded on herself and the other 'bolshevisers'. In fact, the would-be revolutionaries, with Francisco Largo Caballero at their head, had operated in the belief that the mere threat of revolution would bring the right to its sense. When the chosen moment for the revolution came – the entry of the CEDA into the Government on 6 October 1934, Largo Caballero and Amaro del Rosal were notable for their hesitations and passivity.[126]

In her book, Margarita Nelken specifically gave the example of Badajoz where she felt that the numerical superiority of the desperate peasantry provided the basis for a revolutionary triumph. She declared boldly that the accumulated hatred felt for their exploiters should have carried the landless *braceros* to victory. Knives and farm implements should have been enough to permit them to throw off the feudal yoke. That they did not do so, she attributed to poor leadership. The need to blame the reformist leadership of the PSOE and the UGT led her to ignore the demoralisation of the landless labourers after their defeat in the June strike.[127] A few pages later, however, she blamed the harvest strike for exposing peasant militants to beatings and to imprisonment and therefore for leaving the rural revolution decapitated. Her analysis of why the revolutionary movement of October 1934 failed to mobilise the landless peasantry was shrewd and relevant. In general, therefore, she was criticising social democratic reformism. More specifically, however, she was excoriating those who took revolutionary tasks upon themselves and then failed.[128] She mentioned no names but her words might have been applied to Largo Caballero, to Amaro del Rosal, even to her friend Ricardo Zabalza and to herself. In fact, they were directed against the 'historic' Besteirista leadership of the Agrupación Socialista de Badajoz, Narciso Vázquez and Anselmo Trejo.[129] When they were written, in the late summer and early autumn of 1935, her words reflected the views of the Socialist Youth. In many respects they echoed a pamphlet written by the pro-Communist leaders of the FJS, Santiago Carrillo, Amaro del Rosal and Carlos Hernández Zancajo in prison after the events of October. *Octubre – segunda etapa*, (October – second stage) as it was called, became the bible of the 'bolshevisers'.[130] Ironically, by the time that *Por qué hicimos la revolución* was published in the spring of 1936, the Communist Party had abandoned the revolutionary line and was committed to the Popular Front policy of collaboration with reformist social democrats and bourgeois liberals.

Her views on the importance of the peasant revolution reflected her stay in Russia. She wrote, 'In Russia, the revolution began by giving land to the peasants, and in order later, when it was possible, to collectivise it, without clashes of material interests or dashing of hopes. The peasants understood that revolution was theirs.'[131] It was, to say the least, a naïve gloss on the processes of forced collectivisation in the Soviet Union. The influence of her Soviet sojourn was apparent too in attacks on Trotskyism and efforts to draw parallels between the Spanish and Russian revolutions.[132] There was already considerable tension between Margarita and Julián Gorkín, of the more or less Trotskyist Bloc Obrer i Camperol (Workers' and Peasants' Block). In early 1935, they had clashed in Paris on a committee formed by the Socialist Party, its union the UGT, the Partido Comunista de España and the BOC to help Spanish political refugees. Later in the year, Gorkín accused her of helping the Communists to infiltrate the Juventudes Socialistas (Socialist Youth Movement). It was the beginning of a hostility that would haunt Margarita Nelken for years and Gorkín, a man of some malice, would eventually exact a petty revenge.[133]

The opening of the pre-electoral period opened the way for Margarita Nelken to return to Spain at the beginning of 1936. Having, along with Zabalza, firmly embraced Largo Caballero's position that the difficulties of the Republic could only be overcome by a Socialist takeover, she became ever more virulent in her criticisms of more reformist colleagues. Prior to the Popular Front elections of 16 February 1936, she had worked with the local Badajoz left to eliminate the moderates. The Popular Front candidacy for Badajoz should, on the basis of the votes for the left in the 1933 elections, have consisted of eight Socialists, two Republicans and a Communist. In 1933, the Socialists had gained 139,000 votes to the Republicans' 8000. However, in order to exclude the two Besteiristas, Narciso Vázquez, the pioneer of socialism in Extremadura, and Anselmo Trejo Gallardo, the local left now ensured that the candidacy for the 1936 elections would consist of only six Socialists, with two places each for Izquierda Republicana and Unión Republicana, and a Communist. The Socialist candidacy included three members of the Caballerista faction of the PSOE, Ricardo Zabalza, Margarita Nelken and Nicolás de Pablo, and three followers of Prieto, Juan-Simeón Vidarte, José Aliseda Olivares and José Sosa Hormigo. During the electoral campaign, her passionate commitment to the cause of the *braceros* got her into trouble with her own party.

On 17 January, while addressing the Caballerista Socialist Youth in Badajoz, she went so far as to accuse the local leadership of the PSOE of being traitors. As she had insinuated in her book, *Porqué hicimos la revolución*, she blamed the reformists for the failure of revolution in October 1934. She repeated the accusations in a virulent speech in Badajoz on 17 May. Formal complaints were made against her by the Badajoz PSOE group to the PSOE Executive Committee. It was assumed that she was referring to Narciso Vázquez, and the Agrupación Socialista de Badajoz demanded that she be reprimanded and obliged to say openly against whom her remarks were directed.[134] With the national Party in the throes of bitter internecine division, nothing was done.

Exile in Russia had given Margarita an aureola of romantic revolutionism in the eyes of the downtrodden Badajoz day labourers who adored her. Both during the campaign, and after she was successfully re-elected as a deputy for Badajoz, she published a series of articles describing life in Russia in terms both romantic and utopian. The theme of one such article, published in the newspaper of the PSOE bolshevisers, *Claridad*, took the theme 'life is good and joyful in the Soviet countryside'.[135]

Arriving back in Madrid from Moscow, Margarita Nelken had given the impression that – as Gorkín had alleged – she was acting on behalf of the Comintern. It is just as likely that she was simply carried away by her own enthusiasm for what she had seen in Russia. On 25 March, she made a wildly revolutionary speech in the Cinema Europa in Madrid. Her words contributed to the Soviet seduction of Francisco Largo Caballero. In an effort to hasten the unification of the Socialist and Communist Parties, the Comintern had taken to pandering to the vanity of the staid trade unionist by calling him 'the Spanish Lenin'. Margarita recounted – presumably tongue-in-cheek – that, in the Soviet Union, his picture is exhibited everywhere and his work is admired. The speeches of our comrade have been translated there. That alone is sufficient to convince every revolutionary and Marxist worker to feel total confidence in this comrade. When such things happen it is because in Russia they know that Largo Caballero is in the true revolutionary line. And anyone who opposes that line is a counterrevolutionary.

She ended with an attack on the moderate voices of senior Party members:

Sentimentalism is unforgivable during the fight. Young militants, do not let old men oppose you by claiming seniority in the party. Have no respect. Be crushing, be inflexible in your criticisms. Each time that a leader gets up to speak, remember not what he has done in the past but what he must do now![136]

In April 1936, she returned briefly to the Soviet Union. During their exile, Magda had married the young engineer, Adalberto Salas de Eguía, who had helped Margarita flee Spain in December 1934. She had not accompanied her mother back to Spain because she was in late pregnancy. On 23 March 1936, Magda gave birth to a daughter, called Margarita, but known in the family as Cuqui. Margarita had wanted to accompany her daughter during her labour. That being impossible because of her political commitments in Spain, she hastened to be with her as soon as she could. She was present on 7 April when Cuqui's birth was registered. The witnesses were Elena Stasova, who had been Lenin's secretary, and Tomás Sánchez Hernández, the Mexican military attaché in Russia. With Cuqui in his arms, he had provoked general hilarity by prophesying 'this beautiful girl one day will be Mexican, whether you like it or not. You'll see.'[137]

The entire family then made the lengthy journey back to

Spain. Margarita was soon in the thick of the political conflicts within her own Party. Largo Caballero had just prevented the moderate Indalecio Prieto from forming a Government and Margarita Nelken swiftly nailed her colours to the Caballerista mast. She repeated her massaging of Largo Caballero's ego at a meeting in Badajoz on 17 May:

> Why must we have faith in the line laid down by Largo Caballero? We can have faith because there is a fact which is the full guarantee of the rightness of this political line for the triumph of the proletariat. It is that in Russia, in the Soviet Union, the only country in the world which has been able to emancipate the working class and where they are able to judge those who guide the working class, well in Russia, Comrade Largo Caballero is held in the hightest regard. I will never be able to express the emotion that I felt during one of those magnificent events in Moscow's Red Square, the very heart of the USSR, when pictures of Largo Caballero were distributed among the crowd that know all about revolution. There, in Russia, they know who Largo Caballero is, just as every worker in Spain knows, and for that reason, the line that he follows is the true one.[138]

In retrospect, Indalecio Prieto claimed that the seduction of Largo Caballero – in which Margarita played but a small part – was an entirely cynical operation. In fact, her vehemence seemed entirely sincere.[139]

When Margarita Nelken had left Spain in the autumn of 1934, she was the most prominent and popular woman in Spanish politics. By the time that she returned, that position had been taken over by Dolores Ibárruri, Pasionaria. In Margarita's absence, Dolores had come to be the mouthpiece of the victims of the post-October repression. Margarita could never aspire, inside the PSOE, to the prominence enjoyed by

Pasionaria in the PCE. Not only was Dolores on the party executive, but her value as a woman was amply recognised and exploited by the Comintern. In contrast, Margarita was regarded with suspicion by most of the PSOE hierarchy – not least as a result of her incendiary speeches. In the spring of 1936, she played a supporting role to Dolores Ibárruri in the Cortes in attacking the right for the repression in Asturias. This brought both of them, and Pasionaria in particular, into much publicised conflict with the monarchist leader of the right-wingers in the Cortes, José Calvo Sotelo. Those confrontations were later used to construct the Francoist myth that Pasionaria had threatened Calvo Sotelo and therefore instigated his assassination. In fact, Calvo Sotelo was murdered as a reprisal for the shooting by Falangist gunmen on the afternoon of 12 July of a leftist officer of the Republican Assault Guards, Lieutenant José del Castillo. Castillo's was the second name on a black list of pro-Republican officers allegedly drawn up by the ultra-rightist Unión Militar Española, an association of conspiratorial officers linked to Calvo Sotelo's party, Renovación Española. The first man on the list, Captain Carlos Faraudo, had already been shot by Falangists on 7 May. Now, in the early hours of 13 July, furious colleagues of Castillo, determined to avenge his death, kidnapped and shot Calvo Sotelo. There was now virtually open war. The assassination made up the minds of the ditherers among the generals who had been plotting since the elections, most prominent among them Francisco Franco. Within four days, he would be on his way from his post in the Canary Islands to lead the military uprising in Morocco and launch the Spanish Civil War.

The group of Assault Guards (the Republican armed police) responsible for the assassination of José Calvo Sotelo was led by Margarita's friend, Fernando Condés Romero, now a captain in the Civil Guard. It was insinuated later that the handsome thirty-year-old Galician officer had become Margarita Nelken's lover. It was a typical right-wing anti-Nelken rumour. At forty-two years old, she was still extremely attractive and the myths about her easy sexuality still abounded. In fact, as a member of the PSOE, Condés was simply a friend of both Margarita and her husband, Martín. After the crime was committed, he planned initially to take refuge in their house but, given that their friendship was public knowledge, decided against it.[140] Condés would be killed on 30 July 1936, shortly after the outbreak of the Civil War and, at his burial, Margarita delivered a eulogy. Years later, she wrote of remembering him 'deeply stirred, with undying affection'. In her flat in Mexico, she kept a photograph of him, standing in front of a Republican flag. Coincidentally, she knew another member of the squad that murdered Calvo Sotelo. José del Rey Hernández, a member of the Socialist Youth, had been the officer deputed to be her bodyguard.[141]

On 18 July, when news reached Madrid that the military coup had spread from North Africa to the peninsula, the cabinet hesitated to take the daunting step of arming the workers. Margarita Nelken now came into her own. She believed in her bones Largo Caballero's argument that a fascist uprising would be defeated by the workers and pave the way to a revolution. While he, in his strait-laced way, refused to alter his daily routine because of the crisis and declared that he would take the tram in to work at the usual time, she took it upon herself to do something. She led a delegation from the Casa del Pueblo of Madrid to the artillery supply depot where she persuaded the officer in charge, Lieutenant Colonel Rodrigo Gil, a member of the PSOE, to hand over 5,000 rifles.[142] She was furious about the vain attempts made in the course of the day to reach an agreement with the military rebels who contemptuously dismissed any kind of compromise. She was outraged too that, in an effort to appease the generals and the Western powers, a government of colourless Republican liberals was formed under the chemistry professor, José Giral.[143] The real effort to stop the military succeeding was not in government offices but in the streets of Madrid and Barcelona and in the sierras to the north of the capital. Margarita was untiring, zooming around Madrid, trying to make things happen, chivvying Ministers, haranguing groups of workers, advising on the formation of revolutionary committees. When she discovered that Santiago, her fifteen-year-old son, had joined a militia group fighting to repel units of rebel soldiers and Falangists from the north, her feelings were a gut-wrenching mixture of pride in his courage and his politics and a mother's cold terror at the thought of the dangers he faced.

While the uprising was defeated by the workers in Madrid and Barcelona, elsewhere it was successful – in Morocco and in the Catholic agrarian provinces of Old Castile and in major southern towns like Seville, Cádiz and Granada. Within days, Franco had secured the unstinting help of both Hitler and Mussolini. By the end of July, their aircraft were arriving to start lifting the tough Army of Africa across the Straits of Gibraltar. In early August, Franco assembled columns made up of the brutal Foreign Legion and the Moorish mercenaries of the Native Regulars (Regulares Indígenas). They tore through the province of Seville and into Extremadura leaving a wake of slaughter in their wake. Militias were formed in a vain but heroic attempt to stop their progress. Representatives of the UGT Landworkers' Union (the Federación Nacional de Trabajadores de la Tierra) came from the southern provinces to Madrid and sought out Margarita Nelken at the Casa del Pueblo, convinced that only she could get them arms. In her book about the failure of revolution in 1934, she had expressed her ingenuous optimism that, with adequate leadership, unarmed peasants could have seized power. Her views were now to be put to a much harder test, as peasants with old shotguns, farm implements and a few rifles were going to have to face the ferocious African columns moving up from Seville.[144] One of the battalions formed at this time in Extremadura carried the name Margarita Nelken. Another that took her name, of whose volunteers seventy per cent were university students, would play an heroic part in the defence of Madrid.[145]

Mérida fell on 10 August and was witness to the most ferocious repression. Shortly after the fall of the town, in a remarkable display of courage, Margarita went down to Extremadura, along with some other parliamentary deputies. Her efforts to turn the tide of the Africanistas' advance were in vain. Relishing the victorious passage of the Legion, the Francoist journalist, Manuel Sánchez del Arco, wrote that near Mérida there had appeared

> the alien Margarita Nelken, whose name alone brings opprobrium on the regime which put her in parliament, . . . the collapse suffered by the reds in the presence of the Jewish Amazon, Señora Nelken, who can now go and look for another fatherland to betray, just as she betrayed this Spanish fatherland, where she has acted at the service of Russia, spreading poison among the men of Extremadura, who are in rebellion today because of her Marxist preachings.[146]

Margarita was deeply distressed by the slaughter of the peasantry in the South, and also by the obscene radio broadcasts being made by the rebel general in Seville, Gonzalo Queipo de Llano. Every night, he gloatingly recited the exploits of the columns, rejoicing in the rape of left-wing women and the murder of their husbands. In an effort to counteract Queipo's demoralising effect she made a rousing broadcast herself from the Ministry of War on 27 August.

The speech was published by the Federación Nacional de Trajadores de la Tierra, and was prefaced by a tribute to Margarita's identification with the plight of the landworkers of Extremadura from the union's executive committee. In contrast to the sneering right-wing references to the sound of her voice, the FNTT described it as 'tender and soft when she addresses the peasants, hard and steely as a scalpel when she condemns the brutal oppressors of the people'. In his introduction to her speech, Manuel Márquez Sánchez, treasurer of the FNTT and a native of Extremadura himself, spoke of the maternal sentiment with which she had taken to her heart the injustices, miseries and daily calamities suffered by the landless labourers.[147] Her theme was that, having suffered the brutality of life under the *latifundistas*, the landless peasants instinctively understood what the future would be in the event of a right-wing victory in the war. She pointed out that the cruel boasts of General Queipo de Llano in his sordid nightly radio broadcasts would have no capacity to surprise peasants accustomed to the coarseness of their masters. Land given over to hunting reserves and to the breeding of fighting bulls guaranteed unemployment for the labourers and their families who were forced to live in conditions of near-starvation.

In an ironic reversal of the speech made by General Sanjurjo blaming her for the events at Castilblanco, in which he compared the landless peasants to Moroccan tribesmen, she declared:

> When, to add to the shame with which they have already loaded their fake patriotism, the rich 'gentlemen' (*señoritos*) of the Andalusian countryside tried to launch onto Extremadura, to protect *their* fatherland and *their* religion, the mercenaries of the Legion, the dregs of all nations, and the Mohammedans of the Rif, they forgot that the centuries-old experience of the peasants would be enough to block the path of this wave of barbarism. No, they could not be deceived; they knew only too well who their enemies were. The Rif tribesman and the Legionary – the treacherous officer whose marks of honour are called Annual, Monte Arruit, the murder and torture of Asturian miners, unpunished corruption during the dictatorship

of Primo de Rivera – they were the classic and natural
support of the master of the huge estate (*latifundio*), he
who imposed hunger wages and sun-up to sun-down
shifts.

Speaking movingly of the plight of the mothers and children
who had fled before the African columns, she praised the
courage of the men who had stayed behind to fight.[148]
In the early days of the war, Margarita Nelken was an
enthusiastic supporter of the newly created Quinto Regimiento, one of the most professional and effective of the militia
formations. At the invitation of Vittorio Vidali, a Comintern
representative also known as Carlos Contreras, she spoke on
behalf of the PSOE at a ceremony at the headquarters of the
Quinto Regimiento.[149] Thereafter, she advocated the creation
of a fully professional army for the Republic along the lines
of the Quinto Regimiento. When the first Nationalist bombs
fell on Madrid on 27 August, she joined Luis Araquistain in
demanding the resignation of José Giral's Republican Government.[150] In the third week of August, she also went down to
Toledo to raise the morale of the militiamen involved in a
dogged siege of the military rebels who had retreated into the
great fortress that dominates the town, the Alcázar. She spent
time with the 'Compañía Teniente Castillo', named after the
Assault Guard José del Castillo, assassinated by right-wingers
on 12 July, a company commanded by her one-time bodyguard, the now Captain José del Rey.[151] It was later alleged,
absurdly, that it was she who first called for Asturian miners
to be used in an attempt to blow up the fortress.[152] She denied
this vehemently and indeed plausibly, pointing out that her
concern for the art treasures of Toledo would never have
permitted her to approve of such a move. In fact, the suggestion to mine the Alcázar came from the Minister of Public
Works, Julio Just. The decision was taken, after specialist military investigation, at a cabinet meeting.[153]

She did in fact visit the Alcázar on several other occasions both to encourage the attackers and to try to get messages of support in to the hostages taken by the besieged garrison. Spread-eagled against the walls, she tried to reach a window while an anarchist armed with a hand grenade held onto her to forestall any attempt to capture her. However, she was also driven by the need to protect the artistic heritage of the town, a cornucopia of works by El Greco and other great masters. On one visit, she was accompanied by the distinguished French art historian, Elie Faure. As Franco's African columns rapidly closed on the city, in the last week of September, Largo Caballero charged her with a hazardous mission. She was to organise the transfer of the endangered masterpieces of Toledo cathedral to the vaults of the Bank of Spain. 'I brought the treasure in a lorry driven by some comrades. I came behind in a car. To avoid being ambushed on the road, we made it look like any old truck. It was a terrifyingly tense journey until we reached Madrid.'[154]

Throughout August and September, Margarita Nelken was an unsleeping fount of energy. She made daily visits to the front to raise the morale of the militiamen. In Madrid, she organised a campaign both to encourage women to knit jerseys for soldiers and to get hold of the necessary wool. She hassled and harried suppliers to make sure that front-line units got food, blankets and clothing. She made innumerable speeches and wrote regular newspaper articles. Her articles were energetic denunciations of fascism and of defeatism. In this regard, she was especially scathing in her criticisms of the flight from Republican Spain of the philosopher José Ortega y Gasset and the biographer Dr Gregorio Marañón. She applauded the confiscation of the haunts of the rich, herself inaugurating the Socialist Youth recreation centre that had been created from Madrid's luxurious Club de Campo (country club). On several occasions, she spoke at popular concerts of Russian music organised as morale-raising events in requisitioned theatres.

She was a regular visitor to hospitals to talk to the wounded and try to calm their fears about the arrival of ever-nearer Nationalist columns.[155]

Toledo fell on 27 September and Franco delayed his advance while he secured his elevation to supreme military and political commander of the rebels. However, by early November, the African columns led by General Varela were closing in on Madrid. Rumours that the Government was about to abandon the capital to its fate and flee to Valencia were provoking panic. On the morning of 6 November Margarita Nelken was asked to go to rally the defenders of the city in Carabanchel in the southern suburbs. She addressed the crowds until she was hoarse. Returning to the Ministry of War at 2 o'clock in the afternoon, she demanded that a member of the Government accompany her back to Carabanchel. She had an argument with the Cabinet Secretary, Largo Caballero's lieutenant Rodolfo Llopis, who insisted that the cabinet meeting currently in session could not be interrupted. She sent in a message that she would burst in on the cabinet if a minister did not come out. Julio Álvarez del Vayo, the Minister of Foreign Affairs and Ángel Galarza, the Minister of the Interior emerged and told her that no minister was available and begged her to return to Carabanchel alone. This she did. While she was there, in the early evening, the cabinet abandoned Madrid and fled to Valencia. When she returned to the Ministry at eight o'clock, she found it deserted except for a few functionaries. In the echoing corridors, General José Miaja was left to organise the Junta de Defensa de Madrid and the defence of the city. Margarita Nelken became one of his most energetic collaborators.[156]

The unkempt General Miaja immediately called upon her to help in the task of maintaining morale in the terrified city. The atmosphere in the beleagured capital was one of terrified anxiety. It was widely feared that, in the hour of crisis, many imprisoned Nationalist army officers might find a way of implementing General Mola's much-publicised threats about his 'fifth column' within Madrid. In the early hours of the morning of 7 November, Margarita Nelken went to see the Director General of Security, Manuel Muñoz Martínez. The only record of their conversation has her saying to him, 'The Government has abandoned Madrid and here there is no other authority than yours. It falls to you to look out for the fate of us all.' Her visit to Muñoz was later the basis of accusations that she had gone to get documents authorising the Director of the Cárcel Modelo to hand over such prisoners for evacuation and was therefore responsible for the fact that these right-wing captives were later taken from prison and murdered. In fact, there is no evidence linking Margarita Nelken with this horrendous crime, other than the fact that she is known to have visited Muñoz. It is not known on whose orders she was acting. There was considerable anxiety at PSOE headquarters for the safety of these prisoners lest uncontrolled elements took matters into their own hands and it is equally possible – given the scale of the crisis in the capital – either that she had been sent to check on Muñoz's loyalty or indeed to initiate the process of prisoner evacuation and thus to prevent an atrocity which would besmirch the Republican cause. Responsibility for the eventual fate of the prisoners lay elsewhere.[157]

The disappearance of the Government had appalled the defenders of the city.[158] She spoke on the radio on the morning of 7 November, exhorting the entire population of the city to play its part in repelling the attackers. In fact, Miaja was probably glad to find something for her to do. Perhaps mortified not to have been offered a post either in Largo Caballero's cabinet or in the Junta de Defensa which it left behind, she besieged the office of the Delegate for Public Order, Santiago Carrillo. She came to see him 'even at the most absurd times'. 'She was always accompanied by an Assault Guard who acted as her escort which gave rise – without justification, I am sure

– to salacious commentary.' In fact, by this time, Margarita had lost all faith in Largo Caballero and now saw through the emptiness of his revolutionary rhetoric. Her indignation at the Government's undignified evacuation to Valencia had got the better of her and she now pushed for the creation of a great new National Coalition Government, to be based on the Junta de Defensa. As Carrillo pointed out, this would have required a coup d'état. She told Carrillo that she spoke in the name of the Corps of Assault Guards which was ready to support her initiative. Understandably convinced that she had something positive to contribute, she also laid siege to Miaja's office. The middle-aged soldier was immensely flattered by her attentions and by her insinuations that he should preside over the putative coalition. Carrillo protested to Miaja about her intrigues and so the General looked for ways of channelling her turbulent energy. He was glad of his decision. She worked hard, making speeches at the front (now within Madrid's University City), visiting hospitals, and acting as a one-woman foreign ministry, receiving and dealing with foreign delegations.[159]

The defence of Madrid was, as for so many others, Margarita Nelken's finest moment. She could easily have fled. As a parliamentary deputy and a writer of note, she could have been evacuated to Valencia but she remained in the besieged city. Emulating the great propaganda efforts of Pasionaria, she threw herself into the task, speaking to the militias in the Sierra of Guadarrama and Somosierra or in the advanced defence posts of the city itself in the University City.[160] If one admirer is to be believed, the extreme situation of the siege of Madrid had seen the frenetic revolutionary replaced by someone much more mature,

> neither tall nor short, neither pretty nor ugly, dressed with simplicity. Calm in her gestures and mellow in voice. Short-sighted, when she lifts her lorgnettes to her eyes, her gaze becomes profound and inquisitive,

and her interlocutor feels pierced to the very depths of his soul. She asks questions, she gets to the bottom of things, she gets indignant, and she smiles at the boys leaving for the front. She sends telegrams to Valencia and Albacete that demand replies. She inflames the hearts of the women so that, if necessary, they will be ferocious fighters against the Moors and the 'gentlemen' of the Foreign Legion. She calls on them to encourage, to make demands of, to abuse verbally, those who are hesitant, doubtful or just not able to rise to the occasion. When she tongue-lashes the inept or the cowards, she does so with phrases whose sarcasm and irony shatter the most carefully fashioned reputations.[161]

She spoke on the radio to deny rumours spread by the fifth column that the capital was mined and that the water supply had been poisoned. Her ardent harangue did much to lift spirits.[162] Ten days later, on 17 November, the Francoist fifth column excitedly spread rumours that the Moors had penetrated as far as the elegant Paseo de Rosales overlooking the Casa de Campo, the great royal park to the north of the city. Margarita Nelken and Federica Montseny went to see for themselves. On returning to Miaja's headquarters, they each made a broadcast to the workers of Madrid. Margarita declared in a rousing speech:

> I come to give you my word of honour as a Socialist militant not only that Madrid is not taken and will not be taken but also that it is magnificently defended. Everyone at their post and all determined to defend, to the last drop of blood if necessary. At exactly the same moment that ill-intentioned or careless tongues alleged that there were enemy forces in Rosales, Federica Montseny and I were there in Rosales. While enemy radio stations were saying that many houses

were flying white flags because enemy forces had entered Madrid, at that very moment, I can assure you that the only flags that could be seen in Madrid were the tricolour of the national flag, red flags and anarchist black and red flags which speak of the hope placed by the proletariat of the world in a future of greater justice and greater kindness.[163]

Right through the months of the siege of Madrid, Margarita Nelken remained in the capital. She slept on a camp bed in the cellars of the Ministry of War. Whenever troops were retreating Miaja would send her and Federica Montseny to rally and browbeat them back to the front.[164]

For a woman of energy and impetuosity, the failure of the Socialist Party to give Margarita a role of greater responsibility was particularly galling. Perhaps she should not have been surprised. To the rather staid old guard, Margarita Nelken was an embarrassing nuisance. She had not been forgiven for her part in the process that had led to 'historic' local figures losing their places in the Badajoz electoral list in February 1936.[165] Above all, in the patriarchal Socialist Party, she was a woman and a woman who did not know her place. There were simply no senior positions for women in the PSOE. Federica Montseny, who joined Largo Caballero's Government on 4 November 1936 as representative of the anarcho-syndicalist Confederación Nacional del Trabajo, understood the problem only too well. She commented that Largo Caballero 'was categorically opposed to the intervention of women in politics' and that every minister had

> looked at me down their noses when I entered the cabinet. Afterwards, I think that, bit by bit, I was able to overcome this distrust and even hostility, but in the minds of the men of the time there were considerable reservations about, and even outright rejection of, the intervention of women. Since Margarita Nelken,

Pasionaria and I appeared so much at centre stage, we
ran into an especially tense atmosphere.[166]

Of the three, Margarita Nelken faced the most problems.
Dolores Ibárruri had exceptional qualities but she had risen to
the top in the Communist Party when there was little compe-
tition and with the crucial support of the emissaries of the
Comintern. The anarcho-syndicalist movement, while not
without a patronising attitude to women, was sufficiently liberal to encompass the pre-eminence of Federica Montseny.
The Socialist Party, in contrast, never found a place of importance for any of its senior women, whether Margarita Nelken,
María Lejárraga de Martínez Sierra, Isabel de Palencia or Matilde de la Torre.

Nevertheless, throughout the siege of Madrid, Margarita
Nelken was unflagging, working at the Ministry of War, albeit
without an official post – living off her salary as a parliamentary
deputy and her writing. Having attached herself to General
Miaja's staff, she worked interminable hours, trying to make
good the constant drain of deserting officers. She acerbically
criticised the conduct of Largo Caballero as both clumsily and
culpably precipitate in his decision-making. According to the
editor of *El Socialista*, the moderate Julian Zugazagoitia, it
was maliciously rumoured by those whose deficiencies she
highlighted that she was annoyed not to have been sent as
Ambassador to Moscow. 'Intelligent and subtle as she is, she
had not realized how little was the regard felt for her by her
comrades of the revolutionary line.' The fact that she was
given no official Government post finally made her see that
this was the case. According to Zugazagoitia, her resentment
at such treatment by people that she secretly despised, led to
her taking her revenge with acrid sarcasm. She was particularly
hurt not to have been made a member of the Junta de Defensa
de Madrid. Zugazagoitia was one of the most intelligent and
reasonable Socialists and, like Margarita, had courageously

remained to help in the defence of Madrid. As a staunch ally of Indalecio Prieto, he had been subjected to ferocious criticism in the spring of 1936 by the 'bolshevisers' of the PSOE with whom he associated Margarita. Accordingly, this jaundiced his views to the extent of leading him to assume that her criticisms were driven by frustrated personal ambition when, in reality, they derived from indignation at the shortcomings of Largo Caballero's war effort.[167] She visited his office in mid-November and complained that Largo Caballero was responsible for the total chaos in the Ministry of War and the fact that the Communists were filling the vacuum. Manuel Albar, one of Zugazagoitia's colleagues, revealed much about attitudes in the Socialist Party when he commented after she left, 'She's right about most of what she said but she has no business saying it.'

Margarita was sufficiently incensed about the situation to travel to Valencia to make the same points to the Prime Minister himself. She told him that she was a lone Socialist in the Ministry of War trying to do something about the total disorganisation and standing up for the PSOE against the spread of Communist influence. She demanded that he send back from Valencia some of the senior figures who had been so quick to abandon Madrid. Largo Caballero did not take kindly to complaints about the inefficiency in Madrid and even less when they emanated from Margarita Nelken. He had no intention of giving her any authority or staff. It was the last straw and she reacted decisively. Some days later, *Mundo Obrero* published the news that she had joined the Communist Party. Zugazagoitia claimed to be perplexed by the suddenness of the decision coming so soon after her recent diatribes against the Communists. He commented that 'the news provoked joy in me'. He relished the departure from the Socialist Party of someone who had never showed any interest in healing its internal Party divisions and would soon suffer the uncomfortable rigours of the iron discipline of the

Communist Party. Santiago Carrillo – delegate for Public Order in the Junta de Madrid – was also surprised by her switch although he soon came to regard her as 'an active and pretty disciplined militant'.[168]

Clearly her decision to switch parties was motivated by a sense that her own Party did not appreciate her talents as well as genuine, and deeply felt, concern that Largo Caballero was incapable of organising the war effort properly. It may have been because Largo Caballero treated her on the fateful visit with the brusqueness for which he was famous. However, there was also an element of understandable jealousy of the popular acclaim being enjoyed by Dolores Ibárruri. 'When I have done my duty in Valencia', she alleged to have told Zugazagoitia, 'I will return to Madrid to face the same fate as the volunteer militiamen. I'm not one of those always having their picture taken, pretending to be in the front line when the truth is they have never left the rearguard.' Zugazagoitia, although as a moderate Socialist at some distance from Pasionaria, commented that the popularity of Dolores derived from her intelligence and heroism, from the unwavering courage with which she had pursued her political ideals despite immense personal difficulties, in addition to her simple *simpatía* (warmth and charm).[169]

The anarcho-syndicalist Minister of Health, Federica Montseny, commented:

> Perhaps she hoped to occupy in the Communist Party the position that belonged to her because of her qualities, infinitely superior from an intellectual point of view to those of Dolores Ibárruri. But the position was already taken and Pasionaria defended it with tooth and nail. Margarita remained in the background, losing the prestige she had in the Socialist Party and failing to become an influential figure in the Communist Party. It was an error for which she paid dearly.[170]

In fact, her move came at an inopportune moment for the Communist Party. Unaware that she had already made the switch, the Comintern instructed the Spanish Communists to refrain from recruiting high-profile Socialists, specifically naming Margarita Nelken, for fear of arousing the suspicions of Largo Caballero.[171] By the time the cable arrived from Moscow, it was too late. Margarita's affiliation had been announced publicly. There could be no going back. However, the Comintern fear of alienating Largo Caballero did nothing to help her fortunes within the Party.

In the wake of her return from her futile encounter with the Prime Minister, Miaja put her in charge of the transfer of the files and equipment of the Ministry of War to Valencia. Fearing that the enemy could arrive at any moment, the staff frantically emptied filing cabinets and packed papers into boxes. Their nervousness was intensified by the baleful presence of Margarita, staring suspiciously at them, trying to seek out the traitors among them. Given the desperate nature of the situation, she was too impatient to consider the sensibilities of those she lashed with her acerbic wit. There were complaints that she undermined their already feeble morale. The *El Socialista* correspondent in the Ministry telephoned Zugazagoitia, 'Boss, do something to get Margarita out of here or we'll end up with a disaster. She's making mistakes which could cost us dear. There's no one here with a good word for her. They're all beginning to think that she's a spy.' Nevertheless, the person who mattered most in this regard, General Miaja who was responsible for the defence of the capital, remained only too glad to have her energy at his disposal.[172]

Because of her command of languages, she was regularly used to liaise with important foreigners. In the early stages of the siege of the capital, she took George Ogilvie Forbes, the British Chargé d'Affaires, to see the torn bodies of children, women and old people after the Italian bombing and strafing of a Madrid suburb.[173] On some occasions, her unrestrained indignation about such outrages upset the more conservative visitors. In late November 1936, she was deputed to host a group of three English Conservative, one Liberal and two Labour Members of Parliament who were on a fact-finding mission. She urged them to look without prejudice at the situation in Spain and report what they saw to the British people.[174] In a rather sour retrospective account, the English journalist Henry Buckley wrote:

> Their cicerone was singularly ill-chosen in the person of Margarita Nelken, a fierce and imposing woman, a kind of Lady Astor in reverse, Member of Parliament for many years and always quick to criticise and attack. The Socialist Party had sighed with relief when she departed after some stormy discussion and the Communist Party found her a turbulent new recruit. However, her uncompromising manner and directness made her useful in some situations. This was not one of them. She was determined to show the MP's the damage which had been done to Madrid and she literally took them by the nose and dragged them from one wrecked house to another until they cried for mercy.[175]

None of this was even hinted at in the public statements of the MPs. The depth of their awareness of the plight of the people of Madrid indicated rather that Margarita Nelken had done her job well.[176] Later in the war, she accompanied Pandit Nehru on his visit to Republican Spain.[177]

Miaja's headquarters, and his private residence, were in the cellars of the building which housed the Ministry of Finance in Calle Alcalá. Margarita also spent many nights there on a camp bed. Its deep cellars had been chosen as adequate shelter against the constant air and artillery bombardment of Madrid. Late at night, when the turbulence of the day had calmed somewhat, Miaja would relax with his senior staff, favoured journalists and political visitors. It was rumoured that wild orgies took place but the sybaritism went no further than well-lubricated dinners at which Margarita's legendary vitality and sense of humour helped keep up morale. The wine was paid for by means of a curious system of 'anti-erotic fines'. Any time a member of the company was guilty of a double entendre or a sexual innuendo, they were fined five pesetas (the cost of a couple of bottles of good wine). Margarita Nelken was invariably the person who ended up paying most. One of the regulars, the Communist journalist, Eusebio Cimorra, gave an example:

> Margarita would say, 'Madrid will never succumb to frontal assault'. Cimorra would shout 'On guard! On guard!' and, since everyone knew Margarita Nelken's weakness for the Assault Guards, she had to pay an 'anti-erotic' fine. Margarita would laugh along with everyone else.[178]

By the end of November 1936, Franco's assault on Madrid had, at enormous cost, been beaten back. Now, he concentrated on trying to close the circle around the city and close off its lifeline to Valencia. The situation was still desperate and one of the biggest problems was the massive influx of refugees from areas occupied by the Nationalists. Feeding and housing the many thousands of woman and children was a constant anxiety. Margarita Nelken worked feverishly in this area too. The lifelong commitment to child welfare, and her knowledge of the field, out of which had emerged *La condición social de la mujer* and her own nursery, now found a new outlet. Within a week of the outbreak of the war, the Socialist trade union, the Unión General de Trabajadores, requisitioned a large, gloomy, antiquated and underused convalescent home in Madrid belonging to an order of nuns. With Margarita's help and advice, it was converted in the Fifth Regiment Children's Home, (Hogar Infantil del Quinto Regimiento). Reorganised, redecorated and provided with modern medical facilities, it became a model establishment housing three hundred children of men and women on active service at the front.[179]

Margarita was active in the leadership of the principal women's organisation of the Republic, the Union of Spanish Antifascist Women (Unión de Mujeres Antifascistas Españolas). As the war progressed it developed into the main welfare machinery with activities ranging from the provision of food and clothing at the front to looking after children, the aged and refugees in the rearguard. With her background in such areas, it was inevitable that Margarita Nelken would be drawn into such work. At the beginning of the war, she had broadcast to the women of Madrid asking them to overcome their horror at seeing their sons armed and sent to war. Now, in early 1937, she undertook the painful task of persuading mothers to let their children be evacuated from the capital and, where possible, to go with them. She did so with typical vehemence although her own maternal experience informed her words:

> I have no pity for the mothers who wail like wounded beasts for the suffering or loss of their children. What is more, with dagger blows I would stab their pain into them, the pain that they could not or would not avoid . . . What right do you have to decide the fate, the risks and the lives of your little ones? When you brought them into the world, you contracted the sacred duty to be their shelter, their shield, their safety . . . It hurts you to leave your husband? This is hardly the time to be comparing sufferings, but there can be no greater pain than to pass in front of the lifeless body of a toddler and know that its death could have been avoided . . . Face up to reality. Realise that here in Madrid you and your little ones are in the battle-front. War is not a game, nor even a cause for serenity. With serenity and bravery, you can still be bombed.

Face reality, woman, as if your house was on fire, pick
up your babies, hold them to your breast that sustained
them, and without looking back, with the devouring
flames behind you, run, run, faster and take them as
far as possible from the danger.[180]

Two days later, she also wrote a vehement, almost brutal piece,
urging women to leave Madrid because they were 'in the
way'. Her argument was that Madrid was the front line and for
women to be there using crucial food and fuel was damaging to
the war effort.[181]

It was characteristic of the maternal sentiment that underlay
much of Margarita's motivation that she was also capable of
writing movingly of Nationalist conscripts who had died
fighting against the Republic.[182] The wartime activities of her
own son, Taguín, continued to be a source of both satisfaction
and gnawing anxiety. It will be recalled that, when the military
rebellion took place in July 1936, he had joined militiamen
fighting off Mola's forces in the sierras to the north of Madrid.
Since he was barely fifteen and a half, his parents insisted that
he return home. Shortly after doing so, he went off again.
Lying about his age, he enlisted in the Republican army and
entered a course for engineers in Valencia. After three months,
he passed out with a commission as lieutenant. To get him
out of the firing line, Margarita prevailed upon General Miaja
to appoint Santiago to his staff. However, he continued
pressing for a front-line posting and eventually he got his wish.
He took part in the great bloodbath that took place in the
Battle of the Jarama in February 1937 when Franco launched
a major assault on the Madrid-Valencia highway to the east
of the capital. He went into action just a month before his
sixteenth birthday. He was lucky to survive. The casualties
were enormous with the Republic suffering 25,000 casualties.
At the age of seventeen, he fought in the Battle of the Ebro.[183]
Margarita's daughter Magda was a nurse at the front, while

her baby granddaughter Cuqui was sent to Amsterdam where Martín de Paúl was Consul General. Magda was able to see her daughter only on flying visits. Although Margarita was unaware of the fact at the time, her husband had acquired a young lover since arriving in Holland.[184]

On 4 June 1937, Margarita gave a lecture in Valencia to the Friends of the Soviet Union, which was later published as a substantial pamphlet. Her topic was 'Women in the USSR and in the Soviet Constitution'. She enthused unreservedly about the USRR as she remembered it from her stay there two years earlier. 'Here in the West, it is a person's economic situation or social standing that dictates whether a person has more or less independence. In the USSR, that would be incomprehensible. Everyone is the child of their own works.' Her generalised enthusiasm for all things Soviet knew no bounds when it came to the situation of women: 'Every woman has her life according to her aptitudes, her needs and her intelligence, according to her own contribution to the welfare of the collectivity.' There was perhaps an element of wishful thinking when she argued that any Russian girl could study for the career she wished or move to take up the job she wished without family interference and all thanks to the benevolence of the state. Without moral or economic pressures, the Russian woman 'lives how she likes, does what she likes and answers only to her own conscience'. A significant part of the freedom enjoyed by Soviet women was thanks to the efforts of the State in terms of medical and child care. Almost certainly, during her time in Russia, she had been shown facilities which entirely corresponded to her own aspirations for Spain. Such facilities were nowhere near as generally available as she believed. Some of her comments on the freedom enjoyed by women in the USSR no doubt reflected the frustrations that she had suffered herself when her own free lifestyle had come into conflict with the stultifying puritanism of Spain. She talked of taking long walks in Moscow in the early hours of the morning and being able to return to her hotel without having to suffer the malicious smiles and speculations of those who assumed that she was a whore. There was also an element of naïvety about her belief that no one in the Soviet Union could derive benefit from being the close relative of an important party official.[185]

Despite Margarita Nelken's prominence in the Union of Antifascist Women, it remained difficult for the Communist Party to find a suitable political outlet for her remarkable skills and energy. Given its own hierarchical structures, she was not likely to rise to a leadership role. The position of Dolores Ibárruri was unique in that she had transcended the position of token woman by sheer force of personality – something that would not easily be emulated. Margarita Nelken was somewhat downhearted by her own failure to shine within the Party. There was little empathy between her and Pasionaria who regarded her as gratuitously abrasive and ambitious. Nevertheless, it was Dolores Ibárruri's secretary, Irene Falcón, a long-time admirer of Margarita Nelken, who came up with a solution. She had the idea of putting Margarita's considerable journalistic skills at the service of the Communist Party by making her Director of its news agency AIMA. It provided news, largely from Soviet sources, to all the newspapers of the Republican zone. She also wrote vivid reports from the front in the magazine *Estampa*. Margarita's impulsive character constantly ran into problems with the disciplined obedience required by the Party. Her reaction to problems was to demand directly to see Dimitrov or some other senior figure of the Comintern, something which did not go down well with the provincial Spanish Party leadership that was in awe of those who carried the authority of Moscow. Shocked by news of the purge trials in Russia, she often demanded to speak to Stalin on the telephone.[186]

The lack of opportunity to shine in the Communist Party was a serious disappointment but Margarita never stinted her efforts for the war effort.[187] She had clearly changed somewhat under the pressure of Communist Party discipline. The Socialist deputy, Matilde de la Torre, wrote of her participation in the Cortes debates in the Lonja in Valencia on 30 September 1937:

> Margarita has abandoned her inveterate use of the famous pince-nez that had given her the look of an inquisitor. Now she wears some pretty glasses that give her a rather scholarly air. She shows me a photograph of her son in his officer's uniform. He is at the Madrid front, at that legendary front of which we all wish we could say, 'I was there', but where most of us wouldn't dare show our faces. Margarita talks to me about the progress of the war which 'is going badly' because the officers are 'still right-wingers'. Anyway, Margarita's opinions no longer display that combative independent spirit that used to cause discomfort among her enemies and even among her comrades. Now Señora Nelken is a Communist, and she has to temper her judgements to an iron discipline.[188]

She put her oratorical skills and energy at the Communist Party's disposal and played a prominent role in Party propaganda within the army.

So enthusiastic were her efforts in this regard that, in September 1937, she was accused of trying to get her son-in-law, Adalberto Salas, named as a political commissar to a brigade, with the salary of a general. His name was on a list of proposed appointments taken by Julio Alvarez del Vayo, head of the war commissariat, to the Minister of Defence, Indalecio Prieto. It was the only name turned down on the grounds of incompetence. Perhaps as a last throw to get his entire list approved or simply excusing his advocacy of an inappropriate candidate, Alvarez del Vayo tried to throw the blame on Margarita Nelken. He said, 'But who can stand up to that woman?' To which Prieto replied, 'I will stand up to her.' Prieto told Azaña who, drawing on his long-standing antipathy to Margarita Nelken, recounted the story with relish in his diaries. However, given Margarita Nelken's low opinion of her son-in-law, not to mention her complete commitment to the war, with both of her children in situations of considerable danger, it is extremely unlikely that she would be involved in nepotism of this kind.[189] In July 1938, the Madrid press of the anarcho-syndicalist union, the Confederación Nacional del Trabajo, accused her of going around barracks offering promotion to those soliders who agreed to join the Communist Party.[190] She undertook visits abroad on behalf of the Spanish Republic to Denmark, Holland, Belgium, Switzerland and Mexico. She was involved in morale-raising lecture tours on Spanish art. On 16 January 1939, even as Franco's troops forged into Catalonia, she gave a talk at the Barcelona Ateneu on 'Picasso, artist and citizen of Spain'.[191]

Barcelona fell on 26 January. A massive exodus of refugees began to trudge towards the French frontier. The roads were choked with trucks, carts, buses and a huge mass of terrified humanity. The Republican Government crossed into France on 5 February. Margarita Nelken and her daughter Magda managed to do so at the same time and were reunited near Perpignan with her mother and granddaughter, Cuqui. Throughout the first week of February, cold and hungry, the defeated Republican army began to pass into a hostile and unwelcoming France. Men, women and children were herded into rapidly improvised detention camps at Argelès-sur-Mer, St Cyprien, Barcarès and other smaller areas of confinement on the sand dunes. Santiago de Paúl Nelken was one of the last to leave, his unit of engineers having been given the job of blowing up the castle at Figueras, the last town of note before the French border.[192] As the Francoists occupied the last Republican territory of Catalonia on 10 February, important Communist members of the Republican High Command,

Santiago Álvarez, Enrique Líster, Manuel Tagüeña and Juan Modesto crossed the frontier with the battered remnants of the Republican Army of the Ebro. The bulk of their men were forced into the camps, including the not yet eighteen-year-old Santiago de Paúl, whom Margarita believed to be the youngest officer in the Republican army. The senior officers headed for the Spanish Consulate at Perpignan since it constituted Spanish territory. They collapsed starving and exhausted, much to the chagrin of the Consul and his wife who were anxious to see the back of them. Margarita Nelken, aided by her daughter Magda, took it upon herself to alleviate their plight. She had some money in France from fees and royalties and she used it to arrange for food to be bought for the new arrivals. Magda, despite being ill, went out to get civilian clothes for them and arranged their documentation. These senior officers were mainly concerned with making the arrangements for getting back into Spain to continue the struggle, which they did two days later.[193]

On a bitterly cold 12 February, the great cellist Pau Casals visited the Consulate. Margarita recalled the scene both in unpublished memoirs and frequently in her later correspondence with the maestro:

> I shall never forget that in Perpignan, as soon as you saw me, you asked me, 'And what of your son? Did he get out?' Yes, he had led his men out and voluntarily accompanied them to the camp at St Cyprien from which I later managed to get him released.

She never forgot the spontaneous emotion of Casals who embraced her when told that her son was alive in St Cyprien.[194] Margarita managed to get both her son, Santiago, and Dolores Ibárruri's son Ruben, out of the camp. She then took Santiago into the Consulate and introduced him to Modesto, Líster, Tagüeña and Álvarez. Santiago Álvarez, until thrown out when the French Government recognised Franco on

27 February, remained in France to organise help for Spanish Republicans in the fetid camps in the sand dunes. Years later, Álvarez recalled that Margarita gave him sufficient money to buy a suit and get out of his uniform.[195]

The Francoists were implacable in seeking their revenge on all prominent members of the Republic's democratic and left-wing parties. At the end of the war, the house in the Avenida de la Castellana shared by Margarita Nelken and Martín de Paúl was requisitioned by Falangists. Her library, her paintings and her correspondence with many famous Spanish and European writers and artists were looted. Her collection contained signed first editions from many of Europe's literary elite, letters from Unamuno, Auguste Rodin and Gabriela Mistral, as well as many paintings by Spanish and French artists including important canvases by Eduardo Chicharro and Gutiérrez Solana.[196] Margarita herself was never to see Spain again and, now, with her mother and children to look out for, she had to rebuild a life. With typical energy, she pestered officials and used her connections to secure the release from St Cyprien of her son, Santiago, and other young Communists. Since Martín de Paúl was still the Consul General of the Spanish Republic in Amsterdam, she arranged for him to join his father there. In Amsterdam, Martín de Paúl had an affair with a younger woman called Josefina, known as 'Nati'. Years later, Margarita would reach the bitter conclusion that his father's unusual situation prompted Santiago's decision to go to the Soviet Union. Once in Russia, Taguín began to study engineering. Margarita then managed to establish herself in France where she continued to work as a journalist and art critic until emigrating to Mexico. Both then and later, she wrote some articles for the Soviet press and arranged for her fees to be paid to Santiago.[197]

On the orders of President Lázaro Cárdenas, she was given asylum in the Mexican Embassy in Paris. Then, in December 1939, she managed to get her mother, her daughter Magda and her three-and-a-half-year-old granddaughter Margarita (Cuqui) Salas to Mexico on the *Normandie*. She was eventually joined in Mexico in 1940 by her husband, Martín. However, they did not live together in Mexico, as a result of his various relationships with younger women. Margarita, in contrast, never had any other significant relationship after Martín.[198] Shortly afterwards, another casualty of the war was Magda's marriage with Adalberto Salas. He remarried and made not the slightest effort to look after his wife or his daughter. Margarita Nelken thus continued to have sole responsibility for the maintainance of herself, her mother, her daughter and her granddaughter. Not dismayed, she quickly set about resurrecting a career for herself as an art critic, writing a daily article for the Mexican newspaper *Excelsior* and contributing to many other Latin American magazines and newspapers. Her work as a translator was prodigious. She also found a post in the Mexican Ministry of Education, (Secretaría de Educación Pública). She wrote numerous books on Mexican painting and sculpture and acted as adviser to the Mexican Government on artistic matters. According to one commentator, her work as an art critic followed the principles of 'rigorous criticism of established figures; benevolent encouragement for those just starting out, fierce rejection of insincerity and artifice'.[199] She delighted in finding an unknown artist and bringing his or her work to a wider audience. In this respect, she was especially proud of having been the first person to write a serious study of the Spanish expressionist José Gutiérrez Solana.[200]

Despite her absence from Spain, Margarita Nelken was too important as a leftist and a woman to be forgotten by the new regime. Absurdly, since she was in exile and was hardly likely to return to Spain to face mistreatment and a long prison sentence, she was summoned in 1941 to appear before the Special Tribunal for the Repression of Freemasonry and Communism, accused of 'the crime of freemasonry and communism'. The principal evidence of the first half of her 'crime' was that on 27 August 1924, the secretary of the Masonic Lodge Lealtad No.6 of Barcelona had written a letter of recommendation for 'our beloved sister Margarita' when she went on a trip to Italy. In addition to her membership of the Communist Party, she was also considered to be criminal by dint of the fact that she had served on the committee of the Spanish League for Human Rights, been a member of the Socialist Party and attended Spain's most progressive educational establishment, the Institución Libre de Enseñanza (Free Institute of Education). Needless to say, she did not return for the show trial. In her absence, on 14 November 1941, she was tried by a military court presided over by General Andrés Saliquet, the man who had presided over the military uprising in Valladolid. She was found guilty and sentenced to thirty years' imprisonment. In the sentence, her crimes were listed as follows:

> She fomented the revolution of October 1934, for which reason she had to flee abroad. She carried out an intense campaign of lectures and newspaper articles in a demagogic and openly communist manner. She established Red Aid on behalf of those imprisoned during the repression in Asturias and raised three million pesetas. She belonged to the Association of Friends of the USSR and, as its delegate, was in Moscow for several months, soaking herself in bolshevik practices in order to try to impose Communism in Spain. She took part in all kinds of revolutionary and anti-Spanish propaganda work. Before and during the Glorious Movement, she used money and enormous resources in order to take Spain to ruin. At the end of the war, she fled to foreign parts where she continued her campaigns and raised funds in the name of the 'oppressed reds' that permitted her to live in splendour. Proven fact.[201]

By this time, Margarita's son, Santiago, was making rapid progress as an engineering student in Moscow. She lived for letters from him and from friends in the Spanish exile community in Russia who could send her news of him. José Bobadilla, a Party comrade who was studying at the Frunze Military Academy in Moscow, reported in early June 1940 that the twenty-year-old was now a man, mature and dedicated to his studies.[202] After the German invasion in June 1941, along with other young Spanish Communists, Santiago joined the Red Army. In June 1941, she was relieved to hear that Santiago was on leave in Moscow, was well and 'had filled out in the year and a half since we last saw him'.[203]

It has been suggested retrospectively that she feared that her son might be used as a hostage for her good behaviour. If that is the case, it is astonishing that, in Mexico, she was as outspoken as ever on political matters, which did little for any ambition she might have nurtured to be given a leadership role in the Communist Party. She made no secret of her disagreement with policies that she considered mistaken and did nothing to hide her contempt for those party bureaucrats whom she considered to be her intellectual inferiors. This was reflected in an internal party report on the exiled leadership in Mexico sent to Moscow in December 1941.

> There are great difficulties with Margarita Nelken. Her critical relationships with everyone within the Party and the exile have got worse because she does not have an adequate field of action and she feels relegated because she is not brought into the work of the leadership. She is embittered because of this. Her criticisms are not to do with the general political questions of our movement, with which she agrees, but she is against everything that the Party does in fulfilment of this line. She attempts to awaken the discontent of the rank-and-file comrades against certain comrades

of the leadership. She was given the task of drawing up proposals for work among the intellectuals but her ideas were rejected because they amounted to the creation of a new leadership on the grounds that the workers understand nothing about work among the intellectuals. The rejection of her proposals has sharpened Margarita's attitude to the Party. Despite this, the comrades feel that it would not be a good idea to remove her from the leadership. But she is not used except for public speaking in the Party's name and there is much distrust where she is concerned.

She opposed the policy of sending agents into Franco's Spain to work clandestinely since it wasted lives with little or no tangible result. She advocated other means of trying to bring democracy to Spain.[204]

In particular, Margarita Nelken clashed with the mediocre, and slavishly Stalinist, Vicente Uribe, who was running the Spanish Communist Party (PCE) in Mexico. As a Jew, she had been deeply disturbed by the Nazi-Soviet pact of August 1939 although she supported Party policy out of a loyalty intensified by gratitude for Soviet aid to the Republic. Like most exiled Republicans, she followed the fate of the Allies with the keenest interest, although the Party line was to denounce the World War as merely an imperialist squabble. Once the Germans invaded Russia in June 1941, the PCE began to enthuse about a wide anti-fascist front, to be called the Unión Nacional. Since this took the notion of a wide inter-class front to the extent of suggesting a reconciliation with many who had fought on the Nationalist side in the Civil War, Margarita Nelken regarded it as impossibly naïve. The inevitable result was that she was expelled from the Party in October 1942, accused of undermining the policy of Unión Nacional. In fact, she had expressed her disagreement with a policy that sat ill with her fiery commitment to revolutionary radicalism. At a time when the situation could not have been bleaker for the PCE inside Spain, the official line was one of a jaunty triumphalism. Unable to generate the requisite optimism, she was denounced for 'working to sabotage and discredit the policy of Unión Nacional'. After various threats and warnings, she refused to be silenced. It was clear that she had discussed her misgivings about Unión Nacional with others and, for that, she was said 'to have used the dirtiest kinds of corruption typical only of an enemy to bring others into her work of provocation'. In consequence, it was alleged by Uribe's crony, the equally Stalinist Antonio Mije, that she was 'an intriguer', 'an enemy of the people' who felt only 'hatred for the working class'. 'Her uncontrolled ambition had no respect for revolutionary history, for capacity, for honour or for decency.' The Party newspaper which announced her expulsion also issued an official statement in which the PCE 'informed its militants and sympathisers that they must break off all contact with this enemy of the Party and of the people and denounce her conduct'.[205]

What guaranteed her expulsion was the fact that, in opposing Unión Nacional, she was effectively lining up with Jesús Hernández, a Party leader who was engaged in a power struggle with Pasionaria for the right to succeed José Díaz as PCE Secretary General.[206] The public denunciations were exceeded in vitriol by the private comments of erstwhile Party comrades – what the novelist Max Aub called 'the customary stream of insults and abuse' ('*La acostumbrada retahíla de baldones y dicterios*'). Few leapt to her defence. One who did, the poet José Bergamín, was denounced as a traitor for doing so.[207] After her own personal sufferings and the hardships of exile, the hurt that was caused by these denunciations may be imagined. Nevertheless, any fears that she might have had that the change in her position might have repercussions for her son in the Soviet Union were quickly dissipated by a reassuring letter.[208] However, expulsion from the Party had immediate economic consequences for the family in Mexico. Certain publications closed their pages to her. The financial assistance of the Junta de Auxilio a los Republicanos Españoles (Aid Committee for Spanish Republicans), controlled by the Communists, was also closed to her. Important Mexican artists, like David Alfaro Siqueiros and Diego Ribera, being faithful militants of the Mexican Communist Party, turned their backs on her – a serious blow for an art critic. So vicious and long-lasting was their campaign against her that, in 1951, the Mexican Association of Art Critics (La Sociedad de Críticos de Arte de México) gave a dinner in her honour to atone for the disgraceful behaviour of two of its members. The dinner was attended by more than 250 Mexican writers, politicians and artists. Years later, in 1960, David Alfaro Siqueiros publicly begged her forgiveness. Despite her troubles with the Spanish Communist Party, she never criticised the PCE publicly. Indeed, to some extent, she dealt with the issue by denying that it had happened. In private, she continued to speak about political issues as if she were still a prominent figure in the leadership. She still worked actively on behalf of the defeated Republic and maintained her admiration for the Soviet Union. She was secretary-general of the Mexican organisation for Republican prisoners, the Patronato Pro-Presos de Franco.[209]

She wrote a book on the Second World War that was unstinting in its praise of the Russian war effort against the Nazi invaders, dedicating it to 'my son Santiago, combatant for liberty'. Like all of her books, it was lively, readable and extraordinarily well informed. It opened with an enthusiastic hymn of praise for Stalin, with sideswipes at Trotskyists in general, and at Julián Gorkin in particular.[210] In it, she described seeing Stalin during her time in Russia in 1935, portraying him as a humble, shy individual. Nelken's Stalin was gentle and considerate and most comfortable in the company of writers and artists, desperately seeking an ashtray for Emil Ludwig, never missing a performance of Tchaikovsky's

Queen of Spades at the opera house but always slipping out early to avoid applause, allowing the most humble deputies to interrupt him in the Supreme Soviet.[211] In her account of the origins of the Second World War, she mounted a sustained denunciation of appeasement and a defence of the Nazi-Soviet Pact of August 1939. The early failings of the Red Army against the German invaders are attributed to 'the disorder introduced by Trotsky'.[212] It went into three editions. It may have been written in the vain hope of reinstatement but was possibly sincere, since she believed, along with many others, that the war against Nazism had started in Spain in 1936. Moreover, she had visited the Soviet Union only once, in 1935, and been welcomed as a revolutionary of the highest category. Given her gratitude for Russian aid to the Spanish Republic during the Civil War, the fact that she was a Jewish anti-fascist and the fact that her son was a soldier in the Red Army, it is not inconceivable that her admiration for the Soviet Union transcended her local difficulties with the exiled leadership of the Spanish Party.[213]

If it was true, as US intelligence sources believed, that she was an agent of the KGB, the tone of the book sat ill with the need for discretion, not to say deep cover. According to these sources, the Russians had given her the entirely appropriate codename 'Amor'. On the basis of surviving security-service documents, her activities seem to have been extremely low-grade, going no further than suggesting people who might help with border crossings from Mexico into the United States.[214] Julián Gorkín, a Spanish one-time Trotskyist who later worked for the CIA, and a man with a grudge against Margarita Nelken, made more serious allegations. He claimed that Margarita was a Russian agent closely involved with the couple who arranged the murder of Trotsky on 20 August 1940 – Leonid Eitingon and his mistress Caridad Mercader. According to her friend, the exiled Socialist, Aurora Arnaiz, Margarita's link to the Mercaders consisted of sending food, clothes, newspapers and books to the actual assassin, Ramón Mercader, while he was in prison and giving financial assistance to his wife and children. However, her testimony is brought into question because Mercader himself denied that he ever had any children. It is certainly the case that large numbers of Spanish Communists visited Mercader in prison and took him books and other gifts.[215] It is possible, albeit highly unlikely, that – as Gorkin claimed – Margarita Nelken was being black-mailed on the basis of the presence of her son, Santiago de Paúl Nelken, in Russia as a lieutenant in the Red Army. This is extremely far-fetched since, given her background, Margarita would have had every reason to be totally sympathetic to the Soviet Union.

In fact, Santiago was killed in action in the Ukraine on 5 January 1944 while commanding an artillery unit of Katiushka rocket launchers.[216] It was yet another echo of the career of Dolores Ibárruri, whose son Ruben was also killed in action with the Soviet forces. While still unaware of the fate of her son, Margarita wrote a book of poems in praise of the Red Army. Years later, all traces of bitterness gone, she would write, 'he was just twenty-two when he died, remaining for ever under the Soviet earth that he loved so much'.[217] She was, however, deeply hurt by the delay in receiving official confirmation of his death. She believed that the news was deliberately kept from her. The Russian Embassy in Mexico City did not officially inform her of it until eighteen months after the event. The intelligence services of the United States intercepted a letter dated 9 June 1945 from Lieutenant General P. M. Fitin to the KGB residence in Mexico. It contained instructions for the handing over to 'Amor' of the personal effects of Santiago, together with two medals that he had been awarded, the Order of the Patriotic War, First Class, and For the Defence of Moscow.[218] It has been alleged that Margarita was convinced that Dolores Ibárruri was personally to blame for the delay. That seems unlikely. Pasionaria had far too much on her agenda for petty rivalries. In any case, the conditions of the Soviet war effort against Nazi Germany would amply account for the delay in information reaching Margarita Nelken in Mexico. Even senior Spanish Communist cadres in Moscow learned the news after Margarita did. Her friend José Bobadilla, in whose house Santiago had sometimes stayed in Moscow, did not find out until September 1945 and immediately sent her a parcel with some items left there by Taguín.[219]

Margarita was completely inconsolable when she received the news. She never recovered from the blow. There was a strong, resilient, feisty, outspoken, public Margarita Nelken. But the quintessential Margarita Nelken was above all a mother. All her life, she had been able to draw on great reserves of maternal compassion for others. But that same capacity for love was matched by an equal capacity for pain. She adored her son and was infinitely proud of him. Every day for the rest of her life, she would reflect on the boy who had such a short adolescence and reproach herself for not having been able to protect him from the horrors of the Spanish Civil War and the German-Soviet war. To an extent she felt guilty that she was responsible for the very politicisation that led to him volunteering in 1936 and again in 1941. That she was being harshly unfair on herself in no way mitigated her distress. Her inner strength would keep her going but the pain would never diminish.

On 12 June 1945, the President of Mexico, Manuel Ávila Camacho, sent Margarita Nelken a telegram of condolence. Ten days later, Miguel Alemán, the Mexican Minister of the Interior and candidate for the presidency, sent another. These were highly significant indications of Margarita's prestige within Mexican culture.[220] Along with them, many other messages of sympathy flooded in, to no avail. She couldn't eat or sleep or read. Her only consolation was listening to records of Casals playing Bach's cello suites. She threw herself into work – trying, as she told Casals, 'to brutalise myself with work, which is the only way to avoid letting myself be dragged along by the pain'.[221] The theme of work as an analgesic was a constant in her correspondence.

Having been informed of the location of Santiago's resting place, in a war cemetery, in Mitrofanovka, a tiny hamlet in the Ukraine, she made frantic efforts to discover more about it. She wrote to ex-Party comrades in Russia and also to the President of the Soviet of Mitrofanovka begging for details of his last moments, asking if he died immediately, if he suffered, if he had a girlfriend in the district. She requested that a small obelisk be erected and carry the inscription in Russian and Spanish:

> SANTIAGO DE PAÚL NELKEN,
> born Madrid (Spain) 11 March 1921
> Died Mitrofanovka 5 January 1944
> for the USSR, for Spain
> and for the liberty of all peoples.

She requested a photograph and offered to pay for flowers always to be kept on the grave. Her wishes were respected. She was relieved to receive a letter from José Bobadilla in mid-1946 reassuring her that the grave was well looked after and sending her a map with its location.[222]

Recalling her meeting with Casals in Perpignan on 12 February 1939, she wrote to the great cellist in 1948, 'a hero, yes, but I no longer have my son, and it is an old and destroyed mother with that pain which eats away at her day and night, that writes to you now'.[223] Nearly four years later, she wrote again to Casals:

> Regarding myself, I can say only that I work and I just about manage. And, it would appear, this is the most I can hope for with the pain I have plunged in my innards. And I will never forget that in those

terrible moments of the crossing of the frontier, you
were concerned about the possible fate of my son. To
think that he was saved just so that afterwards . . . !
What for?[224]

Margarita's loss was intensified by a moving letter from her
Dutch friend, Germaine Althoff, who had been secretary of
the Republican Consulate in Amsterdam. Germaine evoked
Santiago's brief oasis of happiness in Amsterdam. Her letter
churned up memories of the horrendous experiences of her
son Taguín as a dauntingly young army officer and of his
suffering in the mass exodus over the Pyrenees and in a French
concentration camp. Germaine recalled how he was able to
laugh and be a teenager after the ordeal of the Ebro, the flight
of the refugees from Catalonia and the French camp. The
contrast between what he had been through and the fact that
he was still only an adolescent sprang from the pages of the
letter when Germaine described Taguín's eighteenth birthday
on 11 March 1939. He whooped for joy because it meant he
could go to see movies restricted to over-eighteens. Hitherto,
as a seventeen-year-old escapee from Hades, he had been afraid
of being thrown out of cinemas as 'too young' for violence
on the screen.[225] The letter provoked painful thoughts in Margarita of her innocent child, just out of one inferno and about
to go to his eventual death in another. But although it had
left her in an emotional turmoil, she was avid for more details.

> For someone to speak to me about him makes me
> feel that I haven't lost him altogether. What wouldn't
> I give to have all the details, all his words, all his
> gestures! One of my greatest sufferings is just not
> knowing, exactly, the details of his last moments. At
> times, it drives me mad.[226]

Thinking about Taguín provoked considerable anguish
about her husband, Martín. There were other reasons, of

course. Deep down, she still loved him. His old girlfriend from Amsterdam, 'Nati', was seeking help in applying for compensation for gifts from Martín stolen from her by the German wartime occupiers of Holland. While Margarita worked obsessively to keep her household of women – herself, her mother, her daughter and her granddaughter, Martín was quite prosperous and living with a much younger woman.

> He's got a good job representing a factory with a salary and on commission, and living with a girl young enough, so they tell me, to be not his daughter but his granddaughter. This 'Nati' business, as you say, would be comical if it were not so tragic.

His lack of dignity with his new lover was enough, said Margarita, to make one believe in love potions. She was especially infuriated by the fact that 'he has made no effort to see his daughter or the little one'. She already had reason for distress in that Santiago had repeatedly written to her from Russia lamenting that he never had any word from his father. From there it was but a short step to reflecting that perhaps Martín's behaviour in Amsterdam with Nati had played a part in Santiago's decision to go to Russia.

> If his father had behaved as a father should with a child who joined him directly from the concentration camp and after three years in the trenches, if Martín had not inflicted on him a situation which must have wounded him and which he couldn't stand, I mean the fact that he was living with someone who was occupying his mother's place, perhaps my son would not have wanted to leave for where he would eventually meet his death. Let's just forget it because otherwise I will go mad.[227]

The anniversary of Santiago's death was always terrible for her. She wrote again to Casals:

On 5 January, it will be eight years since my son gave his life believing that he was also fighting for the liberation of Spain. He was almost a child: he had still not had his twenty-third birthday, and since he was fifteen-and-a-half, he, who as a child I had never even allowed to play with toy soldiers, had weapons in his hands. I will never forget that in Perpignan you asked me as soon as you saw me, 'And what about your son? Did he manage to get out?' Yes, he had got out, at the head of his men, and with them he went – voluntarily – to the concentration camp at St Cyprien, from which I eventually managed to get him out. At this time of year, when I feel this pain ever more, I want to tell you how much emotion I feel when I remember that deeply human question of yours.[228]

Shortly before Christmas 1952, she wrote in similar vein to her friends, the celebrated Socialist jurist Luis Jiménez Asúa and his wife Mercedes,

I work like a donkey but I don't complain because it's the best way I have of not thinking. On 5 January, it will be nine years since I lost my son . . . I hardly need to tell you how heavy these days lie on me with all the jollity around.[229]

The death of Taguín lay on Margarita Nelken's conscience for every day of the rest of her life. In 1939, she had thought that the Spanish Civil War had destroyed her life. She had lost all her possessions, her status and her husband. Yet her resilience had carried her through. But all losses in 1939 paled when set beside the hammer blow of Santiago's death.

In one unexpected way, it dampened the fire of her political outspokenness. Víctor Alba, a Spanish Trotskyist whose testimony was distorted because of his understandable hatred of Stalinist Communism, claimed that Margarita told him that she had to remain silent about what she knew about the inner workings of Communism because 'the Russians have something powerful to make me keep quiet: my son's grave'. He portrayed her as nervous, warning the Communist dissident, Jesús Hernández, against publishing his memoirs – which were a virulent attack on Dolores Ibárruri – because 'it would be too dangerous to publish it'.[230] His allegation of Soviet blackmail of Margarita is an exaggeration of things that she often said and is reflected in her reply to a letter from Jesús Hernández in early July 1950. Shortly before, in the wake of the Soviet Union's attacks on Tito's Yugoslavia, Margarita's erstwhile comrades of the Partido Comunista de España were denouncing men who had fought in the International Brigades. She was filled with indignation, yet when Jesús Hernández wrote asking her to sign a collective letter of condemnation, she declined.[231] By way of explanation, she wrote movingly to him:

Above all, I really thank you for thinking of me for the document. You're right. What some of our ex-comrades are doing in relation to people who gave their lives for Spain is indescribable. But, at the end of the day, you and I know them and nothing can now surprise us. I can only tell you that on my last day in Madrid, I went with André Marty to take flowers to the International Brigades cemetery (in Fuencarral) and we stood there together reading the inscriptions on the graves, many, many of which read, underneath the name, 'Yugoslav'. You have to be a real bastard to forget that. And now, you will ask why I don't sign. I'll tell you what I replied to José del Barrio [dissident of the Catalan Communist Party, the PSUC] when he wrote to me about the same business. And I hope that you will understand and forgive me. You know that the misfortune of my son has destroyed me. For me, everything now resolves around it. By 'it', I mean that bit of earth underneath which he lies. I do not want those who look after his grave to see in me an enemy. I want to be able to think that at least they look after it for me. You will say that this is stupid sentimentality, and doubtless you'll be right. But what do you expect? It's something I can't get over. That is why I can't sign. That is why I write nothing about such a repugnant subject, nor about many other things. Just because of that. My entire life I will reproach myself for being unable to save my son; I could not cope if, in addition, I had to reproach myself for cutting off every possibility of at least knowing that his grave was well looked after, or at least to be able to deceive myself that this is the case.[232]

In her grief, Taguín's grave had assumed tremendous importance for Margarita. Her desire not to put in jeopardy what she hoped would be its care and maintenance was understandable. It is, however, some distance from the insinuations of Víctor Alba or the even more dramatic claim that she told her erstwhile enemy, the ferociously anti-Communist Julián Gorkín, that she dare not write her own memoirs because her own life and that of her granddaughter had been threatened.[233] If true that she felt that way, it is astonishing that she should choose to confide in Gorkín of all people and did not say anything remotely similar in her voluminous correspondence with close friends. What had actually happened is that Gorkín, who worked for the CIA-financed Congress for Cultural Freedom, had asked her to write her memoirs, offered her a blank cheque and, to his outrage, she had refused. During the Cold War, the one-time Trotskyist Gorkín had taken his anti-Stalinism far to the right. His task was to besmirch one of the undisputed jewels in the Communist crown – the anti-fascist struggle of the Spanish Republic. He sponsored a number of fiercely anti-Soviet memoirs by repentent ex-Communists – Jesús Hernández, Enrique Castro Delgado and even wrote the 'memoirs' of the illiterate Valentín González, 'El Campesino'.[234]

In a letter to her one-time Party comrade, Enrique Líster, Margarita pointed out that she had been offered very substantial sums for anti-Communist memoirs. She had refused, not out of fear, but out of loyalty to a cause in which she still believed. However, in the same letter, she went on to complain bitterly about the falsifications to be found in the Communist historiography of the war. She protested about the negative distortions of the roles of Largo Caballero and the first wartime prime minister, the Republican José Giral. She was particularly annoyed that, subsequent to her own expulsion from the Spanish Communist Party, her own considerable role in the war had been silenced.[235] She also certainly believed that influential members of the Spanish Communist Party were doing all that they could to make her life difficult. Articles would be commissioned, then mysteriously fail to be published.[236] Of her post in the Mexican Ministry of Education, she wrote, 'Education is full of my ex-comrades. They try to wreck my life whenever they can: I always have to fear some stab in the back that delays or invalidates the best of plans.'[237] However, she was standing up to those acts of hostility and none of her correspondence even hints that she was being blackmailed and threatened by the Kremlin. Indeed, she regularly attended receptions at the Soviet Embassy in Mexico where she was treated with great cordiality.

In late 1947, Margarita took Jeanne Mansberger and Magda and the now eleven-year-old Cuqui to Paris in the hope of re-establishing herself in Europe. She went to Belgium, Holland and Italy to give lectures on Mexican art and to write articles largely for the Mexican press. At one level, she enjoyed the work and the opportunity to see old friends. She even, from Paris, managed to re-establish contact with Ricarda Bermejo Oviedo, who had been her cook in Madrid. For many years already she had been corresponding with Ricarda's sister, Obdulia, the widow of her friend Ricardo Zabalza who had been executed by the Francoists. Margarita had gone to enormous trouble in a vain effort to help Obdulia get out of Orán where she lived and to Mexico.[238] With Ricarda too, Margarita began a correspondence which would continue until her death. For both, it was a link with a better past, the time when their hopes were invested in the Second Republic and both had their families around them. For Margarita, it was a line to Taguín's childhood of which, having fled as a refugee from Spain, she had hardly any souvenirs. Ricarda was suffering considerable privation in Madrid and Margarita occasionally managed to send her money. They had much in common, in the past and in the present. Margarita wrote to Ricarda from Paris: 'when you carry a pain like the one I drag around, life is just obligation: I have to go on because they need me, because for all three I am the only support. And I can tell you that I am seriously short of the will to go on.'

Although busy with her lecture tour, Margarita's thoughts never strayed far from Taguín. In a letter to Ricarda, she reminisced:

> Once he was ill, when we still lived in Calle Goya, he would have been about ten, and he suddenly said 'Oh Mami, I'm going to die. And if I die, how you will suffer!' That was all he was worried about, my suffering. And he has gone to die far from me, among strangers. If he knew that he was going to die and thought of me, what will he not have suffered. The very idea drives me mad, I swear. I'm going to ask you a favour, and I hope that you won't deny me. You say you have a little straw bag from when he brought his homework from school. I know that it is

an important souvenir but can you imagine what it would mean to me? I beg you: send it to me.

Ricarda did.[239]

In general, the European venture did not work out as Margarita had hoped. Post-war austerity made it difficult to find well-paid work. Moreover, in the paranoid atmosphere of the Cold War, things were even more difficult for a well-known Communist. To those on the right, it mattered little that she had been expelled by the party. What mattered was that she had chosen not to join the ranks of the ex-Communists who were shrilly denouncing the God that failed. She was also concerned that she and her family might be trapped in another war. By November 1948, she had decided that it was necessary to go back to the country that was now her home. She wrote to Pau Casals:

> We are returning to Mexico: the four generations, my mother, my daughter and my granddaughter with me. A family now without men, somewhat adrift living from my pen, which tells you enough. We came to Europe, because, after some years in America, there is that nostalgia which bit by bit turns into anguish. And so we went not to our Spain, but at least nearby. But our 'problem' is a long-term one . . . And here life is too uncertain, the difficulties of everyday life too burdensome, for it not to be madness to think in terms of definitively establishing ourselves here without knowing whether one day I might be forced to flee once more with my family: and that would not be easy, with an old woman and a young girl.

The entire family left France en route for Mexico in mid-December 1948. The 'gypsy tribe' ('*tribu gitana*'), as she referred to them, had to travel in a cargo ship. This was a consequence of the fact that Margarita had been refused a visa for the United

States because, she believed, 'I had been a Communist, and above all, because I had lost my son as a hero of the Red Army.' She anticipated a voyage of 25 days. In the event, the family's discomfort lasted well over six weeks.

> At least in Mexico, there is sun, greater facilities for daily life, that is, I will see my family living in better conditions, and one feels more surrounded by friends, more supported there than here, where I know so many people but they are only friends for a visit, they have their own problems and are enclosed within those problems.

One of her hopes in coming to Europe had been that she might visit the grave of Santiago in Mitrofanovka. In the event it was not possible. In 1948, journeys from Paris to the Soviet Union were almost impossible under any circumstances. She was worried that if she made the Herculean effort necessary, it would intensify the hostility of the United States and worsen her family's position:

> I came, more than anything, with the hope of visiting the grave of my son and I will leave even more destroyed than when I came because I haven't done so. But, you have to understand, that to do so at the moment, would be madness. I have to think in terms of looking after those I still have, and if I went there, no one would believe that it was just for 'THAT', and afterwards I wouldn't be allowed to teach courses in Mexico. How awful to think that those who fell, those who gave everything, have made their sacrifice in vain, for a world even more selfish and mean than the one they believed they were going to change . . .[240]

On returning to Mexico, Margarita swiftly acquired massive work commitments. She wrote to Ricarda: 'I'm working like a donkey: it's the only way not to go mad with grief. Everybody intoxicates themselves as best they can.'[241] Cuqui was an ever greater consolation to her but she could never get Taguín from her thoughts.

> Every time I see a boy of his age and I think of how little enjoyment of life my son had, I go mad with grief. I start every day by putting flowers in little vases in front of the photographs of him that I keep in every room and then I'm no good for the rest of the day.

Margarita tried not to let her grief get the better of her. She had to cope with her mother's increasing infirmity, Magda's less than robust health and was often incapacitated herself with sciatica. By 1951, her hair was beginning to turn white. Moreover, in 1951, she slipped and broke her right arm. She could work only by dictating her articles to Magda.[242] A source of solace was her friendship with the exiled Spanish archaeologist, Mateo Papaiconomos. Totally devoted to her, he frequently acted as her amanuensis, often lived with her family and later was a much loved uncle to Margarita's great-grandchildren. They argued about art and politics and their relationship, although platonic, was deep and loving.

Despite her enormous burden of work, her sorrow and her concern to fulfil her duties as head of the Nelken household, Margarita remained obsessed with the fate of Spain's exiles and with the anti-Franco struggle. The internecine squabbles of the exiles were, understandably, given her own expulsion from the Communist Party, a matter of considerable distress to her. In a letter to Casals of late 1951, she expressed her concern about an international situation that every day seemed to favour Franco more. The readiness of the Western democracies to accept the Caudillo filled her with indignation. 'There was never a people so heroic in the defence of its dignity that was so betrayed by those who, even out of self-interest, should have helped it.' But she also felt that the anti-Francoist forces were failing to focus their efforts effectively. Commenting on the spread of Francoist propaganda in Mexico, she wrote:

> its propaganda is unrestrained and this is helped by the absurd divisions among the exiles. If certain sectors of our exile used in the struggle against the common enemy a quarter of the effort that they put into attacking their brothers in the struggle and fellow-sufferers, we would already be back in Spain.[243]

Although not ostensibly involved in local politics, her capacity to stir up controversy did not desert her. In the spring of 1954, it was announced that the noted interpreter and friend of Richard Strauss, Clemens Krauss, was booked to make his debut with the Vienna Philharmonic Orchestra in Mexico City. Margarita immediately denounced both Krauss and his wife for their notorious connections with the Nazi Party and as accomplices of the holocaust. This provoked considerable debate with Margarita being accused of being a wild 'Red'. The cycle of concerts went ahead with great critical acclaim until, shortly after one Sunday-morning performance, on 16 May, Krauss had a heart attack and died in his hotel room. There were those who insinuated that she had in some way contributed to his death which was clearly ridiculous since he had an extremely serious heart condition and had been advised not to travel to Mexico.[244]

Margarita's principal preoccupation was her family – her mother, her daughter Magda and her granddaughter Cuqui. However, things seemed to be improving for Magda. Margarita was delighted that Magda had landed a good job in the Japanese embassy in Mexico City and was learning Japanese.[245] Moreover, she was in love and was soon to be married. Her fiancé, Lan Adomian Waisman, a conductor and composer, was born in the Ukraine in 1906, the son of a Jewish cantor. His family had emigrated to the United States in 1923. He had studied viola at the Peabody Conservatory in Baltimore and composition at the Curtis Institute in Philadelphia where he played under both Leopold Stokowski and Artur Rodinski. A friend of Dr Charles Seeger, father of the folk-singer, Pete, Lan was involved in left-wing causes, writing music for hunger marchers during the Great Depression. Just as he was getting well known, the Spanish Civil War broke out. He joined the Abraham Lincoln Brigade. In addition to service in the trenches, he wrote music. His '*Canción de la Sexta División*' was commissioned and paid for in food and ammunition, by its officers. He wrote songs with words provided by the poet Miguel Hernández. He returned from Spain critical of the Communists. His career began to take off as a composer of radio and documentary films. However, in the early 1950s, he had been placed on blacklists in the United States because of his membership of the Lincoln Battalion. Out of work, he had gone to Mexico to conduct a series of Mozart concerts.[246] There he had met Magda at a fancy-dress party at the home of the great Mexican painter, Rufino Tamayo. They soon fell in love and he decided to stay in Mexico to be with her. To do so, he needed work. That required him to join the composers' union and, in order to do that, he had to be a Mexican citizen. Accordingly, he applied for Mexican nationality which he obtained thanks to her help.

For some months in 1952, Margarita went through agonies of anxiety when Magda was extremely ill, suffering from what was diagnosed as neuritis but she seemed to recover. In mid-1953, Margarita herself had to have a very painful operation to remove a benign tumour (lipoma) from her side.[247] She had barely recovered when, at the beginning of 1954, she was nursing Magda again but this time there was to be no respite. She had cancer of the womb. After what Margarita called 'five months of hell', Magda died on 23 June 1954.[248] Margarita was devastated. She sent a scribbled note to her close friends Luis Jiménez Asúa and his wife Mercedes in Buenos Aires. Her distress can be seen in handwriting scarcely recognisable from her normally careful hand. 'I lost my daughter on the 23rd. Without anyone knowing, she had cancer. You may not believe it but I have still not gone mad. And apparently no one dies of sorrow.'[249]

A moving testimony to her grief appeared in a letter to an old colleague from the Spanish Socialist Party, Enrique de Francisco. She wrote to him six months after Magda's death in apology for not having acknowledged a copy that he had sent her of his *Hacia la humanidad libre* (Towards a Free Humanity). She had delayed because she wanted first to have read his book.

> The fact is, I STILL CANNOT READ. Since my Magda went, I can scarcely glance at the newspapers, and even then not every day. No matter how hard I try, I cannot concentrate. When I start to read, I think and it seems that I'm going mad. I go to exhibitions, when no one is there, to take notes and write, as best I can, the articles which, together with translations, allow me to maintain this house which is now so dreadfully empty, and allow me to look after my mother and granddaughter. But I still can do nothing but the absolutely unavoidable. I've been to the occasional concert . . . but it's useless. In short, I can tell you that, even though I eat well enough, I have lost 27 kilos (60 pounds).

Promising to read his book as soon as she was able, she ended on this terrible note:

> To you and yours, who can still speak of happiness, with all my heart I wish it for you this year and those to come. For your part, if you care for me, wish for me only that, as soon as I have my little girl [Cuqui, now nearly 19] settled in life, that there should be an end to this appalling joke that life plays on me of

waking (on the few occasions when I can sleep) and realising that I am without my children.

The bold, confident signature of her early handwriting was replaced by a tired hand.[250]

One year after her daughter's death, she would write to Jiménez Asú:

> To anyone who didn't know me before, I might seem like a person, but, if I tell you that I have now lost more than 30 kilos (66 pounds, 4½ stone), you can imagine what I'm like. I hardly ever cry nor do I get hysterical, but I'm burning up inside. I cannot go on, day after day, with so much pain.[251]

For more than a year, she dressed entirely in black and intended to do so for the rest of her days until tricked out of her intention by her granddaughter.

It was a cause of particular sorrow to Margarita that Magda had died before fulfilling her wish to marry again. After Magda's death, Lan became like a second son to Margarita, spending time with her and joining her to take flowers to Magda's grave. She felt responsible that the Communists were creating so many problems for him and used her influence to help him secure his naturalization papers. In her letters over the next decade, she made constant reference to him and her satisfaction at his professional successes. He wrote dozens of affectionate letters to her, often beginning 'Dear Mami' – the name by which she was known within the family.[252] Margarita adored his music, which was intensely political in inspiration and profoundly marked by his Spanish experiences and by the holocaust. His Second Symphony, *La Española*, begun during the Civil War contained elements of *cante jondo* and is dedicated to his comrades in the Abraham Lincoln Battalion. Margarita valued most highly of all Lan's *Cantata Elegiaca* for mezzo-soprano, chorus and orchestral ensemble written in memory of Magda. She wrote to Jiménez Asúa to say how deeply moved she had been by its première. She omitted to say that the libretto was by Margarita Nelken. Published in 1956, the text was accompanied by drawings by a remarkable range of artists who loved and admired both Margarita and Magda. They included Rufino Tamayo, Carlos Orozco Romero and Leonora Carrington. The desolation expressed in the text was some measure of the torment she suffered as a consequence of her daughter's death.[253]

In 1963, Lan began to live with María Teresa Toral who had heard his music while in the women's prison of Madrid after the Civil War. A distinguished physicist, as well as a talented artist and musician, Dr Toral had been frequently imprisoned by the Francoists. In October 1946, Nan Green had attended her trial as an observer. After being released from prison, she reached Mexico in 1956. Margarita Nelken had a high opinion of the quality of María Teresa Toral's engravings.[254] The relationship did not diminish Lan's close friendship with both Margarita and Mateo Papaiconomos. On 5 July 1966, Margarita's seventy-second birthday, Lan wrote to her:

> Dear Mami, Yesterday you told me that on this special day you would prefer me not to bring you flowers as in previous years. Well, I had another modest present ready for you. I am dedicating to you the première of my second symphony, La Española. This première is also in memory of Magda, Taguín who together with you, me, Mateo, María Teresa and so many, many, took part in our war for the freedom of our Spain and to avoid the holocaust of the Second World War. We failed. But the ideal lives on.[255]

Margarita's life by this time had become a constant round of frenetic work, partly to earn a living, partly to drive thoughts of her dead children from her mind. She had written to Casals commenting on feeling that she was kept alive only by her responsibilities to her mother and her granddaughter.[256] On 13 April 1955, Pablo Casals wrote to Margarita to inform of the death of Francisca Vidal de Capdevila, his beloved companion:

> My dear friend, I too have passed through a terrible situation. I have lost my partner who was my life's blood. I feel abandoned, without hope. My situation has made me better understand yours, dear friend. How I share your sorrow! But I won't insist, because I too find words of consolation of little use.

She replied in equally gloomy terms:

> I work only to live and keep alive both my mother, now extremely old, and my granddaughter. I believe that when she is on the right road to making her own way in life, I will just go out like a candle that has burned down. Let's hope it's soon.[257]

Margarita's mother's health was failing and, as she retreated into senile infantility, she needed ever greater care. In late 1955, Cuqui married José Ramón Rivas Ibáñez, the son of the playwright, Cipriano de Rivas Cherif, and the nephew of the late President of the Republic, Manuel Azaña. The newly-weds took an apartment next door. Margarita – who initially was not pleased by the Rivas-Azaña link – wrote to Ricarda, 'All alone now with my mother, ever more frail and she's like a little child that you can't scold.'[258] In November 1956, Cuqui gave birth to a baby son, called José Ramón. Margarita wrote: 'I have a great-grandson, now six weeks old but nothing can make me live again.'[259] However, provoked by Cuqui, who cunningly told her that she didn't want her picking up the baby while dressed all in black, she bought some white blouses. Thereafter, according to Cuqui who had three more children over the next nine years, she 'lived for and with my children'. It was a relief from the depressing task of looking after her mother – 'the poor thing, with her progressive arteriosclerosis, she is losing her intellect from one day to the next; she can hardly walk, even in the house, and often falls over.'[260] Jeanne Mansberger's final decline coincided with a period of near-blindness for Margarita. She died in early 1958, aged eighty-five.

On a small table in front of Margarita's sofa, there were framed photographs of Magda and Santiago. Sometimes, when visitors came, she would gaze abstractedly at them and say, 'This is what life has left me: of my two children, just two photographs!'[261] On the fifth anniversary of Magda's death in 1959, Margarita was deeply moved by flowers and messages from friends but the sense of loss still left her feeling incapacitated. 'I cannot cope with this desperation. It's like living on the margins of life, of everything that might help prevent me going mad from my sorrows.' She was cheered slightly by the success of her book on the Mexican painter Carlos Orozco Romero. Even more so, she was thrilled by the birth of Cuqui's second child, a daughter, and by the fact that she named her Magda. Margarita talked of writing memoirs. Her reasons for not doing so had nothing to do with the fears invented by Gorkín. 'What I should do is write an account of my own life in weekly parts. But it would simply be too incredible.' She had increasing difficulties with her eyes. Her handwriting was becoming illegible and she made jokes comparing herself to blind beggars on the streets of Spain.[262] Nevertheless, her spirits revived again when Cuqui gave birth to her third child, a son, and named him Santiago.[263]

In 1962, she suffered a severe bout of bronchitis.[264] She was also upset at the beginning of the year by the death of Martín de Paúl. She had long been bitter that he had not bothered to make contact when both Santiago and Magda had died yet somewhere deep down, she still felt something for him. She visited him in the pauper's hospital where he had been taken. To the astonishment of Cuqui and her husband, José Ramón, who had accompanied her, when Margarita saw Martín, she began to cry. She sat on his bed and lovingly stroked his face. 'My Martín,' she whispered in a voice choked with emotion, 'love of my life, it's me, your Margarita, your little Margarita. All the past is forgotten. I'm here with you now.' After coming to Mexico in 1940, he had twice rebuilt his fortune and twice lost everything gambling in the casino at Cuernavaca. Now, in 1962, he died penniless and forgotten by his various young lovers.[265] The consequence was that Margarita had to take charge of the situation and arranged his funeral. She wrote to Ricarda, 'All kinds of things that I had tried to forget were churned up again. In the end, in memory of our children, I forgave him everything.'[266] But there was more to it than that.

Despite her painful memories of the past, she remained passionate about Spain and, as a result, continued to find herself in conflict with her erstwhile comrades. Nevertheless, she took a leading role in protests about the execution of the Spanish Communist Julián Grimau.[267] Although her commitment to work remained undiminished, the loss of her children and political rejection left her intensely bitter and touchy. In 1964, she prepared a biographical outline at the request of a student, a kind of curriculum vitae. In it, she wrote, 'And now I am just an old woman, torn apart by the pain of the loss of my children, who tries to be as useful as possible and, perhaps fortunately, has to work hard to make a living.'[268] It was ten years since the death of Magda and she wrote of the anniversary 'each year, it is more terrible for me'. Margarita was seventy on 5 July 1964. Earlier in the year, without warning, a doctor had told her point-blank that a tiny lump on her breast meant cancer. In a painful four-hour operation, she had a mastectomy followed by cobalt treatment. 'It's left me a bag of rags. But the worst is that I came round after the operation.' She continued to work as much as her eyesight would allow her. She went to art exhibitions using Cuqui, her friend Mateo, or artist friends such as the muralist Vela Zanetti.[269] She also started to write an account of her life for Cuqui's children.[270] Her health deteriorated. In 1965, she had a heart attack. She sent Ricarda a photograph to show her 'what an old crock I've become'. Jiménez Asúa came to see her and said goodbye with the hope that they would soon meet in Madrid. She wrote to Ricarda, 'Of course I won't return. What would I do without my children, with no husband, with nothing more than my grief and my old age?'[271] In 1966, she had pneumonia, angina and sciatica but fought back. Her love for Cuqui's four children kept her going. Since they lived in the house next door, one of them tended to sleep with her each night, 'and so waking up is less sad'.[272] She received constant visits from Spaniards which made her reflect sadly:

> All that is now too far away. Just to think that I will never see my children there means that Spain is like another planet for me. And yet, it is terrible to think that, whatever happens, I will never return.[273]

Work, her great-grandchildren and her immense prestige in the Mexican cultural world fuelled her energies despite intensifying health problems. In fact, her sufferings were nearly over. On 11 February 1968, she wrote to Luis and Mercedes:

> For the last four months, I've been a disaster. A wrongly applied medicine produced a poisoning which kept me weeks in hospital and several days in a coma. Even now, I still have to have a nurse day and night. I am in a state of weakness which, just as you might expect, has attacked my weakest point, my sight. I still try to work a little. The exhibition organizers bring me paintings to the house and, with the help of Cuqui, I try to do my commentaries. But why even tell you the state of depression into which all this has plunged me.

After this letter was given her to post, Cuqui added, without Margarita's knowledge, the following:

> Mami knows nothing of this, but what is wrong is that she has bone cancer. It has been unmistakably diagnosed in her shoulder, in her ribs, in her hip (all on the left side) and in the cervical vertebrae. Nothing can be done and all we have left is to wait . . . one month, six . . . unfortunately, longer than normal. The best thing for her would be to die now and so avoid the monstrous agony that she has started to suffer. Because the pain is on the left side, she thinks it's her heart. I'm telling you this because I know how much you care for her.[274]

Luis Jiménez Asúa replied to this heart-rending news on 14 March. His letter arrived too late. Margarita Nelken had died in Mexico on 9 March 1968, aged seventy-four.[275]

The novelist Max Aub wrote in his diary on 10 March:

> There can have been few lives with more sorrows, setbacks, disillusionments, misfortunes. She resisted them all until nearly eighty years-old. She was never an easy woman and her sharp tongue must have protected her from her tribulations. She was, it is not necessary to say, very intelligent. She read and saw a lot. She knew how to speak; deputy for Extremadura, she knew the Spanish countryside as well as she knew the museums of Europe.[276]

The anarchist Federica Montseny, who had worked with her during the siege of Madrid, said generously:

> Margarita Nelken's error was her move from the Socialist to the Communist Party; perhaps because she knew that she was a better writer, a better speaker, and better educated than Pasionaria, she thought that

she would become the leading woman in the Party. But the number one spot was occupied by Dolores Ibárruri, who was a deep-rooted myth difficult to displace. The Socialists never forgave her for what they saw as treason and the Communists always regarded her with a certain mistrust and suspicion. That was, for me, Margarita Nelken's tragedy. But Margarita Nelken the art critic, Margarita Nelken the journalist, Margarita Nelken in any field, was a really exceptional asset and a brave woman at all times and in all situations. Perhaps that is, why, because she was an exceptional woman, silence has fallen over her like a heavy gravestone.

The American scholar Shirley Mangini shares Montseny's view that it was Margarita Nelken's 'exceptionality' which tragically consigned her to anonymity.[277] In part, it was simply that her energies and her talents were prodigally scattered over so many fields and causes that she never achieved a commanding position in any one. It was also that she was temperamentally unsuited to the administrative burdens and the duplicity needed for success in political parties. It was Max Aub who best summed up her remarkable life:

> Poor Margarita, I'm really sorry that you're dead! There was something straight and honest about you that always redeemed you: your love for the poor and for beauty.[278]

EPILOGUE

——————————

I N 1931, WHILE PRISCILLA SCOTT-ELLIS's guardian in Spain, the Princess Beatrice of Saxe-Coburg, accompanied Queen Victoria Eugenia into exile. Mercedes Sanz-Bachiller's husband, Onésimo Redondo, was among those who came to bid a mournful farewell to the Queen. The man who gave Mercedes news of her husband's death in 1936, General Andrés Saliquet, presided at the show trial of Margarita Nelken *in absentia* in 1941. Had Margarita not escaped into France and been able to use her influence to get her son Santiago out of the concentration camp at St Cyprien in February 1939, he might have joined Nan Green on the ship *Sinaia* taking Spanish refugees to Mexico instead of dying with the Russian forces in the Ukraine. Nan returned from her Mexican trip on the SS *Normandie* from New York and Margarita Nelken began her Mexican odyssey by sailing on the boat's return trip from Le Havre to New York.

These strange connections are just curiosities of history. They mean little although they serve to remind us of the extent to which these four women lived in extreme times. All four, in their different ways, were exceptional and their stories help us understand something of the emotional costs of the Spanish Civil War. Despite differences of nationality and ideology, Mercedes Sanz-Bachiller, Margarita Nelken, Priscilla Scott-Ellis and Nan Green were remarkable women linked by their courage, initiative and readiness to make personal sacrifices for others. They were not representative other than as examples of the courage and initiative that became a commonplace among women during the war. Like so many others, they confronted the dangers of daily life during the Spanish Civil War with determination, intelligence and compassion. A high price was exacted on all four in terms of their personal and family lives.

That Pip Scott-Ellis and Nan Green were in a position to travel to Spain to contribute to their respective causes was precisely the consequence of the fact that they were not representative. British women may, as a result of technological and material superiority, and because of their being drafted into the public sphere during the First World War, have been somewhat more emancipated than their Spanish counterparts. However, the differences were only relative. Pip and Nan could make the choices that they did because of the exceptional economic and political circumstances of their lives: one was an aristocrat and the other a Communist with comrades ready to help her. Margarita Nelken and Mercedes Sanz-Bachiller, remarkable though they both were in terms of their energy, creativity and humanity, were also unusual in terms of the political and personal circumstances that moulded their roles during the Spanish Civil War.

These stories illustrate the extent to which the Spanish Republic gave much to women and Franco's victory in the Spanish Civil War took away even more. In the five-and-a-quarter years before the right-wing backlash culminated in the military coup of 18 July 1936, cultural and educational reform had transformed the lives of many Spaniards, particularly women – a process in which Margarita Nelken had played an important role. Before 1931, the Spanish legal system had been astonishingly retrograde – women were not permitted to sign contracts, to administer businesses or estates or to marry without risk of losing their jobs. The Republican Constitution of December 1931 gave them the same legal rights as men, permitting them to vote and to stand for parliament and legalising divorce. Pressure for the female vote had come not from any mass women's movement but from a tiny elite of educated women and some progressive male politicians, most notably in the Socialist Party. Accordingly, much of this legislation was excoriated as 'godless' by a majority of Catholic women influenced by their priests. At the same time, the right was far more successful than the left in mobilising newly emancipated female voters to its cause. Nevertheless, in the period from 1931 to 1936, women of both the left and the right were mobilised politically and socially as never before. They were involved in electoral campaigns, trade-union committees, protest demonstrations and in the educational system both through the massive expansion of primary schooling and the opening up of the universities.

Nevertheless, public life remained a predominantly male precinct. The woman rash enough to put her head over the parapet and intrude upon the patriarchal territory of politics faced accusations of being brazen and – as happened to both Margarita Nelken and Dolores Ibárruri – from there it was but a short step to being seen as a whore. Such misogyny was less prevalent in the more cosmopolitan atmosphere of the left in Madrid and Barcelona, although even there it was not uncommon. On the right, female independence was heavily frowned upon. The further one travelled from the metropolis, the more acute the problem became.

There were very few female parliamentary deputies even of the left and centre-left. Indeed, of the 1004 parliamentary deputies of the three Republican Cortes of 1931, 1933 and 1936, only nine were women. One, Dolores Ibárruri, was a Communist, five – Margarita Nelken, María Lejárraga, Matilde de la Torre, Veneranda García, Blanco y Manzano and Julia Àlvarez Resano – were Socialists. Two were left-of-centre Republicans, Victoria Kent and Clara Campoamor. There was

Doves of War

only one women parliamentary deputy on the right, Francisca Bohigas Gavilanes of the Catholic CEDA.

The outbreak of the Spanish Civil War and the need to mobilise society for total war gave women in both zones a dramatically new participation in the functions of both government and society. As in all modern wars, the almost exclusively male preoccupation with violence created the necessity for women to take over the economic and welfare infrastructure. In the Republican zone, women not only played a crucial role in industrial production but also assumed important positions in the political, and even military, establishment. This was not without its complications. The young politically committed women who took up arms and went to fight as militiawomen fought with great courage when they were allowed to do so. However, it was widely assumed by their male comrades that they would be best employed cooking and washing. They were also subjected to considerable sexual pressure and, whether they succumbed to it or not, to the assumption that they were whores.[1] Behind the lines, women ran public services in transport, welfare and health. That, together with the assumption of the role of principal breadwinner, had a dramatic effect on traditional gender relations. It was short-lived and confined to the public sphere. Domestic life was rarely democratised and women continued to take principal responsibility for cooking, cleaning and childcare even as they organised the sinews of war.

As the Francoist forces captured Republican territory, in the Southern provinces in 1936, along the northern coast in 1937 and then all over Spain once the war ended on 1 April 1939, the feminist revolution of the Second Republic was reversed with extreme savagery. In the reactionary atmosphere of the rebel Nationalist zone, there was no comparable emancipation of women, although as the story of Francoist medical services and of Auxilio Social shows, women were enabled to have a public existence hitherto denied them. Nevertheless, the organisation of health and welfare by Auxilio Social and the Sección Femenina would be short-lived. The ideological thrust of the Franco's emergent regime was to stress women's role as homemakers and mothers for Falangist warriors.

Republican women were punished for their brief escape from gender stereotypes by humiliations both public and private. They were dragged through the streets after having their heads shaved, being tarred and feathered or forced to ingest castor oil and thus soil themselves in public. In Nationalist prisons, they were beaten and tortured. Sexual humiliation ranged from being paraded naked, via sexual harassment to rape. The propaganda that denounced all left-wing women as whores justified this.[2]

The full story of the partial emancipation and subsequent repression of women in 1930s Spain has not yet found its historian. Although women made up 50 per cent of the population affected by the war, it is an astonishing fact that of the near 20,000 books published on the Spanish Civil War, probably fewer than 1.0 per cent are by women or about the role of women in the conflict. The women about whom most is known were the middle-class radical female intelligentsia. Although the situation is changing, relatively little is still known of the role of less well-educated working-class women in war production, as nurses, even as soldiers, as farm labourers and as factory workers often in appalling conditions of toxicity, running buses and trams in towns, as teachers in literacy campaigns at the front – as well as continuing to provide food and laundry for men. The repression of the imprisoned and tortured working-class women who were unable to escape into exile is also difficult to reconstruct since often the humiliations to which these women were subjected made them reluctant to relive the experience with interviewers.

It is fortunate that, in the case of the women whose lives make up this book, there survived a unique body of documentary material, letters, diaries and memoirs that has permitted the reconstruction of their biographies and particularly of their roles in the Spanish Civil War and of how that conflict damaged their lives. From their stories, it is possible at least to recreate part of the remarkable history of what happened to women in Spain in the 1930s. More importantly, it is possible to begin to understand something of the emotional cost of the Spanish Civil War.

NOTES

PRISCILLA SCOTT-ELLIS
All for Love

1 Priscilla Scott-Ellis, *The Chances of Death. A Diary of the Spanish Civil War* (Wilby, Norwich: Michael Russell Publishing, 1995).

2 Hugh Thomas, 'Sangre y agallas. El diario sobre la guerra española de una aristócrata británica', *El País*, 15 July 1995.

3 José Luis de Vilallonga, 'Un enigma', *La Vanguardia*, 24 July 1995.

4 Raymond Carr, 'Respuesta a Vilallonga', *La Vanguardia*, 13 September 1995.

5 Margherita, Lady Howard de Walden, *Pages from my Life* (London: Sidgwick & Jackson, 1965) pp.16–23, 31–3, 54–5, 60–1; John Scott-Ellis, *Earls Have Peacocks. The Memoirs of Lord Howard de Walden* (London: Haggerston Press, 1992) pp.44–6; Olga Lynn, *Oggie. The Memoirs of Olga Lynn* (London: Weidenfeld & Nicolson, 1955) pp.50–9.

6 Howard de Walden, *Pages from my Life*, pp.41–6, 81–3.

7 Scott-Ellis, *Earls*, pp.51–2; interview with Gaenor Heathcoat-Amory.

8 Howard de Walden, *Pages from my Life*, pp.85, 111–38.

9 Scott-Ellis, *Earls*, p.85; Gaenor Heathcoat-Amory, Foreword, Scott-Ellis, *The Chances of Death*,

p.ix; Howard de Walden, *Pages from my Life*, pp.173–5; interviews with Gaenor Heathcoat-Amory.

10 Howard de Walden, *Pages from my Life*, pp.185–9.

11 Scott-Ellis, *Earls*, pp.36, 50–1; interview with Charmian Russell (née van Raalte).

12 Howard de Walden, *Pages from my Life*, pp.73–4, 86–7, 93–4, 97, 105–9, 147, 151, 176, 189, 192–4, 199–205; author's interview with Gaenor Heathcoat-Amory.

13 Gaenor Heathcoat-Amory, Foreword, p.ix; author's interview with Gaenor Heathcoat-Amory, 5 February 2001; Scott-Ellis, *Earls*, pp.35–6; Augustus John, *Chiaroscuro Fragments of Autobiography: First Series* (London: Jonathan Cape, 1952) p.225; Lynn, *Oggie*, pp.72–3.

14 Howard de Walden, *Pages from my Life*, pp.89–90; Gaenor Heathcoat-Amory, Foreword, pp.vii-viii.

15 Scott-Ellis, *Earls*, p.85.

16 Howard de Walden, *Pages from my Life*, pp.196–7, 214.

17 Howard de Walden, *Pages from my Life*, pp.234–6.

18 Scott-Ellis, *Earls*, pp.14–22.

19 Juan Balansó, 'Los Infantes de Orleáns', in Priscilla Scott-Ellis, *Diario de la guerra de España* (Barcelona: Plaza y Janés, 1996) pp.269–71; Fernando de Querol Muller, 'El Infante', *Aeroplano*,

Doves of War

No.4, noviembre de 1986,
pp.20–23.
20 Howard de Walden, *Pages from my Life*, pp.62–3, 70–1, 75.
21 José Ramón Sánchez Carmona, *El Infante D. Alfonso de Orleans (Biografía y filosofía aeronáutica)* (Madrid: Instituto de Historia y Cultura Aeronáuticas, 1991) p.38; Querol Muller, 'El Infante', p.24.
22 Juan Antonio Ansaldo, *¿Para qué? . . . (De Alfonso XIII a Juan III)* (Buenos Aires: Editorial Vasca Ekin, 1951) p.18; Alfredo Kindelán, *La verdad de mis relaciones con Franco* (Barcelona: Editorial Planeta, 1981) pp.167, 225. Prince Ali's own account of his journey with the King from Cartagena to Paris is reproduced in Kindelán, *La verdad*, pp.166–8.
23 Minute of S. Gaselee to despatch of Sir Henry Chilton, 19 October 1937, PRO FO371/21300, W91412/1/41; Sánchez Carmona, *El Infante*, pp.28–9; Scott-Ellis, *Earls*, pp.83–4; John, *Chiaroscuro*, p.149; Michael Holroyd, *August John. A Biography II The Years of Experience* (London: Heinemann, 1975) p.31.
24 The diaries of Priscilla Scott-Ellis are deposited at the University of Cardiff (Cardiff University Library Archive; manuscript no. 3/233). References henceforth will be to *DPSE*. *DPSE*, 17, 22 August 1934; Howard de Walden, *Pages from my Life*, pp.218–20.
25 Howard de Walden, *Pages from my Life*, pp.228–9; interviews with Gaenor Heathcoat-Amory and Charmian Russell.
26 *ABC* (Sevilla), 21 November 1936; Alfonso de Orléans Borbón to Alfredo Kindelán, undated, December 1936, reproduced in Kindelán, *La verdad*, p.100;

Sánchez Carmona, *El Infante*, p.30; Querol Muller, 'El Infante', p.23; Gerald Howson, *Aircraft of the Spanish Civil War 1936–1939* (London: Putnam Aeronautical, 1990) pp.201–2.
27 Balansó, 'Los Infantes de Orleáns', pp.272–3; letters of Alfonso de Orléans Borbón and Princess Beatrice of Saxe-Coburg to Kindelán, reproduced in Kindelán, *La verdad*, pp.99–102; *DPSE*, 14 January 1937.
28 *DPSE*, 1 January 1937.
29 *DPSE*, 3, 4 January 1937.
30 *DPSE*, 5, 7, 8, 28 January, 4 February 1937.
31 *DPSE*, 9, 11 January 1937.
32 *DPSE*, 26, 27 January 1937.
33 *DPSE*, 2, 3 February 1937.
34 *DPSE*, 6, 9, 16, 19, 20, 21, 23, 27 February, 17 March 1937.
35 *DPSE*, 6, 8, 16, 20 March
36 *DPSE*, 24, 25, 28, 29 March 1937.
37 Howard de Walden, *Pages from my Life*, p.241; *DPSE*, 30 March 1937.
38 Jim Fyrth, *The Signal was Spain. The Aid Spain Movement in Britain 1936–39* (London: Lawrence & Wishart, 1986) pp.195–6.
39 *DPSE*, 23 March, 2, 3, 4, 5, 6, 7, 8, 9 April 1937.
40 *DPSE*, 13, 14, 15, 19, 28, 29 April 1937.
41 Howard de Walden, *Pages from my Life*, pp.225, 228–9; *DPSE*, 3 May 1937; information provided by Gaenor Heathcoat-Amory.
42 *DPSE* 12, 14 May 1937.
43 *DPSE*, 18, 21, 23, 30 May, 10 June 1937.
44 *DPSE*, 6, 8 June 1937.
45 *DPSE*, 23, 24, 25, 26, 27, 28 June 1937.
46 *DPSE*, 2, 3, 4, 6, 7, 11, 12, 13, 14 July 1937.
47 *DPSE*, 16 July 1937; Nigel

Notes

Tangye, *Red, White and Spain* (London: Rich & Cowan, 1937) pp.11, 157, 187–9.

48 *DPSE*, 19, 20, 22, 26 July 1937; Major Geoffrey McNeill-Moss, *The Epic of the Alcazar. A History of the Siege of the Toledo Alcazar, 1936* (London: Rich & Cowan, 1937) pp.120–34, 309–17 (Badajoz), *passim* (Toledo). On Badajoz and the falsifications of McNeill-Moss, see Herbert R. Southworth, *Le mythe de la croisade de Franco* (Paris: Ruedo Ibérico, 1964) pp.179–88; Mário Neves, *La matanza de Badajoz* (Badajoz: Editora Regional de Extremadura, 1986) *passim;* Julián Chaves Palacios, *La guerra civil en Extremadura. Operaciones militares (1936–1939)* (Mérida: Editora Regional de Extremadura, 1997) pp.106–23.

49 Howard de Walden, *Pages from my Life*, pp.241–2; Scott-Ellis, *Earls*, p.85.

50 Kindelán, *La verdad*, p.225; *DPSE*, 8, 9, 24, 26, 30, 31 August, 3 September 1937.

51 *DPSE*, 7, 9, 10–22 September 1937. On Montagu-Pollock, see Jill Edwards, *The British Government and the Spanish Civil War, 1936–1939* (London: Macmillan, 1979) p.12.

52 Mónica Orduña Prada, *El Auxilio social (1936–1940). La etapa fundacional y los primeros años* (Madrid: Escuela Libre Editorial, 1996) pp.187, 190, 205; Maria Rosa Urraca Pastor, *Así empezamos (Memorias de una enfermera)* (Bilbao: La Editorial Vizcaína, n.d.) p.97.

53 *DPSE*, 21 September 1937.

54 Gertje R.Utley, *Picasso. The Communist Years* (New Haven & London: Yale University Press, 2000) pp.21–5.

55 *DPSE*, 22 September 1937. On the exhibition, see Albert Speer, *Inside the Third Reich* (London: Weidenfeld & Nicolson, 1970) p.81; Piers Brendon, *The Dark Valley* (London: Jonathan Cape, 2000) pp.492–4.

56 *DPSE*, 23, 24, 25, 26 September 1937. On Chilton, see Edwards, *The British Government*, pp.6–8, 114–16, 182–3. On the Junkers Ju 86D-1, see Gerald Howson, *Aircraft of the Spanish Civil War 1936–1939* (London: Putnam Aeronautical, 1990) pp.210–11.

57 *DPSE*, 28, 29, 30 September 1937. Matacán had been built to replace the aerodrome of San Fernando which was too often waterlogged. Franco had been chosen as Caudillo there in late September 1936. It was on part of the estate of Antonio Pérez Tabernero. See Francisco Morales Izquierdo, 'Matacan Base Aereo', in *Aeroplano. Revista de Historia Aeronautica.* December 1987, No 5, pp.84–105.

58 *DPSE*, 1, 2, 3, 4 October 1937. Cf. Chilton to Eden, 21 October 1937, PRO FO371/21300, W19412/1/41, in which it is clear that Chilton has misunderstood the chronology of Prince Ali's return to Spain.

59 *DPSE*, 13, 15, 18, 19, 21, 23, 24, 31 October, 2 November 1937.

60 *DPSE*, 27, 28, 29, 30 October, 2, 3, 4, 5, 6, 7 November 1937.

61 *DPSE*, 9, 11, 14, 20, 25 November, 1, 2 December 1937. On Mercedes Milá, see Priscilla Scott-Ellis, *The Chances of Death* edited by Raymond Carr (Norwich: Michael Russell, 1995) p.13.

62 *DPSE*, 6, 7, 10, 13, 14, 22, 23 December 1937.

63 On the air-force reorganisation, see Coronel José Gomá, *La guerra en el aire (vista, suerte y al toro)* (Barcelona: Editorial AHR, 1958) pp.259–61; Jesús Salas Larrazábal, *La guerra de España desde el aire* 2ª edición (Barcelona: Ediciones Ariel, 1972) p.282. *DPSE*, 23, 24, 25 December 1937.

64 *DPSE*, 24, 25, 26, 27, 28, 29 December 1937, 6, 17, 18, 20 January 1938. On the Condor Legion's move to Alfaro, see Karl Ries & Hans Ring, *The Legion Condor. A History of the Luftwaffe in the Spanish Civil War 1936–1939* (West Chester, PA: Schiller Military History, 1992) p.119.

65 *DPSE*, 18, 21, 22, 23 January 1938.

66 *DPSE*, 24, 25 January 1938.

67 *DGFP*, D, III, p.576.

68 *DPSE*, 28, 29, 30 January 1938.

69 *DPSE*, 1, 2, 3 February 1938.

70 *DPSE*, 4, 5, 6 February 1938; José Manuel Martínez Bande, *La batalla de Teruel* 2ª edición (Madrid: Editorial San Martín, 1990) pp.165–209; Luis María de Lojendio, *Operaciones militares en la guerra de España* (Barcelona: Montaner y Simón, 1940) pp.380–95; Manuel Aznar, *Historia militar de la guerra de España* (Madrid: Ediciones Idea, 1940) pp.569–85; Ramón Salas Larrazábal, *Historia del Ejército popular de la República* 4 vols (Madrid: Editora Nacional, 1973) II, pp.1672–1704.

71 *DPSE*, 8, 9, 10, 11, 12, 13, 14, 16, 27 February, 1 March 1938.

72 *DPSE*, 17, 18, 19, 20, 21, 22, 23, 24 February 1938.

73 *DPSE*, 26 February 1938.

74 Scott-Ellis, *Earls*, pp.85–7.

75 He was born on 29 January 1920 – José Luis de Vilallonga, *Otros mundos, otra vida* (Barcelona: Plaza y Janés, 2001) p.181.

76 Vilallonga, *Memorias*, pp.235–6.

77 Vilallonga, *Memorias*, pp.236–8.

78 José Luis de Vilallonga, 'Un enigma', *La Vanguardia*, 24 July 1995 (where the ambulance is described as a specially prepared Bentley); Enrique Meneses, *José Luis de Vilallonga* (Madrid: Grupo Libro 88, 1993) p.23.

79 *DPSE*, 26 February, 4 March, 9 December 1938.

80 *DPSE*, 10, 11, 12 March 1938.

81 *DPSE*, 13, 14, 15, 16 March 1938.

82 *DPSE*, 17, 18, 19, 21, 23, 24, 26, 27, 28, 30 March 1938.

83 *DPSE*, 31 March, 2 April 1938. On Monasterio, see Teresa Suero Roca, *Los generales de Franco* (Barcelona: Editorial Bruguera, 1975) pp.177–8.

84 *DPSE*, 4, 5, 6, 7 April 1938.

85 *DPSE*, 9, 10, 11 April 1938.

86 *DPSE*, 13, 14, 15, 16, 17, 18 April 1938.

87 Kindelán, *La verdad*, p.225; *DPSE*, 26 April, 11 June 1938.

88 *DPSE*, 27, 28, April, 1, 2, 3 May 1938.

89 Ansaldo, *¿Para qué?* pp.138–44; José Antonio Silva, *Cómo asesinar con un avión* (Barcelona, Editorial: Planeta 1981) pp.40–58.

90 *DPSE*, 30 April 1938.

91 *DPSE*, 4, 7 May 1938; Peter Kemp, *Mine Were of Trouble* (London: Cassell, 1957) p.189.

92 *DPSE*, 4, 5, 19, 20, 21–22 May 1938. In the *Daily Sketch*, 21 April 1938, the front page carried the headline THREE DAYS UNDER FIRE followed by 'For three days and three nights, the place was shelled while we worked desperately in hospital' said Miss Priscilla Scott-Ellis,

Notes

daughter of Lord Howard de
Walden, describing yesterday her
ordeal under fire in Spain. She is
one of four nurses attached to a
mobile unit of Franco's forces.
'A bombardment is terrible
torture to men helpless in bed.'

93 Howard de Walden, *Pages from my Life*, p.242.

94 *DPSE*, 23 May-3 June; Kemp, *Mine Were of Trouble*, pp.170–3.
In his memoirs, Kemp recounted
the same story in greater detail
attributing the actual shooting to
two privates under his command.
He recalls meeting Pip in
Zaragoza on p.189.

95 *DPSE*, 4 June 1938.

96 *Times*, 18, 19 July 1938;
interview with Gaenor
Heathcoat-Amory.

97 *DPSE*, 19, 23, 26 August 1938;
Gomá, *La guerra en el aire*, p.352;
Salas Larrazábal, *La guerra de España desde el aire*, p.402.

98 *DPSE*, 28, 29, 31 August, 1, 2
September 1938. Interview with
Gaenor Heathcoat-Amory 20
December 2000, Gaenor said that
Ali was obsessed with his
children marrying into royalty
and that after Álvaro had married
Carla and Alfonso was killed, the
weight of this requirement fell
on Ataúlfo.

99 *DPSE*, 3, 4 September 1938.

100 *DPSE*, 4, 8, 12, 14, 15, 16, 17
September 1938.

101 *DPSE*, 19, 22, 23, 25, 26, 27
September 1938.

102 *DPSE*, 29, 30 September, 1, 2,
3, 4, 5, 6, 7, 9, 11, 13, 14, 16, 17
October 1938.

103 *DPSE*, 18, 19–28, 29, 30, 31
October, 1 November 1938.

104 *DPSE*, 2, 4, 5, 12 November 1938.

105 *DPSE*, 6, 9, 11, 13 November
1938.

106 *DPSE*, 14, 15, 16, 17 November
1938.

107 *DPSE*, 21, 27, 28, 29, 30
November, 1, 7, 10, 11, 12
December 1938.

108 *DPSE*, 13, 14, 16, 19, 20, 21
December 1938.

109 *DPSE*, 22, 23, 24, 25, 26, 31
December 1938.

110 *DPSE*, 2, 3, 4, 7, 8, 9, 11, 12
January 1939.

111 *DPSE*, 13, 15, 16 January 1939.

112 *DPSE*, 18, 23, 24, 25, 26, 27, 28
January, 2, 4, 5, 6, 7 February
1939.

113 *DPSE*, 15 February 1939.

114 *DPSE*, 8, 16 February 1939.

115 *DPSE*, 21, 23, 24, 28 February
1939.

116 *DPSE*, 4 March 1939.

117 *DPSE*, 6, 7, 10, 11, 12, 14, 15
March 1939.

118 *DPSE*, 28 March 1939.

119 *DPSE*, 29 March 1939.

120 *DPSE*, 30 March, 3, 4, 5, 6, 7,
8, 9 April 1939.

121 *DPSE*, 18, 20, 22, 23, 24, 25,
27, 28 April, 1 May 1939.

122 Howard de Walden, *Pages from my Life*, pp.241–3.

123 *DPSE*, 5, 6, 13, 14, 15, 16 May
1939.

124 On Pollard and British Secret
Services involvement in Franco's
flight, see Michael Alpert, 'El
vuelo del Dragon Rapide' in *La Aventura de la Historia*, Vol.1,
no.9, July 1999, pp.28–35.

125 *DPSE*, 17, 18, 20, 21, 22, 23,
29, 30, 31 May 1939.

126 *DPSE*, 5, 9, 12 June 1939.

127 Gaenor Heathcoat-Amory,
Foreword, pp.ix-x.

128 *DPSE*, 15, 19, 20, 21, 23 June, 3,
4, 10, 11, 12 July, 13 August 1939.

129 *DPSE*, 25, 30 August, 1, 3, 5, 7,
9 September 1939.

130 *DPSE*, 18 September 1939.

131 *DPSE*, 12 October 1939.
132 *DPSE*, 26, 27, 28 September, 1, 9 October 1939.
133 *DPSE*, 12, 13, 14, 15, 17, 18, 22, 25, 27 October 1939.
134 *DPSE*, 1, 7, 8, 13, 15, 16, 17, 18, 19, 20 November 1939; Howard de Walden, *Pages from my Life*, p.243.
135 *DPSE*, 6 December 1939.
136 *DPSE*, 13, 16, 17, 21, 23 December 1939.
137 *DPSE*, 4, 5, 6, 12, 13, 17, 18, 31 January, 2 February, 21 March 1940.
138 *DPSE*, 22 February, 16 March 1940.
139 *DPSE*, 2, 24, 25 March, 5, 6, 8 April 1940.
140 *DPSE*, 22 April, 5, 6 ('niggers'), 7, 10, 12, 15, 17, 19, 21, 23, 24, 25, 26, 28, 29 May, 3, 4, 5, 6 June 1940.
141 *DPSE*, 7, 8, 9, 10, 11, 13, 14, 15, 24, 26, 29 June 1940; Howard de Walden, *Pages from my Life*, pp.246–57.
142 *DPSE*, 2 July 1940.
143 *DPSE*, 7 July 1940.
144 *DPSE*, 18, 31 July, 1, 2, 3, 4, 5, 6, 7, 12, 19, 20, 23, 27, 29 August 1940.
145 *DPSE*, 29 August, 1, 7, 8, 9, 10, 11, 12, 19, 23 September, 15 October 1940.
146 *DPSE*, 6, 9, 18, 27 September; Paul Preston, *Franco. A Biography* (London: HarperCollins, 1993) pp.388–9.
147 *DPSE*, 22 October 1940; Preston, *Franco*, pp.393–400.
148 *DPSE*, 24 October 1940.
149 *DPSE*, 5, 10 November 1940.
150 *DPSE*, 11 November 1940.
151 *DPSE*, 15, 16 October, 5, 11, 14 November 1940.
152 *DPSE*, 19 November, 4 December 1940.

153 The Sikorski Institute could find no record of this title ever being made official. Foreign Office Index – Treaty Section.
154 *DPSE*, 2 January 1941.
155 For this information, I am grateful to the Records Management Department of the FCO Records and Historical Department.
156 I am indebted to Duncan Stewart, the SOE Adviser at the FCO Records and Historical Department, for providing me with material from Pip's SOE Personal File, 7 February 2001.
157 Letter of Duncan Stewart to author, 7 February 2001.
158 Howard de Walden, *Pages from my Life*, p.257; author's interviews with Gaenor Heathcoat-Amory & John de Vilallonga; Scott-Ellis, *Earls*, p.88. It has been possible to reconstruct Pip's life in 1943 thanks to Pip's own captioned photographs, kindly loaned to the author by John de Vilallonga.
159 Interview with Gaenor Heathcoat-Amory 20 December 2000; Scott-Ellis, *Earls*, pp.87–8; Vilallonga, *Memorias*, pp.309–11. Elsewhere, José Luis places the meeting in mid-1939, which is impossible, Meneses, *Villalonga*, pp.24–5.
160 Conversations with Gaenor Heathcoat-Amory, 13 February 2001. Compare the photograph of Pip on the cover of the published version of her diary with the portrait of the Baronesa de Segur on p.3 of the illustrations in Vilallonga, *Memorias*, between pp.160 and 161; the denial on p.298. An almost identical sentence appears

Notes

on his autobiographical novel, *El gentilhombre europeo* (Barcelona: Tusquets Editor, 1993) p.13.

161 Vilallonga, *Memorias*, p.273, 383; José Luis de Vilallonga, *À pleines dents* (Paris: Stock, 1973) p.96, where he declares 'J'adore des putes'.

162 Vilallonga, *Memorias*, pp.314–15; José Luis de Vilallonga, *La nostalgia es un error* (Barcelona: Editorial Planeta, 1980) p.21.

163 Vilallonga, *Memorias*, pp.320–1. On Yagüe, see pp.426–7; on Anders, see pp.412, 427. Vilallonga, *La nostalgia*, p.18.

164 This is what Pip told her son – interview with the author.

165 Vilallonga, *Memorias*, pp.322–3; Meneses, *Vilallonga*, p.26; Vilallonga, *La nostalgia*, pp.21–2; José Luis de Vilallonga, *Otros mundos, otra vida* (Barcelona: Plaza y Janés, 2001) p.43.

166 Vilallonga, *Memorias*, pp.324–31. For the outright accusations – riddled with chronological inaccuracy – that Pip was Prince Ali's daughter, see pp.379–81, 390–2; Meneses, *Vilallonga*, pp.27–8. For a blatant statement that he had married Pip to escape from Spain, Vilallonga, *La nostalgia*, p.28.

167 Gaenor Heathcoat-Amory, Foreword, p.x.

168 Interview with Gaenor Heathcoat-Amory 20 December 2000.

169 Vilallonga, *Memorias*, p.234.

170 Vilallonga, *Memorias*, pp.333–47, 369–83, 394–5. If any of this was true, Pip never mentioned it to either of her later confidants, her son John and her sister Gaenor (authors' interviews with both).

171 Vilallonga, *Memorias*, pp.394–412.

172 Vilallonga, *Otros mundos, otra*

vida, pp.17–39; Meneses, *Vilallonga*, pp.38–9.

173 Vilallonga, *Memorias*, pp.372–3.

174 Vilallonga, *Otros mundos, otra vida*, pp.42–4.

175 As recounted to her son, John (information of John de Vilallonga).

176 José Luis gives contradictory versions in Vilallonga, *Otros mundos, otra vida*, pp.48–53, 67–74; Meneses, *Vilallonga*, p.46; author's interviews with Gaenor Heathcoat-Amory.

177 Scott-Ellis, *Earls*, pp.88–9; author's interview with John de Vilallonga, 11 February 2001; Meneses, *Vilallonga*, p.47; Vilallonga, *Otros mundos, otra vida*, pp.78–95.

178 Vilallonga, *Otros mundos, otra vida*, pp.110–14, 122–3.

179 Vilallonga, *Otros mundos, otra vida*, pp.161–2.

180 *Buenos Aires Herald*, 8 October 1947.

181 Howard de Walden, *Pages from my Life*, pp.264–7.

182 Vilallonga, *Otros mundos, otra vida*, pp.197–205; Scott-Ellis, *Earls*, p.89; interviews with Charmian van Raalte, John de Vilallonga.

183 This account is pieced together from Vilallonga, *Memorias*, p.172; Vilallonga, *Otros mundos, otra vida*, pp.108–9, 120, 171–2, 180–203, 207–22; interviews with Gaenor Heathcoat-Amory and John de Vilallonga.

184 Vilallonga, *Otros mundos, otra vida*, pp.211–12, 253–6.

185 Vilallonga, *Otros mundos, otra vida*, pp.258–9; Meneses, *Vilallonga*, p.49.

186 Interview with Gaenor Heathcoat-Amory, 20 December 2000; interview with John de

Doves of War

Vilallonga, 11 February 2001; correspondence with Carmen de Vilallonga.

187 Vilallonga, *Otros mundos, otra vida*, pp.109–10.

188 Vilallonga, *Otros mundos, otra vida*, pp.289–90, 292–3.

189 Meneses, *Vilallonga*, pp.62–4, 140–2; Vilallonga, *La nostalgia*, pp.246–8; interviews with John de Vilallonga.

190 Interviews with Tatiana Orloff-Davidoff.

191 Interviews with John de Vilallonga, Gaenor Heathcoat-Amory and Tatiana Orloff-Davidoff and correspondence with Carmen de Vilallonga.

192 Meneses, *Vilallonga*, pp.143–5; Vilallonga, *La nostalgia*, pp.170–5, 206.

193 Interviews with John de Vilallonga.

194 Gaenor Heathcoat-Amory, Foreword, pp.xi–xii; interviews with Gaenor Heathcoat-Amory, 5 February 2001; interview with John de Vilallonga, 11 February 2001.

195 Sánchez Carmona, *El Infante*, p.38; Querol Muller, 'El Infante', p.24.

196 *ABC* (Madrid), 14, 15, 16 July 1966.

197 *ABC* (Madrid), 9 October 1974; interviews with Charmian Russell, Gaenor Heathcoat-Amory and Gerarda de Orleans.

198 *ABC* (Madrid), 7 August 1975.

199 Interviews with Tatiana Orloff-Davidoff and Gaenor Heathcoat-Amory.

200 José Luis de Vilallonga, *Inolvidables mujeres* (Barcelona: Plaza y Janés, 1999) pp.243–4; Vilallonga, *Memorias*, pp.277–80; interviews with John de Vilallonga.

201 Gaenor Heathcoat-Amory, Foreword, pp.xii–xiii.

NAN GREEN
A Great Deal of Loneliness

1 Nan Green, 'A Chronicle of Small Beer. The Memoirs of Nan Green' (unpublished MS, kindly made available to the author by Martin Green) pp.1–3. Polly Kemp's father had been successively a boot-boy in a wealthy family in Suffolk, a policeman, then Chief Warder at Wandsworth Prison and finally Governor of H. M. Prison in Devizes, Wiltshire.

2 Green, 'A Chronicle', p.1.

3 *The Studio*, Volume 36, 1906, p.240.

4 'British Involvement in the Spanish Civil War 1936–1939 – Nan Green', Imperial War Museum Sound Archive, Accession No.000815/04, p.1. A substantially abridged version of this interview is reproduced in David Corkill & Stuart Rawnsley, Editors, *The Road to Spain. Antifascists at War* (Dunfermline: Borderline, 1981) pp.63–74.

5 Green, 'A Chronicle', p.6.

6 Green, 'A Chronicle', p.5.

7 Green, 'A Chronicle', p.7.

8 Emily Farrow, *Mem's Memoirs*, annotated by Nan Green (Newlyn: Martin Green, 1997) p.1.

9 Green, 'A Chronicle', pp.9–10.

10 Green, 'A Chronicle', p.11; Farrow, *Mem's Memoirs*, p.3.

11 Farrow, *Mem's Memoirs*, pp.6–8.

12 Green, 'A Chronicle', pp.12–16; Farrow, *Mem's Memoirs*, pp.13–14, 22–3.

Notes

13 Green, 'A Chronicle', pp.15–18.
14 Green, 'A Chronicle', pp.18–19.
15 Green IWM interview, pp.1–2; Green, 'A Chronicle', pp.20–1.
16 Green, 'A Chronicle', pp.21–3.
17 Green, 'A Chronicle', p.24.
18 Green, 'A Chronicle', p.23.
19 Green, 'A Chronicle', p.27.
20 For an account of George's physical appearance and political ideas, Green, 'A Chronicle', p.28.
21 Green, 'A Chronicle', p.34.
22 Interview with Frances Brouard, 3 January 2001.
23 Green, 'A Chronicle', pp.37–8; Green, IWM interview, p.2.
24 Green, IWM interview, pp.2–4; Corkill & Rawnsley, The Road to Spain, pp.64–5; Green, 'A Chronicle', p.43.
25 Green, 'A Chronicle', pp.45–7; poem by Martin Green, 'Heritage'.
26 Green, 'A Chronicle', pp.51–2; Green, IWM interview, p.5.
27 Charles Kahn, 'George Green', Musicians' Union Report, No.27, March 1939.
28 Interview with Frances Brouard.
29 Green, 'A Chronicle', p.52.
30 George Green to Nan Green, 12 May 1937, (Papers of Martin Green).
31 Interview with Frances Brouard.
32 There are several accounts of his extraordinary life in Wogan Philipps, Lord Milford 25.2.1902–30.11.1993 (London: no publisher given, 1994). For the remark on his paintings, Stephen Spender, World Within World (London: Reader's Union, 1953) p.123.
33 Jim Fyrth, The Signal was Spain. The Aid Spain Movement in Britain 1936–39 (London: Lawrence & Wishart, 1986) pp.45–8; Spanish Medical Aid Committee, 'British Medical Aid in Spain', (London: the News Chronicle, n.d.); Bill Alexander, British Volunteers for Liberty. Spain 1936–1939 (London: Lawrence & Wishart, 1982) pp.226–8.
34 Stephen Spender, 'Heroes in Spain', in the New Statesman and Nation, 1 May 1937, pp.714–15; Spender, World Within World, pp.189–90.
35 George Green to Nan Green, 15 May 1937 (Papers of Martin Green).
36 Spender, World Within World, pp.189–90.
37 Ian MacDougall, editor, Voices from the Spanish Civil War. Personal Recollections of Scottish Volunteers in Republican Spain 1936–39. (Edinburgh: Polygon, 1986) p.83.
38 Bill Alexander, 'Wogan Philipps', the Independent, 3 December 1993.
39 Wogan Philipps, 'An Ambulance Man in Spain', New Writing, New Series, Autumn 1938, reprinted in Valentine Cunningham, editor, Spanish Front – Writers on the Civil War (Oxford: Oxford University Press, 1986) pp.48–9.
40 I am grateful to Martin Green for sending me a copy of the long poem in its entirety. A fragment of the poem is reproduced in Fyrth, The Signal, p.62. In a letter of 15 May 1938, George asked Nan about what happened to the poem (Papers of Martin Green).
41 Philipps, p.47.
42 George Green to Nan Green, undated (Papers of Martin Green). The first four pages of this 15-page letter are missing but the detailed content suggests that it was written during the Battle of Brunete. In the copy kept at the Marx Memorial Library, the covering note (in Bill Alexander's

handwriting) states 'Brunete offensive July '37', MML, Box B-3: GRE. On the other hand, there are references throughout George's letters written in May 1937 to a long letter in progress.

43 Jonathan Croall, *The Permanent Rebel of Summerhill* (London: Routledge & Keegan Paul, 1983) pp.246–9.

44 Green, IWM interview, p.6; Green, 'A Chronicle', p.53.

45 Winifred Bates, 'Summary and Critical Survey of my Work in Spain since the Outbreak of the War, Barcelona, September, 1938', Moscow Archive, 545/6/88, pp.1–3; Fyrth, *The Signal*, pp.104–5; Alexander, *British Volunteers*, p.41.

46 Fyrth, *The Signal*, pp.107–8; author's interview with Lou Kenton, 28 October 2000.

47 Nan Green to Fredericka Martin, 4 September 1969, Archives of the Abraham Lincoln Brigade, Brandeis University; interview of Milt Felsen.

48 Milt Felsen, *The Anti-Warrior. A Memoir* (Iowa City: University of Iowa Press, 1989) p.73; Green, 'A Chronicle', pp.55–6.

49 Green, 'A Chronicle', p.57; Green, IWM interview, pp.24–6; Felsen, *Anti-Warrior*, p.73.

50 George Green to Nan Green, 2 April 1938, (Papers of Martin Green).

51 George Green to Nan Green, 1 April 1938, (Papers of Martin Green). On the Activist Movement, see Alexander, *British Volunteers*, pp.202–3.

52 Green, IWM interview, pp.8–9; Green, 'A Chronicle', p.59.

53 Green, 'A Chronicle', pp.61–4; Nan Green to Fredericka Martin, 25 September 1968, ALBA, Brandeis University.

54 In her unpublished memoirs, Nan refers consistently to the medical officer as Austrian and by name Dr Krushmar. However, in a letter written nearly thirteen years earlier, she gives the full name as Herbert Kretzschmar, Nan Green to Fredericka Martin, 17 June 1970, ALBA, Brandeis University.

55 After the Spanish Civil War, Kretzschmar reached Britain and was interned as an enemy alien. He later married an English woman and worked as a GP in Tooting, South London, where he was a much loved member of the local community. He also became a member of the CPGB which suggests that he was fully cleared of any accusations of involvement with drugs. Kretzschmar's life is described in a long letter from his brother, Joachim Kretzschmar to Büro Hager, Sozialistische Einheitspartei Deutschlands, 26 July 1987. The Moscow file describing him as possessing good medical skills and praising his political work was drawn up by Gustav Szinda, 13 February 1940. There are two accounts of his life by Francis K. S. Khoo, 'The spirit of "No Pasaran!"' in the *Morning Star*, 16 August 1986 and 'Tribute to an Internationalist' in *Asian Times*, 26 September 1986. All the above items are held at the Dokumentationsarchiv des Österreichischen Widerstands, Wien. I am deeply indebted to Hans Landauer, the director of the DÖW for his generous help in locating this material and to Francis K. S. Khoo who knew and admired Kretzschmar for his work as a doctor in London and also as an internationalist.

Notes

56 George Green to Nan Green, 30 March 1938, (Papers of Martin Green).

57 Green, 'A Chronicle', pp.60, 67.

58 There are references to Day in MML, IB Archive, Boxes D-7/A-1 & A-2; 29/A/12.

59 MML, IB Archive, Box C-15/5, for the report on this conversation by William Rust.

60 Harvey Klehr, John Earl Haynes & Fridrikh Igorevich Firsov, *The Secret World of American Communism* (New Haven: Yale University Press, 1995) p.180.

61 On Rust, see Charlotte Haldane, *Truth Will Out* (London: The Right Book Club, 1949) pp.131–3; James K. Hopkins, *Into the Heart of the Fire. The British in the Spanish Civil War* (Stanford, California: Stanford University Press, 1998) pp.158–9.

62 Hopkins, *Into the Heart*, p.284. I am indebted to James Hopkins who kindly sent me his notes from Nan Green's Moscow file.

63 The quotation is from the second page of a two-page letter from Rust. The first page with the date and addressee has not survived. MML, Box C: 15/5.

64 Len Crome, 'Walter (1897–1947): A Soldier in Spain', *History Workshop Journal*, No.9, Spring 1980, p.120.

65 Green, 'A Chronicle', pp.59–61.

66 Bates, 'Summary and Critical Survey', Moscow Archive, 545/6/88, p.3.

67 Green, 'A Chronicle', pp.64–5.

68 Bates, 'Summary and Critical Survey', Moscow Archive, 545/6/88, p.6.

69 Penelope Fyvel, *English Penny* (Ilfracombe: Arthur Stockwell, 1992) pp.49–50; Green, IWM interview, pp.11–12; Green, 'A

Chronicle', pp.65–7. On Penelope Phelps, see also 'English Penny' in Frank Jellinek, *The Civil War in Spain* (London: Victor Gollancz, 1938) pp.595–9.

70 George Green to Nan Green, 15 May 1938 (Papers of Martin Green).

71 Green, 'A Chronicle', pp.67.

72 Green, 'A Chronicle', pp.67–8. On Marty, see *inter alia*, R. Dan Richardson, *Comintern Army. The International Brigades and the Spanish Civil War* (Lexington, Kentucky: University Press of Kentucky, 1982) pp.51–2; Rémi Skoutelsky, *L'Espoir guidait leurs pas. Les volontaires français dans les Brigades internationales 1936–1939* (Paris: Bernard Grasset, 1998) *passim*; Alexander, *British Volunteers*, p.27.

73 Moscow Archive, 545/6/93 p.18.

74 Nan Green & A. M. Elliott, *Spain against Fascism 1936–39. Some Questions Answered* 2nd edition (London: The History Group of the Communist Party, 1986) p.22. The irony of this has been underlined by Hopkins, *Into the Heart*, pp.283–4.

75 On Crome and his role with the 35th Division, see Len Crome, 'Walter (1897–1947): A Soldier in Spain', *History Workshop Journal*, No.9, Spring 1980, pp.116–28; Richard Baxell, 'Dr Len Crome', the *Independent*, 11 May 2001; Paul Preston, 'Len Crome', the *Guardian*, 12 May 2001; Fyrth, *The Signal*, pp.110, 149.

76 MML, Box 29: D/9/Aurora Fernández Reminiscences (1980) p.17.

77 Nan Green to Emily Green 28 August 1938 (Papers of Martin Green).

78 Green, 'A Chronicle', p.71; Fyrth, *The Signal*, pp.127–9. Jolly wrote

an important book, *Field Surgery in Total War* based on his Spanish experiences.

79 George Green to Nan Green, 6 August 1938, (Papers of Martin Green).

80 Corkill & Rawnsley, *The Road to Spain*, p.67; Green, '*A Chronicle*', pp.68–73.

81 Nan Green to Emily Green 28 August 1938 (Papers of Martin Green).

82 Nan Green to Emily Green 28 August 1938; George Green to Nan Green, 6 August 1938, (Papers of Martin Green).

83 George Green to Jessie Green, 21 August 1938, (Papers of Martin Green). (Also in MML, Box 50, File GW Green).

84 Wolman's letter was written on 22 July 1937 and is reproduced in Peter N.Carroll, *The Odyssey of the Abraham Lincoln Brigade. Americans in the Spanish Civil War* (Stanford, California: Stanford University Press, 1994) p.74.

85 George Green to Jessie Green, 21 August 1938 (MML, Box 50, File GW Green).

86 Green, IWM interview, pp.14–15; *News Chronicle*, 23 January 1939. Presumably because of errors of transcription by the journalist, this interview contains many errors about dates.

87 Green, 'A Chronicle', pp.74–5; Green, IWM interview, pp.22–3.

88 Walter Gregory, *The Shallow Grave. A Memoir of the Spanish Civil War* (London: Victor Gollancz, 1986) pp.131–4; Alexander, *British Volunteers*, pp.213–15.

89 Bates, 'Summary and Critical Survey', Moscow Archive, 545/6/88, p.6; Hopkins, *Into the Heart*, p.285.

90 Martin Green to Paul Preston, 28 July 2000.

91 Green, 'A Chronicle', p.76.

92 *News Chronicle*, 23 January 1939.

93 Fyrth, *The Signal*, p.203.

94 Charles Kahn, 'George Green', *Musicians' Union Report*, No.27, March 1939.

95 Copy in papers of Martin Green.

96 Green, 'A Chronicle', pp.77–9. Winifred Bates and the official letter, p.78.

97 Conversation of author with Milt Felsen, 6 November 2000.

98 Nan Green to Mrs Fawcett, (MML, Box 41/A/77).

99 Charles Kahn, 'George Green', *Musicians' Union Report*, No.27, March 1939.

100 Minutes of the IBA foundational conference, MML, Box 37/A/3; Report of London Area Meeting of the IBA, 5 March 1939, MML, Box 37/A/5; Bill Alexander, *No to Franco. The Struggle Never Stopped 1939–1975* (London: Bill Alexander, 1992) pp.18–20.

101 Antonio Vilanova, *Los olvidados. Los exilados españoles en la segunda guerra mundial* (Paris: Ruedo Ibérico, 1969) pp.3–22.

102 Nan Green to Irene Grant 12 May 1939 (Papers of Douglas Jolly, kindly made available by Dr Donald Grant).

103 Alexander, *No to Franco*, pp.25–6; David Wingeate Pike, *Vae Victis! Los republicanos españoles refugiados en Francia 1939–1944* (Paris: Ruedo Ibérico, 1969) p.83; Adolfo Sánchez Vázquez, 'Recordando al Sinaia' in *Del exilio en México. Recuerdos en México* (México DF: Editorial Grijalbo, 1997) pp.19–27; Green, 'A Chronicle', pp.79–84; Fyrth, *The Signal*, pp.299–300.

Notes

104 Vilanova, *Los olvidados*, p.13–15.
105 Green, 'A Chronicle', pp.85–6.
106 Green, 'A Chronicle', p.87.
107 Nan Green to Irene Grant, undated April; 4 August 1939, Irene Grant to Nan Green, 9 August 1939 (Papers of Douglas Jolly, kindly made available by Dr Donald Grant); MML, Box 29: D/9/Aurora Fernández, Reminiscences (1980) p.22.
108 Green, 'A Chronicle', pp.86–7; Green, IWM interview, pp.39–40.
109 Fyrth, *The Signal*, p.156.
110 Green, 'A Chronicle', p.89.
111 Green, 'A Chronicle', pp.91–4.
112 Green, 'A Chronicle', pp.96–100.
113 Green, 'A Chronicle', pp.100–2.
114 Green, 'A Chronicle', p.106.
115 Nan Green to Karl Staf, 23 January 1946 (MML, Box 24/ SW/1); Nan Green to Aileen Palmer, 22 March 1946, (MML, Box 24/AL/4).
116 Nan Green to Aileen Palmer, 22 March 1946, (MML, Box 24/ AL/4).
117 Nan Green to Karl Staf, 23 January 1946 (MML, Box 24/ SW/1); Green, 'A Chronicle', pp.100–4; MacDougall, editor, *Voices from the Spanish Civil War*, p.327.
118 Conversation of the author with Santiago Carrillo; Gregorio Morán, *Miseria y grandeza del Partido Comunista de España 1939–1985* (Barcelona: Editorial Planeta, 1986) pp.110–12. See also Dolores Ibárruri, 'Informe ante el Pleno del Partido Comunista de España, celebrado en Toulouse el 5 de diciembre de 1945', *Nuestra Bandera* No.4, Toulouse, January, February 1946, pp.13–14.
119 See Leah Manning, *What I Saw in Spain* (London: Victor Gollancz, 1935). On the visit, see Leah Manning, *A Life for Education (An Autobiography)* (London: Victor Gollancz, 1970) p.140; Alexander, *No to Franco*, p.46. On life in the women's prison at Ventas, see Mercedes Núñez, *Cárcel de Ventas* (Paris: Colección Ebro, 1967) *passim*; Giuliana Di Febo, *L'altra metà della Spagna. Dalla lotta antifranchista al movimento femminista: 1939–1977* (Naples: Luguori Editore, 1980) pp.21–49; and Consuelo García, *Las cárceles de Soledad Real. Una vida* (Madrid: Ediciones Alfaguara, 1983) pp.119–47. For the more or less official view on the benevolence of the Francoist penal regime, see Halliday Sutherland, *Spanish Journey* (London: Hollis & Carter, 1948) pp.43–68.
120 Aurora Fernández to Nan Green, 30 September 1946 (MML, Box 24/CZ/6).
121 Nan Green to Ena Vassie and Margaret Findley, 16 October 1946; Nan Green, 'Madrid 1946', *Spain Today*, November 1946, pp.3–5; Green, Chronicle, pp.113–15.
122 Green, 'A Chronicle', p.111; Martin Green to Paul Preston, 11 October 2000.
123 Richard Crossman, editor, *The God that Failed. Six Studies in Communism* (London: Hamish Hamilton, 1950). On the genesis of the book and on the wider operation, see Frances Stonor Saunders, *Who Paid the Piper? The CIA and the Cultural Cold War* (London: Granta Books, 1999) pp.63–6. On the alliance of extreme leftists and the CIA

Doves of War

to discredit the Spanish Communist Party, see Herbert Rutledge Southworth, 'The Grand Camouflage': Julián Gorkín, Burnett Bolloten and the Spanish Civil War' in Paul Preston & Ann Mackenzie, editors, *The Republic Besieged: Civil War in Spain 1936–1939* (Edinburgh, Edinburgh University Press, 1996). pp.261–310.

124 Spender, *The God*, pp.244–63; Spender, *World Within World*, pp.189–90. On Spender's role in the cultural cold war, see Stonor Saunders, *Who Paid the Piper?*, pp.170–3 et seq.

125 Green, 'A Chronicle', pp.115–18.

126 Green, 'A Chronicle', pp.119–28.

127 Green, 'A Chronicle', pp.129–46; Nan Green, 'On Holiday in People's China', *World News and Views*, 10 September 1955, 715–16.

129 Green, 'A Chronicle', pp.161–2.

130 Green, 'A Chronicle', pp.163–4.

131 Green, IWM interview, p.21; Alexander, *No to Franco*, pp.69–74.

132 The work for this is described in her chapter, Nan Green, 'Nancy Cunard and Spain' in Hugh Ford, editor, *Nancy Cunard. Brave Poet, Indomitable Rebel 1896–1965* (Philadelphia, Chilton Book Co., 1968).

133 Nan Green, 'The Communist Party and the War in Spain', *Marxism Today*, October 1970, pp.316–24.

134 Copy in papers of Martin Green.

135 Nan Green & A. M. Elliott, *Spain against Fascism 1936–39. Some Questions Answered* 2nd edition (London: The History Group of the Communist Party, 1986).

136 Marx Memorial Library, *International Brigades Memorial Archive. Catalogue 1986* (London: MML, 1986) p.v.

137 Nan Green to Fredericka Martin, 31 December 1971, ALBA, Brandeis University.

138 Green, IWM interview, pp.15–16. There is also a copy in Tameside Local Studies Library, Stalybridge, Cheshire.

139 Nan Green to Fredericka Martin, 31 October 1973, ALBA, Brandeis University.

140 Judith Cook, *Apprentices of Freedom* (London: Quartet Books, 1979) pp.132–3.

141 *Morning Star*, 7 April 1984; *Times*, 17 April 1984.

MERCEDES SANZ-BACHILLER
So Easy to Judge

1 Vicente Gay, *Estampas rojas y caballeros blancos* (Burgos: Hijos de Santiago Rodríguez Editores, 1937) pp.84–8, 90–92.

2 Conversations with Mercedes Sanz-Bachiller between 1998 and 2001 (henceforth MSB-PP).

3 MSB-PP.

4 MSB-PP.

5 MSB-PP.

6 José Luis Mínguez Goyanes, *Onésimo Redondo 1905–1936. Precursor sindicalista* (Madrid: Editorial San Martín, 1990) pp.11–18.

7 MSB-PP; José María de Areilza, *Así los he visto* (Barcelona: Editorial Planeta, 1974) p.140.

8 MSB-PP.

9 MSB-PP; marriage certificate in

Notes

Archivo Mercedes Sanz Bachiller (henceforth (AMSB)); Mínguez Goyanes, *Onésimo Redondo*, pp.20–3.

10 Areilza, *Así los he visto*, p.137.

11 José Monge y Bernal, *Acción Popular (Estudios de biología política)* (Madrid: Imp. 'Saez Hermanos', 1936) pp.126–32; Javier Jiménez Campo, *El fascismo en la crisis de la Segunda República española* (Madrid: Centro de Investigaciones Sociológicas, 1979) pp.129–30; José R. Montero, *La CEDA. El catolicismo social y politico en la II República* 2 tomos (Madrid: Ediciones de la Revista de Trabajo, 1977) I, pp.98, 385; Mínguez Goyanes, *Onésimo Redondo*, pp.24–30.

12 *Onésimo Redondo Caudillo de Castilla* (Valladolid: Ediciones Libertad, 1937) pp.19–22. Diary entry for 24 July 1936, Diary of Javier Martínez de Bedoya, in AMSB, (henceforth DJMB), 'I make a promise to write a book to bring to public notice the five terrible years of bitter struggle carried out by Onésimo in the midst of total indifference.'

13 Ángel de Prado Moura, *El movimiento obrero en Valladolid durante la Segunda República* (Valladolid: Junta de Castilla y León, 1985) p.135.

14 *Onésimo Redondo Caudillo*, pp.22–7; Tomás Borrás, *Ramiro Ledesma Ramos* (Madrid: Editora Nacional, 1971) p.284; Mínguez Goyanes, *Onésimo Redondo*, p.36.

15 *Onésimo Redondo Caudillo*, p.9.

16 Eduardo Álvarez Puga, *Historia de la Falange* (Barcelona: Dopesa, 1969) p.25.

17 Ramiro Ledesma Ramos, 'El "caso" Valladolid', *La Patria Libre*, no.6, 23 March 1935, reproduced in Ramiro Ledesma Ramos, *Escritos politicos 1935–1936* (Madrid: Herederos de Ramiro Ledesma Ramos, 1988) pp.255–7; José María Sánchez Diana, *Ramiro Ledesma Ramos: biografía política* (Madrid: Editora Nacional, 1975) pp.125–6; Mínguez Goyanes, *Onésimo Redondo*, p.40; *Onésimo Redondo Caudillo*, pp.34–5.

18 MSB-PP.

19 *Onésimo Redondo Caudillo*, pp.26–37; Ramiro Ledesma Ramos, *¿Fascismo en España?* 2ª edición (Barcelona: Ediciones Ariel, 1968) p.99; Payne, *Falange*, pp.15–18.

20 *Onésimo Redondo Caudillo*, pp.40–7, 51–7; Mínguez Goyanes, *Onésimo Redondo*, pp.42, 170–3.

21 Paul Preston, *The Coming of the Spanish Civil War. Reform, Reaction and Revolution in the Second Republic* 2nd edition (London: Routledge, 1994) pp.58–60, 66–7, 80–4. See also the testimony of Alberto Pastor, a Jonsista farmer from Valladolid in Ronald Fraser, *Blood of Spain. The Experience of Civil War 1936–1939* (London: Allen Lane, 1979) pp.86–9.

22 In his memoirs of this period, Albiñana talks of many visits but does not specifically mention that by Onésimo Redondo, Dr José María Albiñana, *Confinado en las Hurdes (una víctima de la Inquisición republicana* (Madrid: Imprenta El Financiero, 1933) pp.88–92, 117; Mínguez Goyanes, *Onésimo Redondo*, pp.42–3.

23 *Onésimo Redondo Caudillo*, pp.57–8.

24 MSB-PP and conversations with Mercedes Redondo.

25 Ramiro Ledesma Ramos to Onésimo Redondo, undated April, 14 August 1932, (AMSB)

Doves of War

26 Ramiro Ledesma Ramos, ¿Fascismo
   en España? 2ª edición (Barcelona:
   Ediciones Ariel, 1968) p.103;
   MSB-PP; correspondence
   between Onésimo Redondo and
   Andrés Redondo, undated,
   (AMSB); Mínguez Goyanes,
   Onésimo Redondo, pp.45–9.
27 Javier Martínez de Bedoya to
   Onésimo Redondo, 22 April, 1
   May, 15 August 1933, (AMSB);
   Onésimo Redondo Caudillo,
   pp.61–70.
28 Mínguez Goyanes, Onésimo
   Redondo, pp.52–6.
29 Onésimo Redondo Caudillo,
   pp.71–2, 82–4.
30 Onésimo Redondo Caudillo, pp.85–90.
31 MSB-PP.
32 Francisco Bravo Martínez, Historia
   de Falange Española de las JONS 2ª
   edición (Madrid: Editora
   Nacional, 1943) pp.26–7;
   Domingo Pérez Morán, ¡A estos,
   que los fusilen al amanecer! (Madrid:
   G. del Toro Editor, 1973)
   pp.208–9; Ignacio Martín
   Jiménez, La guerra civil en
   Valladolid (1936–1939). Amaneceres
   ensangrentados (Valladolid: Ámbito
   Ediciones, 2000) pp.13, 41.
33 Martín Jiménez, Amaneceres
   ensangrentados, pp.15–16; Onésimo
   Redondo Caudillo, pp.113–30.
34 Alejandro Salazar, Diario, in
   Rafael Ibáñez Hernández, Estudio
   y acción: la Falange fundacional a la
   luz del Diario de Alejandro Salazar
   (1934–1936) (Madrid: Ediciones
   Barbarroja, 1993) p.34.
35 Ian Gibson, En busca de José
   Antonio (Barcelona: Editorial
   Planeta, 1980) pp.63, 208–9. On
   Ledesma as orator, see Javier
   Martínez de Bedoya, Memorias
   desde mi aldea (Valladolid: Ambito
   Ediciones, 1996) p.68.
36 Ledesma Ramos, Fascismo,

pp.197–8; Francisco Bravo
   Martínez, José Antonio. El hombre,
   el jefe, el camarada (Madrid:
   Ediciones Españolas, 1939)
   pp.182–3; Herbert Rutledge
   Southworth, Antifalange; estudio
   crítico de 'Falange en la guerra de
   España' de Maximiano García
   Venero (Paris: Ediciones Ruedo
   Ibérico, 1967) pp.80–1; Martínez
   de Bedoya, Memorias, pp.79–80;
   Angel Alcázar de Velasco, La gran
   fuga (Barcelona: Plaza y Janés,
   1977) p.39.
37 Bravo, José Antonio, pp.82–4;
   Felipe Ximénez de Sándoval, José
   Antonio (Biografía apasionada)
   (Barcelona: Editorial Juventud,
   1941) pp.290–5; Ibáñez
   Hernández, Estudio y acción,
   pp.75–6; Martínez de Bedoya,
   Memorias, pp.80–1; interview with
   Javier Martínez de Bedoya, cited
   by Mínguez Goyanes, Onésimo
   Redondo, p.68.
38 'Las JONS rompen con FE.
   Manifiesto de las JONS', La Patria
   Libre, No.1, 16 February 1935;
   undated letter of Ledesma Ramos
   to Francisco Bravo, in Bravo, José
   Antonio, p.83; Ramiro Ledesma
   Ramos, Discurso a las juventudes de
   España 2ª edición (Bilbao:
   Ediciones Fe, 1938) p.6; Ledesma
   Ramos, ¿Fascismo en España?,
   pp.200–2.
39 Sánchez Diana, Ledesma Ramos,
   pp.210–13, 233–6; Bravo, José
   Antonio, pp.82–4.
40 Mínguez Goyanes, Onésimo
   Redondo, pp.79–80.
41 Onésimo Redondo to President de
   Acción Popular de Valladolid, 20
   January 1936, (AMSB); Onésimo
   Redondo Caudillo, pp.165–19;
   Mínguez Goyanes, Onésimo
   Redondo, pp.80–2.
42 Areilza, Así los he visto, p.145.

Notes

43 Francisco J. de Raymundo, *Cómo se inició el glorioso Movimiento Nacional en Valladolid y la Gesta heróica del Alto del León* (Valladolid: Imprenta Católica, 1936) pp.42–3; José Antonio Primo de Rivera to Onésimo Redondo, 3 July 1936, (AMSB); José Antonio Primo de Rivera, *Textos inéditos y epistolario* (Madrid: Ediciones del Movimiento, 1956) pp.476–7, 480, 491–2, 494, 499, 502–3, 509; Areilza, *Así los he visto*, p.150; Gay, *Estampas*, pp.55–65, 84–92; Onésimo Redondo Caudillo, pp.181–9; Mínguez Goyanes, *Onésimo Redondo*, pp.82–6.

44 Joaquín Arrarás, *Historia de la Cruzada española* VIII vols, 36 tomos, (Madrid: Ediciones Españolas, 1939–43) III, 12, p.308; Gay, *Estampas*, pp.47–52; Francisco de Cossío, *Hacia una nueva España. De la revolución de octubre a la revolución de Julio 1934–1936* (Valladolid: Editorial Castilla, 1936) pp.326–7; Martín Jiménez, *Amaneceres ensangrentados*, pp.24–9, 34; *Onésimo Redondo Caudillo*, pp.189–97; Mínguez Goyanes, *Onésimo Redondo*, pp.86–8, 90–2.

45 *Onésimo Redondo Caudillo*, pp.197–; MSB-PP.

46 Cossío, *Hacia una nueva España*, p.328–31; Gay, *Estampas*, pp.115–30; Arrarás, *Historia de la Cruzada*, III, 12, p.310–21; Raymundo, *Cómo se inició*, pp.6–39; Francisco de Cossío, *Guerra de salvación. Del frente de Madrid al de Vizcaya* (Valladolid: Librería Santarén, 1937) pp.224–9; Pérez Morán, *¿A estos!*, pp.26–32.

47 Martín Jiménez, *Amaneceres ensangrentados*, pp.32–40, 47–65, 76–89, 182–3.

48 MSB-PP.

49 *Diario Regional* (Valladolid) 21 July 1936; Raymundo, *Cómo se inició*, pp.44–6; *Onésimo Redondo Caudillo*, pp.203–16; Arrarás, *Historia de la Cruzada*, III, 12, p.321–2; Martín Jiménez, *Amaneceres ensangrentados*, pp.95, 181.

50 MSB-PP.

51 MSB to Ana Botella de Aznar, 1 May 1995 (AMSB); MSB-PP.

52 Pilar Primo de Rivera, *Recuerdos de una vida* (Madrid: Ediciones Dyrsa, 1983) p.67; Sheelagh Ellwood, *Spanish Fascism in the Franco Era. Falange Española de la JONS, 1936–76* (London: Macmillan Press, 1987) n.23, p.49; José Luis Rodríguez Jiménez, *Historia de Falange Española de las JONS* (Madrid: Alianza Editorial, 2000) p.230; Mínguez Goyanes, *Onésimo Redondo*, pp.92–102.

53 MSB-PP; *Diario Regional* (Valladolid), 26 July 1936; Cossío, *Hacia la nueva España*, p.97; Mínguez Goyanes, *Onésimo Redondo*, pp.101–2; Martín Jiménez, *Amaneceres ensangrentados*, pp.380–2; Julián Casanova, *La Iglesia de Franco* (Madrid: Ediciones Temas de Hoy, 2001) p.65.

54 *Diario Regional* (Valladolid), 26 July 1936; MSB-PP of her conviction that the death of Onésimo Redondo intensified the subsequent repression.

55 The figure of 15,000 is given by Gabriel Jackson, *The Spanish Republic and the Civil War* (Princeton NJ: Princeton University Press, 1965) p.535. A more modest 9,000 is shared by César M. Lorenzo, *Les anarchistes espagnols et le pouvoir* (Paris: Éditions du Seuil, 1969) p.204 and also by 'a Catholic Deputy' in conversation with the British diplomat, Bernard Malley, quoted

Doves of War

by Hugh Thomas, *The Spanish
Civil War* 3rd edition (London:
Hamish Hamilton, 1977) p.265. A
more reasonable 1,600 derives
from a contemporary testimony
cited by 'Juan de Iturralde',
(pseudonym of Father Juan José
Usabiaga Irazustabarrena), *La
guerra de Franco: los vascos y la
Iglesia* 2 vols (San Sebastián:
Publicaciones 'Clero Vasco', 1978)
I, p.448. The semi-official figure
of 1303 derives from Ramón Salas
Larrazábal, *Pérdidas de la Guerra*
(Barcelona: Editorial Planeta,
1971) p.371.
56 Fraser, *Blood of Spain*, p.167; *El
Norte de Castilla*, 25 September
1937, reproduced in Rafael Abella,
*La vida cotidiana durante la guerra
civil. La España Nacional*
(Barcelona: Planeta, 1973) pp.77,
81–2; 'Iturralde', *La guerra de
Franco*, I, pp.447–9; Martín
Jiménez, *Amaneceres ensangrentados*,
pp.220–5; Dionisio Ridruejo, *Casi
unas memorias* (Barcelona: Editorial
Planeta, 1976) pp.69–70.
57 Martín Jiménez, *Amaneceres
ensangrentados*, pp.226–51;
'Iturralde', *La guerra de Franco*, I,
pp.448.
58 Martín Jiménez, *Amaneceres
ensangrentados*, pp.122, 134, 181–2,
199–218.
59 Maximiano García Venero,
*Falange en la guerra de España: la
Unificación y Hedilla* (Paris: Ruedo
Ibérico, 1967) pp.189–92, 282–3,
304, 314; Ridruejo, *Casi unas
memorias*, p.70; Ellwood, *Spanish
Fascism*, p.38; Stanley G. Payne,
Fascism in Spain 1923–1977
(Madison, Wisconsin: University
of Wisconsin Press, 1999)
pp.249–50.
60 MSB-PP; Mónica Orduña Prada,
El Auxilio Social (1936–1940). La

etapa fundacional y los primeros años
(Madrid: Escuela Libre Editorial,
1996) pp.32–3.
61 Martínez de Bedoya, *Memorias*,
p.104.
62 MSB-PP. According to DJMB,
30 August 1936, the pre-war
organisation had 36 members.
63 *Arriba*, No.7, 2 May 1935. The
printing of the fly-sheet in Luis
Suárez Fernández, *Crónica de la
Sección Femenina y su tiempo*
(Madrid: Asociación Nueva
Andadura, 1993) p.39.
64 MSB-PP.
65 Martín Jiménez, *Amaneceres
ensangrentados*, pp.188–96;
Guillermo Cabanellas, *La guerra de
los mil días. Nacimiento, vida y
muerte de la II República española* 2
vols (Buenos Aires: Grijalbo,
1973) II, pp.857–8; Adoración
Martín Barrio, María de los
Ángeles Sampedro Talabán &
María Jesús Velasco Marcos, 'Dos
formas de violencia durante la
guerra civil' in Julio Aróstegui,
Coordinador, *Historia y memoria de
la guerra civil* 3 vols (Valladolid:
Junta de Castilla y León, 1988) II,
pp.396–8.
66 Southworth, *Antifalange*, p.172;
MSB-PP.
67 DJMB, 2, 3, 4, 5, 12, 15, 16
September 1936.
68 DJMB, 25, 27 September 1936.
69 DJMB, 1 October 1936; Martínez
de Bedoya, *Memorias*, p.104.
70 MSB-PP; Southworth, p.171;
Orduña Prada, *El Auxilio Social*,
pp.23–5; Martínez de Bedoya,
Memorias, pp.104–5.
71 MSB-PP; Martínez de Bedoya,
Memorias, pp.104–5; Orduña
Prada, *El Auxilio Social*, p.38.
72 Dionisio Ridruejo, *Escrito en
España* 2ª edición (Buenos Aires:
Editorial Losada, 1964) p.93;

Notes

Ridruejo, *Casi unas memorias*, p.82.

73 MSB-PP.

74 MSB-PP; Martínez de Bedoya, *Memorias*, p.105.

75 Heleno Saña, *El franquismo sin mitos. Conversaciones con Serrano Suñer* (Barcelona: Ediciones Grijalbo, 1981) p.83.

76 DJMB, 2 November, 7 December 1936; García Venero, *Falange y Hedilla*, p.283; Southworth, *Antifalange*, p.173.

77 Ridruejo, *Casi unas memorias*, p.81.

78 MSB-PP; Martínez de Bedoya, *Memorias*, p.105; Southworth, *Antifalange*, p.171; Orduña Prada, *El Auxilio Social*, pp.38–9.

79 Martínez de Bedoya, *Memorias*, p.105.

80 *Diario Regional* (Valladolid) 31 October 1936; Orduña Prada, *El Auxilio Social*, pp.41–2.

81 Ridruejo, *Casi unas memorias*, p.82.

82 Testimony of Miguel Primo de Rivera y Urquijo to the author; Primo de Rivera, *Recuerdos*, pp.75–9; Luis Suárez Fernández, *Crónica de la Sección Femenina y su tiempo* (Madrid: Asociación Nueva Andadura, 1993) pp.50–4.

83 DJMB, 2 November 1936.

84 DJMB, 22 November 1936.

85 DJMB, 7 December 1936.

86 Orduña Prada, *El Auxilio Social*, pp.42–3.

87 Martínez de Bedoya, *Memorias*, pp.106–7; Orduña Prada, *El Auxilio Social*, pp.43–4.

88 Ramón Serrano Suñer, 'Discurso de Clausura del Tercer Congreso Nacional de Auxilio Social' in *De la victoria y la postguerra (Discursos)* (Madrid: Ediciones FE, 1941) pp.85–6.

89 Ridruejo, *Casi unas memorias*, p.80.

90 Primo de Rivera, *Recuerdos*, p.103; Ridruejo, *Casi unas memorias*, p.82. Pilar's memoirs were ghosted by a journalist on the basis of interviews with her (conversation of the author with Miguel Primo de Rivera y Urquijo).

91 Primo de Rivera, *Recuerdos*, p.103; Martínez de Bedoya, *Memorias*, p.107.

92 DJMB, 8 November 1936.

93 DJMB, 7 December 1936.

94 García Venero, *Falange y Hedilla*, pp.290–1; Joan María Thomàs, *Lo que fue la Falange* (Barcelona: Plaza y Janés, 1999) pp.116, 295–6; Payne, *Spanish Fascism*, p.258; Orduña Prada, *El Auxilio Social*, p.49.

95 Martínez de Bedoya, *Memorias*, pp.101, 107; Ridruejo, *Casi unas memorias*, p.68; José Antonio Girón de Velasco, *Si la memoria no me falla* (Barcelona: Editorial Planeta, 1994) p.43; Stanley G.Payne, *Falange. A History of Spanish Fascism* (Stanford: Stanford University Press, 1961) pp.122–5.

96 Martínez de Bedoya, *Memorias*, p.104.

97 DJMB, 10 January 1937.

98 Francisco Bravo, *José Antonio. El hombre, el jefe, el camarada* (Madrid: Ediciones Españolas, 1939) pp.82–4; Rafael Ibáñez Hernández, *Estudio y acción. La Falange fundacional a la luz del Diario de Alejandro Salazar (1934–1936)* (Madrid: Ediciones Barbarroja, 1993) pp.75–6; Martínez de Bedoya, *Memorias,* pp.80–1, 120, 127–8.

99 Hedilla to Martínez de Bedoya, 14 January 1937, (AMSB); Martínez de Bedoya, *Memorias,* pp.107, 109; García Venero, *Falange/Hedilla*, p.283; Southworth, *Antifalange*, pp.171–3.

100 Pedro Lain Entralgo, *Descargo de conciencia (1930–1960)*

(Barcelona: Barral Editores, 1976) p.205.

101 Ramón Serrano Suñer, *Entre Hendaya y Gibraltar* (Madrid: Ediciones y Publicaciones Españolas, 1947) p.42; Saña, *El franquismo*, p.153; García Venero, *Falange/Hedilla*, p.290; Primo de Rivera, *Recuerdos*, p.100.

102 Ramón Serrano Suñer, *Entre el silencio y la propaganda, la Historia como fue*. *Memorias* (Barcelona: Planeta, 1977) pp.170–2; Ridruejo, *Casi unas memorias*, p.77.

103 MSB-PP; Martínez de Bedoya, *Memorias*, p.107.

104 Manuel Tuñon de Lara et al., *La guerra civil española. 50 años después* (Barcelona: Editorial Labor, 1985) p.341.

105 Dionisio Ridruejo, *Casi unas memorias* (Barcelona: Editorial Planeta, 1976) p.68.

106 Ridruejo, *Casi unas memorias*, p.79.

107 Ridruejo, *Casi unas memorias*, p.82.

108 Ridruejo, *Casi unas memorias*, p.82; Martínez de Bedoya, *Memorias*, p.108.

109 Manuel Hedilla, *Testimonio* (Barcelona: Ediciones Acervo, 1972) pp.331–2; García Venero, *Falange Hedilla* (Paris: Ruedo Ibérico, 1967) pp.282–3.

110 Martínez de Bedoya, *Memorias*, p.109.

111 María Teresa Gallego Méndez, *Mujer, Falange y franquismo* (Madrid: Taurus, 1983) p.54.

112 López Bassa to Sanz-Bachiller, 24 May 1937, (AMSB); Martínez de Bedoya, *Memorias*, p.110; Orduña Prada, *El Auxilio Social*, pp.58–9.

113 *Times*, 14 July 1938; Martínez de Bedoya, *Memorias*, p.110.

114 The issues are laid out in an internal report marked *'Secreto'*, Delegación Nacional de 'Auxilio Social', *Réplica a una falsa acusación* (Valladolid, 5 April 1938), in (AMSB); Martínez de Bedoya, *Memorias*, pp.112–13.

115 Martínez de Bedoya, *Memorias*, p.114.

116 Gomá to Vatican, 24 April 1937, reproduced in María Luisa Rodríguez Aisa, *El Cardenal Gomá y la guerra de España: aspectos de la gestión pública del Primado 1936–1939* (Madrid: Consejo Superior de Investigaciones Científicas, 1981) pp.432–5.

117 Martínez de Bedoya, *Memorias*, pp.113–16.

118 MSB-PP; DJMB, 9 August 1937; Orduña Prada, *El Auxilio Social*, pp.144, 232–3; Gallego Méndez, *Mujer, Falange y franquismo*, p.60. MSB-PP made it quite clear that there is no substance to the claim of Suárez Fernández, *Crónica*, p.58; that she was in Germany prior to the foundation of Auxilio de Invierno.

119 DJMB, 30 August, 5 October 1937; MSB-PP.

120 Anselmo de la Iglesia Somavilla to MSB, 13 May 1944 (AMSB).

121 DJMB, 6, 13, 15 September 1937; Orduña Prada, *El Auxilio Social*, pp.156–7.

122 DJMB, 15 September 1937; Orduña Prada, *El Auxilio Social*, pp.62–3.

123 MSB-PP; DJMB, 29 September 1937; Sanz-Bachiller, 'Notas sobre mi trayectoria', unpublished notes written in 1972, (both in (AMSB)).

124 DJMB, 5 October 1937.

125 Reprinted in Javier Martínez de

Notes

Bedoya, *Siete años de lucha. Una trayectoria política* (Valladolid: Artes Gráficas Afrodisio Aguado, 1939) pp.130–1.

126 Ellwood, *Spanish Fascism*, p.34. See also Pedro Carasa, 'La revolución nacional-asistencial durante el primer franquismo (1936–1940)', *Historia Contemporánea* (Bilbao), No.16, 1997, pp.89–140.

127 Pilar Fidalgo, *A Young Mother in Franco's Prisons* (London: United Editorial, 1939) p.31.

128 Florence Farmborough, *Life and People in National Spain* (London: Sheed & Ward, 1938) pp.38–41.

129 Merwin K. Hart, *America Looks at Spain* (New York: P. J. Kennedy & Sons, 1939) pp.105–10.

130 Ernesto Giménez Caballero, *La infantería española* (Madrid: Ediciones de la Vicesecretaría de Educación Popular, 1941) pp.62–3.

131 Martínez de Bedoya, *Memorias*, pp.116–17; Suárez Fernández, *Crónica*, pp.68–9, 90–1; Orduña Prada, *El Auxilio Social*, pp.202–8; Gallego Méndez, *Mujer, Falange y franquismo*, pp.59–66, 91–5; Rosario Sánchez López, *Mujer española, una sombra de destino en lo universal. Trayectoria histórica de Sección Femenina de Falange (1934–1977)* (Murcia: Universidad de Murcia, 1990) pp.35–40.

132 MSB-PP.

133 Martínez de Bedoya, *Memorias*, p.120.

134 Serrano Suñer to Martínez de Bedoya, 21 February 1938, (AMSB); Martínez de Bedoya, *Memorias*, pp.120–1.

135 Martínez de Bedoya, *Memorias*, pp.127–8.

136 Martínez de Bedoya, *Memorias*, p.130.

137 Martínez de Bedoya, *Memorias*, p.120; Orduña Prada, *El Auxilio Social*, pp.64–9, 293–303.

138 Javier Martínez de Bedoya, 'La liberación de las JONS', in *Patria Libre*, 16 February 1935; Ximénez de Sándoval, *José Antonio*, pp.290–5; *Onésimo Redondo Caudillo*, pp.143–4.

139 Martínez de Bedoya, *Memorias*, pp.134–9; Manuel Valdés Larrañaga, *De la Falange al Movimiento (1936–1952)* (Madrid: Fundación Nacional Francisco Franco, 1994) pp.125–6; Girón de Velasco, *Si la memoria*, pp.52–6; Orduña Prada, *El Auxilio Social*, pp.69–73.

140 Muñoz Grandes to Martínez de Bedoya, 30 August 1939, (AMSB).

141 ¡Madres! (Madrid: Ediciones Auxilio Social-FET y de las JONS, 1939); *La mujer en la familia y en la sociedad* (Madrid: Ediciones Auxilio Social-FET y de las JONS, 1939); *Puericultura en el hogar (complementada con nociones de medicina casera e hygiene)* (Madrid: Ediciones Auxilio Social-FET y de las JONS, 1939); *Corte y confección* (Madrid: Ediciones Auxilio Social-FET y de las JONS, 1939); *Ciencia doméstica* (Madrid: Ediciones Auxilio Social-FET y de las JONS, 1939) – each with a prologue by Mercedes Sanz-Bachiller.

142 Martínez de Bedoya, *Memorias*, p.141; Ridruejo, *Casi unas memorias*, p.79.

143 Mercedes Sanz Bachiller, 'Breves reflexiones', unpublished manuscript (AMSB).

144 Ramón Serrano Suñer, 'Discurso

Doves of War

de Clausura' in *De la victoria,*
pp.90–2; Martínez de Bedoya,
Memorias, pp.142–4.
145 Ramón Serrano Suñer, 'Discurso
de Clausura' in *De la victoria,*
pp.88–9.
146 Guillermo Cabanellas, *La guerra
de los mil días. Nacimiento, vida y
muerte de la II República española* 2
vols (Buenos Aires: Grijalbo,
1973) II p.878; Suárez Fernández,
Crónica, p.121.
147 MSB to Muñoz Grandes, 15
January 1940 (AMSB).
148 MSB to Lorente Sanz, 14 April
1940; Gamero to MSB, 25 April
1940, (AMSB).
149 – MSB-PP; Martínez de
Bedoya, *Memorias,* pp.144–6;
Ridruejo, *Casi unas memorias,*
p.79; Orduña Prada, *El Auxilio
Social,* pp.73–7, 145–6.
150 Orduña Prada, *El Auxilio Social,*
pp.106, 191.
151 Martínez de Bedoya, *Memorias,*
pp.141–2, 151–3, 159.
152 Martínez de Bedoya, *Memorias,*
pp.154, 160–2, 164–6.
153 *The Times,* 25 April 1941.
154 Pereira to Salazar, 7 March 1941,
Pedro Teotónio Pereira,
*Correspondência de Pedro Teotónio
Pereira para Oliveira Salazar, II
(1940–1941)* (Lisbon: Presidência
do Conselho de Ministros, 1989)
pp.226–7.
155 *Arriba,* 3 May 1941.
156 Miguel Primo de Rivera to
Franco, 1 May 1941, *Documentos
inéditos para la Historia del
generalísimo Franco* 2 tomos
(Madrid: Fundación Nacional
Francisco Franco, 1992) II-2,
pp.141–4.
157 Stanley G. Payne, *The Franco
Regime 1936–1975* (Madison,
1987) pp.286–6.
158 *ABC,* 6, 8 May; *El Alcázar,* 6

May; *Arriba,* 10, 11 May; *Boletín
Oficial del Estado,* 10 May 1941.
159 *Arriba,* 21, 22 May 1941;
Martínez de Bedoya, *Memorias,*
pp.170–3; Paul Preston,
*¡Comrades! Portraits from the
Spanish Civil War* (London:
HarperCollins, 1999) pp.130–2.
160 Serrano Suñer, *Memorias,*
pp.200–1.
161 Garriga, *Franco-Serrano Suñer,*
pp.133–4; Payne, *Franco Regime,*
pp.291–3.
162 Martinez de Bedoya, *Memorias,*
p.173.
163 Salvador Merino to Sanz
Bachiller, 3 July 1941, (AMSB);
Martinez de Bedoya, *Memorias,*
pp.174–7.
164 MSB-PP.
165 Martínez de Bedoya, *Memorias,*
pp.199, 215–16.
166 Martínez de Bedoya, *Memorias,*
pp.224–5, 229–32, 240–1, 247.
167 Sanz Orrio to MSB, 26 February
1947; MSB to Sanz Orrio,
undated, (AMSB); MSB-PP.
168 Martínez de Bedoya, *Memorias,*
pp.250–1.
169 MSB-PP; Martínez de Bedoya,
Memorias, pp.267, 279–82, 287,
292–6.
170 Martínez de Bedoya, *Memorias,*
pp.296–302, 315–16, 324–8,
335–6, 343–6.
171 Martínez de Bedoya, *Memorias,*
pp.351–3, 367.
172 *Ya,* 13 October 1967; Rodolfo
Argamentería García to MSB, 13
October 1967 (AMSB).
173 *ABC,* 19 March 1991.
174 Sección Femenina, *Anuario de
1940,* reproduced in Luis Otero,
La Sección Femenina (Madrid:
Editorial EDAF, 1999) p.126.
175 Falange Española Tradicionalista
y de las JONS, *La Sección
Femenina. Historia y Misión*

Notes

(Madrid: Sección Femenina de
FET y de las JONS, 1951)
pp.16–18.

MARGARITA NELKEN
A Full Measure of Pain

1 Francisco Casares, *Azaña y ellos*
(Granada: Editorial y Librería
Prieto, 1938) pp.197–8, 200.
2 Roy Campbell, *Light on a Dark
Horse. An Autobiography 1901–1935*
2nd edition (London: Hollis &
Carter, 1969) p.328.
3 Casares, *Azaña y ellos*, pp.198–9,
200. See also Juan Pujol, 'Cuando
manda Israel' in *ABC* (Sevilla), 20
December 1936; Chilton to Eden,
31 December 1936, PRO
FO371/21/281, W342/1/41.
Pujol's article accuses Indalecio
Prieto of being a Jew 'although he
does not know it' ('*sin saberlo*').
4 Manuel Sánchez del Arco, *El sur
de España en la reconquista de
Madrid (diario de operaciones glosado
por un testigo* 2ª edición (Sevilla:
Editorial Sevillana, 1937) p.80.
5 I recall the lewdly enthusiastic
comments about Margarita
Nelken's physical attractions made
to me in Madrid in 1972 by her
Socialist contemporary Amaro del
Rosal. Similar remarks were made
by Amaro del Rosal to an
American scholar – Shirley
Mangini, *Memories of Resistance:
Women's Voices from The Spanish
Civil War* (New Haven: Yale
University Press, 1995) pp.32. For
the generalised nature of
speculation about Margarita's
sexuality, see Andrés Carabantes &
Eusebio Cimorra, *Un mito llamado
Pasionaria* (Barcelona: Planeta,
1982) p.98.

6 The birth was registered by her
father on 6 July 1894, Expediente
de Margarita Nelken, Archivo del
Congreso de los Diputados, legajo
481, exp.27. See also María Gloria
Núñez Pérez, 'Margarita Nelken:
una apuesta entre la continuidad y
el cambio' in *Las mujeres en la
guerra civil española* (Madrid:
Ministerio de Cultura, 1989)
p.165; Jacobo Israel Garzón
& Javier Mordejai de la Puerta,
'Margarita Nelken, una mujer en
la encrucijada española del siglo
XX' in *Raíces. Revista Judía de
Cultura*, Vol.20, autumn 1994,
p.32; Antonina Rodrigo, *Mujer y
exilio 1939* (Madrid: Compañía
Literaria, 1999) p.35. The
nationality and place and date of
birth of Margarita Nelken are
frequently given erroneously by
scholars. In a short curriculum
vitae that she composed in 1964,
Margarita gave the date correctly
as 5 July 1894, 'Datos biográficos
de Margarita Nelken enviados,
por ella misma, a una alumna de
la Facultad de Leyes de Salamanca
en 1964'. I am grateful to
Margarita Salas de Paúl for
supplying me with a copy of this
document. It is reproduced almost
entirely by Josebe Martínez
Gutiérrez, *Margarita Nelken*
(Madrid: Ediciones del Orto,
1997) pp.15–19. Elsewhere in the
same book, p.8, the author,
incidentally, gives Margarita's date
of birth as 5 July 1896. One
scholar managed, in a single
sentence, to state incorrectly her
name, date and place of birth –
Robert W. Kern, 'Margarita
Nelken: Women and the Crisis of
Spanish Politics' in Jane Slaughter
and Robert Kern, *European Women
on the Left: Socialism, Feminism, and*

the *Problems Faced by Political Women, 1880 to the Present* (Westport, Conn.: Greenwood Press, 1981) p.147.

7 Rodrigo, *Mujer y exilio*, p.36.

8 Rodrigo, *Mujer y exilio*, pp.35–60; Carmen Baroja y Nessi, *Recuerdos de una mujer de la generación del 98* prólogo, edición y notas de Amparo Hurtado (Barcelona: Tusquets Editores, 1998) p.220; Montserrat Alvira, coordinadora, *El exilio español en México 1939–1982* (México DF: Fondo de Cultura Económica, 1982) p.764; Carlos Martínez, *Crónica de una emigración* (México DF: Libro Mex, 1959) p.139.

9 Author's interview with Margarita Salas, 26 July 1999.

10 Author's interview with Enrique de Rivas Ibáñez, 20 September 1999.

11 Margarita Nelken, *Glosario: obras y artistas* (Madrid: Librería Fernando Fé, 1917) p.147.

12 Margarita Nelken, *Presencias y evocaciones* (unpublished essays) Archivo Histórico Nacional, Madrid, Archivo Margarita Nelken) pp.139, 172. See her article on Chicharro in *The Studio*, Vol.57, no.237, 15 December 1912, pp.258–61.

13 See her interview with Artemio Precioso, 'A manera de prólogo' in Margarita Nelken, *La aventura de Roma* (Madrid: La Novela de Hoy, 1923) pp.3–4, Germaine Picard-Moch & Jules Moch, *L'œuvre d'une révolution. L'Espagne républicaine* (Paris: Les Éditions Rieder, 1933) pp.82–3; Antonina Rodrigo, *Mujeres de España (Las silenciadas)* (Barcelona: Plaza y Janés, 1978) pp.160–1; Rosa María Capel Martínez, *El sufragio femenino en la segunda República española* (Madrid: Horas y Horas,

1992) pp.162–3. See also the autobiographical frontispiece in Margarita Nelken, *Goethe* (Madrid: Ediciones Biblos, n.d. [1928]).

14 Interview with Artemio Precioso, Nelken, *La aventura de Roma* p.6.

15 Margarita Nelken, *Glosario: obras y artistas* (Madrid: Libreria Fernando Fé, 1917) pp.7, 159–71.

16 Max Aub, *Diarios (1939–1972)* (Barcelona: Alba Editorial, 1998) pp.409–10.

17 *The Studio*, Vol.84, No.355, 14 October 1922, pp.225–6.

18 Margarita Nelken, *La trampa del arenal* 2ª edición (Madrid: Editorial Castalia, 2000) pp.168–9.

19 Rodrigo, *Mujeres de España (Las silenciadas)*, p.161; Martínez Gutiérrez, *Margarita Nelken*, p.22; Santos Torroella, *Exposición de Esculturas. Julio Antonio (1889–1919)* (Madrid: Dirección General de Bellas Artes. Comisaría de Exposiciones, 1969) p.16.

20 Nelken, *Presencias y evocaciones*, pp.17–18; author's conversations with Margarita Salas.

21 *The Studio*, Vol.84, No.355, 14 October 1922, pp.226–8.

22 Picard-Moch & Moch, *L'œuvre d'une révolution*, pp.82–3; Alvira, *El exilio español*, p.822.

23 Margarita Nelken, *Johann Wolfgang van Goethe* (Madrid: Biblos, [1928]).

24 Margarita Nelken, *La condición social de la mujer en España: su estado actual, un posible desarrollo* (Barcelona: Editorial Minerva, [1919?]); *En torno a nosotras* (Madrid: Páez, 1927); *Maternología y puericultura* (Valencia: Generación Consciente [192?]).

25 Margarita Nelken, *Por qué hicimos la revolución* (Barcelona: Ediciones Sociales Internacionales, 1936).

26 For a lengthy, albeit incomplete,

Notes

list, see Núñez Pérez, 'Margarita Nelken', pp.170–1. See also her own 'Datos biográficos', pp.1–2.

27 Nelken, *Presencias y evocaciones*, pp.7, 16–17, 46, 163, 179, 181; 'Datos biográficos', p.4.

28 Precioso, 'A manera de prólogo', p.7.

29 Nelken, grant application, Archivo de la Secretaría de la Junta para Ampliación de Estudios e Investigaciones Científicas (1907–1939), Residencia de Estudiantes (Madrid).

30 Picard-Moch & Moch, *L'œuvre d'une révolution*, p.83; Rodrigo, *Mujeres de España (Las silenciadas)*, p.163; Garzón & De la Puerta, 'Margarita Nelken', p.34; Capel Martínez, *El sufragio femenino* p.164.

31 Nelken, *La condición social de la mujer*, pp.160–9.

32 Nelken, *La condición social de la mujer*, p.157.

33 Interviews with Margarita Nelken in Precioso, 'A manera de prólogo', pp.6–7 and in Picard-Moch & Moch, *L'œuvre d'une révolution*, p.82; Margarita Nelken 'Datos biográficos', p.1; '*El Orden*' in Gonzalo Santonja, editor, *Las novelas rojas* (Madrid: Ediciones de la Torre, 1994) p.358. See also María Aurelia Capmany, 'Un libro polémico sin polémica' prólogo a Margarita Nelken, *La condición social de la mujer en España* 2ª edición (Madrid: CVS Ediciones, 1975) p.22; Rodrigo, *Mujeres de España (Las silenciadas)*, p.162.

34 Precioso, 'A manera de prólogo', pp.3, 5.

35 Nelken, *La condición social de la mujer*, pp.135–54. See also Geraldine Scanlon, *La polémica feminista en la España contemporánea 1868–1974* (Madrid: Akal, 1986)

pp.78–9, 91, 99–101, 116, 120–1.

36 Nelken, *La condición social de la mujer*, pp.132, 126–7

37 Irene Falcón, *Asalto a los cielos. Mi vida junto a Pasionaria* (Madrid: Temas de Hoy, 1996) pp.47–8.

38 Margarita Nelken, *La mujer ante las Cortes Constituyentes* (Madrid: Editorial Castro, 1931) p.99.

39 Nelken, *La trampa*, p.197; conversations with Margarita Salas.

40 Author's interview with Margarita Salas, 26 July 1999. Aub, *Diarios (1939–1972)*, p.410, wrote 'Se tuvo que divorciar'.

41 Esperanza García Méndez, *La actuación de la mujer en las Cortes de la II República* (Madrid: Ministerio de Cultura, 1979) p.37.

42 Nelken, Margarita, *La aventura de Roma* (Madrid: La Novela de Hoy, 1923); *Una historia de adulterio: una novela inédita* (Madrid: La Novela Corta/Prensa Popular, 1924); *Mi suicidio: novela inédita* (Madrid: La Novela Corta/Prensa Popular, 1924); *El milagro* (Madrid: Los contemporáneos, 1924).

43 Shirley Mangini, *Las modernas de Madrid. Las grandes intelectuales de la vanguardia* (Barcelona: Ediciones Península, 2001) pp.88–92; Shirley Mangini, *Memories of Resistance: Women's Voices from The Spanish Civil War* (New Haven: Yale University Press, 1995) pp.6–7; María Teresa León, *Memoria de la melancolía* (Buenos Aires: Losada, 1970) p.311.

44 Baroja, *Recuerdos de una mujer*, pp.104–5.

45 Margarita Nelken, *Tres tipos de Vírgenes* (Madrid: Cuadernos Literarios, 1929) pp.7–8, 78–9.

46 Margarita Nelken, *Las escritoras españolas* (Barcelona: Editorial Labor, 1930) pp.10, 83–114.

47 This is the message of her book

En torno a nosotras. See also Nelken, *La mujer ante las Cortes Constituyentes*, p.6.

48 Archivo de la Secretaria de la Junta para Ampliacion de Estudios e Investigaciones Cientificas (1907–1939), Residencia de Estudiantes (Madrid); Artemio Precioso, 'A manera de prólogo' in Margarita Nelken, *La aventura de Roma* (Madrid: La Novela de Hoy, 1923) pp.3–5; *The Studio*, Vol.78, no.320, 15 November 1919, pp.81–5.

49 Federica Montseny, interview in 1978 with Antonina Rodrigo, Rodrigo, *Mujeres en España*, p.170.

50 Aurora Arnaiz, *Retrato hablado de Luisa Julián* (Madrid: Compañía Literaria, 1996) p.74.

51 Mangini, *Memories of Resistance*, pp.30–1.

52 Nelken, *Presencias y evocaciones*, pp.121, 126.

53 Miguel Utrillo Jr, 'Hablando con Margarita Nelken', *La Calle*, 27 November 1931; Esperanza García Méndez, *La actuación de la mujer en las Cortes de la II República* (Madrid: Ministerio de Cultura, 1979) p.83.

54 Interview with Margarita Nelken, *Heraldo de Madrid*, 27 November 1931.

55 Conversation with Margarita Salas.

56 Fernando Claudín, *Santiago Carrillo. Crónica de un secretario general* (Barcelona: Planeta, 1983) pp.13–14; Núñez Pérez, 'Margarita Nelken', p.171, n.20bis.

57 For the circumstances of her selection, the reactions within the Socialist Party and the mistaken views about her marriage and her acquisition of Spanish nationality, see Vidarte, *Las Cortes Constituyentes*, pp.83–5.

58 Junta Central del Censo electoral de Badajoz, 8 October 1931; Declaración de Margarita Nelken al Presidente de la comisión de Actas, 12 November 1931, Archivo del Congreso de los Diputados, exp. Margarita Nelken legajo 481, exp.27; Diario de sesiones de las Cortes Constituyentes de la República española, comenzaron el 14 de julio de 1931, 12 November 1931.

59 Juan Simeón Vidarte, *Las Cortes Constituyentes de 1931–1933* (Barcelona: Grijalbo, 1976) pp.84–5, 109.

60 Picard-Moch & Moch, *L'œuvre d'une révolution*, p.84.

61 Author's interview with Margarita Salas, 26 July 1999. See also Garzón & De la Puerta, 'Margarita Nelken', p.35.

62 *Excelsior* (Mexico City), 18, 19 June 1947.

63 José Luis Gutiérrez Casalá, *La segunda República en Badajoz* (Badajoz: Universitas Editorial, 1998) pp.114–19; Rafael Salazar Alonso, *Bajo el signo de la revolucón* (Madrid: Librería de San Martin, 1935) p.221.

64 Archivo del Congreso de los Diputados, exp. Margarita Nelken legajo 481, exp.27. See also Concha Muñoz Tinoco, *Diego Hidalgo, un notario republicano*, (Badajoz: Diputación Provincial, 1986) pp.49–51.

65 María Martínez Sierra, *Una mujer por caminos de España* 2ª edición (Madrid: Castalia, 1989) pp.219–21.

66 Nelken, *La mujer ante las Cortes Constituyentes*, pp.22–36.

67 Clara Campoamor, *El voto femenino y yo* 2ª edición (Barcelona: Edicions de les Dones, 1981) pp.220–2; Concha Fagoaga, & Paloma Saavedra, *Clara*

Notes

Campoamor. La sufragista española 2ª edición (Madrid: Instituto de la Mujer, 1986) pp.90–121.

68 Her interest in the Badajoz situation was apparent in a correspondence with Besteiro – Nelken to Besteiro, 11 June 1932, FPI, AJB-201–53. Her passionate concern for the problems of the landless peasantry is evident in Margarita Nelken, *Las torres del Kremlin* (México DF: Industrial y Distribuidora, 1943) pp.258 ff.

69 Gabriel Morón, *El fracaso de una revolución* (Madrid: Gráfica Socialista, 1935) p.81.

70 Manuel Albar, 'Sobre unos sucesos. El verdadero culpable', *El Socialista*, 2 January 1932. For a description of Castilblanco, see Vidarte, *Las Cortes Constituyentes*, pp.308–9.

71 Jesús Vicente Chamorro, *Año nuevo, año viejo en Castilblanco* (Madrid: Ediciones Albia, 1985) p.80.

72 *ABC*, 1, 2, 3, 5 January; *El Debate*, 2 January 1932. The accusation was repeated for many years thereafter. See, for example, George Hills, *Franco The Man and his Nation* (New York: The Macmillan company, 1967) p.179.

73 Morón, *El fracaso*, pp.97–8; Vidarte, *Las Cortes Constituyentes*, pp.296–7; Chamorro, *Año nuevo*, pp.117, 183.

74 *Diario de Sesiones de las Cortes Constituyentes*, 5 January 1932, p.291.

75 *Diario de Sesiones de las Cortes Constituyentes*, 5 January 1932; Vidarte, *Las Cortes Constituyentes*, pp.297–304; Muñoz Tinoco, *Diego Hidalgo*, pp.54–5; Nelken, *Por qué hicimos la revolución*, pp.62–3.

76 Manuel Azaña, *Obras completas* 4 vols (México DF: Ediciones Oasis, 1966–1968) IV, pp.295–6.

77 On Azaña's attitude to women, see María Gloria Núñez Pérez, 'Sentimiento y razón: las mujeres en la vida de Azaña', in Alicia Alted, Ángeles Egido y Maria Fernanda Mancebo eds, *Manuel Azaña: pensamiento y acción* (Madrid: Alianza, 1996) pp.167–195.

78 Manuel Azaña, *Diarios, 1932–1933. 'Los cuadernos robados'* (Barcelona: Crítica, 1997) p.193.

79 Vidarte, *Las Cortes Constituyentes*, p.308.

80 Regina García, *Yo he sido marxista. El cómo y el porqué de una conversión* (Madrid: Editora Nacional, 1952) pp.95–6. For a list of the thirteen villages in the province of Badajoz where Nelken made speeches, see Federación Nacional de Trabajadores de la Tierra, *Memoria que presenta el Comité Nacional de este organismo al examen y discusión del Congreso ordinario que ha de celebrarse en Madrid durante los días 17 y siguientes del mes de septiembre de 1932* (Madrid: Gráfica Socialista, 1932) pp.53–5.

81 *El Socialista*, 6 January; *La Rioja*, 6, 8, 9, 10, 12 January 1932; Edward E. Malefakis, *Agrarian Reform and Peasant Revolution in Spain: Origins of the Civil War* (New Haven: Yale University Press, 1970) pp.310–11.

82 *El Socialista*, 24, 26 December 1931, 31 January 1932. The accusations and her declarations in FC-Tribunal Supremo – Recursos, Legajo 85, 1906/932, Legajo 89, 6/933, Archivo Histórico Nacional, Madrid.

83 Morón, *El fracaso*, p.128.

84 Lázaro Somoza Silva, *El general Miaja (biografía de un heroe)*

Doves of War

(México DF: Editorial Tyris, 1944) p.169.

85 'Memoria sobre la gestión de la Comisión Ejecutiva del Partido Socialista desde el último Congreso hasta la fecha', FPI, AH-19–18, p.8; *El Socialista*, 5 February, 18, 31 May 1932; Núñez Pérez, 'Margarita Nelken', p.168.

86 Gutiérrez Casalá, *La segunda República en Badajoz*, pp.140–71.

87 *Diario de sesiones de las Cortes Constituyentes*, 20, 21 October 1932, 10 January 1934; Nelken, *Por qué hicimos la revolución*, pp.60–2.

88 *Diario de Sesiones de las Cortes Constituyentes*, 1 April, 20 October 1920; *El Debate*, 2 April, 21 October 1932.

89 Casares, *Azaña y ellos*, p.199. For another example of right-wing ridicule, see Antonio Pérez de Olaguer, Antonio, *El terror rojo en Andalucía* (Burgos: Ediciones Antisectarias, 1938) p.41.

90 Conversation of the author with Santiago Carrillo, 21.02.00.

91 *El Sol*, 11 March 1933.

92 'En la Casa del Pueblo,' *El Socialista*, 28 October 1933.

93 Nelken, *Por qué hicimos la revolución*, p.69.

94 *El Socialista*, 28, 30 October 1933: Gutiérrez Casalá, *La segunda República en Badajoz*, pp.153,169, 187, 190.

95 Nelken to Pi Sunyer, 21 November 1933, Arxiu Carles Pi Sunyer, Barcelona.

96 Margarita Nelken, 'Las Actas de Badajoz: Con el fango hasta la boca', *El Socialista*, 30 November 1933; Nelken, *Por qué hicimos la revolución*, pp.69–70; Juan-Simón Vidarte, *El bienio negro y la insurrección de Asturias* (Barcelona:

Grijalbo, 1978) pp.151–2; Gutiérrez Casalá, *La segunda República en Badajoz*, pp.193–9.

97 *El Socialista*, 18 May 1932.

98 Nelken, 'Con el fango hasta la boca', *El Socialista*, 30 November 1933.

99 *Diario de las sesiones de Cortes, Congreso de los Diputados, comenzaron el 8 de diciembre de 1933 (DSC)* 25 January 1934.

100 Margarita Nelken, 'Para que la tierra se entere', *El Obrero de la Tierra*, 24 March 1934; FC-Tribunal Supremo – Recursos, Legajo 99, 259, AHN, Madrid.

101 Nelken, *Por qué hicimos la revolución*, pp.114–15. See the encounters between Margarita Nelken and Salazar Alonso, *DSC*, 25 January, 6 February 1934.

102 *SOE*, Año I, no.1, May 1934; FC-Tribunal Supremo – Recursos, Legajo 97, 163, AHN, Madrid.

103 Francisco Largo Caballero, *Mis recuerdos. Cartas a un amigo* (México D.F.: Editores Unidos, 1954) p.224.

104 Arrarás, *HSRE*, IV, p.162; Luis Romero, *Por qué y cómo mataron a Calvo Sotelo* (Barcelona: Planeta, 1982) p.61. See also Víctor Alba, *El Partido Comunista en España* (Barcelona: Planeta, 1979) p.142, where it is alleged that she was working on behalf of the PCE within the PSOE from 1933.

105 Paul Preston, *The Coming of the Spanish Civil War: Reform Reaction and Revolution in the Second Spanish Republic 1931–1936* 2nd edition (London, Routledge, 1994) pp.148–53.

106 Salazar Alonso, *Bajo el signo*, p.153.

107 *DSC*, 7 June 1934.

Notes

108 Margarita Nelken, 'Para la España obrera y campesina. Cuando se dice que no pasa nada', in *El Socialista*, 27, 28, 29, 30 June 1934.

109 FC-Tribunal Supremo – Recursos, Legajo 109, 266, Legajo 112, 428, AHN, Madrid.

110 Guillermo Cabanellas, *La guerra de los mil días* 2 vols (Buenos Aires: Grijalbo, 1973) I, p.254; Nelken, *Por qué hicimos la revolución*, pp.118–19; David Jato, *La rebelión de los estudiantes (Apuntes para una Historia del alegre SEU)* (Madrid: CIES, 1953) p.109; Stanley G. Payne, *Falange. A History of Spanish Fascism* (Stanford: Stanford University Press, 1967) pp.57–8.

111 FC-Tribunal Supremo – Recursos, Legajo 97, 163, Archivo Histórico Nacional, Madrid.

112 Nelken, *Por qué hicimos la revolución*, p.120.

113 Although retrospective, her enthusiasm can be deduced from Nelken, *Por qué hicimos la revolución*, p.122. It is all the more striking coming, as it does, after the failure of armed insurrection in October 1934 and the subsequent repression.

114 Amaro del Rosal, *1934: el movimiento revolucionario de octubre* (Madrid: Akal, 1983) pp.207–9; Manuel Tagüeña Lacorte, *Téstimonio de dos guerras* (México DF: Ediciones Oasis, 1973) pp.61–6; Santos Juliá Díaz, *Historia del socialismo español (1931–1939)* (Barcelona: Conjunto Editorial, 1989) pp.105–6.

115 Preston, *The Coming of the Spanish Civil War*, pp.139, 166–8.

116 *El Socialista*, 27 September 1934; FC-Tribunal Supremo –

Recursos, Legajo 112, 413, AHN, Madrid.

117 Segundo Serrano Poncela, *El Partido Socialista y la conquista del poder* (Barcelona: Ediciones L'Hora, 1935) pp.122–7.

118 Rosal, *1934*, pp.217–18; Arrarás, *HSRE*, II, p.459. With the exception of Condés, efforts to subvert the Civil Guard came to little, Nelken, *Por qué hicimos la revolución*, p.142.

119 FC-Tribunal Supremo – Recursos, Legajo 132, 28, AHN, Madrid.

120 Henry Buckley, *Life and Death of the Spanish Republic* (London: Hamish Hamilton, 1940) p.149; Nelken, *Presencias y evocaciones*, pp.54, 60–1, 74–5, 100, 110; 'Datos biográficos', pp.2–3; author's conversations with Margarita Salas; José Ruiz-Castillo Basala, *Funcionario republicano de reforma agraria y otros testimonios* (Madrid: Biblioteca Nueva, 1983) p.114: Santos Juliá Díaz, *Historia del socialismo español (1931–1939)* (Barcelona: Conjunto Editorial, 1989) p.352.

121 Alsing to Adler, 7 March; Nelken to CE del PSOE, 1 April; Vidarte to Adler, 9 April 1935, FPI, AH-73-38.

122 Nelken, *Presencias y evocaciones*, pp.74–5, 100, 110; 'Datos biográficos', p.3.

123 Eduardo Comín Colomer, *Historia del Partido Comunista de España* 3 vols (Madrid: Editora Nacional, 1967) II, pp.474–8.

124 Margarita Nelken, 'A los Trabajadores Socialistas de la Provincia de Badajoz', Archivo del Partido Comunista de España, Caja 132, carpeta 13; *Frente Rojo*, No.7, July 1935.

125 Nelken, *Por qué hicimos la*

Doves of War

revolución, pp.129–140; Preston,
*The Coming of the Spanish Civil
War*, pp.124–43, 155–6, 162–3.

126 Grandizo Munis, *Jalones de
derrota, promesa de victoria* (México
DF: Editorial Lucha Obrera,
1948) pp.130–40; Joaquín
Maurín, *Hacia la segunda
revolución: el fracaso de la República
y la insurrección de octubre*
(Barcelona: Ediciones Alfa, 1935)
pp.144–67; testimony of Madrid
CNT secretary, Miguel González
Inestal, to the author, January
1970; Enrique Castro Delgado,
Hombres made in Moscú
(Barcelona: Luis de Caralt, 1965)
pp.176–83; Andrés Nin, *Los
problemas de la revolución española*
(Paris: Ruedo Ibérico, 1971)
pp.156–7; Santos Juliá Díaz,
'Fracaso de una insurrección y
derrota de una huelga: los hechos
de octubre en Madrid', *Estudios
de Historia Social*, No.31,
October-December 1984; Santos
Juliá, *Historia del socialismo español
(1931–1939)* (Barcelona: Conjunto
Editorial, 1989) pp.126–9.

127 Nelken, *Por qué hicimos la
revolución*, pp.140–4.

128 Nelken, *Por qué hicimos la
revolución*, p.142. The prologue to
the book is dated September
1935.

129 Nelken, *Por qué hicimos la
revolución*, pp.143–8.

130 Carlos Hernández Zancajo,
Octubre – segunda etapa (Madrid:
Editorial Renovación, 1935).

131 Nelken, *Por qué hicimos la
revolución*, p.147.

132 Nelken, *Por qué hicimos la
revolución*, p.267–70.

133 This led, at their Fourth
Congress, to the Juventudes
Socialistas de Valencia declaring
their 'incompatibility' with

Gorkín. Andrew Charles Durgan,
*B.O.C. 1930–1936. El Bloque
Obrero y Campesino* (Barcelona:
Editorial Laertes, 1996) p.324;
Víctor Alba, *El marxismo en
España (1919–1939)* 2 vols
(México DF: 1973) I, pp.226–7.

134 Juan-Simeón Vidarte, *Todos
fuimos culpables* (Mexico DF:
Fondo de Cultura Económica,
1973) pp.38–9; Agrupación
Socialista de Badajoz to
Comisión Ejecutiva del PSOE,
undated, FPI AH-61–20; *El
Socialista*, 17, 28 May 1936;
Gutiérrez Casalá, *La segunda
República en Badajoz*, p.190,
mistakenly attributes this incident
to November 1933.

135 Articles in *La Libertad* (January
1936) – Cf.Arrarás, *HRSE*, IV,
p.213; 'Cómo se vive en la
Unión Soviótica. El
funcionamiento de un koljós',
Claridad, 16 May 1936.

136 *El Socialista*, 26 March 1936.

137 Author's interview with
Margarita Salas, 26 July 1999. See
also Garzón & De la Puerta,
'Margarita Nelken', p.37.

138 *El Socialista*, 26 March; *Claridad*,
19 May 1936.

139 Indalecio Prieto, *Palabras al viento*
2nd ed. (México DF: Ediciones
Oasis, 1969) pp.128–130.

140 Ian Gibson, *La noche en que
mataron a Calvo Sotelo* (Barcelona:
Argos Vergara, 1982) pp.104,
117, 151. For the allegation that
Margarita and Condés were
lovers, see George Hills, *The
Battle for Madrid* (London:
Vantage Books, 1976) p.35; Hills,
Franco, p.228; Arrarás, *HSRE*,
IV, pp.348, 360; Carabantes &
Cimorra, *Un mito*, p.98.

141 For the funeral oration, *Claridad*,
31 July 1936; David Jato

Notes

Miranda, *Madrid, capital republicana* (Barcelona: Ediciones Acervo, 1976) p.244. For her later comment, Nelken, *Las torres del Kremlin*, p.258. For the photograph, author's interview with Margarita Salas.

142 According to Margarita Nelken in an interview with Burnett Bolloten in 1939, Burnett Bolloten, *The Grand Camouflage. The Spanish Civil War and Revolution, 1936–39* (London: Pall Mall, 1968) p.29.

143 Luis Romero, *Tres días de julio* 2ª edición (Barcelona: Ariel, 1968) pp.202, 222.

144 Margarita Nelken, *La epopeya campesina. Texto íntegro del discurso pronunciado ante el micrófono del Ministerio de la Guerra, el día 27 de agosto de 1936* (Madrid: Aldus, 1936) p.10. (This pamphlet does not contain page numbers. Those given here simply follow the sequence of printed pages.)

145 Luis Roldán Rodríguez, *Militares de la República. Su segunda guerra civil* (Madrid: Ediciones Vosa, 2000) p.28; Mauro Bajatierra, *La guerra en las trincheras de Madrid* (Barcelona: Ediciones Tierra y Libertad, 1937) pp.58–60.

146 Nelken, *Las torres del Kremlin*, p 261; Sánchez del Arco, *El sur de España*, pp.78–80.

147 Nelken, *La epopeya campesina*, pp.1–3.

148 Nelken, *La epopeya campesina*, pp.6–7, 9–10.

149 *Milicia Popular*, No.15, 12 August 1936; Nelken to Enrique Líster, 7 July 1967, AHNMN, legajo 3238–65.

150 On the air-raid, see Gerald Howson, *Arms for Spain. The Untold Story of the Spanish Civil War* (London: John Murray,

1998) p.98. On Margarita Nelken's reaction, see Aurora Arnaiz, *Retrato hablado de Luisa Julián* (Madrid: Compañía Literaria, 1996) p.40.

151 Nelken, *La epopeya campesina*, pp.8–9; Frank Jellinek, *The Civil War in Spain* (London: Left Book Club, 1938) p.426.

152 Cecil D. Eby, *The Siege of the Alcázar* (London: The Bodley Head, 1966) pp.110–11; Peter Wyden, *The Passionate War. The Narrative History of the Spanish Civil War* (New York: Simon and Schuster, 1983) p.124; Ángel Palomino, *Defensa del Alcázar. Un epopeya de nuestro tiempo* (Barcelona: Editorial Planeta, 1998) pp.146, 178. Palomino is under the impression that Margarita Nelken was a minister.

153 Rafael Casas de la Vega, *El Alcázar* (Madrid: G. del Toro, 1976) pp.221, 259; Isabelo Herreros, *Mitología de la Cruzada de Franco: El Alcázar de Toledo* (Madrid: Ediciones Vosa, 1995) pp.54–5.

154 Nelken, *Presencias y evocaciones*, pp.67–76; Professor Holman Hamilton, University of Kentucky to Margarita Nelken, 6 February, Nelken to Hamilton, 10 February 1966, (Archivo Histórico Nacional, Archivo Margarita Nelken, [henceforth AHNMN] legajo 3237–2).

155 Pietro Nenni, *La guerra de España* (México D.F.: Ediciones Era, 1964) p.108; Margarita Nelken, 'El doctor astracán', *Mundo Obrero*, 12 February 1937; Jato, *Madrid*, pp.310, 333, 400–1, 432, 512, 520.

156 Margarita Nelken, 'Defensa de Madrid', *España Popular* (México D.F.), 9 November 1940.

157 Jato, *Madrid*, p.655; Rafael Casas de la Vega, *El terror: Madrid 1936. Investigación histórica y catálogo de víctimas identificadas* (Madrid: Editorial Fénix, 1994) pp.175, 193–4, 206, 234; Carlos Fernández, *Paracuellos del Jarama: ¿Carrillo culpable?* (Barcelona: Argos Vergara, 1983) p.102.

158 *Mundo Obrero*, 10 November 1936.

159 Santiago Carrillo, *Memorias* (Barcelona: Planeta, 1993) p.213; Nelken, *Presencias y evocaciones*, pp.42, 50–1. Numerous conversations of the author with Santiago Carrillo.

160 Antonio López Fernández, *Defensa de Madrid. Relato histórico* (México DF: Editorial A. P. Márquez, 1945) pp.114–15, 134.

161 Somoza Silva, *El general Miaja*, pp.168–9.

162 Antonio López Fernández, *Defensa de Madrid. Relato histórico* (México DF: Editorial A. P. Márquez, 1945) pp.114–15; Robert Colodny, *The Struggle for Madrid. The Central Epic of the Spanish Conflict 1936–1937* (New York: Payne-Whitman Publishers, 1958) p.53.

163 *Milicia Popular*, No.102, 17 November 1936. See also López Fernández, *Defensa de Madrid*, pp.177–8.

164 Carmen Alcalde, *Federica Montseny. Palabra en rojo y negro* (Barcelona: Argos Vergara, 1983) p.62.

165 Cf. Kern, 'Margarita Nelken', p.154.

166 Federica Montseny, interview in 1978 with Antonina Rodrigo, Rodrigo, *Mujeres en España*, p.170; Agustí Pons, *Converses amb Frederica Montseny* (Barcelona: Editorial Laia, 1977) pp.162.

167 'She visited us at the paper, a building she had not deigned to visit for some months, considering it not worthy of her revolutionary stance' – Julian Zugazagoitia, *Guerra y vicisitudes de los españoles* 2nd ed., 2 vols (Paris: Librería Española, 1968) I, p.186.

168 Zugazagoitia, *Guerra y vicisitudes*, I, pp.186–7; Carrillo, *Memorias*, p.213.

169 Zugazagoitia, *Guerra y vicisitudes*, I, p.187.

170 Burnett Bolloten, *The Spanish Civil War: Revolution and Counterrevolution* (Hemel Hempstead: Harvester Wheatsheaf, 1991) p.786, n.29.

171 Antonio Elorza & Marta Bizcarrondo, *Queridos Camaradas. La Internacional Comunista y España, 1919–1939* (Barcelona: Planeta, 1999) pp.338–9.

172 Zugazagoitia, *Guerra y vicisitudes*, I, p.188.

173 Nelken, *Las torres del Kremlin*, p.47, where she locates the bombing in Leganés when it was more probably Getafe. She also suggests wrongly that Ogilvie Forbes was immediately transferred out of Spain because of writing a report denouncing the Axis bombing of Madrid. Ogilvie Forbes was the British Chargé d'Affaires from 10 August 1936 until April 1937. In early January 1937, he was ordered to move the Embassy to Valencia. Jill Edwards, *The British Government and the Spanish Civil War, 1936–1939* (London: Macmillan, 1979) pp.8, 182; Julio Alvarez del Vayo, *Freedom's Battle* (London: Heinemann, 1940) pp.231–2.

174 *Mundo Obrero*, 24, 26 November

Notes

1936; *Milicia Popular*, No.112, 27 November 1936.

175 Buckley, *Life and Death*, p.268.

176 *Milicia Popular*, No.119, 4 December 1936.

177 Nelken, *Las torres del Kremlin*, pp.159, 275–7.

178 Federica Montseny, *Mis primeros cuarenta años* (Barcelona: Plaza y Janés, 1987) p.107; Carabantes & Cimorra, *Un mito*, p.149.

179 Margarita Nelken, *Niños de hoy, hombres de mañana* (Madrid: Ediciones SRI, n.d. [1937]) (unpaginated but pp.1–2 of text).

180 Margarita Nelken, 'In memoriam', *Mundo Obrero*, 13 January 1937.

181 Margarita Nelken, 'Para una compañera', *Mundo Obrero*, 15 January 1937.

182 Margarita Nelken, *Mundo Obrero*, 18 January 1937.

183 Nelken to Director de la Escuela '16, Moscow, 23 February 1946, AHNMN, legajo 3235–153; Nelken to Líster, 7 July 1967, AHNMN, legajo 3238–65.

184 Nelken, *Las torres del Kremlin*, p.245; author's interviews with Margarita Salas de Paúl, 26 July 1999, 17 March 2001.

185 Margarita Nelken, *La mujer en la URSS y en la constitución soviética* (Valencia: Publicaciones de los Amigos de la US, 1938) pp.7–8, 14.

186 Author's conversations with Irene Falcón, 9 May 1999. See also Falcón, *Asalto*, pp.154, 156.

187 Author's conversations with Irene Falcón, 9 May 1999.

188 Matilde de la Torre, Apuntes, 'Cortes en la Lonja de la Seda', 30 September 1937, FPI AH-ARLF-LXII.

189 Azaña, *Obras*, IV, p.786.

190 Azaña, *Obras*, IV, pp.733, 786;

Alba, *El Partido Comunista*, p.241. For a savagely hostile account of her demagogy, see Blanca Lydia Trejo, *Lo que vi en España* (México DF: Editorial Polis, 1940) pp.67–9.

191 Nelken, *Presencias y evocaciones*, p.115; Nelken, 'Datos biográficos' p.3; Rafael Abella, *Finales de enero, 1939. Barcelona cambia de piel* (Barcelona: Planeta, 1992) p.78.

192 Nelken to Director de la Escuela 16, AHNMN, legajo 3235–153.

193 Nelken to Líster, 7 July 1967, AHNMN, legajo 3238–65.

194 Nelken to Casals, 31 December 1951, (Fundació Pau Casals, Fons Pau Casals, 04.01 Corresponden-cia rebuda: Margarita Nelken (1948–1955), 13 unitab u.i.122); Nelken, *Presencias y evocaciones*, pp.30–2.

195 See Pike, *Vae victis*, pp.213–14; *Testimonio de dos guerras*, pp.300–1; Juan Modesto, *Soy del quinto regimiento (Notas de la guerra española)* (Paris: Colección Ebro, 1969) pp.273–5; Santiago Álvarez, *Memorias III La lucha continúa . . . El exilio. La 2ª Guerra Mundial. El regreso clandestino a España. (1939–1945)* (La Coruna: Ediciós do Castro, 1988) p.26; *Memorias V La larga marcha de una lucha sin cuartel (1954–1972)* (La Coruña: Ediciós do Castro, 1994) pp.105–6.

196 Nelken, *Presencias y evocaciones*, pp.139, 144, 163.

197 This situation can be deduced from correspondence concerning the fact that, on leaving Amsterdam, Martín had presented his household effects (which legitimately belonged to his wife) to Josefina. (Althoff to Nelken 12 April, Nelken to

Althoff, 19 April 1949,
AHNMN, legajo 3233–78).

198 Author's interview with
Margarita Salas, 26 July 1999.
Aub, *Diarios (1939–1972)*, p.410,
wrote 'Se tuvo que divorciar'.

199 Alvira, *El exilio español*, pp.469,
491, 822; Martínez, *Crónica*,
pp.104, 127.

200 Nelken, *Presencias y evocaciones*,
p.144.

201 Tribunal especial para la
represión de la masonería y el
comunismo: Juzgado Especial
no.2 año 1941, sumario no.83,
no.207 contra Margarita Nelken
de Paúl, Archivo General de
Salamanca, Legajo 19, expediente
13.

202 Bobadilla to Nelken, 1 June
1941, AHNMN, legajo
3234–136.

203 Bobadilla to Nelken, 1 June
1941, AHNMN, legajo
3234–132.

204 'Marta', Informe sobre el Trabajo
y la situación de la Dirección del
Partido Comunista de España en
México, 3 December 1941,
Archivo del Comité Central del
Partido Comunista de España,
Caja 102, Carpeta 6.5. Aub,
Diarios (1939–1972), p.410;
Arnaiz, *Retrato hablado*, pp.258–9.

205 *España Popular*, 23 October 1942;
Gregorio Morán, *Miseria y
grandeza del Partido Comunista de
España 1939–1985* (Barcelona:
Planeta, 1986) p.67; David
Wingeate Pike, *In the Service of
Stalin. The Spanish Communists in
Exile 1939–1945* (Oxford:
Clarendon Press, 1993) pp.153,
335–6; Manuel Vázquez
Montalbán, *Pasionaria y los siete
enanitos* (Barcelona: Planeta,
1995) p.131.

206 Jesús Hernández, *En el país de la*

gran mentira 2ª edición (Madrid:
G.del Toro, 1974) pp.177–82;
Martínez Gutiérrez, *Margarita
Nelken*, pp.42–3.

207 Aub, *Diarios (1939–1972)*,
pp.170–1, 410, 487.
Conversation of the author with
José Bergamín in Madrid, 1977.

208 Santiago de Paúl to Nelken, 24
June 1943, AHNMN, legajo
3249–31.

209 Patronato Pro-Presos de Franco,
*Denunciar el terror franquista es
ayudar a la lucha de las democracias*
(México DF: Ediciones
Patronato Pro-Presos de Franco,
1942) pp.3, 5, 9. Arnaiz, *Retrato
hablado*, p.260.

210 Nelken, *Las torres del Kremlin*,
pp.14–15.

211 Nelken, *Las torres del Kremlin*,
pp.18–26, 30–1.

212 Nelken, *Las torres del Kremlin*,
pp.33, 37–68.

213 Her indignation at French and
German anti-semitism is evident,
Nelken, *Las torres del Kremlin*,
pp.191–217; her sense that her
son is fighting in a just war,
p.245.

214 National Security Agency: Radio
transmission from KGB residence
in Mexico City to Moscow, 31
March 1944, Venona Project
Documents, Ref: 3/NBF/T712.

215 Gorkín, *Les communistes*, p.197;
Arnaiz, *Retrato hablado*,
pp.259–60; Luis Mercader &
Germán Sánchez, *Ramón Mercader
mi hermano* (Madrid: Espasa-
Calpe, 1990) pp.92, 97. See letter
of Ramón Mercader to his
brother, Luis, written in 1955,
ibid., p.268.

216 Manuel Tagüeña Lacorte,
Testimonio de dos guerras (México
DF: Ediciones Oasis, 1973)
p.488. Antonio Vilanova, *Los*

Notes

olvidados (Paris: Ruedo Ibérico,
197) pp.496–7; Daniel Arasa, *Los
españoles de Stalin* (Barcelona:
Editorial Vorágine, 1993)
pp.348–9.

217 Margarita Nelken, *Primer frente*
(México DF: Angel Chapero,
1944); Nelken, *Presencias y
evocaciones*, p.29.

218 National Security Agency: Fitkin
to KGB residence in Mexico
City, 8 August 1945, Venona
Project Documents, Ref: 3/
NBF/T851.

219 Morán, *Miseria y grandeza*, p.154.
See Bobadilla (Moscow) to
Nelken, 20 September 1945,
AHNMN, legajo3234–134.

220 AHNMN, legajo 3233–207.

221 Nelken to Casals, 18 January
1948, Fundacio Pau Casals, Fons
Pau Casals, 04.01 Corresponden-
cia rebuda: Margarita Nelken
(1948–1955), 13 unitab u.i.122
(henceforth FPC).

222 Nelken to President of Soviet of
Mitrofanovka, 23 February 1946,
AHNMN, legajo 3240–109;
Bobadilla (Moscow) to Nelken,
23 May 1946, AHNMN, legajo
3234–135.

223 Nelken to Casals, 18 January
1948, FPC.

224 Nelken to Casals, 19 October
1951, FPC.

225 Althoff (Amsterdam) to Nelken,
12 April 1949, AHNMN, legajo
3233–78.

226 Nelken to Althoff, 19 April 1949,
AHNMN, legajo 3233–79.

227 Nelken to Althoff, 19 April 1949,
AHNMN, legajo 3233–79,
Santiago de Paúl to Nelken, 9
June 1940, 30 February 1941, 24
June 1943, AHNMN, legajo
3240–19, 20, 31.

228 Nelken to Casals, 31 December
1951, FPC.

229 Nelken to Jiménez Asúa, 21
December 1952, FPI, ALJA-
418–7.

230 Víctor Alba, *Sísifo y su tiempo.
Memorias de un cabreado
(1916–1996)* (Barcelona: Laertes,
1996) pp.290–1.

231 José del Barrio to Nelken, 27
March 1950, AHNMN, legajo
3233–240.

232 Nelken to Hernández, 4 July
1950, AHNMN, legajo 3237–78.

233 Julián Gorkín, *Les communistes
contre la révolution espagnole* (Paris:
Pierre Belfond, 1978) pp.196–7.

234 Gorkín, *Les communistes*,
pp.16–18; Herbert Rutledge
Southworth, ' "The Grand
Camouflage": Julián Gorkín,
Burnett Bolloten and the Spanish
Civil War' in Paul Preston &
Ann L. Mackenzie, editors, *The
Republic Besieged. Civil War in
Spain 1936–1939* (Edinburgh:
Edinburgh University Press,
1996) pp.261–310.

235 Nelken to Líster, 7 July 1967,
AHNMN, legajo 3238–65.

236 Nelken to Alejandro Quijano &
to Fernando Benítez, 16 May
1949, AHNMN, legajo
3240–115, –116.

237 Nelken to Jiménez Asúa, 21
December 1952, FPI, ALJA-
418–7.

238 Their voluminous
correspondence is in the large
number of letters from Obdulia
Bermejo Oviedo in AHNMN,
legajo 3234–28–86.

239 Nelken to Ricarda Bermejo
Oviedo, 10 October 1948,
AHNMN, 3234–29.

240 Nelken to Casals, 28 February
1948, FPC.

241 Nelken to Ricarda Bermejo
Oviedo, 28 February 1949,
AHNMN, 3234–31.

242 Nelken to Ricarda Bermejo
Oviedo, 2 September 1949, 28
April, 30 September, 30 December
1950, 11 February, 29 December
1951, 4 July 1952, AHNMN,
3234–33, 37, 39, 40, 44, 47.
243 Nelken to Casals, 31 December
1951, FPC; Casals (Prades) to
Nelken, 11 January 1952,
AHNMN, legajo 3234–229.
244 Martínez, *Crónica*, pp.47–8. On
Krauss's Nazi sympathies, see
Marcel Prawy, *The Vienna Opera*
(London: Weidenfeld &
Nicolson, 1969) pp.143–6.
245 Nelken to Jiménez Asúa, 13
September 1953, FPI, ALJA-
418–7.
246 Peter N. Carroll, *The Odyssey of
the Abraham Lincoln Brigade:
Americans in the Spanish Civil War*
(Stanford, California: Stanford
University Press, 1994) pp.321–2;
Lan Adomian, 'Biographical
Notes' (files of G. Schirmer, Inc.,
New York); Al Prago, 'Lan
Adomian – A Tribute', *The
Volunteer* (New York) vol.VIII,
no.2, July 1985. Lan died on 9
May 1979, see *Excelsior*, 10 May
1979. I am immensely grateful to
Peter Carroll for making available
to me his files on Adomian.
247 Nelken to Ricarda Bermejo
Oviedo, 4 July 1952, 9 August
1953, AHNMN, legajo
3234–47, 53.
248 Nelken to Ricarda Bermejo
Oviedo, 3 February 1955,
AHNMN, legajo 3234–56.
249 Nelken to Jiménez Asúa, undated
but received 5 July 1954, FPI,
ALJA-418–7.
250 Nelken to Enrique de Francisco,
9 January 1955, FPI, AEFG-
154–64. She repeated the claim
about losing 27 kilos in a letter
to Ricarda four weeks later,

Nelken to Ricarda Bermejo
Oviedo, 3 February 1955,
AHNMN, legajo 3234–56.
251 Nelken to Jiménez Asúa, 30 May
1956, FPI, ALJA-418–7.
252 Adomian to Nelken,
correspondence in AHNMN,
legajo 3233.
253 Nelken to Jiménez Asúa, 30 May
1956, 29 March 1962, 25
December 1963, FPI, ALJA-
418–7. The text was published as
Elegía para Magda (México DF:
UNAM, 1956); the music as
Cantata Elegiaca (New York: G.
Schirmer, 1962).
254 Rodrigo, *Mujer v exilio*,
pp.391–3.
255 Adomian to Nelken, 5 July 1966,
AHNMN, legajo 3233–59.
256 Nelken to Casals, 4 June 1955,
FPC.
257 Casals (Prades) to Nelken, 13
April 1955, AHNMN, legajo
3234–235; Nelken to Casals, 4
June 1955, FPC.
258 Nelken to Ricarda Bermejo
Oviedo, 9 December 1955,
AHNMN, legajo 3234–57.
259 Nelken to Jiménez Asúa, 26
December 1956, FPI, ALJA-
418–7.
260 Nelken to Ricarda Bermejo
Oviedo, 12 March 1957,
AHNMN, legajo 3234–59.
261 Arnaiz, *Retrato hablado*, p.260.
262 Nelken to Jiménez Asúa, 26 June
1959, FPI, ALJA-418–7.
263 Nelken to Obdulia Bermejo
Oviedo, 16 June 1962,
AHNMN, legajo 3242–125.
264 Nelken to Jiménez Asúa, 29
March 1962, FPI, ALJA-418–7.
265 Conversation of the author with
Margarita Salas.
266 Nelken to Ricarda Bermejo
Oviedo, 16 June 1962,
AHNMN, legajo 3234–67.

Notes

267 Nelken to Jiménez Asúa, 16 May
     1963, FPI, ALJA-418–7.
268 'Datos biográficos de Margarita
     Nelken'. For a harsh account of
     Margarita's irritability, see Arnaiz,
     Retrato hablado, p.258.
269 Nelken to Jiménez Asúa, 27 June
     1964, FPI, ALJA-418–7; Nelken
     to Obdulia Bermejo Oviedo, 6
     May 1964, AHNMN, legajo
     3242–126; Nelken to Ricarda
     Bermejo Oviedo, 3 August 1964,
     AHNMN, legajo 3234–72. See
     also Arnaiz, *Retrato hablado*,
     pp.255–6. For the information
     on Vela Zanetti, I am indebted
     to Eduardo Aguirre Romero of
     the Fundación Vela Zanetti of
     León.
270 Author's interview with
     Margarita Salas, 12 August
     1999.
271 Nelken to Ricarda Bermejo
     Oviedo, 6 March 1965,
     AHNMN, legajo 3234–73.
272 Nelken to Ricarda Bermejo
     Oviedo, 4 February, 10 July
     1966, AHNMN, legajo
     3234–77, 78.

273 Nelken to Jiménez Asúa, 10 July
     1966, FPI, ALJA-418–7.
274 Nelken to Jiménez Asúa, 11
     February 1968, FPI, ALJA-
     418–7.
275 Dolores Ibárruri, *Memorias de
     Pasionaria 1939–1977* (Barcelona:
     Planeta, 1984) p.57; Morán,
     Miseria, p.154.
276 Aub, *Diarios (1939–1972)*, pp.409.
277 Rodrigo, *Mujeres en España: Las
     silenciadas*, pp.169–70; Mangini,
     Memories of Resistance, pp.30–1.
278 Aub, *Diarios (1939–1972)*, p.410.

EPILOGUE

 1 Mary Nash, *Defying Male
    Civilization: Women in the Spanish
    Civil War* (Denver, Colorado:
    Arden Press, 1995) pp.50–4,
    115–16.
 2 Shirley Mangini, *Memories of
    Resistance: Women's Voices from the
    Spanish Civil War* (New Haven:
    Yale University Press, 1995) chs
    5 & 6, pp.127–30.

A NOTE ON THE ILLUSTRATIONS

The Author and Publishers gratefully acknowledge the invaluable help of the following in obtaining the rare photographs reproduced in this book: Juan Alfonso de Vilallonga for the Priscilla Scott-Ellis photographs; Martin Green for those of Nan Green; Margarita Salas for those of Margarita Nelken; and Mercedes Sanz-Bachiller.

INDEX

Index

Index

offensive 53, 161; rescinds order that all captured foreigners be sh shot 61; directs counteroffensive at the Ebro 67–8, 166; final offensive against Barcelona 71, 73, 180; recognised by Britain and France 78, 375–6; inequalities of regime 192; strikes Martínez de Bedoya from cabinet list 274–5; and Second World War 92, 95, 100; and Mercedes' resignation from Auxilio Social 280, 282, 283; and Serrano Suñer 284; meeting with Hitler at Hendaye 96, 290; removes Mercedes from Consejo Nacional 288; allows Prince Ali to become Don Juan's representative 116; defends Mercedes' membership of Instituto Nacional de Previsión 289; speaks with Mercedes in Portugal 291; vetoes Martínez de Bedoya's appointment as Undersecretary 291; international acceptance angers Margarita Nelken 396–7; permits Martínez de Bedoya to resign as press attaché in Paris 291

French Government: and Spanish refugees 180, 297–8, 374, 375–6

Frente Rojo 343

Frentes y Hospitales, La Delegación Nacional de Asistencia a 35, 59, 79, 80–1, 84

Friends of the Soviet Union 371

Gabor, Magda 106, 107

Galarza, Ángel 358

Galarza, Colonel Valentín 285

Galatea, HMS 93

Gamero del Castillo, Pedro 281, 284, 286

Gandesa 56–7, 166

Garcerán, Rafael 247

García, Alvaro 25–6

García, Tomás 283

García, Regina 326

García de Diego, Colonel Joaquín 231, 235

García Lorca, Federico 306–7

García Morato, Joaquín 80

García Pelayo, Concepción 311, 312

García Quintana, Antonio 227

García Valdecasa, Alfonso 276

Geddes, John 30, 87

General Strike (1926) 20

George VI: coronation 30

German Workers' Front 6

Gielgud, John 85

Gil, Lt Colonel Rodrigo 352

Gil Albarellos, Ángeles 411

Gil Robles, José María 220, 339

Gili, Gustavo 102

Gilon, Etienne 91

Giménez Caballero, Ernesto 268–9, 313

Giménez Cendón, Teodoro 238, 240

Giral, José 352, 356, 392

Girardon, Michelle 115

Girón de Velasco, José Antonio 248–9, 284–5, 286, 287, 291

God that Failed, The (ed. Crossman) 193

Gomá, Cardinal Isidro 259

Gómez, Trifón 319

González, Valentín (El Campesino) 392

González Bueno, Pedro 270, 271

Göring, Hermann 6, 261

Gorkín, Julián 347, 348, 382, 383, 391–2, 403

Grace, Ann Hamilton 30

Grado, Joaquín del 339

Graffy, Count Laszlo 109, 110, 112

Grant, Irene 181, 183

Greco, El 145, 303, 357

Green, Frances: birth 133; childhood 121, 122, 134, 136; and father's departure for Spain 137, 138; schooling 150, 182, 184, 185; and father's death 175–6, 177; and mother's remarriage 186; at Battersea Polytechnic 188; married in Mauritius 195, 196, 197

Green, George: meets and marries Nan 130–2, 133; has affairs 133–4, 135; becomes interested in politics 135, 136; goes to fight in Spain 121–2, 137–8; friendship with Wogan Philipps 138, and Spender

Index

Index

Index

Index

Index

Index